GEOGRAPHIES OF CUBANIDAD

CARIBBEAN
STUDIES
SERIES

Anton L. Allahar and Natasha Barnes
Series Editors

GEOGRAPHIES OF CUBANIDAD

Place, Race, and Musical Performance in Contemporary Cuba

Rebecca M. Bodenheimer

University Press of Mississippi / Jackson

www.upress.state.ms.us

The University Press of Mississippi is a member of the
Association of American University Presses.

Lyrics of Clave y Guaguancó's song "Para Gozar, La Habana" reprinted
courtesy of Cuba Chévere.

Lyrics of Los Van Van's song "La Habana No Aguanta Más" reproduced courtesy of Termidor Musikverlag and Timba Records.

Lyrics of Orquesta Original de Manzanillo's song "Soy Cubano y Soy
de Oriente" reproduced courtesy of Tumi Music.

Lyrics of Adalberto Álvarez y Su Son's song "Un Pariente en
el Campo" reproduced courtesy of Bis Music.

Lyrics of Afrocuba de Matanzas's song "Tambor" reproduced courtesy
of Francisco Zamora Chirino.

Lyrics of Afrocuba de Matanzas's song "Baila mi Guaguancó" reproduced courtesy of Francisco Zamora Chirino.

Lyrics of Afrocuba de Matanzas's song "Caridad" reproduced courtesy
of Francisco Zamora Chirino.

All images courtesy of the author unless otherwise noted.

Photo of Pancho Quinto playing *guarapachangueo* reproduced courtesy of Sven Wiederholt.

Portions of chapter 1 and chapter 2 first appeared in a 2009 article
published in the *Musical Quarterly* (Bodenheimer 2009).

First printing 2015

∞

Library of Congress Cataloging-in-Publication Data

Bodenheimer, Rebecca M., author.
Geographies of cubanidad : place, race, and musical performance in contemporary Cuba / Rebecca
M. Bodenheimer.
pages cm. — (Caribbean studies series)
Includes bibliographical references and index.
ISBN 978-1-62846-239-5 (cloth : alk. paper) — ISBN 978-1-62674-684-8 (ebook) 1. Popular music—
Cuba—History and criticism. 2. Music and race—Cuba—History. 3. Regionalism in music. I. Title.
ML3486.C82B64 2015
781.64097291—dc23   2014048860

British Library Cataloging-in-Publication Data available

For Julián, and in memory of
my dear Tutu, for whom music was everything

Contents

Acknowledgments

No es fácil—"It's not easy." This most ubiquitous of Cuban expressions extends to the process of conducting research on the island. The research and writing of this book has only been possible with the support and collaboration of many different individuals and institutions in Cuba and the United States, and I feel extremely fortunate to have been able to freely conduct fieldwork on the island for the past decade.

As a Mellon Postdoctoral Fellow in the Arts and Humanities at Hamilton College from 2010 to 2012, I was provided with generous research funds that allowed me to conduct research in Cuba in 2011, particularly in Santiago, and to begin writing this book. I also received funding and assistance from a number of divisions at the University of California, Berkeley, including the Music Department, the Graduate Division, and the Center for Latin American Studies. I had the privilege of working with various prominent scholars at UC Berkeley—particularly in the departments of African American Studies, Ethnic Studies, and Geography—and my theoretical frameworks and methodological approaches owe a great deal to the guidance of these individuals, specifically Percy Hintzen, Alex Saragoza, Allan Pred, and Nelson Maldonado-Torres. The Music Department was a supportive and intellectually stimulating environment for my formation as a scholar and teacher. I am grateful for the generous financial assistance I was given and want to especially acknowledge the longstanding trio of ethnomusicologists in the department—Bonnie Wade, Ben Brinner, and Jocelyne Guilbault—and to thank them for their encouragement over the past decade. I feel fortunate to have worked with Bonnie Wade, a leading figure in and champion of our discipline, who has always shown a great deal of interest in my professional development. Ben Brinner has always reminded me of the importance of engaging with musical sounds and provided insightful, candid feedback about my writing. Jocelyne Guilbault has consistently cheered me on and offered sage professional advice and invaluable comments and critiques about my writing. Her attention to cultural politics—specifically the ways that race and national identity are imbricated with musical performance—is mirrored in my own research interests. Most importantly, she introduced me to cultural studies literature, particularly the work of a scholar whom I believe to be one of the most important intellectuals of the past half century, Stuart Hall (RIP); his theorizations related to Afro-diasporic identity and cultural hybridity, and his emphasis on the importance of deconstructing discourse, have guided this study's modes of analysis more than the work of any other scholar.

There are a number of US-based Cuba scholars who have assisted me in my professional development over the past ten years. I want to especially acknowledge the late ethnomusicologist Katherine Hagedorn, *que descanse en paz*. Katherine's ethnographic narratives inspired me with their theoretical originality and creative self-reflexivity. She was a generous mentor to me, and it's still hard to believe that I won't ever feel her infectious warmth again or see her smiling face at SEM every year. The UC-Cuba Multi-Campus Research Program, which has gathered an impressive range of Cuba scholars from the University of California system and beyond, has been an ongoing source of financial and professional support, and I thank Raúl Fernández for his encouragement of my research. I have collaborated with many other US-based Cuba researchers who have influenced my thinking, including Susan Thomas, Kevin Delgado, David Garcia, Ken Schweitzer, Sarah Blue, Lani Milstein, Grete Viddal, Nolan Warden, and Lara Greene. I thank Ariana Hernandez-Reguant for her foresight and work in creating a fabulous, productive network of Cuba scholars on Facebook, the EthnoCuba group. Robin Moore has been a particularly generous and important colleague to me over the past decade, and I cannot thank him enough for his genuine encouragement of me as an emerging scholar and for the professional opportunities he has facilitated. Finally, I am profoundly grateful to Peter Manuel for his thoughtful, detailed, and candid feedback on my manuscript; my writing and arguments are surely stronger because of his comments and critiques.

There are many people in Cuba who have facilitated my research over the years. I was very fortunate to be granted an affiliation with La Fundacíon Fernando Ortiz and want to thank Miguel Barnet, María Teresa Linares, Jesús Guanche, and all the other scholars and staff not only for welcoming me into their institution but also for the crucial and innovative intellectual work they support in the field of anthropology. At the Ministerio de Cultura, Oscar Verdeja almost single-handedly made my visa approval happen and was a friendly and welcoming presence in an otherwise daunting bureaucratic institution. I spent many hours conducting archival research at the library of the Center for the Research and Development of Cuban Music (CIDMUC), and the resident librarian, Tamara Sevila Salas, was extremely helpful in locating materials that I would not have otherwise found. I also conducted archival research at the library of the Casa del Caribe in Santiago, where Pura and León Estrada were of great assistance. A number of Cuban musicologists and scholars—including Radamés Giro, Helio Orovio, Olavo Alén Rodríguez, Ana Casanova, Caridad Diez, María Elena Vinueza, Neris González Bello, Liliana Casanella Cué, Julio Corbea Calzado, and Olga Portuondo—provided me with invaluable information and sources. I appreciate the opportunities I had to engage in academic conversations with these eminent local scholars, and to establish friendships with them.

While these institutional contacts were fundamental for the realization of my research, it is the Cuban musicians with whom I worked that deserve the most recognition. Musicians from many rumba and folkloric groups extended their generosity in allowing me to attend rehearsals, ask an endless stream of questions, record their performances, and travel with them to gigs. These groups—with whom I worked to varying degrees—include Afrocuba de Matanzas, Yoruba Andabo, Los Ibellis, Clave y Guaguancó, Cutumba, Kokoyé, Los Muñequitos de Matanzas, and Raíces Profundas. A few individuals must be singled out for their collaboration. Francisco "Minini" Zamora, director of Afrocuba de Matanzas, and all of the group's musicians and dancers allowed me to participate in their dance classes despite my lack of knowledge, and to become an intimate observer of the inner workings of this truly special folkloric group. A special thank you to the current and former Afrocuba musicians whom I interviewed—Minini, Dolores Pérez and Juan García, Reinaldo "Wichichi" Alfonso, Pedro "Pello" Tápanes, and Sandy Pérez—who were so generous with their information. In Santiago, I was privileged to interview two members of the famed folkloric group Cutumba, "Pablo" and Ramón Márquez, and a former percussionist of the rumba group Kokoyé, Mario "Mayito" Seguí, all of whom spoke frankly about regionalist antagonisms and highlighted the variety and richness of eastern Cuban folklore. I am particularly grateful to Mayito, whom I first met and took percussion lessons with in 2005, as he has facilitated my networking with musicians in Santiago and become a good friend.

In Havana, I was fortunate to work closely with two of Cuba's best rumba groups, Yoruba Andabo and Clave y Guaguancó. Several members of Yoruba Andabo—including Geovani del Pino, Ronald González, Gerardo de Arma, and Francisco "Frank" Queralta—were generous with their time in our interviews and conversations, and brought to light interesting and unexpected issues. Amado Dedeu, director of Clave y Guaguancó, was also an important source of information, and I appreciated his candor in speaking about sensitive topics. Los Chinitos welcomed me to their home in San Miguel del Padrón for their annual Mother's Day rumba, and I thank Irián López for sharing his invaluable knowledge about *guarapachangueo* in our interview and for the demonstrations that were the basis for my transcriptions. Ban Rarrá director Isaias Rojas offered a unique perspective as an eastern Cuban musician who has lived, established a successful career, and led a folkloric group in Havana for two decades. Finally, I want to particularly acknowledge my Havana percussion teacher, Daniel Rodríguez. Daniel was the first rumba musician with whom I established a relationship in Cuba, and he has always been extremely generous with me, both in terms of his deep musical knowledge and the information he has shared with me about the Havana rumba and Afro-Cuban religious scenes. He opened many doors for me, particularly by introducing me to other *rumberos* with whom I would conduct research and letting me tag along to his *tambores* and *cajones*. Daniel, estoy muy agradecida para toda tu ayuda en los últimos diez años y me he divertido un montón aprendiendo de tí—no solo eres un gran músico y profesor, sino también un gran amigo.

Beyond Daniel and Mayito, I want to thank all of the musicians who have served as my percussion and song teachers throughout the past ten years. Bay Area–based Cuban percussionist Jesus Diaz introduced me to rumba and folkloric music and in this sense pointed me in the direction of rumba as a topic of research. Beyond his incredible talent as a percussionist, vocalist, composer, and bandleader, Jesus is an amazing teacher and has always shared his knowledge generously with his students. In Matanzas, Miguel Angel "El Negro" Dreke shared with me his prolific knowledge of Afro-Cuban song, and Luisito (then a percussionist with Afrocuba and now with Los Muñequitos de Matanzas) taught me the basics of Matanzas-style rumba percussion.

I want to recognize a few women with whom I established close friendships and whose support and companionship have been crucial to my well-being in Cuba. From the first time I traveled to Matanzas in 2004, Ana Pérez, longtime singer and dancer with Los Muñequitos, welcomed me wholeheartedly into her home and family, which boasts many folkloric musicians and dancers. I was a daily presence in Ana's household for almost three months, eating almost all of my meals and spending most afternoons and evenings in her Pueblo Nuevo home. Her daughter Yurien has become one of my closest friends on the island, and I am grateful to have found such a wonderful confidante. Ana y Yurien, gracias por haber compartido conmigo tantos momentos maravillosos y divertidos con Uds. y su gran familia. In Havana, my oldest and closest friend in Cuba, Martica Pérez, along with her husband Ernesto and daughters Sheyla and Shirley, adopted me into her family almost immediately, and her friendship provided the most consistent source of support for me during my research. Martica, siempre me has apoyado y escuchado en mis momentos dificiles, y hasta me has criticado cuando me lo merecía—estoy muy agradecida por haber encontrado una amiga tan buena y sincera.

I very likely would not have arrived at the decision to pursue a career in academia if not for the long and illustrious background of scholars in my family. My paternal grandparents (Edgar and Brigitte Bodenheimer), both of my parents, and several aunts and uncles all dedicated their lives to the pursuit and dissemination of knowledge in various fields. My maternal grandmother, Hilda Jonas, deserves much of the credit for my choice of discipline, music. A professional harpsichordist and piano teacher, she instilled in her children and grandchildren not only a love of music but also the importance of this pursuit. I feel so fortunate to have grown up with her and my grandfather (Gerald Jonas), who were like second parents to me and who always encouraged me in my educational and personal goals. My aunts and uncles—Rosemarie Bodenheimer, Andy von Hendy, Linda and David Schroeder, and Peter Bodenheimer—also offered support and sage advice about the various stages of a career in academia.

My choice of research site proved to be auspicious, as I have gained not only a deep love for Cuban music but also a husband and a wonderful Cuban family. Para mi familia cubana, quiero agradecerles a todos para su gran generosidad y apoyo—desde el primero momento me hicieron sentir bienvenida y parte de la familia, y los quiero mucho. A mi suegra Guillerma, eres como mi madre y no puedo imaginar una mejor suegra con quien puedo reírme tanto. A mi cuñada Nidia, eres como una hermana verdadera—gracias por tu amistad y apoyo. A mi cuñado Diógenes, gracias por cuidarme como una hermana y para acompañarme a los eventos en Santiago. Quiero reconocer también a mis otros cuñados—Pupy, Dorita, Guillermo, y Leonorcita—a las sobrinas, y a todos los tios y primos. Finalmente, quiero recordar con mucho cariño a mi suegro, Diógenes Moncada Figueredo, quien fue un gran hombre y padre y quien me hizo sentir como una hija verdadera. Te fuiste demasiado temprano y te echamos mucho de menos, que descanses en paz.

I am especially grateful to my immediate family—Susanne Jonas, Tom Bodenheimer, Sara Syer, Anna Landau, and (RIP) Tom Holleran—for all the years of support and encouragement. Mom and Dad, I have always admired your commitment to social justice, which has influenced me in ways that are impossible to express, and I feel fortunate to have been raised in such an incredible and unique community of activists. I am proud of the great work that you continue to do, which I am always reminded of when I randomly meet someone who sings your praises or who asks with admiration, are you Susanne Jonas's/Tom Bodenheimer's daughter? Thank you for the endless amount of love and support you have given to me, Lázaro, and Julián.

Finally, I must thank my husband, Lázaro Moncada Merencio, and the beautiful, brilliant, hilarious light of my life, Julián Santiago Moncada. Lázaro has been my companion since I began conducting research in Cuba and throughout the writing of this book. His experience as a *santiaguero* in Havana influenced my perspectives in the most fundamental ways, and he has always kept me grounded in my moments of professional angst. Nunca me imaginé que encontraría mi media mitad en Cuba, y le doy las gracias al universo por haberte conocido en el Callejón de Hamel ese domingo, un 4 de julio. Gracias por apoyarme y animarme por todo este proceso, por siempre recordarme de las cosas verdaderamente importantes—el amor, la familia, y la risa—y por darme el mejor regalo del mundo, nuestro amadísimo y lindísimo hijo. Julián, you have given my life meaning and purpose beyond what I thought possible—thank you for teaching me to be more patient, flexible, and present, and for showing me the true meaning of unconditional love.

GEOGRAPHIES OF CUBANIDAD

Introduction

Derived from the late-nineteenth-century writings of Cuban national poet and hero José Martí, the notion of *Cubanidad* (Cubanness) has always imagined a unified, hybrid nation where racial difference is nonexistent and where nationality trumps all other axes of identification. This projection of absolute national unity became even more crucial following the 1959 Cuban Revolution led by Fidel Castro that ushered in the socialist regime, and has been continually utilized to combat the ongoing political threat to the island's sovereignty represented by the United States and neoliberal capitalism in general. Since the fall of the Soviet bloc in 1990, Cuba has found itself with very few allies in the fight against capitalism's global domination.[1] Despite the continuing celebration of national race mixture in the rhetoric of the Cuban government and many intellectuals on the island, many scholars have highlighted the contradictions inherent in the gap between these discourses of racial harmony, and the realities of inequality faced by Cubans of African descent since independence in 1898. In this book, I posit that it is not only the recognition of racial difference that threatens to divide the Cuban nation, but that popular regionalist sentiment further contests the notion of Cubanidad that has been hegemonic for over a century. Through the examination of several national musical practices, I will elucidate the various ways that race and the politics of place, an analytic I explain below, are articulated in contemporary music making in Cuba.

Traditional musical practices in Cuba are commonly associated with the particular places from which they emerged, as is evident in the notion that the Afro-Cuban percussion-based genre *rumba* is from western Cuba, and the traditional dance genre *son* is from eastern Cuba (Robbins 1990; Gómez Cairo [1980] 1998). Taking as my point of departure the notion that the island's music functions as a prominent signifier of Cubanidad, both on and off the island, I propose that musical practices play an important role in the construction of regional and local, as well as national, identities.[2] Furthermore, in addition to the impact of local social histories on the formation of local and regional identity within Cuba, I argue that the racial and cultural tropes attached to these places—which circulate in part through musical texts and which I refer to as "racialized discourses of place"—are constitutive of this process of place-based identification. Notions about places, in other words, impact local identity formation. Thus, the musical practices I examine in this book—including contemporary Cuban dance music, rumba, Afro-Cuban folkloric (sacred) practices from both western and eastern Cuba, and son—will be presented as examples of the entangled relationship between regional/local identity formation, racialized discourses of place, and music making.

Despite the recent interest in theorizing space and place in relation to identity and cultural practices, there has been no published work exploring the impact of regional identity on, and the ways it is articulated within, Cuban musical performance. I conceive of the politics of place—an analytic that borrows frameworks from nonmusicological disciplines, specifically cultural studies, cultural geography, and anthropology—as consisting of two distinct yet related discursive formations. The first is constituted by the widespread expressions of regionalist sentiment within Cuba, which have a long history on the island but which are also, as I have observed during many years of fieldwork on the island, a particularly pervasive source of tension in contemporary Cuban society. Expressions of regionalism, which are often antagonistic, are evident both in everyday social relations in Havana among Cubans from different provinces and in the lyrics of songs from various genres, including *timba* (post-1990 Cuban dance music) and rumba. One of my book's main goals is to suggest that regional/local provenance is an influential axis of identity formation that can foster divisiveness, and that popular regionalist sentiment betrays the cracks in the wall of Cuban national unity and socialist egalitarianism.

The second discursive formation entailed in the politics of place is constituted by the aforementioned racialized discourses of place, which conjure up isomorphic links between racialized cultural practices and particular places/regions. The western Cuban city of Matanzas, for example, is known as *la cuna de la cultura afrocubana* (the cradle of Afro-Cuban culture), while Havana is represented as the center of contemporary innovation and hybridity (both racial and cultural). The construction of Matanzas as a historic space of authentic blackness is a clear example of the widespread tendency to correlate race and place, and an illustration of how the two often stand in for each other discursively. My study will explore this discursive conflation, particularly the ways that Cuban genres tend to be discussed in racialized terms and as emplaced in particular locales in academic scholarship.

In order to set the stage for a detailed consideration of regionalism and the ways that race and place are entangled in Cuba—the subject of chapter 1—in this chapter I aim to provide a summary of the scholarship on race in Cuba, with a focus on the nationalist hybridity discourse. I will then outline the theoretical approaches that have informed my ethnography, which are drawn primarily from cultural geography and anthropology.

Race in Cuba and the Hegemony of *Mestizaje*

While the recognition of the inherent hybridity of all cultural practices is relatively new in the Euro-American academic milieu, the promotion of this concept has a very long history in the Caribbean and Latin America. *Mestizaje*, which translates roughly to race mixture, has been the conceptual centerpiece of many Latin American nationalist discourses since the nineteenth century. Related promotions of hybridity can also be identified in the Francophone Caribbean with the concepts of *antillanité* and *creolization* (Bernabé et al. 1990), and in the Anglophone Caribbean with the notion of *creole* or *callaloo* (Hintzen 2002; Puri 2004). Each country's nationalist hybridity discourse varies according to the racial makeup of its particular population,[3] and some Latin American countries have not endorsed mestizaje.[4] Nonetheless, one overriding similarity among them has been, as race theorist David Theo Goldberg (2008) points out, the goal of promoting homogeneity, paradoxically through the auspices of racial hybridity and the assertion that "we are a country of mixed-race people."[5] Thus, national hybridity is conceived in totalizing terms with the presumption being that individuals who identify themselves in monoracial terms—i.e., white, black, or indigenous—cannot be recognized as part of the hybrid national body. Beyond constituting an exclusionary definition of the nation that renders nonmixed people invisible—particularly blacks, indigenous people, and East Indians—Caribbean hybridity discourses also maintain Eurocentric ideologies and colonial structural conditions in the postcolonial context by denying the role that racial difference plays in access to political power, economic resources, and land ownership. In addition, while these discourses of mestizaje have been successful in discursively distancing nationalist elites (largely white) from their former European colonizers, they have also been utilized to proclaim the triumph of racial equality as an automatic result of decolonization, thus marginalizing and sometimes silencing any debate on race. Addressing the widely held assumption in Latin America that a large mixed-race population is mutually exclusive with structural racism, political scientist Mark Sawyer states: "Rather than eliminate racial hierarchy, miscegenation has only created more steps on the staircase of racial hierarchy" (2006, 138).

In his writings during the late-nineteenth-century wars of independence, José Martí was the first intellectual not only to assert the uniqueness of hybridized Cubanidad, but also to proclaim mestizaje as a symbol of pride for all nations of the Americas (Isfahani-Hammond 2005). Ethnomusicologist Robin Moore (1997) problematizes the nationalist promotion of hybridity that was asserted in the decades following the 1902 establishment of the Cuban Republic. He discusses how Martí's idealistic vision of racial progress in postindependence Cuban society was appropriated by the white elite as a way of denying the continuing socioeconomic inequalities experienced by Afro-Cubans after independence from Spain (R. Moore 1997, 28). Caribbeanist scholar Shalini Puri issues a more pointed critique, accusing Martí himself of manipulating the notion of hybridity for his nationalist agenda: "Martí's claim of racial transcendence is beyond doubt false. . . . [E]lsewhere in the essay, he himself betrays the residual discursive pull of racial types" (Puri 2004, 54). She also identifies a civilizing impulse within Martí's writings, stating that "the primary agency in 'Nuestra América' [the famous 1891 essay in which Martí first advocated mestizaje] seems reserved for elite white and mulatto Christians who would 'rescue the Indian' and 'make a place for the competent Negro'" (54).

Latin Americanist scholars have highlighted the fact that, while proclaiming the victory of racial harmony, early-twentieth-century governments in Brazil, Cuba, Colombia, and elsewhere simultaneously pursued policies of *blanqueamiento* (whitening) by encouraging European immigration to their respective countries (Wade 1993; R. Moore 1997; Marx 1998; de la Fuente 2001; Sheriff 2001). During the first three decades of the twentieth century there was a huge wave of in-migration to Cuba—1,293,000 people, 57 percent of whom were Spanish and 25 percent of whom came from other Caribbean islands to fill the demand for cheap labor in the American-dominated sugar industry (Comité Estatal de Estadísticas 1979, 70). Blanqueamiento was intended to literally embed European values and physical traits within the racially hybrid population for the purposes of diluting and eventually expunging "atavistic" African traits, traditions, and superstitions from the national body and culture. As noted by historian Aviva Chomsky, even celebrated anthropologist and later champion of Afro-Cuban culture Fernando Ortiz initially advocated blanqueamiento (Chomsky 2000, 426). This literal and figurative move toward whiteness was thought to be a necessary step for postcolonial nations like Cuba to enter Western modernity.[6] Nevertheless, the desire to whiten the Cuban population conflicted with the need for cheap labor, and some prominent black intellectuals highlighted the hypocrisy displayed by elites who encouraged Spanish immigration while opposing black Antillean immigration (de la Fuente 2001, 51). Ultimately, as Cuban historian Alejandro de la Fuente asserts, economic interests superseded racist constructions of Cubanidad: by allowing the importation of hundreds of thousands of Antilleans, mostly Haitians and Jamaicans, "[t]he Cuban government had sacrificed whitening to sugar production because, as a popular saying put it, 'sin azúcar no hay país' (without sugar there is no country)" (102).

Although the political orientation of the government changed markedly after 1959, the mestizaje discourse has remained hegemonic. Unlike the leaders of the first half of the twentieth century, however, Fidel Castro took an active role in highlighting African contributions to Cuban culture and in redefining Cubanidad as "Latin-African" (Castro 1976).[7] Castro's rearticulation of national identity was likely linked to the heavy Cuban intervention in and support of African liberation struggles in the mid- to late 1970s, particularly in Angola, Mozambique, and Ethiopia. This discursive Africanization of Cuba has been interpreted by some critics of the revolution, like black Cuban exile Carlos Moore (1988), as a calculated move designed to gain support, especially among Afro-Cubans, for the military campaigns. Nonetheless, the revolution's commitment to desegregation and racial equality in the public sphere undoubtedly resulted in higher literacy rates and living standards among Afro-Cubans. However, revolutionary nationalist discourse has continued to gloss over socioeconomic inequalities between different racialized groups, and Afro-Cubans are still underrepresented in positions of power and suffer from disproportionate poverty, racial profiling, and high incarceration rates (de la Fuente 2001; Sawyer 2006; Blue 2007). In addition, they are still somewhat invisible in high-profile cultural arenas, such as television and film, where black characters tend to be either absent or marginal to the storyline (Knight 2000). Mark Sawyer (2006) asserts that Cuba might be considered a "pigmentocracy," since lighter skin—independently of one's racial self-identification—is positively correlated with higher social and economic status. Finally, as Pedro Pérez Sarduy and Jean Stubbs write (1993), the socialist government's claims to have eradicated racism and other forms of discrimination have had the impact of shutting down public debate on issues of race in contemporary Cuba. Carlos Moore (1988) has gone further, arguing that asserting a *black* Cuban identity in a "raceless" society has often been interpreted by the government as counterrevolutionary. Moore's recent memoir (2008) chronicles his detention at the hands of authorities in the early 1960s when he attempted to highlight continuing racism under the revolution.

Alejandro de la Fuente (2008) asserts that in recent years black artists and intellectuals have succeeded in pushing the government to publicly recognize and begin to address issues of racial inequality, and to admit that full equality for blacks was never achieved under the revolution. However, there have yet to be instituted any policy changes to counteract racist and discriminatory practices, particularly those that have arisen since the Special Period with the introduction of market-oriented economic measures (see de la Fuente 2001).[8] In addition, the defensive response on the part of Cuban intellectuals to a 2009 public condemnation by African American leaders (including prominent intellectuals like Cornel West and Julianne Malveaux) of the racism that blacks have faced under the Castro regimes, suggests that the academic elite is still not ready to fully acknowledge the extent of the problem.[9] Among other arguments, revolutionary intellectuals have often attributed continuing racism to the private sphere (i.e., to prejudicial attitudes toward blacks held by individuals and within families), thus implying that the state should not be held responsible (Pérez Sarduy and Stubbs 2000). Finally, in March 2013 a new racial controversy arose in which prominent black scholar Roberto Zurbano was stripped of his leadership position at the prestigious research institution Casa de las Américas after publishing an editorial in the *New York Times* arguing that Afro-Cubans had not yet gained full equality under the revolution.[10]

I now move on to detail the theoretical framework that undergirds my research, the politics of place. Subsequent chapters will return to a discussion of race and its entanglements with regional identity formation, discourses of place, and music making.

The Politics of Place: Theoretical Approaches

Discussions of space and place often go hand in hand. However, the two have traditionally been theorized as opposites, with space regarded as an "empty," "universal," and sometimes "alienating" entity and place fetishized as the "local," the comforting, familiar site of cultural specificity. This study focuses on the production of place and the ways that locales come to have racialized associations and to signify certain types of music making. For example, as I will discuss in chapters 4 and 5, Matanzas is linked to blackness and a traditional style of rumba, whereas Havana is represented as a racially and culturally hybrid place defined by fusion and innovation. Thus, I am primarily engaging with theorizations of "place" and not "space" as such, although I find that the distinction between the two is not always clear, even in the work of geographers. Nonetheless, I follow geographer Doreen Massey's conceptualization of the relationship between place and space, in which she argues against the traditional polarization of the two within her field. She notes that the "persistent counterposition of space and place . . . is bound up with a parallel counterposition between global and local [that] resonates with an equation of the local with realness, with local place as earthy and meaningful, standing in opposition to a presumed abstraction of global space" (Massey 2005, 183). Massey also views the relationship between space and place in terms of scale, with place existing on a reduced scale as compared to space and constituting a "particular envelope of space-time." She states: "If . . . the spatial is thought of in the context of space-time and as formed out of social interrelations at all scales, then one view of place is as a particular articulation of those relations, a particular moment in those networks of social relations and understandings" (Massey 1994, 5). In this vein, I treat Matanzas, Havana, and Santiago—the sites in which I conducted ethnographic research—as places produced by and through social relations manifested at a particular point in time, the early twenty-first century, although very much informed by their respective demographic and social histories.

In *Music and Urban Geography* (2007), Adam Krims makes a similar critique of the polarization of space and place. Rather than seeing space as the homogenizing force of globalization and place as a liberatory site of cultural specificity, he conceives of the two as mutually constitutive, noting that the precondition for the romanticization of place as local/intimate/resistant—which is in turn necessary for successful tourism marketing strategies—is the current economic climate of neoliberal capitalism. In other words, space and place work in tandem: the symbolic value of place helps sell it to tourists and is thus crucial in the economic restructuring of cities into tourist/service hubs following deindustrialization. Krims states, "*place* itself provides one of the fundamental symbolic values for many of these commodities and services . . . whether one is visiting a city that has remade itself (or parts of itself) as a tourist destination or whether one is simply shopping for ethnic food or world music, routes through post-Fordist cities are often laden with the signposts of place. . . . [T]he omnipresence of place in our cultural life, as well as (importantly) the scholarly interest in place that has so permeated music studies, has undergone its vast recent expansion for a reason; it is not a matter of coincidence but, rather, an aspect of the changing developmental circumstances of the capitalist world" (Krims 2007, 36–37). With this more complex conceptualization of the relationship between space and place in mind, I turn to more specific theorizations of place that inform my work.

Challenging Sedentarist Metaphysics: A Nonessentialist Notion of Place

Anthropologists James Clifford (1992), Akhil Gupta and James Ferguson (1992), and others have critiqued ethnographers' long-held assumption of a natural link between particular cultural groups, seen as unitary and homogeneous, and the territories they inhabit, what Liisa Malkki calls a "sedentarist metaphysics" (Malkki 1997). Malkki describes this sedentarism as "deeply moral, sinking 'peoples' and 'cultures' into 'national soils' and the 'family of nations' into Mother Earth. . . . [I]t actively territorializes our identities, whether cultural or national" (Malkki 1997, 61–62). Addressing the role that ethnographers play in the construction of a sendentarist metaphysics, Gupta and Ferguson call on their colleagues to examine their own *production* of spatialized difference, and the ways that these naturalized assumptions about "others" contribute to what Arjun Appadurai calls the "spatial incarceration of the native" (Gupta and Ferguson 1992, 14). In his ethnography *Suffering for Territory: Race, Place, and Power in Zimbabwe*, anthropologist Donald Moore presents a similar critique of this "spatial incarceration," which he describes as the "ethnic spatial fix," a divide-and-conquer colonial strategy in which "affixing [ethnic] identities in tribal territories" was used as a tool of domination and control over Africans (D. Moore 2005, 14).

My framework is strongly informed by these anthropological interventions that have problematized the naturalized links between place, culture/ethnicity, and identity. However, following Massey (1994; 2005) and others (Bennett 2000; Turino 2000), I also wish to emphasize the importance of what Massey terms "locality studies." She offers an alternative theorization of place, one that sees places as defined not by fixed essences nor by "some long internalized history but . . . constructed out of a particular constellation of social relations, meeting and weaving together at a particular locus" (Massey 1994, 154). My analytic draws on this reconceptualization of place, which, as noted above, eschews the traditional fetishization of place as a "safe haven" from the supposedly alienating effects of increasing globalization. Instead, places are characterized by porous, shifting boundaries and social relations that are inevitably entangled with extra-local political and economic conditions (Massey 1994, 133–34). Ethnomusicologist Thomas Turino similarly asserts: "For me, *local* simply indicates a place where face-to-face interchanges are common, likely, or at least possible. . . . My use of the word does not necessarily indicate cultural distinction or a binary opposition in relation to cosmopolitanism (as in 'local-global')" (Turino 2000, 17–18). Donald Moore goes a step further when he posits the hybridity of the "local," stating: "Place emerges as a distinctive mixture, not an enduring essence, a nodal point where these translocal influences intermesh with practices and meanings previously sedimented in the local landscape" (D. Moore 2005, 20). In the frameworks of Massey, Turino, and Moore, then, places are porous, relational, heterogeneous, and even hybrid, a conceptualization that is very productive for my own project, particularly chapter 5, in which the notion of hybridity is so central.

The Politics of Place

The politics of place, as I conceive of it, includes the following elements: the "spatiality of identity," regionalist sentiment among Cubans of different provinces, racialized discourses of place and their links with musical practices, and localized notions of hybridity. The first is a notion that undergirds the study as a whole, and I will thus detail it here, while the other three will be elucidated in depth in subsequent chapters. My research seeks to build on the recent body of literature theorizing space and place in relation to identity and cultural practices, which has proliferated particularly in popular music studies (see, for example, Cohen 1994; Bennett 2000; Forman 2002; Connell and Gibson 2003; Whiteley et al. 2004; and Krims 2007). In this vein, my study argues that music and place mutually constitute each other and that musical practices often inform the construction of local identities. In *Ethnicity, Identity, and Music: The Musical Construction of Place*, ethnomusicologist Martin Stokes states: "I would argue therefore that music is socially meaningful not entirely but largely because it provides means by which people recognize identities and places, and the boundaries which separate them" (Stokes 1994, 5). In *Music, Space and Place: Popular Music and Cultural Identity*, Sheila Whiteley and her coauthors further suggest that "music plays an important role in the narrativization of place . . . the way in which people define their relationship to local, everyday surroundings" (Whiteley et al. 2004, 2). This notion of music "narrativizing" place is particularly useful for my discussion of discourses of place (chapter 4) and the ways these discourses are entangled with musical and cultural production. Finally, while the bulk of scholarship concerning the relationship between music and place has been written by cultural geographers and popular music scholars, this book contributes to the few music studies (e.g., Stokes 1994) that ground theorizations of place in ethnographic research.[11]

A central part of my framework relates to what cultural geographer Don Mitchell characterizes as the "spatiality of identity" (Mitchell 2000, 62). As a basic tenet of cultural geography, this notion points to the powerful effects that space and place have on the production of social identities, whether they are locally, regionally, nationally, and/or transnationally defined. In *The 'Hood Comes First: Race, Space, and Place in Rap and Hip-Hop*, Murray Forman highlights the fascinating cross-cultural assumption of a "latent relationship between spatiality and identity" (Forman 2002, 30), evidenced by the ubiquitous tendency to ask someone where he or she is from as a way of gaining insight into his or her character. In the context of contemporary music making in Cuba (and elsewhere), the spatiality of identity is inevitably entangled with processes and discourses of racialization. As Forman and anthropologist

Peter Wade (1993) have noted, there is a widespread tendency to correlate race and place, and the two often stand in for each other discursively, as will be evidenced by the entanglements between the two that I discuss in chapter 1.

As chapter 1 will elucidate, I view regionalism as a significant—albeit understudied—social issue in Cuba, one that deeply informs relationships among Cubans from different provinces, particularly in Havana. Despite the state's rhetoric espousing national unity, regional provenance is an influential axis of identity for Cubans, and this sometimes entails feelings of hostility toward people from other provinces. As this is the focus of the following chapter, I won't expound on my argument here. I do want to emphasize that, rather than suggesting that regional or local identity supplants national identity or that they are mutually exclusive, I find that these loci of identity coexist in a state of contradictory tension. In sum, Cubans are famously proud of their nationality—and Cubanidad is very much a rallying point and source of social cohesion for those living abroad—but I also believe that Cubans are very much defined by their specific regional and local identities.[12]

The second element of my analytic is constituted by what I call racialized discourses of place, which posit naturalized links between race and place/region/province and which I examine in various chapters in relation to different musical practices. For example, whereas Havana is represented as the center of contemporary innovation and hybridity, Matanzas is known as "the cradle of Afro-Cuban culture" and constructed as the site of authentic blackness. While the two cities share many of the same Afro-Cuban musical traditions, they have been inserted into polarized racial and cultural discourses. My extensive fieldwork with rumba and folkloric groups in both Havana and Matanzas leads me to complicate these widely held assumptions about where tradition is "located" and where hybridity "takes place" in Cuba, as they obscure the diversity that animates both cities' folkloric scenes. Thus, another main objective for me in scrutinizing discourses of place is to highlight that there is "no authenticity of place" (Massey 1994, 121). However, although these tropes entail a problematic essentialization of the cultural identities of the two cities, they nonetheless enjoy widespread currency both in Cuba and abroad and cannot simply be dismissed, particularly because of the material effects they have on the livelihoods of folkloric musicians (see chapter 4).

Finally, in relation to racialized discourses of place, I aim to highlight localized conceptions of musical hybridity by examining the creation of two rumba innovations in recent decades, one from Matanzas and one from Havana. Chapter 5 will thus focus on the entanglements of local identity formation with hybridizing practices and broader notions of musical fusion.

Methodological Issues

This study is based on ethnographic research in three Cuban cities: Havana, Matanzas, and Santiago. My dissertation, from which chapters 2, 4, and 5 are roughly drawn, was the result of fieldwork conducted in Havana and Matanzas from 2004 through 2008. My focus was on contemporary rumba performance and innovations, and my decision to conduct fieldwork in these cities was guided primarily by their long histories in this tradition. I conducted the bulk of my fieldwork between August 2006 and May 2007, a stay that had been preceded by four shorter research trips between 2004 and 2006. I spent roughly six and a half months in Havana, which allowed me to conduct ample ethnographic research with the three following rumba groups: Yoruba Andabo, Clave y Guaguancó, and Los Ibellis. Although known primarily for the performance of rumba, all three groups also include Afro-Cuban sacred music and dance traditions within their repertoires. I spent three months in Matanzas conducting ethnographic research with the folkloric group Afrocuba de Matanzas, focusing my inquiries on their 1973 creation of the rumba hybrid *batarumba* and their expansion of repertoire to the sacred domain in 1980.

For this book, I have expanded my sites of research to include Santiago and broadened my focus from one genre—rumba—to various traditions. The musical practices I will be discussing include rumba, Cuban dance music (sometimes called Cuban salsa), *folklore oriental* (eastern Cuban folklore, which includes various traditions), and son. In addition, sacred Afro-Cuban traditions from western Cuba—such as *Santería, Palo,* and *Abakuá*—will be discussed at various moments in relation to both rumba and folklore oriental. My primary research trip to Santiago took place in summer 2011, although I had become familiar with local traditions and conducted preliminary fieldwork during several visits to the city dating back to 2003. The musicians I interviewed and with whom I primarily engaged were members of the celebrated folkloric troupe Cutumba and the rumba group Kokoyé. During the same research trip (summer 2011), I also conducted research with an eastern Cuban folkloric group in Havana, Ban Rarrá, formed in Guantánamo but now based in the capital. I should note that although at times I will be discussing the entire region of Oriente, or its southeastern part (consisting of the provinces of Santiago and Guantánamo), I have conducted ethnographic research only in Santiago and not in other locales in eastern Cuba. However, throughout the book I have tried to avoid discursive slippage between "Santiago" and "Oriente"—geographic categories that I certainly do not want to conflate—and attempted to be specific about the locales to which I am referring.[13]

My primary methodological approach consisted of ethnographic observations of rehearsals and performances by rumba/folkloric groups, and interviews with members of these groups. In addition to attending many performances by each of the abovementioned groups, I regularly attended other weekly and biweekly rumba events in Havana, which provided me with a broad perspective concerning the capital's contemporary rumba scene. I also attended performances by other rumba/folkloric groups in Matanzas and Santiago—such as Los Muñequitos de Matanzas and the Ballet Folklórico de Oriente—although these types of events are much less frequent than in the capital. I attended all the rehearsals of Afrocuba de Matanzas during my stay in Matanzas but was able to attend only a few rehearsals of each of the Havana- and Santiago-based groups. In addition to formal interviews, musicians' perspectives were drawn from the many casual conversations, or "unstructured interviews" (Knauer 2005), that I've engaged in during my many trips to the island.[14] Besides formal interviews and conversations, I found that some very provocative issues and questions arose within the context of my percussion and song lessons, particularly in relation to the contemporary reality of rumba and Afro-Cuban folkloric musicians.[15] Thus, the music lessons that I took—primarily in Havana and Matanzas—constituted a crucial ethnographic activity for my research.

Beyond ethnography, this study engages fairly heavily in discourse analysis, particularly in chapter 4 but also in chapters 1, 3, and 5. This approach relates to one of my primary goals, which is to critically examine musicians' expressions of regional/local identity and their perspectives on racialized discourses of place, and the ways these notions impact their musical creations. Textual analysis has also been an important method for my study. Chapter 2 analyzes song texts—primarily in Cuban dance music but also in rumba—as evidence of the regionalist sentiment I detail in chapter 1. Chapter 6 also relies heavily on textual analysis, examining scholarship on rumba and son as an elucidation of how regionalism informs the production of knowledge. Musical analysis, while not present in all chapters, is a major element of chapter 5, as I detail two innovations in rumba performance. Finally, I conducted archival research in several libraries on the island, spending many hours at Cuba's primary music research institution, the Center for the Research and Development of Cuban Music (CID-MUC), and at the library at the Casa del Caribe in Santiago. The examination of texts—including books, magazine and journal articles, and theses conducted by Cuban university students—allowed me to become familiar with the publication of local materials related to rumba and eastern Cuban folklore.

Terminology

As is evident from my discussion of the nationalist hybridity discourse, racial categorization in Cuba (and in most of Latin America) is distinct from the black/white binary that is still hegemonic in the United States. Far from adhering to the "one-drop rule," mixed-race ancestry has long been recognized and distinguished from blackness, with a separate census category that dates back to the first count after independence, in 1899. In addition to the three official terms used to identify a Cuban's racial identity—*blanco* (white), *negro* (black), and *mulato/mestizo* (mulatto/mixed-race)—Cubans use various "in-between" categories to make further distinctions in skin color and other phenotypic features. Common terms are *jabao* (a light-skinned mulatto), *trigueño* (a person who is even lighter than jabao and has straighter hair), and *prieto* (a black person with very dark skin). Cubans draw even further racial distinctions by pinpointing "contrasting" phenotypic traits. For example, I have often heard Cubans speak of a *negra con pelo bueno*, a black woman with "good," or relatively straight, hair, a trait that presumably offsets the negative associations of her skin color and assumes a greater level of attractiveness. Thus, whenever possible I make a distinction between blacks and mulatos, as is the norm in Cuba, in order to avoid imposing a US-derived system of racial categorization. However, this does not mean that I believe the Cuban racial taxonomy is inherently less racist than that of the United States, or that the official recognition of mixed-race people translates to more structural racial equality.

The term "Afro-Cuban" is often used outside of Cuba to refer to black and mixed-race Cubans. On the island, however, the Spanish term *afrocubano* is not generally used by Cubans to refer to their racial identity but rather to refer to African-derived religious and musical traditions. The term is used quite indiscriminately and can potentially refer to any practice with some degree of African derivation—for example, even though son features more audible traces of European influence than rumba, both can be and are discussed as Afro-Cuban musical practices. I suspect that since the term *afrocubano* glosses over the distinction between *mulato* and *negro*, it is not useful for most Cubans in terms of racial identification, because they tend to be extremely distinguishing about physical differences indexing race, sometimes revealing racist overtones or ideas.[16] I thus use "Afro-Cuban" primarily to refer to cultural and religious practices that display heavy African influences. In line with the ways that Cubans identify themselves, I avoid using the term to refer to an individual's racial identity. That said, in order to avoid overly wordy descriptions, I do utilize the term "Afro-Cuban" to refer to Cubans of African descent as a large population group (including both black and mixed-race Cubans), and primarily when discussing historical contexts, as is common among US-based Cuba scholars (for example, Helg 1995; R. Moore 1997; de la Fuente 2001).

The second issue of terminology relates to my use of the terms "rumba" and "folkloric" to refer to groups with whom I have conducted ethnographic research. Although I generally use one or the other, depending on the group discussed, I want to emphasize that there is an ambiguous politics of naming involved in identifying groups as such. This is because many rumba groups also perform Afro-Cuban "folkloric" (generally meant to mean "sacred") traditions, and vice versa. However, I retain the distinction between "rumba" and "folkloric" groups in order to signal a difference in the proportion of repertoire that is dedicated to rumba and Afro-Cuban sacred traditions, respectively. For example, since becoming a folkloric group in 1980, Afrocuba de Matanzas's performances tend to be more oriented toward the latter rather than rumba. In fact, the group has become so strongly associated with folkloric/sacred musical practices that many are not aware that Afrocuba began as a rumba group. For these reasons I refer to the group as "folkloric." In contrast, the Havana rumba groups with whom I conducted research are all known primarily for rumba performance, despite the fact that they perform Afro-Cuban religious traditions as well. Thus I refer to these as "rumba" groups. One other distinguishing factor is the number of dancers in the group: full-fledged folkloric troupes have larger corps of dancers and focus on choreographed pieces, whereas rumba groups often only have a few dancers.

Structure of the Book

This study is designed to be triangular. I am considering the relationship between music, race, and place in three sites on the island—Havana, Santiago, and Matanzas—but I also perform comparisons of each of the three relationships: Havana-Santiago, Havana-Matanzas, and Santiago-Matanzas. The early chapters focus on the juxtaposition of Havana/western Cuba and Santiago/eastern Cuba. Chapter 3 will step away from a comparative framework temporarily in order to hone in on the contemporary situation of folklore oriental (eastern Cuban folklore), which has enjoyed relatively little academic attention. Chapters 4 and 5 are centered on the discursive polarization of Havana and Matanzas. My final chapter, although not focused primarily on the relationship between Matanzas and Santiago, will include a discussion of the different notions of blackness that adhere to the two cities. Nonetheless, as will be obvious, this third pairing is considered in much less depth than the Havana-Matanzas and Havana-Santiago relationships.

In terms of the various elements of the politics of place this book explores, regionalism will be the focus of chapters 1 and 2 and will carry over into the discussion of folklore oriental in chapter 3. Chapter 4 will turn to the racialized discourses of place associated with Havana and Matanzas, respectively, with a heavier focus on the trope attached to Matanzas, "the cradle of Afro-Cuban culture." Chapter 5 will continue this comparison of Havana and Matanzas, albeit with a somewhat different theoretical focus—localized notions of hybridity as exemplified in rumba innovations. Finally, chapter 6 will engage with both issues of regionalism—related to the national musics associated respectively with eastern and western Cuba—and racialized discourse of place, this time in a comparison of Matanzas and Santiago. Following are brief summaries of each chapter.

My first chapter chronicles the pervasiveness of regionalist sentiment within contemporary Cuban society. I first present a genealogy of regionalism on the island from the early colonial period through independence in order to contextualize the present situation and challenge the notion of a unified hybrid nation put forth by the Cuban state. The discussion of contemporary regionalism will focus on relationships among Cubans in Havana and the effects of large-scale migration from Oriente to the capital. The second part of the chapter elucidates the intersections between race and place, taking into account the racial demographics of each region both historically and in the present moment.

Chapter 2 elaborates on the ways regionalist tensions are performed through the lyrics of Cuban dance music and rumba and conducts textual analyses of several songs that explicitly comment on this issue. These first chapters will provide ample evidence of regionalist sentiment gathered from various sources, including subjective perspectives, ethnographic observation, song lyrics, and published scholarship.

Chapter 3 will provide a detailed discussion of the current status of eastern Cuban folklore in terms of both academic scholarship and performance. Because this realm of cultural production has been marginalized within national scholarship and has been discussed in very few English-language publications, I feel it necessary to present a comprehensive overview of folklore oriental. I utilize various sources and methods in this chapter, including a review of regional scholarship on these traditions, interviews with musicians, discourse analysis, and musical description and analysis.

Chapter 4 entails a critical examination of racialized discourses of place in the academic and popular realms, focusing on the ways that the cities of Havana and Matanzas are represented in polarized racial and cultural terms. I argue that while these discourses of place do not accurately characterize the folkloric scenes in either city, they serve an important function—particularly in the smaller and more isolated city of Matanzas—in that they impact musicians' ability to benefit financially from cultural tourism.

The fifth chapter details two hybridizing practices within contemporary rumba performance, one in Matanzas (*batarumba*) and one in Havana (*guarapachangueo*). I employ Stuart Hall's concept of *situated hybridity* (Chen 1996) in order to argue that these innovations are informed by the histories and discourses of place attached to the two respective locales. In discussing these innovations, I employ oral histories and in-depth musical analyses of both. Finally, I elucidate how these innovations are illustrative of the different approaches toward rumba-based fusion in the two cities in general, and thus of how musicians "perform" local identity.

My final chapter returns to the relationship between eastern and western Cuba, and to the discussion of regionalism more broadly. It takes up an exploration of how historical regional inequalities and the overall hegemony of Havana-based and western Cuban traditions may have informed the scholarship on the two most important national music traditions, son and rumba.

The Particularities of Conducting Ethnographic Research in Cuba

The long-standing political antagonism between the Cuban and American governments at times seems to present an insurmountable challenge for US researchers who conduct fieldwork on the island. The obstacles I and other Cuba researchers have faced due to the lack of diplomatic relations between the two countries primarily relate to the serious difficulties in obtaining research funding and the legal issues involved in traveling to and residing for a period of time on the island.[17] Nonetheless, the December 17, 2014, announcement by President Obama that his administration would restore diplomatic ties between the two nations was a very promising development that will surely facilitate the research process for Americans in the future. For each research trip I took while completing my doctoral degree, I was required to obtain permission from the University of California to use their special license to travel to Cuba, academic institutions being one of the few entities exempted from the economic embargo that constitutes a de facto travel ban. In addition to the impediments imposed by my own government, the Cuban government has historically made it very difficult for foreign researchers to legally undertake ethnographic research on the island (see Knauer 2005). The Ministry of Culture—the apparatus that oversees many cultural and research institutions such as La Fundación Fernando Ortiz in Havana, which generously provided me with an institutional affiliation for my fieldwork—may approve a research visa, although this is not a given at all. Additionally, there is no guarantee that a researcher will be able to stay for the length of time needed to conduct an in-depth project. In fact, many US and foreign researchers conduct their research "illegally," under the auspices of a tourist visa, which lasts for thirty days and can only be extended for one month. While I arrived in Cuba on a tourist visa for my extended period of fieldwork from August 2006 to May 2007, I was extremely fortunate to get my research visa approved after two months without having to leave the island, and to be given the amount of time I requested, ten months.[18] When it comes to research in Cuba, the stars must be aligned for both adequate funding and long-term visa approval to fall into place.

In addition to the logistical and economic difficulties of conducting research in Cuba, there are a number of ethical issues that have arisen for Cuba scholars as a result of the government's responses to the economic crisis of the Special Period. The growth of the tourism industry and the installation of a dual economy have meant a reexacerbation of income inequality among Cubans, which had been greatly reduced in the prior three decades of the revolution. Cubans have been made to feel like second-class citizens owing to the privileged treatment accorded to tourists and other foreigners in terms of the products and services that are offered in *divisa* (hard currency or dollars, in which foreigners operate) versus Cuban pesos (the national currency in which Cubans are *meant* to operate, although they often gain access to some dollars through various means).[19] As Cuba researchers quickly come to learn, there is an economic aspect of all relationships created between Cubans and foreigners due to the inequality in the dual currency system, for there is no denying that even a graduate student making $15,000–$20,000 per year is viewed as wealthy in the eyes of Cubans, most of whom earn $200–$400 per year. Thus, while Cubans are likely to tell a foreign researcher who has spent long periods of time on the island that he or she has become "almost Cuban," the awareness of the difference in economic means between themselves and the non-Cubans is always lingering in the air.[20] This issue took on an added significance for me when I began a relationship with a Cuban during an early research trip that eventually resulted in his immigration to the United States and our marriage in 2008.

This almost constant awareness of economic difference can be difficult for researchers, who often feel an obligation to help Cuban friends and collaborators by giving them money periodically or buying them groceries, all the while trying to stretch research funds as far as possible within a tourist currency whose value has been inflated. These circumstances are also uncomfortable for Cubans, who are generally very proud and think of themselves as self-sufficient. There is an exchange of resources that occurs between a (usually Western) researcher of culture and a (generally non-Western) collaborator: the former often provides much-needed financial help through gifts and/or payment for private lessons, while the latter imparts intangible resources such as knowledge of a given phenomenon or connections that facilitate entry into a particular social network. Nevertheless, the possession of economic resources, or the lack thereof, is an incredibly influential factor that impacts the quality of life one has in Cuba, and money is the prime issue around which power relations are constructed. Thus, I want to emphasize that the complex and sometimes uncomfortable dynamics of interrelation between Cubans and foreigners must be understood as a product of Cuba's post-Soviet economic situation, and the almost universal desperation and deprivation suffered by its citizens in the 1990s.

Being cognizant of the economic differences between myself and the Cubans with whom I worked does not necessarily mean, however, that there was an abyss that could not be bridged. Over the past ten years, I have created close, affectionate relationships and experienced many moments of warmth and shared laughter with Cuban musicians and friends beyond my husband's family. At the same time, my experiences living in Cuba and my reactions to difficult situations have taught me, to my chagrin, how culturally conditioned I am as an American in certain ways. I often found myself cursing the inefficient bureaucracy that presented obstacles to conducting research and hampered the creative activities of the musicians with whom I worked, and distressed by the inaccurate assumptions friends and musicians made about my ability to help them financially for a sustained period of time. Thus, I have become, as Jocelyne Guilbault terms it, a "commuter." She states: "What this commuting has led me to develop is a series of affinities and a special connection with particular circuits of the transnational Caribbean space" (Guilbault 2007, 15–16). I feel a tremendous sense of affinity and intimacy with many Cubans and their music that, despite the thorny and unavoidable issues of economic—and often racial—inequality that arise in relationships between Cubans and foreigners, impels me to return to the island again and again.

The Politics of Representation

As various Cuba scholars have noted, anything published by a US scholar on a Cuban topic is inevitably politicized, because the discourse and views about the island have been polarized for so many years. For this reason, it has become de rigueur to address the politics of representation entailed in the publication of lengthy work on a Cuba-related issue, particularly when the scholar is an ethnographer. However, while Cuba is usually held up as an exception in almost all matters—politics, research, and otherwise—I do not believe that an extra level of self-reflexivity is necessarily warranted in order to discuss Cuba-related topics as compared to those associated with other countries in the "global South." Following the wealth of literature on the politics of representation during the so-called anthropological crisis of the 1980s, it is now well acknowledged that researchers can never fully or objectively represent the culture of an "other" or even of a community to which they belong without recognizing their own role in the production of "the field" and the power dynamics surrounding the given phenomenon. Along these lines, I do not view a US scholar discussing Cuban musical performance as inherently more problematic or complex than if the researcher were Canadian or Italian, or than if I were researching music in a country "friendly" to the United States. After all, most of the world's cultural traditions are impacted by postcolonial relations and researched by people of a different class and/or national background than their practitioners. In my view, it's important not to reinforce the discourse of exceptionalism associated with Cuba.

Contrary to widespread belief in the United States that Cubans are brainwashed by their socialist government to hate all things American, many have professed to me that they feel more affinity with Americans and our culture than with Europeans. They often explain their feelings in terms of the Latin American tradition of hemispheric solidarity—advocated strongly by José Martí—which views the whole Western hemisphere as *Las Américas*, a geographical entity that entails elements of shared history (the experience of European colonization) and culture. Thus, it would be a mistake to reify the notion that the political hostilities between the US and Cuban governments have succeeded in producing similarly polarized attitudes between the citizens of the two countries. Nevertheless, I do not want to dismiss the significance of the antagonisms that have developed over the past half century, and thus recognize the need to discuss my own positioning as an American researcher in Cuba. Ethnomusicologist Robin Moore makes an eloquent statement that reflects my feelings very closely: "I consider myself sympathetic to the goals of socialism and believe that many of its basic precepts are more humane than those driving decision-making in capitalist countries. However, this has not blinded me to the oppressiveness of many aspects of life in Cuba today. I hope that readers on the left and right of the political spectrum will agree that it serves no one's interest to gloss over mistakes made by any government" (R. Moore 2006, xiv).

In terms of my own relationship to the long-standing US-Cuba conflict, I was raised in San Francisco by leftist parents who actively opposed US imperialist ventures into Latin America in the 1970s and 1980s. The Cuban Revolution was held up as the one permanent victory in Latin America's struggle for sovereignty and self-determination, and as a significant thorn in the side of the United States and our historical hegemony within the Americas. Thus, while it is the extraordinary allure of Cuban music that primarily drove my decision to conduct research on the island, I also recognize that my choice was informed by a certain romanticization of Cuban socialism that pervaded both my childhood and the larger environs of the San Francisco Bay Area. Like Moore, I continue to believe that the revolution's social reforms have been beneficial for a majority of Cubans and that Cubans enjoy a level of education and a welfare safety net unmatched in Latin America, and probably in North America.[21] However, Cuba's first- and second-wave exile community, and its positioning on the extreme right of the US political spectrum, has resulted in a polarized discourse around Cuba that has forced leftists into the position of being apologists for the Castro regime. In response to the rabid anticommunism of the Miami exile power elite and mafia-style intimidation of any moderate Cubans or others who dare to suggest a normalization of relations with the island, leftists have often expressed a complete and unproblematic endorsement of the Castro regimes, despite their nonprogressive agendas in several arenas.[22] These have included well-known policies—like heavy repression of political dissent and lack of freedom of expression and the press—and the imprisonment of citizens considered to be counterrevolutionary such as gays and lesbians, advocates for black empowerment, religious practitioners, and other "undesirables" (in Fidel Castro's words) during the first three decades of the revolution.[23]

Although revolutionary Cuba is often held up by leftists as a symbol of resistance, I want to follow sociologist Sujatha Fernandes's assertion that it is necessary to problematize the notion of "resistance." She states: "I am cautious about speaking of 'resistance' in the Cuban context. . . . Notions of 'rebellion' and 'revolution,' which may stir up the imaginations and energies of citizens elsewhere, have been co-opted by the state in Cuba. Official discourse continually refers to 'resistance' to colonialism, US imperialism, and global capitalism" (Fernandes 2006, 185). Thus, while some of the musical practices I am examining and musicians I have worked with have been subject to marginalization, it is precisely because of the co-optation of the notion of "resistance" by revolutionary socialist discourse that I eschew this term in my book. I am not arguing that musicians' actions/beliefs should never be interpreted as challenging the policies of a state that is repressive in certain arenas;

elsewhere (Bodenheimer 2013) I have focused specifically on the marginal-ization of rumba musicians due to the continued racialization of the genre. Nonetheless, I believe that the situation on the ground is much more complex than the notion of "resistance" offers and that most Cubans hold nuanced, conflicted views of the state and its policies; they support certain ones and feel oppressed by others. Moreover, it must be recognized that there has never developed in Cuba an organized and mass movement of resistance against the socialist regime. While the reasons for this continue to elude most Cuba researchers (myself included), this fact might suggest that most Cubans do not feel oppressed to such an extent that they are willing to risk their lives to impel a change in government—as occurred during the revolution and the fight against Fulgencio Batista's dictatorship—and that they still recognize some basic benefits of a socialist system.

Stuart Hall's scrutiny of the "essential black subject" in his essay "New Eth-nicities" has helped me in framing my conflicted feelings about the Cuban government, which are shared by many progressive Americans who have experienced the contradictions of Cuban society firsthand. He states: "Once you abandon essential categories, there is no place to go apart from the poli-tics of criticism and to enter the politics of criticism in black culture is to grow up, to leave the age of critical innocence" (Hall [1989] 1996b, 448). To recognize that the Cuban Revolution has allowed for the continuation of racial discrimination and the introduction of preferential treatment for for-eigners in the 1990s is to realize that the government is not necessarily and always "right on" just because it calls itself "socialist" or opposes US imperial-ism and hegemony; it is to "leave the age of critical innocence."

Finally, I feel it necessary to acknowledge how my personal choices and relationships have informed this study. Although this book attempts to paint a nuanced portrait of the effects of regionalism on musical performance and to represent a diversity of viewpoints on the matter, it would be naïve to believe that my research interests, objectives, and analytical interpretations were not influenced and positioned to a certain extent by my relationship with a Cuban from Santiago. We met in 2004 at an early stage of my dissertation research, and, while Lázaro was neither an active collaborator nor a participant in my fieldwork activities, our relationship served as a constant backdrop for my research. I was witness to the police harassment and snide comments he was sometimes subjected to in Havana because of his identity as an eastern Cuban, and I understand that my own research perspectives were colored by these experiences. One way in which I am sure readers will recognize this position-ing is in my interpretation of the statements of many of my collaborators as influenced by their regional/local identities. Although I feel a profound duty

to represent musicians' perspectives as faithfully as possible (while recognizing my own mediating role), I realize that some readers may disagree with my
analyses. I do hope, in any case, that this study will contribute a new perspective to the already rich body of scholarship on the relationship between musical performance and contemporary social issues in Cuba.

Chapter One

Regionalism and the Intersections of Race and Place in Cuba

> I just bought a pair of gym shoes, Nikes. Because I am black and an Oriental,
> everyone will call me a hustler. . . . I work hard for my money, but people
> think I am a pimp because I am black and from Santiago de Cuba.
> —Mark Sawyer, *Racial Politics in Post-Revolutionary Cuba*

My introduction presented an overview of racial politics in Cuba, emphasizing how the recognition of racial difference has been considered to be detrimental to a unified national identity. This chapter posits that in a similar fashion, regionalism—constituted by both a centuries-long history of regionalist antagonism between the eastern and western parts of the island and contemporary regionalist sentiment among the population—contests the notion of Cubanidad that has been hegemonic for over a century. My secondary goal is to elucidate how race and the politics of place historically and currently intersect with each other. I will ultimately argue that the racialization and regionalization of Cuban society, which are reflected in a variety of musical practices that I will discuss in subsequent chapters, challenge the nationalist notion of a hybridized and unified Cubanidad.

My interest in investigating the politics of place in contemporary Cuba stems from observations since my first research trip to the island in 2004 that expressions of regionalism are longstanding and pervasive. I employ "regionalism" and its related terms to refer to popular discourses that assume a set of naturalized distinctions between Cubans from different provinces of the country. Although there is a distinction to be made between regions and provinces within Cuba—in that each region is made up of various provinces—I use the term "regionalism" in a broader manner that sometimes glosses over the differences between the two geographical categories. Acknowledgment and examination of this issue is largely absent from both Cuban and US academic scholarship, a lacuna that is surprising given the frequency of assertions of regionalist sentiment in both popular discourse and music. Such assertions are evident mostly in the arena of popular, mass-mediated music, but also in rumba songs, as will be demonstrated in the following chapter. Despite the revolutionary government's official rhetoric, which stresses national unity and celebrates the population's ongoing dedication to socialist ideals of egalitarianism and cooperation, many Cubans cling tightly to their regional identities. This means not only a fierce loyalty to one's province of birth but often an explicit antagonism toward people from other provinces, particularly between *habaneros* (people from Havana) and *orientales* (people from the eastern provinces). As will be evident, these regionalist antagonisms are often entangled with racialized discourses. Thus, I want to examine the ways that race is mapped onto different regions and cities on the island. My analysis in this chapter foregrounds the importance of what cultural geographer Don Mitchell terms the "spatiality of identity" (2000, 62), which recognizes the powerful effects of space and place on the production of social identities.

A Genealogy of Regionalism in Cuba

In order to contextualize my discussion of the politics of place in contemporary Cuban society and its relation to musical performance on the island, this section performs a genealogy of regionalism. Michel Foucault (1977) elucidates his analytic of "genealogy" in contrast with traditional historiography, drawing on Friedrich Nietzsche's notion of "wirkliche Historie" (effective history), which emphasizes the discontinuities and ruptures in the development of humankind. Foucault states, "The search for descent is not the erecting of foundations: on the contrary, it disturbs what was previously considered immobile; it fragments what was thought unified; it shows the heterogeneity of what was imagined consistent with itself" (1977, 147). In this vein, I aim to offer a rather detailed summary of regionalism in Cuba in order to disrupt the narratives of national unity that have been so pervasive not only since the revolution but since the birth of the island as an independent nation.

Cuban Historiography and the Significance of a Regional Perspective

Published histories of Cuba have been fairly silent on the issue of regionalism. While there have been regional histories written about various provinces on the island, I am familiar with only one Cuban scholar, Hernán Venegas Delgado, who has framed the issue as a more fundamental problem in terms of the historiography of the nation. In *La Región en Cuba* (2001), Venegas

Delgado points out a number of underlying assumptions within Cuba historiography, most notably the fact that historians have neglected to consider the histories of all regions beyond western Cuba. Speaking about one of the first histories of the island to be written (during the colonial period), he states: "His homeland is not Cuba, it is Havana, and more than the province [of Havana], the city" (Venegas Delgado 2001, 60; my translation). In a similar critique, Cuban American historian Miguel Bretos begins his book chronicling the history of Matanzas thus: "Over the years, the allure of the Cuban capital has seduced all comers to the point of nearly subsuming the nation's identity, as if Cuba were the hinterland of Havana instead of Havana the capital of Cuba" (Bretos 2010, xiii).

Among Venegas Delgado's more significant critiques, he discusses the impact of the development of the sugar industry on national history, noting that because the largest sugar mills during the boom of the nineteenth century were in the west, colonial economic conditions in the central and eastern regions have been ignored. In fact, by the mid-nineteenth century, the bulk of sugar production had moved away from the province of Havana and toward the western-central region, concentrated in the provinces of Matanzas and Las Villas, and by the early twentieth century it had moved further east, coming to be concentrated in Camagüey and northeastern Cuba (Venegas Delgado 2001, 103). Venegas Delgado's larger point is that if the history of sugar was so crucial to the economic foundation of the nation, it should also take into account regions beyond western Cuba. He also repeatedly stresses that the provinces of the western region tend to be lumped together and discussed as one entity, meaning that Matanzas and the westernmost province of Pinar del Río tend to be discussed as extensions of Havana, despite the fact that they have their own historical processes and events (99–101). The history of Pinar del Río is particularly neglected, even though it is characterized by unique agricultural conditions—it is the primary tobacco producer on the island and was never a center of sugar production.

One other major critique by Venegas Delgado concerns the birth of nationalist sentiment—often attributed to Havana—and the role of the independence struggles in its development. Referring to the fact that the large majority of combat during the thirty-year independence struggle took place in the east, he states: "In those eastern and central regions the emergence of Cuban nationalism has occurred with the most strength, and this requires a very serious foundation in national history" (Venegas Delgado 2001, 117). Finally, he finds that regionalist antagonism was one of the primary reasons why the Ten Years' War (the first sustained independence struggle) failed to succeed in liberating the island from Spanish control (141); in other words, the east and west were too divided to wage a successful war. Venegas Delgado's critique of Cuba's rather myopic historiography is an important one, as it comes from an intellectual on the island who has experienced firsthand the hegemony of Havana and western Cuba in nearly all aspects of life.

Historic Differences and Tensions between Eastern and Western Cuba

Olga Portuondo Zúñiga, who currently holds the distinguished title of historian of the city of Santiago de Cuba and has written extensively on the history and culture of the eastern city, asserted in a conversation that regionalist sentiment dates back to the early colonial period and is related to how Spain founded the different villas, or cities, on the island (pers. comm. 2011). In fact, Columbus first arrived in the east in 1492, coming from the nearby island of Hispaniola (present-day Haiti and Dominican Republic), and Cuba's easternmost city of Baracoa was the first Spanish settlement to be established, in 1512. After its founding in 1515, Santiago de Cuba, currently the island's second-largest city and de facto capital of Oriente (eastern Cuba), became the home base of the colony's first governor, famed Spanish conquistador Diego Velásquez, and thus the first capital of the island. In 1553, the Spanish Crown ordered the governor to relocate to the villa of Havana, which grew in significance throughout the sixteenth century, and the western city was formally established as the capital of the island in 1607 (Louis Pérez 2006). During the first century of colonization, the island was considered to be one province, but in 1607 a royal decree split Cuba into two halves—Havana and Santiago de Cuba—each with its own independent government.[1] In 1774, there was a new geographical demarcation, with the Departamento Occidental o de La Habana (Western Department or Havana) constituting almost three-fourths of the island's land mass and the Departamento Oriental o de Santiago de Cuba (Eastern Department or Santiago de Cuba) making up the rest. By 1827, the population growth on the island necessitated a division of the island into three departments: *occidental* (western), *central* (central), and *oriental* (eastern). Since then, there have been several divisions of the island into varying numbers of provinces, with a current total of sixteen (see figure 1.1). Nonetheless, the island is still discussed, both by the government and within popular discourse, as having three principal regions, with each containing five or more provinces.

Portuondo asserted that by the beginning of the seventeenth century, western Cuba came to be the focus of the colonial government and its commerce, and the Departamento Oriental began to be marginalized, resulting in a tendency to segregate the two regions and the growth of autonomous

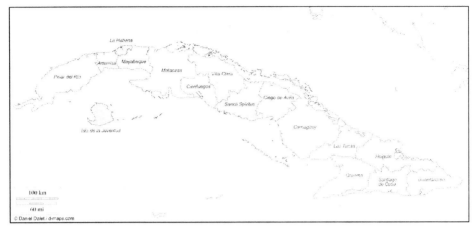

Figure 1.1: Map of Cuba's sixteen provinces after the most recent administrative division in 2011. Occidente is composed of La Habana, Pinar del Río, Artemisa, Mayabeque, Matanzas, and Isla de la Juventud. Centro includes Cienfuegos, Villa Clara, Sancti Spíritus, Ciego de Ávila, and Camagüey. Oriente is made up of Las Tunas, Granma, Holguín, Santiago de Cuba, and Guantánamo. Source: http://d-maps.com/carte.php?&num_car=38497&lang=en.

sentiment in Oriente (pers. comm. 2011). She thus documented a long-standing precedent by the colonial government of privileging Havana and western Cuba in resources and technological development, a dynamic that continued after independence into the period of American occupation (1898–1902). Portuondo further asserted that even within colonial-era Oriente there was a tendency toward localist sentiment: planters in the cities of Bayamo and Holguín routinely opposed the centralization of power in Santiago. Joel James, José Millet, and Alexis Alarcón (2007, 39) attribute the historic rivalry between Holguín on the one hand and Santiago and Bayamo on the other to a large influx of Spaniards into Holguín that created differences in racial composition. Santiago and Bayamo were thereafter composed of a more mixed-race population, while Holguín has long been considered the "whitest" city in Oriente.

Cuba historian Louis Pérez also discusses the growing isolation of Oriente after the establishment of Havana as the capital of the colony, asserting that colonial officials rarely traveled to the east, leaving it somewhat defenseless against incursions by other European powers, including several attacks by the French and the English in the seventeenth century (2006, 30). Ironically, this colonial neglect set the stage for an increase in contraband and illicit trade with other Caribbean colonies, such as Jamaica and Barbados. Pérez states, "The distinctions between east and west would deepen with the passage of time, but already at the end of the century of conquest, both Havana and Santiago de Cuba occupied sharply different places on the social continuum of colonial Cuba. From these two contrary points would emerge competing views of *cubanidad*, of what it meant to be Cuban. The west flourished as a result of the official presence, in defense of colonial policy; the east flourished as a result of official absence, in defiance of colonial policy" (31). Pérez paints Oriente as "Cuba's frontier land," noting of its distinct geography, "Oriente appeared too remote, the terrain too inhospitable, to justify large-scale settlement and extensive commercial exploitation" (8), and arguing that its remoteness made it "the most Cuban region of all of Cuba, less susceptible to outside influences, more committed to ways local and traditional" (9). Considering the history of migration from other parts of the Caribbean to Oriente since the early nineteenth century (see below), I view this as a somewhat essentialist statement that seems to romanticize Oriente as a pristine outpost, immune to foreign influence. In fact, the diverse histories of migration to the two regions can be viewed as another important factor that contributed to divisions between east and west: the late eighteenth and early nineteenth centuries saw not only a major wave of Franco-Haitian migration to eastern Cuba but also a huge growth in the importation of African slaves primarily to western Cuba.

Historian Ada Ferrer's *Insurgent Cuba: Race, Nation, and Revolution, 1868–1898* (1999) also discusses the historical tensions between Havana and Oriente as a result of the distinct social and economic conditions of the two regions under Spanish colonialism. In the mid-nineteenth century, while central and western Cuba were enjoying the economic boom produced by high levels of slave-driven sugar production, eastern Cuba was suffering from an economic downturn and the effects of harsh taxation by the colonial government (Ferrer 1999, 18–21). In contrast to the monocrop nature of western-central Cuban agriculture, dominated by sugar plantations, eastern Cuba's agricultural production had always been more varied—including coffee, tobacco, and cattle in addition to sugar estates.[2] Furthermore, the eastern plantations were generally smaller and less technologically advanced, with a significant percentage of free workers of color (18–21).[3] Louis Pérez asserts that the free population of color constituted 63 percent of the total nonwhite population in the east, but only 32 percent in the west (2006, 66). These social and economic conditions contributed greatly to what Ferrer terms the "geography of insurgency" (Ferrer 1999, 17), or the fact that eastern Cuba was the site of the first rebellion in 1868 that began the thirty-year struggle for independence.[4] Pérez states, "Already politically marginal, in varying degrees of economic decline, not as burdened by the weight of slavery, they [easterners] had less to fear from disorder, more to gain from change. The economic problem was seen as an aspect of the political problem: if the eastern zones were poor, backward, and miserable, it was because of the malfeasance and misgovernment by Spain. The only solution was a political one" (Louis Pérez 2006, 89).

In contrast to the spirit of rebellion characterizing nineteenth-century Oriente, Havana and much of western Cuba remained loyal to the Spanish Crown until 1895, three years before independence. The *Grito de Yara* (Cry of Yara) on October 10, 1868, in the southeastern jurisdiction of Manzanillo constituted the first call to arms against Spanish rule, thus beginning the Ten Years' War (1868–1878). The rebellion was led by plantation owner Carlos Manuel de Céspedes, who freed his slaves on that day and invited them to join the independence struggle.[5] Ada Ferrer suggests that the initiative taken by white eastern elites in advocating abolition and armed struggle against Spain was more about their adverse economic situation and resentment of colonial taxation laws than it was about humanitarian ideals of equality and freedom (Ferrer 1999, 17–23). Notwithstanding the white planters' intentions, another major chasm between east and west was created with the terms of the Pact of Zanjón, which ended the Ten Years' War and reestablished Spain's hegemony: de facto abolition was decreed in the central-eastern region of the country (where the war was based), and a continuation of slavery in all the provinces west of Camagüey (James et al. 2007, 41).[6]

Historian Aline Helg's *Our Rightful Share: The Afro-Cuban Struggle for Equality, 1886–1912* (1995) also foregrounds regional differences as they impacted the Cuban independence struggle, viewing them as an important factor that hampered Afro-Cubans from presenting a united front in their demands for equality after emancipation in 1886. Like Ferrer, Helg emphasizes the distinct socioeconomic conditions in different regions, illustrating the particular patterns of land ownership by blacks and mulatos[7] in different provinces. In the western province of Matanzas and the central province of Santa Clara, the sites of the largest concentrations of slaves, Afro-Cubans owned or rented land at a much lower percentage than whites. In Oriente, where a large rural free population of color had been concentrated before emancipation, the two racial groups owned land at approximately equal rates (Helg 1995, 26). Correspondingly, racial barriers were stronger and more rigid in Matanzas and Santa Clara than in Oriente, where, in addition to having twice the proportion of a free population of color, slaves had been more widely distributed on smaller plantations (32). Support for the *mambises* (insurgents during the independence struggles) was always strongest on the eastern end of the island. Not surprisingly, Cuban plantation owners in the western and central provinces were firmly opposed to abolition, and by extension the independence struggles, which were led primarily by a mulato native of Oriente, Antonio Maceo.

Arguably the most effective tactic used by colonial authorities to keep white Cuban planters loyal to Spain was the specter of a race war led by black Cubans, in the vein of the Haitian Revolution. In addition to conveying a racial threat, this propaganda also included crucial dimensions of regional hostility; as I discuss in more detail below, Oriente has a significant population of Haitian descent dating back to the early nineteenth century. Whereas western Cuban provinces such as Havana and Pinar del Río had always been Spanish colonial strongholds, the east was characterized by a spirit of rebellion and independence fervor, partly due to the Franco-Haitian presence. In other words, racist colonial propaganda that conjured up the image of Haitian slaves expelling and massacring their white masters was also regionalist propaganda, the goal of which was to marginalize eastern Cuba. Helg states, "The Spanish authorities cleverly propagated the rumor that Maceo's real aim was to establish a separate black state in eastern Cuba with the support of the Liga Antillana (Caribbean League), an organization allegedly made up of blacks and mulattoes from Haiti and Santo Domingo" (Helg 1995, 51).

The racial anxiety caused by the imagined threat of a Haitian-style black revolution ultimately succeeded in containing the major rebellions in Oriente for twenty-eight years, until Antonio Maceo successfully invaded the western part of the island in early 1896. Even important Afro-Cuban intellectuals became swept up in this racist hysteria; for example, Matanzas-born Juan Gualberto Gómez attempted to disprove parallels between Haiti and Cuba by emphasizing the different African provenances of slaves imported to the two respective countries. Gómez asserted that while Haitian slaves had been taken principally from warlike tribes in Senegal and Dahomey (modern-day Benin), Cuban slaves had largely come from more "submissive" and "gentle" tribes of the Congo basin (Helg 1995, 52).[8] Given the regionalist logic underpinning these assumptions about different African ethnic groups, not to mention the history of regional tension in Spain,[9] perhaps it is not surprising that regionalist sentiment has been such a long-standing and divisive issue in Cuba.

Helg provides a fascinating breakdown by province of the racial composition of the independence rebels in the final War of Independence (1895–1898): Oriente's rebels were divided into two main regions, one battalion led by a wealthy white planter from Holguín, and the other led by Guillermón Moncada, a black carpenter from Santiago, representing the poorer and blacker southeastern part of Oriente. In the neighboring province of Camagüey, the rebels were mostly white, and in fact throughout the war they weakened rebel unity by pitting themselves against the darker-skinned *orientales* (easterners). The central Santa Clara Province was made up of a diverse range of Cubans, including landowners and former slaves. While the Matanzas rebels were largely of rural Afro-Cuban descent, regionalist sentiment was operative here as well and divided the mambises: Matanzas insurgents were hesitant to follow leaders from Oriente moving westward. Helg notes that despite these regional antagonisms, Antonio Maceo fostered cross-regional unity as he moved westward across the country and gained the respect and admiration of both black and white rebels. Although Havana and Pinar del Río, the latter with a majority of Spanish and white Cuban-born peasants, had supported Spain during the Ten Years' War, Maceo was finally successful in invading the latter in January 1896. Helg views this victory as the strategic key in winning the war that led to Cuban independence and notes that it was only at that point that "the independence struggle had acquired a truly national dimension" (Helg 1995, 74). She thus suggests—echoing Venegas Delgado's assertion above—that Cuba could have only gained independence by overcoming, albeit temporarily and only partially, the regionalist antagonisms between the eastern and western provinces.

Helg foregrounds the disillusionment faced by Afro-Cubans after independence, when they saw their disproportionately high military participation in the defeat of Spain downplayed in public discourse and their hopes for full racial equality denied by continuing segregation and discrimination. The Partido Independiente de Color (Independents of Color Party, or PIC) was formed in 1908 by Afro-Cuban political leaders as a response to the continuing inequalities faced by blacks and mulatos, and by 1910 had grown to constitute roughly 44 percent of Afro-Cuban voters (Helg 1995, 156). An overwhelming number of party leaders were from southeastern Oriente, where the party had its stronghold. This regional association, in addition to the party's organization along racial lines, was identified as a threat to Havana's mainstream political leaders, who were opposed to the eastern provinces having a stronger influence on national politics (158). By 1910, a racist campaign was launched by the Havana government and the media against the PIC, resuscitating imagined threats of a Haitian-style black revolution. This new bout of racial panic eventually led to the massacre in 1912 of thousands of blacks and mulatos in Oriente, including the vast majority of the PIC leaders and many suspected sympathizers, by a combination of government forces and white militias.

Oriente's tradition of rebellion did not of course end with the wars of independence. The Cuban Revolution officially began on July 26, 1953, with a failed attack on the Moncada barracks in Santiago by a group of rebels led by Fidel Castro, a native of Holguín in northwest Oriente. In an homage to the failed rebellion, which led to the death or jailing of many of the conspirators, Castro named his group of revolutionaries El Movimiento 26 de Julio (the 26th of July Movement). After being released from jail in 1955 and spending a year in exile gathering forces for another invasion in Mexico, Castro (along with Ernesto "Che" Guevara) landed in the southeastern province of Granma in late 1956. From that point on, guerrilla activity against dictator Fulgencio Batista's forces was based in the Sierra Maestra range in the provinces of Santiago and Granma. Thus, like the struggle for independence from Spain, the Cuban Revolution has been unequivocally linked to Oriente, evidenced by the fact that Santiago is known as *la cuna de la Revolución* (the cradle of the Revolution). Political scientist Mark Sawyer states that during the early years of the revolution, "Castro himself suggested that the capital be moved from Havana to Santiago de Cuba, a largely Afro-Cuban city, as a symbol of the priorities of the Revolution" (Sawyer 2006, 57).

Olga Portuondo asserted that during the early decades of the revolution, Havana continued to hold a privileged position over the other provinces, including in its relationship with the USSR, which provided Cuba with subsidized food and other products during the two countries' thirty-year partnership. Nonetheless, as Louis Pérez notes, the Castro regime attempted to produce more egalitarian living conditions across the island, evidenced by the large-scale construction of health care facilities in rural areas, particularly in central and eastern Cuba, in the 1960s and 1970s (2006, 276). Portuondo also noted that during the 1980s the revolution shifted to a more balanced approach and began to focus on other regions beyond Havana, partially due to the new administrative division of the country into fourteen provinces in 1976 (from the previous division into just six) and the need to develop provincial capitals; in fact, she was involved in this policy shift as the government promoted the development of regional histories. In addition, the trend toward urbanization since independence was somewhat weakened as the revolution strove to increase standards of living and access to education and health care in the rural and neglected areas of the country.[10] Similar to Portuondo's perspective, Venegas Delgado recognizes that since the revolution there has been a greater effort to focus attention on regions beyond the capital and to support research on regional histories. However, he also notes the erosion of some of these projects since the economic crisis of the Special Period (Venegas Delgado 2001, 145) and highlights the need to study interregional migration within this context, particularly the movement of eastern Cubans to the central and western regions in recent decades (125). As will be evident in the following discussion, this phenomenon constitutes a crucial issue informing contemporary regionalist antagonism in Havana.

Contemporary Regionalist Sentiment in Cuba

Eastern Migration and Regionalist Antagonism on the Streets of Havana

While both Cuban and foreign historians provide illuminating analyses of the social and economic foundations for regionalist tensions between eastern and western Cuba during the colonial era, there has been almost no scholarly attention to the enduring effects of this antagonism on contemporary social relations, identity formation, or popular culture in Cuba. While several scholars have broached the subject in passing—for example, Yvonne Daniel (1995) and Alejandro de la Fuente (2001)—there has not been an in-depth exploration of the ways that regional identity informs societal and individual beliefs or musical creativity in Cuba, or the ways it can provoke tensions between Cubans from different provinces. Moreover, it is not only the legacy of the historical strains between eastern and western Cuba that is brought to bear on the current situation but also newer, present-day pressures that continue to fuel this regionalist sentiment.[11] The level of hostility has grown since the Special Period as a result of the marked increase in migration to Havana by Cubans from *el campo* (the countryside), particularly orientales, due to the economic crisis that has disproportionately affected the outer provinces.[12]

Like the natives of many capitals throughout the world, habaneros consider every locale outside the capital to be el campo, even large cities like Santiago and Camagüey. A revealing example of the enduring force of regionalism is the pervasive use in Havana of the term *palestinos* (Palestinians) to refer to eastern Cubans, a word that not only reveals the long-standing unequal power dynamics between Havana and eastern Cuba but also contains racialized overtones. While I haven't been able to ascertain exactly how long this term has been in existence with this specific meaning, it should be made clear that it does not refer to any actual history of Palestinian presence or ancestry in eastern Cuba.[13] Rather, the term imagines a parallel between the longstanding political conflict in Palestine/Israel and the antagonism between habaneros and orientales in the Cuban capital. One Santiago-based folkloric musician noted that there are even orientales who use the term *palestino* to refer to other eastern Cubans, apparently in order to discursively distance themselves from their own roots. In fact, even the seemingly neutral term *oriental* (easterner) often functions as a discursive stand-in for rural and/or poor blackness, and backwardness generally. Another term utilized to refer to orientales is *nagüe* (slang that translates roughly to "brother"), a regionally specific way of referring to a male friend in Oriente, which habaneros sometimes invoke in mocking fashion, presumably to highlight orientales' backwardness.

Alejandro de la Fuente briefly addresses this issue in his influential book *A Nation for All: Race, Inequality, and Politics in Twentieth-Century Cuba* (2001). In elucidating the racial inequalities that have crept back into the Cuban public sphere since the Special Period and the expansion of the tourism sector, he states, "the migration of people from the eastern provinces to Havana has been frequently interpreted as a black assault on the city" (de la Fuente 2001, 327). He further highlights widespread assumptions concerning the link between race and region with a quotation from a white male professional who asserts, "These *negros orientales* [blacks from Oriente] are taking over" and who refers to them as palestinos (327–28). De la Fuente also emphasizes the racialization and regionalization of access to dollars since that currency was legalized in 1993: not only are black Cubans much less likely to be the recipients of remittances sent from relatives living abroad, principally from immigrants in the United States who were overwhelmingly white until recent years, but the remittances are disproportionately sent to residents of the capital rather than the outer provinces (327–28).[14]

In the eyes of many habaneros, orientales have colonized large sections of their city, packing themselves and their numerous relatives into crumbling, colonial apartment buildings and thus contributing greatly to the deterioration of the capital's once-great architectural accomplishments. The overcrowding is especially intense in the center of Havana, in the municipalities of Habana Vieja (Old Havana) and Centro Habana (Central Havana).[15] Furthermore, habaneros tend to paint orientales as the main culprits responsible for petty theft and hustling-oriented crime targeting tourists.[16] Many habaneros assume that orientales' intentions in migrating to Havana are sinister, whether to try to make a living *jineteando* (hustling tourists, which can involve a large variety of activities including the exchange of sex for material goods or money), or to engage in the illicit buying and selling of goods on the black market. As evidenced in the quotation reproduced at the beginning of this chapter, orientales often feel doubly criminalized—for their race and for their regional identity—and are seen as either *jineteros* (hustlers) or palestinos. Considering the fact that Israelis occupy significant portions of Palestinian land, the use of the term *palestino* to refer to orientales is curious because the latter are characterized by habaneros not as the occupied (the situation of actual Palestinians) but as the occupiers of Havana. Nonetheless, the use of the term seems to be related partly to the perception that eastern Cuban migrants are like refugees from a foreign country who have no real homeland, which is sometimes the way that exiled Palestinians are depicted.

While it is true that the Centro Habana neighborhoods of Colón, San Leopoldo, and Cayo Hueso are the destinations for many Cubans from the eastern provinces, my observations and conversations with habaneros have led me to identify certain contradictory tendencies in their comments about orientales. For example, many of these "natives" either migrated to Havana with their families during childhood, or have parents from Oriente or other Cuban provinces. Habaneros do not deny this irony, in fact often joking that there are no more "real" habaneros left in Havana (i.e., those who can boast a capital-based identity for longer than one generation) and that they have all left for el yuma (the United States or Europe).[17] Thus, the term habanero has become infused with many different meanings and regional subjectivities, and the line between habanero and oriental is sometimes quite blurry.

Another principal source of tension between eastern and western Cubans is the composition of the police force: many officers are recruited by the state from the interior and eastern provinces. A commonly held view among habaneros is the notion that Fidel Castro has routinely practiced regional bias during his regime by recruiting government officials and police officers from Oriente, of which his native province of Holguín is a part. Given that the police function as the main agents constricting Cubans' freedom of movement, orientales represent by proxy the repressive state forces that Havana residents collide with on a daily basis. Policing technologies take on a variety of forms in contemporary Havana, the most common one being the random detention of citizens on the street to ask for identification, particularly if they are black Cubans walking with (white) foreigners. I have been party to this experience in many different circumstances, in which my husband, friends, or musicians were stopped and questioned about what they were doing with me. Habaneros engaged in black market activities—from nonlicensed taxi driving to the illicit buying and selling of goods—often rail against the "palestino" cops for curtailing their economic ventures and enforcing the heavy-handed policies outlawing nonlicensed, individual private enterprise. Furthermore, this regionally inflected antagonism directed at the police is not limited to a certain sector of the Havana population but is more pervasive across class/ occupational sectors. Black Cuban intellectual Roberto Zurbano, known for his critique of continuing racism under the revolution and recently embroiled in a controversy (see introduction), discusses the police harassment of young blacks on the Havana streets thus: "Young police officers in Havana generally come from rural areas, and therefore are not familiar with the cultural dynamics of a city expressing itself through myriad fashions, aesthetic affiliations, and other visible marks characteristic of diverse cultural identities, such as rockers, religious groups, homosexuals, and tourists. The police often confuse these differences with marginal or possibly delinquent behaviors" (Zurbano 2009, 152). In a condescending tone suggesting the cultural backwardness of non-Havana natives, Zurbano apparently views the capital as the only place on the island where diverse identities and cosmopolitan ideas can be found and expressed.

The irony in the fact that a significant proportion of the police force is from the eastern provinces, is that the most heavily criminalized and policed population in Havana are orientales themselves. When the police randomly detain Cubans on the street, one of the first things they check is the citizen's place of residence. If the citizen does not have a Havana-based residence listed on their *carnet* (identification card), they are questioned as to the purpose of their stay in the capital, the result of a 1997 law called Decree 217 that restricts migration to the capital and requires that Cubans from the outer provinces get authorization from the local police to be in Havana.[18] While it has been possible in the past for Havana residents to add non-Havana residents to the registry of occupants in a given domicile, thereby providing the latter with legal residency in the capital, the state authorities have been curbing these permits since the late 1990s due to overpopulation within individual homes and within Havana generally.[19] Owing to stereotypes of orientales as petty criminals and hustlers and the already large proportion of them in the capital, they are less likely to be given authorization to stay in Havana for a non-work-related reason, and many do in fact stay in Havana "illegally." One oriental caustically likened himself to an undocumented Mexican in the United States, asserting that in addition to *palestino*, the term *indocumentado* (undocumented) has recently entered the popular lexicon as a way of referring to orientales. In fact, the analogy is apt in many ways: orientales, like undocumented Mexicans in the United States, are employed disproportionately in low-paying manual labor jobs in Havana such as construction and housecleaning. Anthropologist Jacqueline Nassy Brown discusses a parallel situation faced by people from Liverpool who live in other English cities: "Bournemouth residents, the newspapers, and Liverpudlians themselves were all describing Scousers [people from Liverpool] as immigrants without the proper papers, as trespassers in a place perceived to belong not commonly to the people of Britain but exclusively to the people of Bournemouth" (Brown 2005, 159).

I have witnessed what I deem to be "regional profiling" when orientales are stopped by the police.[20] Not only does the officer radio in to the precinct to check if the detained citizen has a criminal record, but, even if that person has no prior convictions, he or she may be automatically brought in to the precinct in a police car and subjected to a long wait while the authorities conduct a more in-depth investigation. At the very least, people who are detained for this reason are held at the precinct for several hours and sometimes released after midnight. If they have had prior convictions or *advertencias* (warnings) on their record, they are sometimes deported back to their province of origin and prohibited from coming back to Havana for a certain period of time.[21] While it is disconcerting to recognize that the criminalization of orientales in Havana is often perpetrated by their regional compatriots, it is also important to note that the police officers recruited from Oriente and other provinces often have very few occupational options and in the end are constrained to carry out orders issued to them from above.[22] In sum, orientales function as scapegoats for a whole range of social problems in contemporary Havana: housing shortages, the crumbling infrastructure, police repression, black market activities, petty crime, hustling, and prostitution.

Regionalist Sentiment in El Campo

While habaneros view the rest of the country as "el campo" and assume a certain level of backwardness in people from other provinces, many of these other Cubans, including orientales, also hold quite negative views of the *capitalinos* (natives of the capital) and go out of their way to distinguish themselves from habaneros. Several of the Santiago-based musicians I interviewed expressed a certain hostility toward habaneros. Generalizing about the relationship between eastern and western Cubans, percussionist Mario Seguí Correoso (known as "Mayito") stated: "People from the west always paint the easterner as inferior to themselves" (pers. comm. 2011).[23] Although at times he spoke of a general regionalist antagonism between easterners and westerners, he also specified several times that the greatest hostility was between habaneros (i.e., people from the capital specifically, and not other western Cubans) and orientales—whom he described as "eternal rivals." In other words, he did not view anti-eastern prejudice as coming from Cubans from the center of the country, or even from all western Cubans, noting that he never had problems with people from Pinar del Río or Matanzas. He discussed the long history of antagonistic relations particularly between *santiagueros* (people from Santiago) and habaneros, owing to the centuries of hostility between east and west discussed above and the fact that Santiago is the island's second-largest city and de facto capital of Oriente. Mayito further asserted that habaneros often single out santiagueros as targets of their contempt, and that people from Holguín, Guantánamo, and other eastern cities and provinces are not subject to the same treatment. He discussed the baseball rivalry between the two cities as being a particularly incendiary source of tension, noting that television commentators, who should be neutral, often openly betray their regional identities and their preference for western Cuban or Havana-based teams.

Mayito also drew some hard and fast lines between people from Havana and orientales, stating that they were completely opposite from each other. He stated that easterners are more sincere, hospitable, and friendly, and that habaneros are "plastic" (i.e., only interested in appearances), money hungry, untrustworthy, and unlikely to share, say "hello" on the street, or invite you into their home (pers. comm. 2011). In fact, he saw habaneros as different from all other Cubans, whom he found to be hospitable and friendly. He also painted people from the capital as lazy and interested in acquiring money without having to work for it. Mayito's recognition of a basic difference between habaneros and orientales was buttressed by the views of other eastern Cuban musicians, such as Ramón Márquez Domínguez, longtime percussionist with the Santiago-based folkloric group Cutumba. Ramón noted that habaneros often ridicule the oriental accent—the latter are often described as "singing" when they speak and are mocked for "eating their s's" or omitting the letter s in their pronunciation. He countered this notion by stating that it is actually habaneros who speak badly, with an accent that is hard to understand (pers. comm. 2011).[24] Musicologist Radamés Giro, a Santiago native who has lived in Havana for many years, also spoke about the differences between the two cities, noting distinct food and alcohol preferences, such as the stereotype that santiagueros prefer to drink rum while habaneros prefer beer (pers. comm. 2011). Countering much of the elitism expressed by habaneros, Radamés also felt that Havana's culture is more "vulgar" and less refined than that of other cities—he mentioned Bayamo in particular—and that other Cuban locales are much cleaner than Havana.[25] While habaneros were the main targets of critique for the Santiago-based musicians I interviewed, several of them also spoke with disdain about orientales who relocate to the capital and seem to forget their roots, an issue I explore in chapter 2 vis-à-vis popular music lyrics. Pablo, a folkloric singer from Santiago,[26] criticized eastern Cubans who have migrated to Havana and do not feel the desire or need to return to Oriente, presumably because they feel superior about the rise in economic and social status that has accompanied their move (pers. comm. 2011). He stated, "viven en el aire"; they live with their heads in the clouds, or with an unrealistic, false sense of who they are.

One interesting notion espoused by several eastern Cuban musicians whom I interviewed was that, while there was often regionalist antagonism in everyday dealings on the streets of Havana, this hostility did not transfer to the world of *el arte*, or the professional artistic sphere. Pablo suggested that artists (such as himself) tend to look beyond regional identities and evaluate each other strictly in terms of competence and talent. He stated, "Entre los artistas no hay eso," meaning that there was no competition between artists on the basis of their regional identity or background, and that the ethics of their profession precluded this sort of petty antagonism. He felt that the audience response serves as the best indication of which performers are valorized or not and that, in terms of reception, the public evaluates performers based on their competence, not on their region of origin. Isaias Rojas Ramírez, director of the eastern Cuban folkloric group Ban Rarrá—which has been based in Havana since 1994—expressed a similar opinion, noting that in the capital there are many eastern Cuban musicians and dancers who are members of Havana groups, and that he also counts a number of habaneros in his own group (pers. comm. 2011). I found it interesting that several of the oriental musicians buttressed the nationalist discourse when discussing regionalist sentiment in the artistic world, stating that their identity as Cubans supersedes the place-based antagonisms that exist in other realms of Cuban society and that "we all defend Cuba." I discuss this issue in further depth in chapter 3.

While this chapter has focused primarily on regionalist tensions between habaneros and orientales, and the long history of divisions between the east and the west more generally, I also observed a certain antagonism directed toward the capital during my extended periods of research in the small western city of Matanzas. The degree of hostility between habaneros and *matanceros* (people from Matanzas) is generally much less pronounced. In fact, Havana-based musicians and religious practitioners often express reverence both in conversation and in song for "the cradle of Afro-Cuban culture," as Matanzas is known. One of the main reasons why habaneros express less hostility toward matanceros than orientales concerns the micropolitics of regionalism's manifestations in Cuba. Although I use regionalism as a more generalized phenomenon that at times conflates the differences between region and province, there is a distinction to be made between one's regional identity and one's provincial identity. As noted above, Cuba is divided up into three main regions, each of which comprises several provinces. Thus, at the level of regional identification, people from Havana and Matanzas are both *occidentales* (westerners). This regional solidarity often comes into play during the national baseball championship. During 2007's championship, Havana's team was pitted against Santiago's team, a historic rivalry, needless to say. Most orientales, whether from Santiago, Guantánamo, or Las Tunas, rooted for Santiago. Many habaneros stated that if their team hadn't made it to the finals, they would have thrown their support behind Pinar del Río's team. Another example of this intraregional solidarity between habaneros and matanceros is the fact that I have also heard the derisive term *palestinos* used in Matanzas to refer to orientales. Furthermore, Havana and Matanzas share many Afro-Cuban religious and musical traditions, owing to their physical proximity to one another. Finally, both have historically been important port cities, and matanceros have a long history of migration to the capital.

While many habaneros display respect for Matanzas as the birthplace of Afro-Cuban religious and musical traditions, they also often speak about Matanzas in terms of an orientation toward the past, and as a culturally conservative and even backward place. Ethnomusicologist Katherine Hagedorn states that matanceros are "considered to be Havana's 'country cousins'—sweet and well meaning, but out of step, and a little 'behind the time'" (2003, 101). Despite Matanzas's identity as a rich fount of Afro-Cuban culture, matanceros are still considered to be *gente del campo* (people from the countryside) with antiquated customs and beliefs, an issue I discuss in more depth in chapter 4. In a similar fashion, people from Pinar del Río are often stereotyped as being ignorant, undoubtedly because it is the most rural province in *Occidente*.[27] In other words, notwithstanding their common regional identity with habaneros as western Cubans, people from the other provinces in western Cuba are subject to the reification of the urban/rural binary and essentialized notions about the antimodern and provincial nature of their customs and beliefs.

While habaneros at times express condescension toward their "country cousins," matanceros display as much regionalist sentiment, if not more, toward habaneros. Matanceros are very proud of being from Matanzas. This pride arguably has much to do with the discursive value attached to the Afro-Cuban religious and musical traditions that are thought to have emerged from the city and province; Matanzas folkloric musicians generally conceive of their cultural practices as unique and special. Although many concede that they may not be the sole proprietors of these traditions, most of which have long histories in Havana, they do feel that their manifestations are the closest to the "original" African practices. Conversely, their evaluations of Havana's manifestations of these same cultural practices—whether Santería worship or rumba performance—tend to be negative. As will be evident in chapter 4, they often express the view that Havana folkloric musicians are solely responsible for the commercialization of Afro-Cuban culture and religion, especially Santería. In the eyes of matanceros, habaneros are always *inventando*, making things up, to render Afro-Cuban cultural practices more appealing to foreign tourists.

Beyond the matter of differences in cultural identity, many natives of Matanzas seem to take pains to differentiate themselves from habaneros in more fundamental ways. Echoing the perspectives of the eastern Cuban musicians discussed above, one Matanzas-based folkloric percussionist spoke of habaneros as completely distinct from matanceros in every way. He stated, "The habanero speaks very differently from the matancero, even though both speak the same language, Spanish.... The habanero can be distinguished from the matancero, their way of being, their way of walking, their way of carrying themselves, in everything" (Alfonso García, pers. comm. 2007).[28] The image of the habanero that predominates in Matanzas is that of an arrogant, loud person with a superiority complex who is always *especulando* (displaying wealth conspicuously). Thus, although matanceros may look down on orientales much as habaneros do, they do not display the same hostility toward the former as they do toward the latter. Perhaps more importantly, matanceros do not feel like they have anything to prove in distinguishing themselves from orientales, whom they already view as quite different. Instead, it is the capitalinos from whom matanceros wish to set themselves apart, asserting that Matanzas breeds people who are more considerate and genuine. Indeed, historian Miguel Bretos, a Matanzas native, characterizes matanceros as "cordial, polite, a trifle too trusting, generous, and infinitely hospitable" (2010, 261). In chapter 4 I elaborate on views expressed to me by folkloric musicians in both Havana and Matanzas regarding the complex relationship between the two cities and their respective folkloric scenes.

The Racialization of Place

In *Blackness and Race Mixture: The Dynamics of Racial Identity in Colombia*, anthropologist Peter Wade theorizes "the regionality of blackness," stating, "race is often spoken of in a locative voice, as it were, and this is because racial identities are broadly regionalized.... [R]ace relations are regional relations" (1993, 54). Wade's critique of the Colombian nationalist notion of mestizaje is accompanied by a nuanced analysis of the "regionalization" of mestizaje, or the different manifestations of and discourses about racial and cultural mixture on the Atlantic coast, on the Pacific coast, and in the interior of the country, respectively. In this section I want to begin to explore the ways that race is regionalized and region is racialized in another Latin American country in which the discourse of mestizaje is hegemonic. As I will elaborate in chapter 4, the construction of Matanzas as the "cradle of Afro-Cuban culture" is a clear example of the widespread tendency to correlate race and place, and the ways that the two often stand in for each other discursively. Jacqueline Nassy Brown's insightful ethnography *Dropping Anchor, Setting Sail* (2005) also serves as an excellent model for analyzing the ways that race and place are entangled. What is unique about Brown's argument is her emphasis on how race is shaped by notions of place in Liverpool; that is, she gives place primacy in the relationship and attributes to place the power to shape racialized subjectivity. She states, "I argue here that the cultural logics of localness and place have profoundly shaped racial identity and community formation—so much so that the local could be profitably understood as a racial category. I show localization as racialization" (Brown 2005, 31–32). She concludes her book thus: "I remain convinced that *place* not race was the more pronounced, palpable 'structure of feeling' among the folks who eventually became Black. In its appropriation of 'birth,' the term *Liverpool-born Black* shows place dominating race. One is not 'born' Black; one is *Liverpool*-born. That place is the more powerful category" (248).

As noted above, Oriente is often assumed to be the "blackest" region of Cuba in terms of racial demographics.[29] On the other hand, Camagüey is commonly racialized as white and viewed by many Cubans as the most racist region—in terms of peoples' individual attitudes—in the country.[30] I believe that these notions constitute a simplification of the "geography of race" on the island that has been consistently reified in both academic and popular discourse. For example, problematizing the association of Camagüey with whiteness is the fact that the province is home to one of the largest populations of Afro-Haitian and West Indian descent on the island. Regarding the racialization of Oriente, one of the primary reasons for revisiting the normative narrative is the fact that there are provinces in the east such as Holguín and Las Tunas that have historically been home to high proportions of white Cubans (James et al. 2007). Another important demographic fact is that at the pinnacle of slave importation to Cuba, from 1790 to 1860,[31] the highest concentration of Africans was in western-central Cuba due to the location of the largest sugar plantations there. By 1778, western Cuba contained more slaves (and inhabitants) than Oriente, but the proportion of slaves within the respective populations was roughly equal in both regions, about 32 percent (La Rosa Corzo 2003, 74). Nevertheless, this was before the majority of Africans were imported to the island. Cuban ethnographer Jesús Guanche generalizes that the "African component" of the nation (in addition to the Spanish and Chinese populations) tended toward the central-western end of the island (Guanche 1996, 134), and the *Atlas etnográfico de Cuba* (Centro de Investigación y Desarrollo de la Cultura Cubana Juan Marinello, 1999) presents figures showing that the percentage of African-born people on the island was increasingly concentrated in the west throughout the late eighteenth and nineteenth centuries: in 1774 almost 70 percent, in 1817 about 75 percent, and in 1899 more than 90 percent. Given these demographics, I propose that the notion that Oriente is the "blackest" region on the island requires reconsideration. It may be that within this discursive formation, blackness functions as a signifier for criminality, and that discursively blackening Oriente simultaneously acts to "whiten" western Cuba and signal its modernity. My final chapter further fleshes out this argument, linking it to the literature on national musical traditions.

My goal is not to portray Oriente as "whiter" than Occidente but rather to suggest that it is more racially hybrid. Racial demographics indicate that the amount of race mixing is higher in Oriente than in the west and less polarized in racial terms; in other words, eastern Cuba has a lower proportion of people who either self-ascribe or are identified by others as "white" or "black" (i.e., in monoracial terms). In addition—as is the case in Colombia (Wade 1993)—the particular composition of race mixture in Oriente is not the same as in Occidente. As Guanche (1996) and other scholars have noted, there is a substantial population of mixed-race people with some indigenous heritage in Oriente, which, although impossible to measure statistically, is apparent in the physical traits of some eastern Cubans. More importantly, the Antillean immigration to Cuba has been overwhelmingly concentrated in the east, beginning first in the wake of the Haitian Revolution in 1791 and then reinforced in the early decades of the twentieth century due to the demand for cheap labor to work in the US-dominated sugar industry. Given the importance of Antillean, particularly Haitian, immigration to eastern Cuban society and culture, I believe that it would be productive to provide an in-depth discussion of this history to understand some of the fundamental demographic differences between east and west.

Antillean Immigration to Cuba

In their book on the practice of *vodou* in Cuba, Joel James, José Millet, and Alexis Alarcón discuss the "conciencia de caribeñidad" or "Caribbean consciousness" that characterizes the southeastern part of the island. Nonetheless, as noted by ethnomusicologist Benjamin Lapidus, in national narratives "Oriente's importance as a crossroads between the Spanish, French, and English-Caribbean is ignored" (Lapidus 2008, xviii). The origins of this distinct regional identity can be traced back to the first wave of Franco-Haitian migration to eastern Cuba in the years between the outbreak of the Haitian Revolution and the establishment of the independent Haitian nation, from 1791 to 1804 (James et al. 2007, 27). Cuban scholars likely use the term "Franco-Haitian" to refer to this wave because it easily encompasses a diverse group of people and national origins: the roughly thirty thousand migrants included more than seven thousand French nationals, between eight and ten thousand mixed-race individuals, and the rest black slaves (Venegas Delgado 2001, 138).[32] Cuban musicologist Olavo Alén asserts that the immigrants, regardless of their place of birth and race, preferred to be regarded as "French," because the word "Haitian" signaled potential danger and rebellion to the Spanish colonial authorities; the term *francés* was also used to refer to their cultural traditions (Alén 1986, 10).[33] In addition, this first wave of migration—occurring during a struggle for independence—predated the formation of a distinct Haitian national identity.

The immigrants settled primarily in the provinces of Santiago and Guantánamo, partly due to their proximity to Haiti, but also, Alén asserts, because land was cheaper there than in the west. French planters and their slaves contributed in important ways to the region's economic development, particularly in the realm of coffee production, which was almost nonexistent before their arrival.[34] In 1807, 83 percent of the coffee plantations in the Santiago region were owned by French immigrants from the former Saint-Domingue (Bergad et al. 1995, 95), and between 1803 and 1807 coffee production increased tenfold. In 1830, already during the peak years of sugar production, Cuba still exported a larger proportion of coffee than sugar to the global market (Alén 1986, 11–12). At the time, owning a coffee plantation was a sign of cultural sophistication (Millet and Brea 1989, 20), and French planters constructed big, ostentatious mansions in the mountainous zones of Santiago and Guantánamo. In fact, coming from the most developed colony in the Caribbean, the French refugees considered themselves to be superior to the "backward" *peninsulares* (the Spanish) (Millet and Brea 1989, 18). In addition to their contributions to agricultural production, a significant portion of the city of Santiago was built by the French immigrants, as is evident even today in the historic neighborhood of Tivolí, and they reinvigorated the city's cultural life with French theater, opera, and contredanse. The French cultural influence was quite significant until around the mid-nineteenth century and the onset of an economic crisis in the coffee industry precipitated by a spate of hurricanes, and the beginning of independence struggles in the later 1860s. Many "French" slaves from coffee plantations subsequently incorporated themselves into the rebellion forces during the Ten Years' War, and after full emancipation in 1886 they migrated to urban areas to look for employment (Alén 1986, 16–17).

The second major wave of Haitians occurred a century later, in the early years of the Cuban Republic, when North American capital dominated the agricultural sector.[35] Interestingly, as noted by James, Millet, and Alarcón

(2007, 96) there were few common bonds between the first and second waves of immigrants, who were separated not only by a century but also by class and national affiliation: whereas the first wave of migrants considered and referred to themselves as "French" (an identity that was passed on to their descendants with all of its accompanying class and racial connotations), laborers arriving in the twentieth century were desperately poor, uneducated, overwhelmingly black, and Haitian-identified. There are some discrepancies in the literature regarding the total number of immigrants who arrived or were imported to fill the labor shortages on US-owned sugar plantations during this period. Historian Matthew Casey asserts that over half a million Antilleans, composed primarily of Haitians and Jamaicans in that order, were imported to Cuba from 1913 to 1931, the last year they could arrive legally (Casey 2001, 6–7).[36] Unlike Spanish immigrants arriving in the same period, the Antilleans were conceived of as *braceros*, temporary contract laborers who would not stay on the island permanently.[37] The source of Casey's number is not clear, and it is difficult to make direct comparisons with figures cited by other scholars, as they use different year ranges. Joel James, one of the preeminent researchers on Haitian-derived culture and religion in Cuba, also provides the figure of more than five hundred thousand Haitians arriving between 1913 and 1930, in addition to seventy-five thousand Jamaicans between 1913 and 1921 (James et al. 2007, 29). According to James, Millet, and Alarcón, Haitians and Jamaicans made up 95 percent of the braceros who came to the island. They also state that Antilleans constituted not 25 percent of all immigration to Cuba in the first three decades of the twentieth century (the number provided by the *Atlas demográfico de Cuba*) but 40 percent (James et al. 2007, 29). James later estimates the number of Antilleans who arrived in Cuba during this period to be closer to one million, due to high instability in the work force and frequent coming and going, but also clarifies that the population of Antillean braceros was never close to a million at any one time (55).[38]

Presenting more conservative statistics, two Cuban sources cite a figure of around 150,000 Antillean immigrants between 1913 and 1921 (Guanche 1996, 97; Venegas Delgado 2001, 144), and another source cites an additional number of around 153,000 Antillean arrivals (mostly Haitian) from 1921 to 1933 (Guanche and Moreno 1988, 17). These combined statistics add up to 300,000 rather than 500,000. A more recent Cuban source, taking information from government records, asserts that exactly 337,875 Antillean braceros came into Cuba legally between 1906 and 1931,[39] but that if we take into account the many immigrants who arrived illegally, the figure is probably over 500,000 (Álvarez Estévez and Guzmán Pascual 2008, 34). While I do not want to cast doubt on James's high figures—as it is clear from many sources that there was considerable undercounting of Haitians and other immigrants, partly relating to illegal entry to Cuba—it might be relevant to note that in general his narrative tends to emphasize, perhaps overly so, the impact of Haitian immigration and culture on rural eastern Cuba. For example, he asserts that, considering the underpopulation of rural areas in central-eastern Cuba, it is possible that Haitians constituted a majority in many zones and that in the exchanges between rural Cubans and Haitians the cultural traditions of the latter generally predominated (James et al. 2007, 100–102).

In terms of the geographic distribution of Antillean immigrants within Cuba, Guanche notes that in 1907 80 percent of Antilleans were concentrated in Oriente and Camagüey, a figure that rose steadily throughout the century, peaking at 97 percent in 1953 (1996, 95). The *Atlas demográfico* indicates that, by 1931, the former province of Puerto Príncipe (currently Camagüey) had the highest ratio of foreign-born people at 18 percent (Comité Estatal de Estadísticas 1979, 71–72), which corresponds to the dramatic growth of the sugar industry in that province. While 15 percent of the island's sugar was produced in Camagüey in 1901, by the 1920s and 1930s the province was producing over half of the island's sugar (Casey 2001, 6). Unsurprisingly, Caribbean migrants contributed to a massive growth in the populations of Oriente and Camagüey from 1907 to 1919—increases of 60.6 percent and 93.6 percent, respectively—while the population increase on the whole island during this period was only 33 percent (Casey 2001, 6).

Needless to say, the immigration waves of the early twentieth century resulted in further divisions and cultural distinctions between eastern and western Cuba, as the majority of the Spanish immigrants settled in the latter—84 percent of them in 1907 (Guanche 1996, 42)—and most Caribbean immigrants in the former. It is interesting that precisely at the most important moment of nation building for the newly formed Cuban Republic, not only were large numbers of immigrants arriving but the two halves of the country were being populated with very different people. In addition, unlike the situation of the Spanish arrivals, the Antillean immigrants faced racist and xenophobic sentiment from Cubans who, foreshadowing the neoconservative, anti-immigrant rhetoric in the United States today, accused the Haitians and Jamaicans of stealing their jobs and driving down wages (McLeod 1998; Casey 2001). While Antillean immigrants certainly accepted lower wages, they worked primarily as cane cutters, a job that most Cubans were not willing to do. Scholars have described the extremely exploitative and harsh conditions in which the immigrants worked, with Jesús Guanche and Dennis Moreno going so far to describe the importation of Haitians as a "new slave trade" of the twentieth century (1988, 12). They assert that immigrants were often tricked into going to Cuba by their Haitian compatriots who worked as contractors for American sugar planters, and who lied about the working conditions and wages (19). They also discuss the internal migration of Haitian immigrants within Cuba during the "dead time" of the sugar harvest in order to survive economically: from January to April they worked on sugar plantations, but they would migrate to the mountains, largely in Guantánamo, for the coffee harvest in September (26).

It is also relevant to note that these black immigrants were arriving at a moment of disproportionately high racial tension in the nation: 1912 had seen the massacre of thousands of members of the Partido Independiente de Color and random Afro-Cubans by government forces and white militias. At a time in which Afro-Cubans were attempting to integrate into mainstream Cuban society, the arrival of hundreds of thousands of (mostly uneducated) black, non-Spanish-speaking immigrants put them in a position of having to reinforce racist, nativist rhetoric. In fact, despite the depiction of the PIC by the Havana government as a group of race agitators in the vein of the Haitian revolutionaries, the PIC did not unilaterally support the immigration of black Caribbean laborers and in fact adhered to José Martí's vision of a "post-racial" Cuba where national identity trumps racial allegiance (Chomsky 2000, 429). Nonetheless, historian Aviva Chomsky suggests that Haitian and Jamaican immigrants may have participated in the PIC rebellions because, as they were unfolding, the Cuban government prohibited ships with immigrants from landing in Oriente (2000, 433). Chomsky states, "Thus West Indian immigrants were dangerous to Cuban nationhood on two fronts, and both replicated the dangers inherent in African slaves. They might rebel, and [because they were used by American landowners as cheap labor] they kept white Cubans dependent on foreign domination" (434). Chomsky reflects on the difficult situation of Cuban-born blacks, particularly intellectuals advocating racial equality, thus: "The very process of independence, emancipation, and nation-building had transformed Cuban blacks so that they became, instead of Cuban blacks, black Cubans. 'Race' became a cultural and historical attribute rather than a biological one, and a virulent racism against [foreign] blacks could coexist with an ideology of racial inclusiveness. And yet, it was a racial inclusiveness predicated upon racism" (435–36). The irony of this situation is that the massacre of the PIC members and sympathizers in 1912 created a greater demand for foreign laborers to work on the sugar plantations.

The nativist rhetoric of the late 1920s and 1930s resulted in various repatriation campaigns, but only for black Antillean laborers, not for Spanish immigrants, who were more numerous. Haitians were particularly singled out as dangerous elements who needed to be removed. Historian Marc McLeod explores the differential treatment of Haitians and British West Indians (mostly Jamaicans) during this period, beginning with the question of why thirty-eight thousand Haitians were deported in the mid- to late 1930s while the British West Indians were allowed to stay or leave voluntarily. He states, "The radical Cuban nationalism of the 1930s affected all foreigners in Cuba, especially Afro-Caribbean immigrants. But Haitians alone suffered the horrors of forced removal. . . . Haitian immigrants thus remained closely linked to the main target of Cuban nationalism—US domination of the Cuban economy, especially the sugar sector" (McLeod 1998, 613). Haitians in particular were scapegoated for the economic crisis precipitated by the global drop in sugar prices in the late 1920s, and subjected to several rounds of deportation throughout the 1930s. Both Guanche and Moreno, and James, Millet, and Alarcón, note that many times Haitians were rounded up with no notice, and that much of their livestock and produce—the wealth they had been able to accumulate in Cuba—was stolen by the Rural Guard.[40] Although there are no records documenting what happened to these deported immigrants, some of James's informants claimed that many Haitians never arrived back to their country because they were thrown overboard in order to save gas and time (James et al. 2007, 59–60).[41] Although foreign blacks were the primary target of racist xenophobia during the late 1920s and 1930s, Spanish immigrants were also adversely affected by a 1933 decree declaring that at least 50 percent of all positions in all occupations were to be performed by native Cubans (de la Fuente 2001, 104).[42]

Returning to the issue of the differential treatment of Haitians and British West Indians, McLeod notes the advantages held by the latter due to their English-language skills (thus giving them access to jobs beyond the sugar plantation, such as being servants and nannies for American planters), their relatively high rates of literacy (only 9 percent were illiterate), the skills they possessed before arriving in Cuba, and the more equal gender ratio of the immigrants (almost 19 percent were women, allowing for reproduction within their communities). Haitians, on the other hand, were at a distinct disadvantage in terms of their language skills, their extremely low rates of literacy (84 percent illiterate), their lack of employment options, and the fact that only 6 percent of immigrants were women (McLeod 1998, 607–9). Furthermore, their different residential patterns affected their assimilation into Cuban society: Haitians tended to live in more rural, isolated, and ethnically homogeneous communities, whereas British West Indians were more likely to migrate to the cities and integrate themselves into the larger society. These residential patterns in turn impacted the rates of schooling for the children of the two immigrant groups; fewer Haitian children attended school, further cementing their isolation. In addition to the outside discrimination they faced, Haitians also self-isolated to a certain extent as they strived to preserve their linguistic and cultural differences (McLeod 1998, 609). Finally, religious differences constituted a major distinguishing factor between the two Antillean groups: while Haitians practiced vodou, which was subject to the same racism and outrageous charges of cannibalism as the Afro-Cuban religion Santería, British West Indians were largely Christian and thus seen as more respectable. McLeod notes that the latter received aid from the Episcopal Church and helped expand their mission in Cuba, although they were still subject to racism and segregation: two services were held, one for Americans and one for Antilleans (610–11).

Interestingly, as discussed by Andrea Queeley (2010), British West Indians not only faced less prejudice and marginalization than Haitian immigrants but also considered themselves to be superior to and more respectable than both Haitians and Cuban blacks. Queeley asserts that the discursive trope of black West Indian respectability has endured throughout the twentieth century to the present day, as descendants of laborers from the former British colonies (primarily Jamaica) still view themselves as more respectable and dignified than blacks of other national origins. She states of her fieldwork experience, "I was repeatedly told that *los jamaicanos* were clean, respectful, disciplined, pious, hard working, invested in education and self-betterment, and proud of being black. Regardless of a shared racial identity, they were perceived to be markedly distinct from Haitian immigrants, who were thought to be more likely illiterate, confined to agricultural labor, and devoted to *brujería* [witchcraft], and from black and working-class Cubans, who were said to use foul language and were loud, crude, and prone to disorder" (Queeley 2010, 201). Incidentally, just as there has been an increased visibility for the traditions and contributions of ethnic minorities to Cuban national culture (an issue that will be discussed in chapter 3), there has been a recent surge of interest on the part of the descendants of West Indian migrants in recapturing their cultural roots and creating ethnically defined organizations to reflect their complex identities.

It is not easy to determine how many Antillean immigrants remained in Cuba after the 1930s. The 1943 census numbers suggest a marked decrease in foreigners overall as compared to 1931, with the Spanish-born population down by 100,000 and a 60 percent decline of non-Cuban blacks from a little over 100,000 to around 40,000 (de la Fuente 2001, 104–5). Nevertheless, de la Fuente suggests that the number of Antilleans in Cuba in 1943 was massively underestimated, noting that the Haitian minister in Havana estimated the number to be closer to 80,000 (104–5). In addition, Rolando Álvarez Estévez and Marta Guzmán Pascual (2008, 128) assert that there were around 40,000 Jamaicans on the island in 1950. The 1953 census counted 27,543 Haitians—many of whom continued to live in relatively isolated, rural communities such as Caidije in Camagüey—and 14,421 British West Indians (McLeod 1998, 613). The *Atlas demográfico de Cuba* cites a figure of 25,000 Haitians in Cuba in 1970 (Comité Estatal de Estadísticas 1979, 74), although by this time there were also many Cubans born of Haitian parents. As a testament to the continuing influence of Afro-Antillean culture in eastern Cuba, folkloric dancer Isaias Rojas stated that during his youth in the 1970s and 1980s three languages could regularly be heard circulating in his neighborhood in the city of Guantánamo: Spanish, English, and Haitian Creole (pers. comm. 2011). Beginning with the 1981 census, people were no longer asked about their place of birth (Centro de Investigación y Desarrollo de la Cultura Cubana Juan Marinello 1999), so it is difficult to determine how many foreigners have lived in Cuba in recent decades. Nevertheless, a source discussing the 2002 census count asserts that more than 15,000 foreigners currently live on the island, of whom 10 percent (around 1,600) are Antillean, with 919 Haitians and 292 Jamaicans (Álvarez Estévez and Guzmán Pascual 2008, 230).

The Racial Composition of Oriente

While I argue that the discursive "blackening" of Oriente often functions to marginalize the eastern region, this widespread notion likely results from the racial demographics of the southeastern part of the region, which seem to have been consistent for the past 150 years. Statistics suggest that, while not necessarily "blacker," the provinces of Santiago and Guantánamo have historically been and still remain the most nonwhite areas of the island, partly due to the waves of Antillean immigration detailed above. Nonetheless, it is important to remember that Oriente is not constituted only by these two provinces but also includes Holguín, Granma, and Las Tunas. In 1862, only 19 percent of the Cuban population lived in Oriente, but 52 percent of its residents were slaves and free people of color. In addition, around 40 percent of the total free population of color on the island lived in Oriente (Louis Pérez 2006, 66). At that time, both slaves (86 percent of the island's total) and whites (84 percent) were overwhelmingly concentrated in the west, creating a more polarized racial climate there, but also a whiter population overall (Louis Pérez 2006, 66). The 1899 census, taken during the American occupation, counted the proportion of the "colored population" to be highest in Santiago (45 percent) and lowest in the province of Puerto Príncipe (20 percent), which is current-day Camagüey (Gannett 1900, 283).[43] In the 1907 census, the white population in Santiago was 43 percent, with a 57 percent nonwhite population, while Guantánamo's population was 61 percent nonwhite (Castro Monterrey 2010, 30). At the same time, the western cities of Guanabacoa (a municipality on the outskirts of Havana) and Matanzas were 70 percent and 68 percent white, respectively. The eastern city of Manzanillo (in the province of Granma) was 61 percent white, while the central Cuban city of Trinidad was evenly split between whites and nonwhites (Castro Monterrey 2010, 30). At the time of the 1907 census, all nonwhite people were referred to as "persons of color," making it difficult to distinguish the black population from the mulato population.[44] However, we do know that in 1907 Santiago's *black* population was 24 percent (Castro Monterrey 2010, 30). In 1910, at the height of the popularity of the PIC, the Afro-Cuban population (both blacks and mulatos) in Oriente—which then included "blacker" municipalities like Santiago and Guantánamo and "whiter" ones such as Holguín—constituted 43 percent of the total population, the highest number of all regions in Cuba. While Matanzas was the second "blackest" region, at 38 percent (Helg 1995, 156), the PIC had the weakest representation and popular support there, likely because of the large concentration of sugar plantations and slaves there during the nineteenth century.

Notwithstanding the demographic statistics, which pinpoint Oriente as having a high proportion of "colored people" in the late nineteenth and early twentieth centuries, one event from the 1930s also clearly evidences the discursive power of the association of the region with blackness. In 1932, the Cuban Communist Party proposed the creation of an independent black state within Cuba, to be made up of the municipalities in Oriente that constituted the *faja negra* or "black belt," where more than 50 percent of the population was of African descent. These included the cities of Santiago, Guantánamo, and Baracoa, in addition to the smaller municipalities of El Caney, Palma Soriano, La Maya, Songo, San Luis, El Cobre (all in the province of Santiago), and parts of Bayamo (in the province of Granma) (Corbea Calzado 1996; Barcia Zequeira 2004). Cuban scholars now consider this proposal to have been a misguided attempt to promote racial equality that was influenced by American binary racial thinking, following in the line of a Jim Crow "separate but equal" ideology. They argue that this type of solution was not appropriate for a nation with a large proportion of mixed-race people (for example, see Barcia Zequeira 2004; Massón Sena 2009). Caridad Massón Sena (2009) further critiques this proposal by noting that only 22 percent of African-descended people on the island (including blacks and mulatos) lived in the "black belt" during this period, and that, in any case, it was erroneous to assume that Cuba's black population was substantially different from the

rest of the nation in cultural and economic terms.[45] Thus, while the proportion of nonwhites to whites was certainly higher in Oriente than in other
regions in the first half of the twentieth century, less than one-fourth of blacks
and mulatos on the island lived there because of the overall concentration of
the population in western Cuba. In turn, the discourse of blackness attached
to Oriente should be viewed as an incomplete representation of the island's
racial demographics.

The 1953 census showed a continuation of the overall demographic trend
of the first half of the twentieth century. Whites were heavily represented in
the western and central provinces and less so in eastern Cuba: of the six provinces, all except Oriente had a proportion of 77 percent white or higher, while
the eastern province had a figure of 59 percent (Oficina Nacional de los Censos 1953, 49–50); this was still, however, a majority. Oriente had a much higher
incidence of mixed-race people, roughly 26 percent, but had an almost equal
number of blacks, 14.6 percent, as compared to the otherwise white province
of Pinar del Río (14.2 percent) (Oficina Nacional de los Censos 1953, 49–50).
I want to emphasize that census results in mixed-race countries are generally difficult to interpret because the numbers depend on who is determining
racial identity (an enumerator or the subject). Moreover, even when people
self-identify, they often "whiten" themselves. In other words, individuals who
could be considered mulato might identify themselves as white, and dark-
skinned persons could present themselves as mulato instead of black.[46]

The census counts after 1953 are distinct, mainly due to the ideological
shift that accompanied the triumph of the Cuban Revolution. The revolution is notorious for not collecting data on racial demographics, which corresponds to the broader silence on the issue and the assumption that the
socialist redistribution of wealth automatically eradicated racial inequality. Concerning the 1970 census, Cuba scholar Lisandro Pérez notes that
although race data was collected, the results were never released. He states,
"It was argued that the race item was not tabulated because it was decided
after the census was taken that questions of race are not relevant in a socialist society" (1984, 157). However, Pérez notes that the next census, in 1981,
also collected data on race, proving the hypocrisy of the aforementioned
statement. He continues, "Perhaps the cross-tabulation of the figures on race
and education did not show the expected elimination of racial differentials
in educational attainment that has been a major goal of the revolutionary
government's redistributive educational program since 1960" (157). The 1981
census was the first conducted after the 1976 division of the island into fifteen
provinces (whereas previously there had been only six); thus, a direct comparison is impossible. Nevertheless, the trend of a whiter western and central

region continued, except for Ciudad Habana (the province that contains the various municipalities that make up the capital), which was tabulated as 63 percent white. As expected, Oriente's population showed some inconsistencies, with the southern part of the region having a heavy majority of nonwhites—Santiago and Guantánamo had white populations of 30 percent and 26 percent, respectively—while the provinces of Las Tunas and Holguín had white populations of 74 percent and 79 percent, respectively (Comité Estatal de Estadísticas 1984). In fact, racially mixed people were predominant in the three southeastern provinces of Santiago, Granma, and Guantánamo: 47 percent, 53 percent, and 55 percent, respectively (Comité Estatal de Estadísticas 1984). Also telling is the fact that the two provinces on the island with the lowest percentages of blacks were both in Oriente—Holguín with 6 percent and Granma with 4 percent—although the eastern region was also home to the provinces with the highest percentages, Santiago at 22 percent and Guantánamo at 19 percent; for comparison, Ciudad Habana had a 16 percent black population (Comité Estatal de Estadísticas 1984).

More recent national censuses were conducted in 2002 and 2012. The first presented results that many researchers (at least outside Cuba) consider to be deeply flawed, in that the figures seem to continue the general trend of statistical "whitening": the overall population was reported as approximately 65 percent white, 25 percent mixed race, and 10 percent black (Oficina Nacional de Estadísticas 2006, 112). These figures can be compared to the overall numbers from the 1981 census—66 percent white, 22 percent mestizo, and 12 percent black—and seem especially dubious when taking into account that the large majority of the Cuban émigré population that has come to the United States since 1959 is white. In other words, Cuba should be (and is viewed by most people as) a demographically blacker nation now.[47] The 2002 census results did not break down the racial identity of the population by region, so it is impossible to compare the numbers with those of 1953 and 1981.

The preliminary results of the 2012 census show an overall continuation of the racial demographics of the nation in the revolutionary period, with small decreases in the white and black populations and an increase in the mixed-race category—64.1 percent, 9.3 percent, and 26.6 percent, respectively (Oficina Nacional de Estadísticas 2013). Interestingly, in this census the government released information on the racial demographics not only of each province but of each municipality. The central Cuban provinces of Villa Clara and Sancti Spíritus, and the eastern province of Holguín, had the highest proportions of whites, all over 80 percent, while Santiago and Guantánamo continued to have the lowest percentages, both around 25 percent. La Habana (which was renamed from Ciudad Habana in 2011 after the rural province formerly known as La Habana was divided into two provinces, Mayabeque and Artemisa) and Santiago had the highest percentages of blacks (15.2 percent and 14.2 percent, respectively), while the eastern provinces of Guantánamo, Santiago, and Granma had the highest incidences of mulatos (62.8 percent, 60.2 percent, and 54.3 percent, respectively). These numbers are especially interesting with regard to the black population: the capital city is now the location with the greatest percentage of blacks on the island, which is ironic considering the widespread racialization of Oriente as the "blackest" part of the island. These recent numbers demonstrate that Oriente is not necessarily blacker than the rest of the nation, but is in fact overwhelmingly populated by people of mixed race. Chapter 6 will revisit this issue, linking it to the history of son and introducing subjective perspectives on the matter.

Conclusion: Popular Regionalist Sentiment as a Challenge to the Nationalist Discourse

In a recent publication, prominent Cuban folklorist Rogelio Martínez Furé rejects the notion of a unified national cultural identity, instead arguing for a "multiethnic, pluricultural identity." He states, "A mulatto Cuban from Baracoa, the descendant of Haitian émigrés in a coffee-growing area, is not the same as a black Cuban descendant of Arará from the province of Matanzas, a sugar-growing area, or a fair-skinned Cuban from Pinar del Río, a tobacco-growing area, the descendant of Canary Islanders. They are all Cuban, but there are differences in food, speech, psychology, religious beliefs, and phenotype. I believe it is important to accept plurality and free ourselves from that monomania, according to which we're all the same" (Martínez Furé 2000, 157). While this statement could certainly be interpreted as somewhat essentialist—as it draws a homology between race and region and naturalizes racial/ethnic difference (even while making distinctions between different types of African-derived people)—it is also a strong counterargument to the hegemonic nationalist discourse, which tends to discount racial and regional distinctions among the population.

The articulations of regionalist sentiment I have examined in this chapter present a similar challenge to Cuba's nationalist discourse. The revolutionary government has always projected a picture of absolute national unity to the world, which is symbolized by a prominent billboard one encounters when driving from the Havana airport toward the city center that asserts, "Welcome to Havana, capital of *all* Cubans!" During his nearly fifty years in power, Fidel Castro consistently utilized this discourse of national unity to shore up support for the state's political system, arguing that socialist principles better address and conform to the needs and desires of the majority of the Cuban population. While serving as a declaration to the international community, this unifying rhetoric was also directed at Cuban citizens and displayed the "educative and formative," as opposed to merely the coercive, role of the state in establishing and maintaining hegemony (Gramsci 1971). Stuart Hall notes that this Gramscian formulation of the state targets "the ethical, the cultural, the moral" (Hall [1986] 1996a, 428–29).[48] Much of Castro's staying power can be explained by his ability to generate popular consent, through the use of his formidable rhetorical skills and hyperbolic discourses, which were designed to convince the national population and the rest of the world of Cuba's unimpeachable morality. One of his most frequent assertions in this vein was to simplistically attribute all of Cuba's internal social problems to the US embargo.

The expressions of regionalist sentiment that I have detailed here, and will continue to explore in chapter 2, betray the cracks in the wall of Cuban national unity and socialist egalitarianism and illuminate how regional provenance is an influential axis of identity formation that can foster divisiveness. Many scholars have productively examined the contradictions contained in the gap between the nationalist hybridity discourse, sometimes referred to as the "myth of racial equality" (Helg 1995), and the realities of inequality faced by Cubans of African descent since independence. I have argued here that expressions of regionalist sentiment further contest the notion of a unified nation proclaimed by all Cuban governments during the twentieth century, but particularly by the Castro regime. After all, the state's own policies that restrict and criminalize internal migration to Havana belie this unifying rhetoric. This discourse of unity also disregards the on-the-ground regionalist tensions among the populace that are influential in shaping daily social relations in the nation's capital.

The state's apparent unwillingness to publicly address this problem likely relates to the revolution's socialist political project. Cuba is still a socialist nation, at least in name if not entirely in terms of its economic system.[49] In a country that has faced long-standing political isolation and repeated threats to its sovereignty by the United States, and that has strived almost single-handedly to rescue socialism from the onslaught of neoliberal capitalism, admitting to any form of difference within the population may open the door to dissension and political unrest. Thus, perhaps more than the majority of countries in the world, the stakes are higher for Cuba in terms of maintaining national unity, or at least in projecting this image to the world.

Chapter Two

"La Habana No Aguanta Más":
Regionalism in the Lyrics of Cuban Popular Music

Para gozar, La Habana	To have fun, Havana
Para disfrutar, La Habana	To enjoy yourself, Havana
Está llena de emigrantes que llegan y no se van	It's full of emigrants who arrive and never leave
Siempre son bien recibidos y se les brinda amistad	They are always welcomed and offered friendship
Los encantan las mujeres y el ambiente popular,	They are captivated by the women and the down-home atmosphere,
Y es que encuentran en La Habana el paraíso terrenal	and it's simply that in Havana they find heaven on earth

—"Para Gozar, La Habana," Clave y Guaguancó[1]

The above lyrics, from a 2006 song by Havana-based rumba group Clave y Guaguancó, get to the heart of this chapter's focus: the ways the regionalist sentiment I detailed in the previous chapter is expressed in musical performance. Packed into these five lines of text are several provocative statements about regional/local pride within Cuba and the prickly issue of internal migration to the capital by *gente del campo*, or people from the outer provinces. The lyrics of this rumba song reveal much both about Havana natives' attitudes toward Cubans who migrate to the capital seeking better economic opportunities, and about their assumptions concerning these migrants' intentions in moving there. However, such regionally inflected assertions are not uncommon within the realm of popular music, as will be evident in three songs by premier dance bands that will also be analyzed in the chapter—Los Van Van's "La Habana No Aguanta Más," Orquesta Original de Manzanillo's "Soy Cubano y Soy de Oriente," and Adalberto Álvarez's "Un Pariente en el Campo." I will also analyze in detail the rumba song whose lyrics open this chapter, although expressions of regionalist sentiment are not as common in rumba. Assertions of local or regional pride are not infrequent in Cuban dance songs; two examples are NG La Banda's early hits "La Expresiva," which shouts out and extols the virtues of various Havana neighborhoods, and "Los Sitios Entero," which includes a rumba in the middle of the song.[2] However, fewer songs explicitly address the thornier regionalist tensions between Cubans of different provinces. Taking my evidence from these songs' lyrics, I will argue that notions of regional identity are being negotiated and contested through Cuban dance music and rumba in ways that threaten to undermine the unifying nationalist discourse.[3]

Expressions of Regionalism in Cuban Dance Music

Cuban dance music constitutes a particularly rich terrain of interpretation for exploring contemporary expressions of regionalism.[4] The country's elite bands often combine eminently danceable music with socially relevant lyrics that issue critiques in veiled terms so as to evade censorship by state cultural officials (Perna 2005). While my interpretations of the songs discussed below are gleaned largely through textual analysis, my conclusions are deeply informed by my fieldwork experiences and the many informal discussions I have had with Cubans—both musicians and others—about regionalism and the ways it is addressed in musical performance. Correspondingly, I have inserted quotations and other ethnographic commentaries about the songs where relevant.

"La Habana No Aguanta Más"

The title of this chapter, "La Habana No Aguanta Más" (Havana Can't Take Anymore), is borrowed from a hit song recorded in 1984 by Los Van Van, Cuba's premier dance band since its formation in 1969. The band's longevity has inspired the nickname *El tren de la salsa*, the salsa train; the word *tren* is used to refer to something/someone that just keeps going and going.[5] Los Van Van is beloved and critically esteemed both for its unparalleled musical creativity, drawing on and combining diverse popular music influences principally from Cuban and African American sources, and its ability to evolve over time and tap into the hippest sounds at any given moment. The band has also created a widespread and loyal fan base by utilizing its songs as vehicles for social and political commentary, sometimes explicitly, but principally through veiled messages and double entendres. Los Van Van's bandleader and principal composer since its inception, Havana-born bassist Juan Formell, displayed a continuous ability to pinpoint the relevant social concerns of urban dwellers at different moments in the past five decades, thus providing affirmation of the daily realities and struggles of average Cubans. Formell passed away suddenly on May 1, 2014, which constituted a major loss, as he was perhaps the most influential Cuban musician since the revolution; his death inspired many official and unofficial tributes and a massive public funeral in Cuba. While presumably Los Van Van will carry on under the direction of Formell's son Samuel, the group's drummer and unofficial leader in recent years, there are certainly questions about the band's future in the wake of Formell's death.

"La Habana No Aguanta Más" was recorded during a particularly fruitful period of composition for Formell and the band, the 1980s, when Los Van Van's repertoire is considered to have achieved an almost perfect synthesis of catchy, danceable music and satirical commentary on diverse social issues and controversies. As noted in the liner notes of the compilation album *The Legendary Los Van Van: 30 Years of Cuba's Greatest Dance Band* (1999), Los Van Van's hit songs during that decade included "El Negro No Tiene Na'" (The Black Guy Doesn't Have Anything, 1984), responding to rumors that lead singer Pedro Calvo had contracted AIDS; "La Resolución" (The Resolution, 1985), which criticized the ungrateful gossip mongering of Cuban partygoers who are never satisfied with the generosity of their hosts; "La Titimanía" (Young Girl Fever, 1987), exposing the trend of older men taking up with younger women; and "No Soy de la Gran Escena" (I'm Not from the Big Stage, 1989), an explicit critique of a well-known Cuban television program called *La Gran Escena* that features performances only of "high art" genres such as opera and ballet, while shunning Cuban popular and folkloric music and dance (Faro and Mauleón 1999).

"La Habana No Aguanta Más" belongs to this category of social commentary songs, as it laments the constant influx of people migrating from other provinces to Havana in search of greater economic prospects. Among other assertions, its lyrics remind Cubans that housing and job opportunities are available all over the country and that there is no need to overcrowd the capital.[6] Following are the song's lyrics in their entirety.[7]

Verse 1

He recibido un telegrama de Cachito y Agustín,	I received a telegram from Cachito and Agustín,
Son mis primos que me dicen	They're my cousins and they tell me

(Coro) Que en La Habana quieren vivir

(Solista) Somos siete de familia

con dos perros además.

Con cuidado, mis parientes,

¡Que La Habana no aguanta más!

(Chorus) That they want to live in Havana

(Lead) There are seven of us in the family

with a couple of dogs too.

Take it easy, my folks,

'Cause Havana can't take anymore!

Bridge

(Coro) Y ya tú ves que en Cuba entera

(Chorus) And now everyone knows that there are good living conditions all over Cuba

hay condiciones para vivir

Y hasta se han hecho pueblos nuevos por montones, de verdad

And they've even built a bunch of new towns, it's true

Verse 2

(Solista) Sin embargo aquí en La Habana

se me quieren colar

Con cuidado, mi familia,

¡Que La Habana no aguanta más!

(Lead) Even so, here in Havana

everyone's trying to squeeze in

Take it easy, my family,

'Cause Havana can't take any more!

Montuno (call-and-response) section[8]

(Coro) ¡Qué va! ¡Qué va, está bueno ya!

¡Que La Habana no aguanta más! (3x)

Come on! Come on, enough already!

'Cause Havana can't take any more! (3x)

(*Coro* alternates with instrumental repetition of chorus)

(Solista) ¡Con cuidado, mi familia!

(Coro, shortened) ¡Que La Habana no aguanta más!

(Solista) Mis parientes, vamos a ser conscientes

– Qué problema me voy a buscar si viene mi hermana Pastora

– Con sus seis vejigos que son candela

– Sin embargo aquí en mi casa se me quieren colar

Take it easy, my family!

'Cause Havana can't take any more!

My folks, we have to be conscious

What problems I'll have if my sister Pastora comes

With her six kids that are trouble

Even so, here in my house everyone's trying to squeeze in

– *Y además de todo eso mi mujer quiere tener otro negrito*	And besides all that my wife wants another (black) baby
(Instrumental interlude)	
(Solista, spoken*) ¡Manolo, el tumbador de la sonrisa amplia! ¡YA!*	Manolo, the conga player with a big smile! ENOUGH!
(Coro) ¡Que La Habana no aguanta más! (4x)	'Cause Havana can't take any more! (4x)
(*Coro* alternates with instrumental repetition of chorus)	
(Improvised flute solo)	
(Solista, spoken*) Sopla Armando, ¡sopla!*	Blow Armando, blow!
(Sung) *Bibliotecas, cines de estrenos, y un buen bailable*	Libraries, new movie theaters, and a good dance club
(Coro) En toda Cuba vas a encontrar	You'll find them all over Cuba
(Solista) Sí, una pizzería y un Coppelita, mamita	Yes, a pizzeria and a Coppelita,[9] baby
– *Apartamentos bien amueblados*	Well-furnished apartments
– *Hay que aclararle esto a mis parientes*	We have to make this clear to my relatives
(Coro) ¡Que La Habana no aguanta más!	That Havana can't take any more!
(Solista) Yo no sé que va a pasar si mi hermana se decide llegar	I don't know what I'll do if my sister decides to come
– *Porque como yo le dije, trae seis vejigos que son de ajá*	Because like I told you, she'll bring six restless kids
– *Oye, ahora que en mi casa me la quieren llenar*	Listen, now they want to fill up my house
– *Qué va, qué va, no aguanta más*	Come on, come on, it can't take anymore
(*Coro,* until fade out)	
(Solista, spoken over *coro) Por eso yo me quedo en La Jata*	That's why I'm staying in La Jata
Allí voy a hacer un doce plantas	There I'm gonna build a twelve-story building[10]
Pregúntale, pregúntale a Bomba, el limpiabotas	Ask, ask Bomba, the shoe shiner.
¡Oye! ¡Sígueme!	Listen! Follow me!

The song is framed as a sort of morality tale directed at the narrator's relatives (and by extension the relatives of Havana residents who were born elsewhere), in which he makes an appeal for them to consider the greater social good, and not just their own individual desires to move to the capital. The solista's "call" early in the *montuno* (call-and-response) section borrows a word commonly used in socialist ideology, *consciente* (meaning to be socially conscious or aware), in order to elicit a feeling of duty in the population not to overcrowd the capital city. This notion recalls the admonitions of Fidel Castro, who during his lengthy time in power often called upon Cubans to sacrifice their individual desires for the good of the country and for the purposes of advancing socialist ideologies during periods of economic and social crisis, most recently during the Special Period. The references in the bridge and montuno section to the construction of housing, educational institutions, and entertainment and food venues all over the island serve to detail the attractive living conditions outside Havana, and to try to convince people to stay in their own provinces. The narrative technique of appealing to the social conscience of listeners can be interpreted as a hegemonic move in the Gramscian sense, particularly in relation to the necessity of gaining popular consent in order to perpetuate hegemonic moments and configurations (Hall [1986] 1996a, 424). The reproduction of socialist notions in this song—such as the importance of citizens being *conscientes* and sacrificing for the greater public good—is evidence of the state's success in (to paraphrase Stuart Hall) making its hegemonic ideologies popular (426).

The most interesting part of the song's narrative strategy lies in the fact that the subject is clearly not a Havana native, which seems to render the message more effective because it is an outsider addressing other outsiders. It is almost as if the regional identity of the narrator is used to forestall possible accusations of regionalism and divisiveness that could be launched at Los Van Van for defending Havana against "foreign" invaders. Instead, the song appears to be making an objective argument, free from the biases of regional identity, about the ways that overmigration contributes to Havana's crumbling infrastructure and disrupts the narrator's life. While the narrator never provides any autobiographical details, the meanings of this message, and the probability that it is directed primarily at *orientales*, must be inferred in light of the regional identity of lead singer Pedro "Pedrito" Calvo. Undeniably one of Los Van Van's most visible and beloved stars, who played a major role in the group's popular ascent in the 1970s and 1980s, Calvo is from Santiago. Rachel Faro and Rebecca Mauleón state, "No visual icon represents Los Van Van's identity more than lead singer Pedro Calvo, with his broad-rimmed hat, his overwhelming sexuality (both physically and vocally), and his ebullient humor" (1999, 20). Indeed, many of the songs he is famous for—such as "Sandunguera" and "La Fruta"—utilized sexualized double entendres and lyrics, and his dancing style when he was performing with Los Van Van reinforced this association.[11] However, Calvo's visual presence—with his broad-rimmed "farmer's" hat, bandana, and long, bushy moustache—also conjured up the image not of an elite urban dweller representing the capital's most famous dance group, but of a *campesino* (peasant from the countryside).

What sort of message can be inferred from having a Santiago native, whose image signifies him as an outsider to Havana, police the boundaries of the capital in this song? Whatever the intentions of Formell (a habanero) in composing and Calvo (a santiaguero) in interpreting this song, it is clear that the meanings are much more complex than a simple regionalist defense of one's city from overcrowding by other Cubans. Formell seems to have been prophetic in writing this song several years before the fall of the Soviet bloc and the onset of the Special Period, which provoked much larger waves of migration to Havana. Faro and Mauleón state, "In 1996 the government initiated a resolution (which may or may not have been inspired by the song) to 'thin out' the capital city by encouraging those Cubans who migrated from other provinces to return to their original homes" (1999, 22). In fact, Decree 217 (discussed in chapter 1) did more than "encourage" non-Havana natives to return to their homes; it has often meant "regional profiling" of them by police officers in the capital and has sometimes resulted in deportations.

In order to contextualize the song's multivalent meanings vis-à-vis regional identities and antagonisms, it is worth highlighting the career trajectory of Formell and the band's founding members prior to the formation of Los Van Van. Complicating the direct association of the band with the capital city is the fact that Formell, whose family has roots in Santiago, received much of his musical formation during the years he spent with the pioneering dance band Orquesta Revé. Formed in 1956 and led by Guantánamo native Elio Revé until his death in 1997, Orquesta Revé has arguably been the most important dance band associated with Oriente of the twentieth century.[12] Vincenzo Perna states: "Such extensive use of coros [choral refrains], now a feature common to practically all contemporary MB [*música bailable*, or dance music], was spearheaded by Elio Revé, the now defunct leader of a band that has functioned as an incubator for many important names of contemporary Cuban dance music" (2005, 140).[13] These musicians include Formell, Chucho Valdés, and Juan Carlos Alfonso, leader of the timba group Dan Den.[14] Ethnomusicologist Benjamin Lapidus similarly refers to the group as a "school-like institution" (2008, 115), asserting that around three hundred musicians have passed through its ranks. While pioneering many elements that would later come to be associated with timba—some, in fact consider Revé to be "the father of salsa"—the band also drew on Guantánamo's musical roots in various ways. First, the band was assembled as an updated *charanga francesa*—an ensemble featuring flutes and violins that became popular around the turn of the twentieth century[15]—and second, Revé incorporated various musical features associated with and lyrical references to the traditional *changüí* genre.[16] Before joining Orquesta Revé in the mid-1960s, Formell had been drawn more toward rock and jazz than Cuban dance music (Perna 2005, 36). In fact, he introduced rock elements to Orquesta Revé such as electric guitars and the trap set, musical features he carried over to Los Van Van a few years later (Faro and Mauleón 1999, 8). More importantly, he effectively decimated Orquesta Revé when he left to start his own band, taking at least nine core members with him, including the man who would become Los Van Van's other principal composer, pianist Cesar "Pupy" Pedroso (Faro and Mauleón 1999, 9).[17]

The fact that Los Van Van's founding members and most influential musicians began their professional careers with Orquesta Revé or other eastern Cuban dance bands (see below) suggests a strong legacy of musical creativity that has moved from east to west. In fact, timba, the dominant style of Cuban dance music since the early 1990s, would probably not have developed into its current manifestation if not for the musical schooling of many of its principal innovators within eastern Cuban dance bands formed in the 1950s. Beginning their careers with Ritmo Oriental—a highly influential dance band that emerged as an offshoot of Orquesta Revé in 1958—were Los Van Van's Pedrito Calvo and several other future timba stars. Vincenzo Perna states, "In the 1970s the band [Ritmo Oriental] was known in Cuba as the charanga with the best percussion, and had a powerful, spectacular presence, featuring two musicians who would become key figures of timba, David Calzado (the future leader of La Charanga Habanera) and Tony Calá (the singer of NG La Banda)" (Perna 2005, 42). Indeed, La Charanga Habanera and NG La Banda are perhaps the two bands most intimately associated with timba, albeit for very different reasons: the former has enjoyed almost unparalleled mass popularity among Cuban youth since its emergence in the 1990s, and the latter is widely viewed as the first band to pull together all the musical elements that define *timba* (Perna 2005; R. Moore 2006).

"Soy Cubano y Soy de Oriente"

Addressing precisely this issue of the formative influences of eastern Cuban musical creativity, and speaking/singing back to the defensive posture of "La Habana No Aguanta Más," the eastern Cuban dance band Orquesta Original de Manzanillo (founded in 1963 with a charanga format featuring flute and violin) released "Soy Cubano y Soy de Oriente" (I'm Cuban and I'm from Oriente) in 1985. The discursive counterattack was led by singer Cándido Fabré, from the small town of San Luis near Santiago and widely considered to be one of the best vocal improvisers in Cuban popular music. Fabré is famous not only for his spontaneous composition of songs that comment on the social issue or situation of any given moment but also for his prolific body of work; his compositions have been interpreted not only by other Cuban musicians but by international salsa stars like Celia Cruz and Oscar D'León. "Soy Cubano y Soy de Oriente" contradicts the notion that orientales always travel to Havana with intentions of staying and asserts the significance of Oriente's musical contributions to Cuban popular music as a whole.[18] I reproduce the song's lyrics in their entirety in order to illustrate the various narrative strategies used by Fabré to respond to Los Van Van, and specifically to fellow santiaguero Pedrito Calvo.[19]

Verse

Yo que pensaba en las vacaciones llegar a La Habana,	I thought I would go to Havana for my vacation,
para pasear con Pedrito, con mi familia y con Juana	to take a stroll with Pedrito, with my family and with Juana
Llegarme por Tropicana, pasar por el malecón,	Go to the Tropicana, stroll on the malecón,[20]
visitar el capitolio y escuchar al Aragón	visit the capital building and go hear the [Orquesta] Aragón[21]
Porque vivo convencido que en toda Cuba hay escuelas,	Because I am convinced that all over Cuba there are schools,
hay hospitales, trincheras, casas, mujeres y cines	there are hospitals, trenches,[22] houses, women, and cinemas,
Y yo por eso no vine las vacaciones pasadas	And because of this I didn't come during my last vacation
Y aunque soy del monte adentro, nadie me puede engañar	And although I'm from the boondocks,[23] no one can fool me
No existe otro capitolio, ni he visto otra catedral,	There is no other capital building, nor have I seen another cathedral,
igual que no hay en La Habana ninguna Sierra Maestra	just like in Havana there is no Sierra Maestra[24]

No hay ningún Cuartel Moncada,	There's no Moncada Barracks,
no hay Gran Piedra, no hay Caney,	there's no Gran Piedra, no Caney,
no hay Granjita Siboney,	there's no Granjita Siboney,
no hay Bayamo, no hay Glorieta	there's no Bayamo, no Glorieta[25]
Tampoco existe otra fiesta criolla como la mía	Nor is there another creole [Cuban] party like mine,
que empieza por la mañana y termina al otro día	that begins in the morning and ends the next day
Pero como me enteré que ya La Habana no aguanta más,	But since I found out that Havana can't take anymore,
¿Porqué no cogen al son y me lo mandan pa'cá?	Why don't they send the *son* back to me?
¿Porqué no cogen al son y lo devuelven pa'cá?	Why don't they return the son back here to Oriente?
(Coro) Soy cubano, yo soy de Oriente	I'm Cuban, I'm from Oriente
¿Pero qué pasa en La Habana,	What's going on in Havana,
qué le pasa a mi gente?	what's going on with my people?
(Instrumental repetition of coro)	

Montuno section

(Coro) Soy cubano, yo soy de Oriente	I'm Cuban, I'm from Oriente
¿Pero qué pasa en La Habana,	What's going on in Havana,
qué le pasa a mi gente?	what's going on with my people?
(Solista) En cualquier parte se puede vivir,	(Lead) You can live well in any place,
lo voy a decir a gritos:	I'm going to yell it at the top of my lungs:
¡Cuba es la tierra más linda que ojos humanos han visto!	Cuba is the most beautiful country that human eyes have ever seen!
– Pero por eso no hay razón pa' que me digan que ya La Habana no aguanta más	So there's no reason for them to tell me that Havana can't take anymore
Mañana temprano recojo lo mío y con mi familia me voy pa'llá	Tomorrow I'll gather my things early and go there with my family[26]
– ¡Pedrito! Dale la mano al que llega,	Pedrito! Lend a hand to he who arrives,
bríndale hospitalidad,	offer him hospitality,
Que cuando él vea que no cabe solito se marchará	Because when he sees that there's no room for him, he'll leave by himself

– *En Oriente tengo un humilde bohío con un techado de guano*	In Oriente I have a humble hut with a roof made of palm leaves
Que tiene la puerta abierta para todos los cubanos	Whose door is open for all Cubans
(Instrumental interlude)	
(Shortened coro) *Soy cubano, yo soy de Oriente*	I'm Cuban, I'm from Oriente
(Solista) *Antonio Maceo nació en Majaguabo y fue a morir a Occidente*	Antonio Maceo was born in Majaguabo[27] and died in the West
– *José Martí que nació en La Habana y vino a caer en Oriente*	José Martí who was born in Havana and died in Oriente
– *¡Ay, esos grandes corazones cayeron en opuestas regiones!*	Oh, those two brave hearts died in opposite regions!
- *Ay, pero por eso le voy a cantar que venga, si quiere, Alberto y Vicente*	Oh, because of this I'll sing for Alberto and Vicente to come if they want
- *Que tengo esta rumbita, esta rumbita caliente*	'Cause I have this little rumba, this hot little rumba
– *Vamos a gozar, ¡que baile toda la gente!*	We're gonna have fun, everyone dance!
(Shortened coro) *Yo soy de Oriente*	I'm from Oriente
(Solista) *Hace tiempo esta es la tierra caliente*	This has always been the "hot land"[28]
– *A ver, Usted, Usted, ¿de dónde es?*	Let's see, you, you, where are you from?
– *El sol sale por aquí, y se esconde en Occidente*	The sun rises here and hides in the West
(Coro, with instrumental response replacing solo voice)	
(Flute solo added on top of call-and-response, then fade out)	

Fabré utilizes different narrative techniques to respond to Los Van Van's assertions concerning the availability of housing and other social services all across the island. He affirms that this statement is true in both the verse and montuno sections, hence suggesting that one need not travel to Havana and that any Cuban city provides the necessary conditions for living well. However, by listing the monuments and attractions unique to the capital and to other locales in Oriente, Fabré also makes a broader statement about the diversity that characterizes the island. He asserts that just as the capital building, the cathedral, and the *malecón* are unique to Havana, Oriente has unparalleled sites of natural beauty and historic importance, such as the colonial city of Bayamo and Santiago's Moncada Barracks, where the Cuban Revolution was launched in 1953. This counters Los Van Van's homogenizing rhetoric implying that all places offer more or less the same amenities. Just as Fabré details eastern Cuba's attractions, the song's title, "I'm Cuban and I'm from Oriente," discursively emplaces eastern Cuban identity at the center of Cubanidad and thus challenges the implication that orientales are not as native to Cuba as habaneros are—a notion that is currently more pervasive than ever in Havana with the term "undocumented" used to refer to eastern migrants.

With the line "Although I'm from the boondocks, no one can fool me," Fabré wears his "countryness" and regional identity proudly, thus flipping the traditional denigration of people from el campo on its head and admonishing Calvo for not acting hospitably toward other easterners in Havana. He assures habaneros that orientales will recognize when Havana has reached its full capacity and have the moral sense to leave without being told to do so.[29] He juxtaposes Calvo's (and habaneros') unwelcoming behavior with his own hospitality, stating that although his home is humble, the doors are always open for all his countrymen, no matter where they're from.

Fabré issues perhaps his most witty and caustic barb at the end of the verse when referencing the origins of Cuba's national genre, singing, "Why don't they [habaneros] return the *son* back here to Oriente?" Here he alludes to the history of son, which originated in Oriente and was subsequently brought to the capital in the first decade of the twentieth century, where it became a symbol of Cubanidad both on the island and abroad.[30] The implication is that son (and eastern Cuban musical creativity in general) has been appropriated by habaneros and redefined as the island's quintessential musical practice.[31] Furthermore, Fabré could be interpreted as issuing a veiled critique at the many eastern Cuban musicians, such as Calvo, who have abandoned Oriente for the capital and apparently forgotten their regional roots. In fact, he constitutes a rare case in that even after leaving Orquesta Original de Manzanillo in 1993 to form his own band, Fabré never relocated to Havana, preferring to maintain his home base in Oriente. When asked by a journalist in 2013 why he had never moved to Havana like so many other eastern Cuban musicians, he responded, "Someone has to stay in this region to continue representing Oriente from here, which means to continue representing one single nation named Cuba" (Gaínza Moreno 2013; my translation).[32]

In line with this perspective, the second part of the montuno section, with the shortened choral refrain, reveals two very different and conflicting discursive aims. The first appears to be a call for cross-regional unity, as evidenced in Fabré's invocation of the two most celebrated figures in the struggle for Cuban independence—Antonio Maceo, the military leader, and José Martí, the intellectual leader—and the fact that both were born and died in "opposite regions" fighting for the same noble cause. This unifying discourse, which corresponds to the quotation reproduced above, is also displayed in his suggestion in the song that the island's beauty lies in its diversity and in his assertion that all Cubans would be welcome at his home. The last several lines of the montuno section, however, are characterized by a more aggressive, critical tone that could be viewed as a *puya*, a verbal challenge/battle.[33] He sings: "Let's see, you, you, where are you from?," thus challenging Calvo and other musicians from Oriente living in Havana to come out of the regional closet and reveal their true identity. Finally, the last line of the song is loaded with double meaning: "The sun rises here and hides in the west." There are certainly other words that Fabré could have used to refer to the sun's daily trajectory, like the obvious choice of "sets," but he chose the word "hides," lending the phrase a more sinister tone. Once again, he seems to be implying that musical creativity and brilliance (the shining sun) originate in Oriente and travel to Occidente, never to be heard from again, thus leaving the east bereft of its talent. While there are other ways of interpreting Fabré's veiled references, my discussions with folkloric musicians from Santiago (relayed in the following chapter) suggest that this is a common perspective among easterners in general.

Lázaro Moncada Merencio, a Santiago native, told me that the regionalist "battle on wax" constituted by "La Habana No Aguanta Más" and its response song, "Soy Cubano y Soy de Oriente," stirred up quite a popular controversy in the mid-1980s, and that many orientales felt vindicated by Fabré's passionate defense of his region (pers. comm. 2008). However, unlike the Los Van Van song, Fabré's composition seems to have been largely forgotten in Cuban dance music historiography, a lacuna that is perhaps related to the nature of Cuba's regional politics and the hegemony of Havana's cultural production vis-à-vis the rest of the island.[34] Furthermore, the message relayed in the Los Van Van song has continued to be relevant to the present day and has perhaps increased in significance since the Special Period and augmented migration from the provinces to Havana.

This chapter is largely excerpted from my 2010 dissertation, but during my fieldwork in Santiago in 2011 I was alerted to the existence of an analysis of these two songs by Cuban writer Odette Alonso Yodú, which provides an interesting and somewhat surprising counterpoint to my interpretation.[35] Alonso, who is from Santiago, wrote a brief opinion piece, "Una polémica innecesaria" (An unnecessary controversy), about the songs in 1986, cementing Lázaro's assertion that they had both gained widespread popularity and caused a stir. Alonso's basic argument is that Fabré's response song constituted an over-reaction riddled with "a ridiculous regionalism" (Alonso Yodú 1986, 15; my translation). Her reasons for defending Formell's composition are threefold: first, Formell wasn't directing his comments at anyone in particular, and the family discussed in the song could have been from any region of the country; second, his targets were not people who travel to the capital to visit but only those who decide to stay; and third, she finds that the tone of the song was not offensive in the least. In contrast, she views the Fabré song as emanating a disproportionate bitterness, and critiques (among other things) his treat-ment of son as a "postal package" that can simply be reclaimed by orientales. Alonso finds this phrase particularly vexing because, she argues, son is the cultural heritage of the entire nation, not just one region (Alonso Yodú 1986, 16). Furthermore, she takes Fabré's line about being from the "boondocks" as evidence of his inferiority complex, wondering why anyone would want to try and fool him. Her piece concludes with a strong reaffirmation of the unify-ing nationalist discourse discussed in the previous chapter: she invokes the oft-cited expression "desde la punta de Maisí hasta el Cabo de San Antonio" (from the tip of Maisí [the easternmost point on the island] to the Cape of San Antonio [the westernmost point]) in order to signify the sentiment of national unity shared by all Cubans, particularly in their goal of advancing the revolution.

While reading Alonso's critique of "Soy Cubano y Soy de Oriente" has not convinced me to discard my own analysis of the song, it does signal to me the significance of the broader social context in which popular culture is cre-ated, enacted, and received. I interpret these songs from the vantage point of the twenty-first century, more than two decades removed from the start of the Special Period, and within the context of continuing large-scale migra-tion from eastern Cuba and other provinces to the capital and beyond (i.e., abroad). During my first trips to the island, I found myself surprised by the amount of animosity directed at "palestinos" by Havana natives. My interest in and sensitivity about this issue only increased as I began a relationship with Lázaro, a santiaguero who was living and working in Havana. Is my reading of the songs discussed in this chapter colored by my particular positioning? Undoubtedly. Might my analysis be overreaching in finding animosity in the lyrics of the Los Van Van song? Possibly. However, the agenda guiding Fabré's song is more transparent in that it is a clear regionalist defense of Oriente; thus, Los Van Van's song was interpreted as an attack by Fabré and, most likely, other orientales. In contrast to the contemporary moment, Alonso was writ-ing at a time when the different regions of the island were probably as equal as at any point in Cuba's history; after all, one of the main goals of the revolution was to provide education, medical care, and institutional infrastructure to the neglected areas of the country, and it succeeded quite well in this task. In addition, as a supporter of revolutionary goals, her analysis likely seeks to reaffirm both the hegemonic nationalist discourse and the assertions about the overall equality of all Cubans—urban and rural—and uniformity of living conditions across the island. Alonso states, "this business of the 'boondocks' is becoming, every day with more certainty, a bad reminder of a past that has luckily been overcome" (Alonso Yodú 1986, 16; my translation). Thus, she finds the idea that someone would be looked down upon because they are from *monte adentro* to be obsolete, due to the successes of the revolution. Unfortunately, I believe that my ethnographic research and personal experiences are a testament to Alonso's miscalculation.

"Un Pariente en el Campo"

Whereas the two songs examined above suggest that overcrowding in the capital and hostilities between habaneros and orientales were significant concerns in the mid-1980s—during a period of relative economic and social stability—regionalist sentiment has become increasingly hostile since the economic crisis of the Special Period. A recent timba song that addresses this issue and the presence of migrants in Havana is Adalberto Álvarez's "Un Pariente en el Campo" (A Relative in the Countryside). Álvarez is from the city of Camagüey, in the province of the same name, which until the revolution constituted part of Oriente (see chapter 1). However, he was born "by accident" in Havana while his mother was visiting the capital.[36] During the early years of his career he helped form the dance band Son 14 in Santiago, a fact that adds Álvarez to the list of pioneering musicians who gained their musical formation with eastern Cuban bands. After four years with Son 14, Álvarez left for Havana in 1984 to form his current group, Adalberto Álvarez y Su Son, which has come to be one of the most successful and durable Cuban dance bands of the past quarter century.[37] Following in the footsteps of Los Van Van, many of Álvarez's compositions are topical and include elements of social commentary or humorous interpretations of social trends.[38] "Un Pariente en el Campo," a major hit from Álvarez's 2005 album *Mi Linda Habanera*, provides a fascinating commentary on the manifestations of regionalist sentiment in twenty-first-century Havana.[39]

Verse 1

Mira qué linda es La Habana,	Look how lovely Havana is,
como La Habana no hay	there is no other place like Havana
Verdad que se ve bonita,	It's true that it's pretty,
por donde quiera que vas	no matter where you go
Y según cuenta la historia,	According to history,
hace ya más de 100 años	more than 100 years ago
en La Habana no había tanta gente,	there weren't so many people in Havana,
pero de pronto se empezó a llenar	but suddenly it began to fill up
Vinieron de todas partes	They came from all parts of the country
porque La Habana es la capital.	because Havana is the capital.

Verse 2

Y así se fueron uniendo el campo y la capital,	This is how the countryside and the capital began to come together,
y se formaron familias,	and families were formed,
los de aquí con los de allá	those from here with those from there
Por eso cuando te veo	That's why when I see you
inocente y especulando, te digo	acting innocent and showing off,[40] I tell you
que aquí él que más, él que menos	that here everyone, more or less,
tiene un pariente en el campo. ¡Ay Dios!	has a relative in the countryside. Oh boy!

Montuno section

(Coro) *Como se goza en La Habana,*	(Chorus) Havana is so much fun,
por eso me gusta tanto	that's why I like it so much
Aquí él que más, él que menos	Here pretty much everyone
tiene un pariente en el campo	has a relative in the countryside
(Solista) *Qué linda luce la capital de toditos los cubanos*	(Lead) What a beautiful place the capital of all Cubans is
Cuando los veo caminar de la mano, mi compay, de su pariente del campo	When I see them walking hand in hand, my brother, with their relative from the countryside

(Whole four-line coro)

(Solista) *Lo importante es la familia,*
el cariño y el amor

The important thing is family,
affection and love

Jardín que no se cultiva
jamás te brinda una flor

[Proverb] A garden that isn't cultivated
will never bring forth a flower

– ¡No, no! No importa de donde vengas,
siempre te daré mi mano

No, no! It doesn't matter where you're from,
I'll always shake your hand

Y sacando bien la cuenta, caballero, toditos
somos cubanos.

After all, man, we're all Cubans.

(Instrumental interlude, then coro)

(Shortened coro) *Tiene un pariente en el*
campo

Has a relative in the countryside

(Solista) *El caballo en Santa Fe hace poco*
se hizo santo, tú ves

The guy in Santa Fe just "made santo,"[41]
you see

– Y la chica de la esquina que me gusta
tanto

And the girl who lives on the corner whom I
like so much

– Michila de Centro Habana, la que siempre
está bailando

Michila, from Central Havana, the one
who's always dancing

– ¡La mayoría de la gente que ahora a mí
me está escuchando!

The majority of the people listening to me
right now!

(Coro)

(Solista, spoken): *Bueno caballeros, voy a*
mencionar a todo él que tiene un pari-
ente en el campo. Voy pa'llá, ¡mira!

Ok guys, I'm gonna mention everyone who
has a relative in the countryside. Here I
go, listen!

David Calzado, Manolito Simonet, José Luis
Cortés, Elito Revé, Pachito Alonso, Juan
Formell, Isaac Delgado, y Eduardo Pérez
que ahora me está grabando. ¡Ahí!

David Calzado, Manolito Simonet, José Luis
Cortés, Elito Revé, Pachito Alonso, Juan
Formell, Isaac Delgado and Eduardo Pérez,
who is recording me right now. Yeah!

¡Vaya, Andrea de Baracoa!

Hell, Andrea from Baracoa![42]

(Sung) *Por la forma en que me hablas*
ahora yo decirte quiero,

Because of the way you're speaking to me I
want to tell you right now,

(New coro) *¡Como te gusta hacerte el*
habanero!

How you like passing yourself off as
habanero!

(Solista) *Tú le vas a Los Industriales, pero*
eres guantanamero

You root for the Industriales [Havana's baseball team], but you're from Guantánamo

– Deja las boberías y ve a ponerte tu
sombrero

Stop being silly and go put on your
[country] hat

– *Verdad que La Habana es linda, pero lo tuyo primero*	Havana really is beautiful, but your own [city] comes first
(Coro alternates with instrumental response, 3x)	
(Alternating choral refrains, 4x):	
(Coro 1) *Pero hay, lo hay*	But they exist, they exist
(Coro 2) *¡Como te gusta hacerte el habanero!*	How you like passing yourself off as habanero!
(Solista, spoken) *¡Mi gente de Camagüey!*	My people from Camagüey!
(Instrumental repetition of coro, 2x)	
(Solista) *Tú vives en Centro Habana pero eres de Niquero*	You live in Central Havana but you're from Niquero[43]
(Coro) *¡Como te gusta hacerte el habanero!*	How you like passing yourself off as habanero!
– *Viniste de visita y ahora, ¿como te llevo?*	You came to visit and now, how can I make you go back home?
(Solista, spoken) *Oye, La Habana, Santiago, Camagüey, Pinar del Río, ¡Cuba!*	Listen, Havana, Santiago, Camagüey, Pinar del Río, Cuba!
¡Qué linda es Cuba!	Cuba, what a beautiful place!

Upon initial analysis of the song, it seems to make similar declarations to those in "La Habana No Aguanta Más": there is a recognition of the increase in migration from other provinces to the capital and a complaint about relatives coming to visit and never leaving. However, there are also references that position this song squarely in the post-Soviet era: there is an explicit perpetuation of the notion that there are no more "pure" habaneros left in Havana and a pointed critique of Cubans who affect certain styles of dress, comportment, and beliefs associated with Havana natives, while denigrating or denying their own eastern Cuban and/or rural customs. Interestingly, despite his identity as a *camagüeyano* (Camagüey native) from el campo, Álvarez does not proudly defend his region like Fabré does; he simply critiques non-Havana natives who do not display regional pride or who effectively attempt to pass as habaneros. The main refrain in the second half of the montuno section—"¡Como te gusta hacerte el habanero!"—is definitely the most catchy (and probably the most pointed) lyric in the entire song, and audiences love singing along with it. In fact, timba group Manolito y Su Trabuco inserted this refrain into a 2008 ode to the capital called "La Habana Me Llama."[44] Álvarez's critique of this trend of attempting to pass as habanero also brings to mind Jacqueline Nassy Brown's commentary on the profound import of one's place-based identity and the futility of trying to hide this aspect of one's background: "[T]here must be something about place that defines one's personhood on some terribly deep level. This woman's origins, if discovered, would immediately associate her with everything that marks Liverpool's difference; an abject class positioning would only be the beginning. Indeed, the trenchant emphasis on *origins*, which connotes fixity and nature, implies that one can no more reverse the effects of birthplace by, for example, migrating, than one can change one's 'race.' But one can try to 'pass'" (Brown 2005, 15).

While there are certain parallels to the stance taken in the Los Van Van song, a closer analysis of "Un Pariente en el Campo," paired with information concerning Adalberto Álvarez's intentions in writing it, illustrates a somewhat different perspective. In an interview with journalist Jorge Smith Mesa, the bandleader states that one of his main objectives with the release of the album *Mi Linda Habanera* was a "crusade against provincialism" (Smith Mesa 2005; my translation). Álvarez stated that although he was born in a Havana hospital, he considers himself to be a native of Camagüey, and continued: "It's funny . . . in my concerts here [in Havana], when I ask, how many habaneros are there here? many people raise their hand, and when I investigate further, asking, how many come from the countryside? no one speaks, they even get irritated" (Smith Mesa 2005; my translation). Álvarez lamented the "shame" that many feel in not being "pure habaneros" and the fact that they deny their roots, stating, "True national pride begins with a love and pride for the place where one is born" (Smith Mesa 2005; my translation). The call in the montuno section that asserts, "Havana really is beautiful, but your own [city] comes first," correspondingly highlights the importance of the "spatiality of identity." Furthermore, Álvarez effectively "outs" the most important bandleaders in timba as either being born in or having roots in el campo, including those mentioned earlier in the chapter—Calzado, Revé, and Formell—and four others, Manolito Simonet, José Luís Cortés, Isaac Delgado, and Pachito Alonso.[45]

Although the song condemns non-Havana natives for denying their regional roots, it also advocates cross-regional relationships within the capital. This stance is evidenced in the song's second verse and in the conclusion, which "shouts out" different provinces of the country and implies that their diversity is what constitutes the beauty of Cuba. These portions of the song recall one of the narrative strategies used by Cándido Fabré, who also invokes the beauty of Cuba; this fact suggests that both songs—despite their respective critiques—imagine a national unity that can overcome regionalist tensions. However, while encouraging orientales and Cubans from other provinces to assume their regional identity proudly, Álvarez does not address the underlying issues that result in this shame, specifically the pervasive prejudice they encounter in the capital. Far from "singing back" to habaneros like Fabré does, Álvarez apparently exempts capitalinos (natives of the capital) from charges of regionalist transgressions in "Un Pariente en el Campo," as his principal targets of critique are nonnatives who, ashamed of their heritage, try to pass as habaneros. Further evidence of Álvarez's oblique alliance with habaneros and their perspectives in this matter can be found on the title track of the album, "Mi Linda Habanera." This song is an homage to the capital's beauty, symbolized by the figure of a *habanera* (a woman from Havana), who functions as the narrator's creative muse and whom he never stops thinking about when traveling and performing far from home.

The unifying discourse represented by the song's closing lyrics, which declare that Cuba's regional diversity is what makes the country beautiful and unique, reverberates with the nationalist hybridity discourse. As noted in the introduction, this discourse foregrounds racial unity over difference and presumes that racial equality stems directly and automatically from the fact of being a nation with a long history of racial mixing. In other words, whether black, white, or of racially mixed ancestry, Cubans are all committed to the cause of antiracism because Cuba is a hybrid nation. Similarly, in Álvarez's song, whether from Havana, Santiago, Camagüey, or Pinar del Río, everyone is Cuban, and, as the capital, Havana belongs to all. This is a message that Cubans and foreigners alike are encouraged by the state to adopt, as illustrated by the prominent billboard in Havana that I discussed in chapter 1 that states, "Welcome to Havana, capital of *all* Cubans!" Despite the realities of regional profiling within contemporary Havana and popular expressions of regionalist sentiment, the state is very invested in the notion that regional differences take a backseat to national unity.

According to Lázaro, "Un Pariente en el Campo" was extremely well received in Oriente, as it seemed to speak a truth that many orientales felt deeply and had experienced in very personal ways, namely the shame of being labeled a "palestino" in Havana and the consequent obligation to suppress or at least downplay their regional identity (pers. comm., 2008). However, it was an extremely popular song all over Cuba, and Lázaro suggested that habaneros loved it for a different reason: the song seemed to "prove" their superiority by publicly acknowledging the attempts by other Cubans to imitate their mannerisms, slang, and fashion trends. One could even say that the shame felt by eastern Cubans was a point of pride for people from the capital. Furthermore, the song gave "real" habaneros an outlet to police the boundaries of local identity: Álvarez's technique of calling out the timba stars who had either been born in or whose parents had come from el campo provided them with a model by which to differentiate themselves, as native-born habaneros, from their neighbors who perhaps had moved to Havana from Oriente ten years earlier and were now identifying as capitalinos.

A casual conversation I had with a young man in Camagüey in May 2008 provided another interesting perspective concerning Álvarez's assertions, both in his song and in his statements, regarding the importance of regional identity. In speaking about Álvarez, I was surprised to hear the young man express feelings of disillusionment toward his fellow camagüeyano. He stated that Álvarez does not return often to his hometown to perform, and when he does, his concerts never last for more than sixty or even thirty minutes. He asserted that many camagüeyanos view Álvarez as a traitor to his province. Thus, ironically, much like his own singling out and critique of non-Havana natives for abandoning their roots in "Un Pariente en el Campo," some of Álvarez's fellow camagüeyanos seem to accuse him of the same thing. Even more fascinating was the young man's subsequent statement that in Camagüey people love Cándido Fabré for his legendary propensity to perform long concerts (as compared to those of Álvarez) that last into the early hours of the morning.[46] I suspect that the admiration displayed for Fabré by this young man also has partly to do with the singer's brazen displays of regional pride, and his reputation as someone who discursively "stood up" to Havana. Finally, it is not irrelevant that Camagüey was part of Oriente until the revolution, in that some older camagüeyanos may still consider themselves to be orientales.

Expressions of Regionalism in Rumba Music and Performance

Expressions of regionalism in rumba performance are generally harder to pin down, largely because rumba does not enjoy the amount of mass mediation, specifically radio circulation and recording opportunities, available to Cuban dance music groups. In addition, the themes of rumba songs, while varying widely, are often quite distinct from those of Cuban dance music. Although many rumba songs address contemporary social issues, they tend much more than dance music to pay homage to certain people, places, or things, including the genre of rumba itself, past *rumberos* (rumba musicians or dancers), or different aspects of Afro-Cuban culture, history, and/or religion. Other common themes include boasting about one's own skills as a rumbero and recounting important events in Cuba's history. One prevalent theme among "tribute" songs is extolling the virtues of one's city/province of birth, or of another Cuban city that has a distinguished history in some aspect of national culture. Famed rumba group Los Muñequitos de Matanzas, for example, recorded an ode to Santiago's revolutionary history on their rumba *guaguancó*[47] called "Inspiración a Santiago."[48] The first phrase reproduces a popular phrase about the eastern capital: "Santiago, fuiste rebelde ayer, hospitalaria hoy, serás heróica siempre" (Santiago, you were a rebel yesterday [in the past], hospitable today, you will always be heroic). The lyrics link Santiago to the heroic activities of independence war heroes José Martí and Antonio Maceo, and suggest that this ode to Santiago constitutes a fulfillment of the group's duty to support and remember the origins of the Cuban Revolution.

While Los Muñequitos' song goes against the grain of regionalist sentiment (which does not necessarily imply anything about the personal views of the group members vis-à-vis regionalism), the rumba song "Para Gozar, La Habana" (To Have Fun, Havana) by Havana-based rumba group Clave y Guaguancó is reminiscent of the attitudes underlying "La Habana No Aguanta Más." The lyrics of the second verse, which open this chapter, refer to the endless stream of internal migrants arriving in Havana with intentions of staying indefinitely.[49]

Verse 2

Para gozar, La Habana	To have fun, Havana
Para disfrutar, La Habana	To enjoy yourself, Havana
Está llena de emigrantes que llegan y no se van	It's full of emigrants who arrive and never leave
Siempre son bien recibidos y se les brinda amistad	They are always welcomed and offered friendship
Los encantan las mujeres y el ambiente popular,	They are captivated by the women and the down-home atmosphere,
Y es que encuentran en La Habana el paraíso terrenal	and it's simply that in Havana they find heaven on earth

The lyrics declare that nonnatives are always treated with hospitality and welcomed with open arms by habaneros. More generally, the song extols the virtues of the capital, emphasizing the principal attractions for other Cubans—beautiful women and *el ambiente popular* (the down-home atmosphere)[50]—and characterizing Havana as "heaven on earth." As opposed to the narrative strategy of Los Van Van's song, which attempts to convince possible migrants that living conditions are just as good in their home provinces, this song lists some reasons why people might want to migrate to Havana. As in the previous songs discussed, the montuno section of "Para Gozar, La Habana" contains many provocative statements regarding regionalist sentiment. Following are the transcribed and translated lyrics.

Montuno section

(Coro) *Para gozar, La Habana*	(Chorus) To have fun, Havana
(Solista) *No mandan ni un telegrama*	(Lead) They don't even send me a telegram
– *Llegan sin saberlo yo*	They arrive without me knowing it
– *Se alojan en el Vedado*	They stay in the Vedado [neighborhood]
– *Se alojan en Luyanó*	They stay in Luyanó [neighborhood]
– *Trajeron la barbacoa*	They brought the *barbacoa*[51]
– *¡Caballero, que familia!*	Man, what a big family!
– *No me mandan ni un recado*	They don't even send me a message
– *¿De dónde sale tanta gente?*	Where do all these people come from?
– *¡Qué cosa más grande, negra!*	It's unbelievable, girl!

Spoken interlude (Woman's voice with an exaggerated eastern Cuban accent, spoken over montuno singing):[52]

Corre y echa los trapos en un cubalse,	Hurry and throw the clothes in a bag,
¡que nos vamos para La Habana!	'cause we're going to Havana!
¿Sabes lo que dice Silvio,	You know what Silvio,
el babalao de las estrellas?	the babalao[53] to the stars, says?
Que tiene por allá un cuarto, por allá por	That he has a room over there in El Cerro
El Cerro que me lo va a prestar, y que	[Havana neighborhood] that he's going to
podemos mandar a buscar a toditico	lend me, and that we can send for absolutely everyone
Oye, ¿tú conoces a Jorge, el esposo de Isely?	Hey, do you know Jorge, Isely's husband?
Ése es que nos va a mandar la plata.	He's the one who's gonna send the money.
Sí, sí, nos va a mandar la plata para	Yeah, yeah, he's gonna send us the money
nosostros ir todo el mundo a La Habana	So that all of us can go running to Havana
corriendo	
Ay hermanita, ay, a mí me da mucha lás-	Oh sister, I'm so sad that we have to leave
tima dejar el buey jabao	the *jabao*-colored ox[54]

¿Dónde lo vamos a meter?	Where are we going to put him?
Pero tenemos que cargar con él en el tren	We have to bring him on the train
¡Corre, niña, que se va el tren!	Run, girl, the train is leaving!
Pero después voy a mandar a buscar a todo el mundo	After a while I'm gonna send for everyone
Voy a mandar a buscar a Panchito, a Chichí, a Pancrasio, a Manyoli, sí, Manyoli, la hija de Guillermo.	I'm gonna send for Panchito, for Chichí, for Pancrasio, for Manyoli, yeah, Manyoli, Guillermo's daughter
Oye, y también podemos mandar a buscar a Mayito.	Hey, and we can also send for Mayito.
Así dice la Cáterin, que también es de por allá	That's what Cáterin says, she's also from there
Cáterin, ¿te acuerdas de ella?	Cáterin, do you remember her?
¡Ay, dios mío, se quema mi familia!	Oh Lord, my family is such a mess!
Mi familia es un dibujo.	My family is a drawing[55]
Ay comay, acuérdate echar una merendita también allí porque en el tren no hay na'.	Oh sister, remember to throw a snack in too, because there's nothing on the train
Pónme un pepino con agua, y no sé cuantas cosas más, pero ¡apúrate niña, corre!	Bring me a bottle of water, and I don't know what else, but hurry up girl, run!
Corre, que se nos va . . . ¡ah muchacha!	Run, 'cause it's leaving . . . oh, girl!

(End of spoken interlude, return to coro)

(Solista) *Para que choques con la verdad*	So that you face the truth
(Coro) *Para gozar, La Habana*	To have fun, Havana
(Solista) *La Habana tiene sus cosas*	Havana has its distinctiveness
– *La Habana tiene misterios*	Havana has mysteries
– *Oye, ¡La Habana no aguanta más!*	Listen, Havana can't take any more!
– *Pero, vienen de Pinar del Río*	Oh, they come from Pinar del Río
– *Oye, vienen desde Camagüey*	Listen, they come from Camagüey
– *También de Santiago de Cuba*	From Santiago de Cuba too
– *Y todos son bien recibidos*	And all are welcomed
– *Los encantan las mujeres*	They are captivated by the women
– *En La Habana son muy lindas*	In Havana they're very pretty

(Fade out)

As is evident from many of the solista's lines during the montuno section, Clave y Guaguancó's song explicitly references the Los Van Van hit recorded roughly twenty years earlier. Not only does it directly quote "La Habana No Aguanta Más" but it also includes references to the stereotypical large family migrating from the outer provinces and the resultant overcrowding of Havana neighborhoods, and emphasizes the inconvenience and irritation this causes to the Havana native. However, this song also includes updated, post–Special Period cultural references such as the architectural phenomenon of the *barbacoa* (see note 51). The notion that Havana constitutes a terrestrial paradise for *orientales* and other migrants, but not for *habaneros* themselves who are forced to cohabitate with them, betrays the attitudes of superiority held by many *capitalinos*. The stance put forth suggests that migrants would not wish to stay in their home province, even if there existed economic and entertainment opportunities equal to those found in Havana. The narrative thus ultimately obscures the primary reason for such large increases in migration to the capital since the Special Period—the inability of these Cubans to survive economically in their home provinces.

My transcription and translation of the spoken interlude inserted into the middle of the montuno section (beginning at 3:43) cannot adequately convey what I consider to be the inflammatory nature of this parody of eastern Cubans. Although there are no direct references to specific regions in Cuba, the woman's exaggerated accent screams out "oriental!"; in fact, I believe it's necessary to hear the recording to fully understand its message. In addition, there are elements of eastern Cuban dialect inserted, such as the words *cubalse* (plastic bag) and *comay* (an abbreviated version of *comadre*, a close female friend). Beyond these elements, the words seem rather innocuous when read on paper, apart from the absurd idea of bringing an ox on the train, which is clearly meant to signify the woman's backwardness. However, although there are no specific identifiers in the spoken interlude, and the solista mentions Cubans from various provinces in the montuno, the song's principal target of critique immediately becomes explicit to all Cubans and to foreigners with a good working knowledge of regional dialects within the country. The scenario painted here seems to be a manifestation of Pedrito's worst nightmare, and, given the links to the Los Van Van song, the woman speaking could even be imagined as the sister he sings about who wants to bring her large eastern Cuban family (and even non–family members!) to Havana to impose on him. This brief dramatization of the politics of regionalism in contemporary Cuba presents a sharp contradiction to the assertions in both the verse and toward the end of the song that all migrants enjoy a warm welcome when they arrive in the capital.

I do not presume to know how a migrant from Oriente might feel upon hearing his/her accent parodied in this manner by a Cuban from a different province, much less by a Havana-based rumba group. I also recognize that what I may interpret as offensive might not be perceived as such by a Cuban or someone from a different cultural background. I have observed, for example, that Cubans often find hilarious jokes and statements that many Americans would find insulting or not "politically correct"; for example, jokes that perpetuate hypersexualized stereotypes about black people are extremely pervasive on the island.[56] In this vein, I asked Lázaro to listen to the song and describe to me his reaction. In fact, this vignette did not provoke the same feelings of indignation that it incited in me. He stated, "La letra es fuerte, pero no hiere" (The lyrics are strong/provocative, but they don't wound; pers. comm. 2008). He did not view the song as a major affront because, as he emphasized, this type of parody of orientales' manner of speaking has become completely normalized in popular media in contemporary Cuba: one can frequently hear and view similar caricatures of eastern Cubans on radio and TV programs. He asserted that if the song had come out in the 1980s, around the same time as "La Habana No Aguanta Más" and before the Special Period, there would have been more of an outcry on the part of orientales; they would have defended themselves more vigorously, and perhaps there would have even appeared a response song such as the one composed by Cándido Fabré.[57] Lázaro thus framed his reaction in relation to the distinct economic situations in Oriente before and after the Special Period, respectively: during the era of Soviet patronage, eastern Cubans were not as anxious to leave their homes for the capital, and when they did go to Havana, it was often for a visit and not to migrate. Since the Special Period, however, orientales have found themselves in desperate situations, and their regional pride has taken a backseat to their economic imperatives.

Conclusion

In the absence of an official recognition of the divisiveness that regionalist sentiment can incite, dance bands and rumba groups have taken it upon themselves to address this thorny issue in their lyrics. In *Timba: The Sound of the Cuban Crisis* (2005), Vincenzo Perna details the crafty textual strategies used by Cuban timba musicians to comment upon and stimulate popular debate about topics in post-Soviet Cuba that are considered to be subversive by the government, such as state censorship, increasing racialized class inequalities, and sex tourism. In a similar manner, the dance music and rumba songs discussed in this chapter unearth a popular debate about regionalism that simmers just beneath the surface of the capital. These narratives can be interpreted as implicitly challenging the unifying nationalist discourse that remains silent on the matter. While the recent unstable economic conditions and constantly shifting state solutions to these problems have certainly deepened regionalist hostilities since the Special Period, as the songs by Los Van Van and Cándido Fabré attest, these tensions existed at the height of Cuban socialism's success and are not exclusively the result of economic crisis.

The songs analyzed above present contesting claims about regionalism and migration to Havana in contemporary Cuba. "La Habana No Aguanta Más" and "Para Gozar, La Habana" effectively police the boundaries of the capital, assuming a defensive stance against "foreign" invaders. Nonetheless, the two songs utilize different narrative strategies that seem to be determined by the subject positions inhabited by their respective lead singers. In other words, while Clave y Guaguancó's song represents the subjectivity of the Havana native through the voice of the leader of the group, Amado Dedeu Hernández, Los Van Van's song constitutes a more complex utterance due to the santiaguero identity of the lead singer, Pedrito Calvo. Also, as suggested by Odette Alonso Yodú, there is nothing overtly offensive or antagonistic about "La Habana No Aguanta Más"; its critiques are issued in a respectful manner. The Clave y Guaguancó song, on the other hand, is quite incendiary with its brazen ridiculing of migrants from Oriente.

Both "Un Pariente en el Campo" and "Soy Cubano y Soy de Oriente" represent perspectives that contrast with the Havana-identified songs. Similar to the narrative position of Calvo, Adalberto Álvarez's song presents the point of view of an outsider, albeit one who has been accepted into habaneros' hearts and minds because of his superior compositional skills.[58] Therefore, he has earned a certain amount of clout that allows him to critique the regionalist antagonisms between habaneros and Cubans from el campo. However, while certainly advocating a more tolerant attitude toward regional difference, it should be reiterated that the main targets in the song are not habaneros but, as in the previous two songs, *gente del campo*. The Álvarez song indicts migrants to Havana for attempting to pass as habaneros and not wearing their regional identity with pride in the capital, and simultaneously seems to acquit habaneros of any responsibility for the hostile attitudes faced by these migrants. Ultimately, "Soy Cubano y Soy de Oriente" represents a more forceful counterclaim to "La Habana No Aguanta Más." It derives from the perspective of a proud oriental, Cándido Fabré, who unapologetically and unabashedly asserts eastern Cuban identity as central to Cubanidad and rejects the notion that Havana is a universally desired location of residence for all citizens.

Finally, it must be emphasized that although expressions of regionalist sentiment and hostility toward orientales in particular are pervasive in contemporary Havana, there are many habaneros who do not display prejudicial or disparaging attitudes toward Cubans from the outer provinces. While the lyrics of the songs I have discussed foreground the tensions that exist between Cubans of different provinces, particularly within the diverse matrix of the capital, it is also crucial to note that the three Havana-based music groups discussed above—Los Van Van, Adalberto Álvarez y Su Son, and Clave y Guaguancó—boast regionally diverse memberships. This fact suggests that regional differences do not always result in discord and that musical competence and charisma may trump regionalist antagonisms. Nonetheless, what this chapter has attempted to demonstrate is that regionalist sentiment in contemporary Cuban popular music is a pressing issue that has not been given voice, but that merits scholarly attention and analysis.

Chapter Three

"Conciencia de Caribeñidad": Regionalism, *Folklore Oriental*, and Santiago's Caribbean Connection

This chapter continues my exploration of the cultural and musical manifestations of regionalism, with a focus on the current status of *folklore oriental*, or eastern Cuban folklore, within the national context. One of my primary arguments is that the traditions associated with Oriente are both relatively neglected in the national academic realm and less visible in the performative realm than their western Cuban counterparts, which are often presented as *the* national folklore and thus assumed to represent all Cubans. Although my hypotheses about the regional inequalities within the representation of folkloric traditions were in many ways buttressed by my ethnographic research with musicians from Santiago de Cuba, our conversations also suggested that gains have been made in the performance of folklore oriental outside of Oriente. Furthermore, what became clear in my interviews was that, regardless of the status of eastern Cuban folklore, musicians view the situation through a regionally inflected lens. Thus, much like the situation with contemporary Cuban dance music, here I argue that regional identity strongly informs the perceptions and aesthetic preferences of folkloric musicians, even when they deny its impact. In order to contextualize my discussion of folklore oriental, I will first discuss the ways that national folkloric traditions have been represented in racialized and regionalized terms, and how long-standing regional inequalities have impacted the scholarship on the subject.

Race, Region, and the Representation of National Folklore

Racialized Taxonomies of Cuban Music and the Denial of Indigenous Influence

Despite the discursive valorization of mestizaje as the defining essence of Cubanidad since independence (see chapter 1), the persistence of Eurocentric binary racial thinking is evidenced in a particular paradox found in Cuban hybridity discourses: while proponents of national hybridity advocate racial equality and eschew racial difference, there has been a consistent attempt by folklorists and intellectuals to parse the different elements of Cuban identity and culture into hierarchical, neatly bounded categories of Spanish and African influence, thus reifying notions of racial purity. In subscribing to these racial taxonomies, promoters of Cuban nationalism simultaneously deny *and* maintain racial difference: they assert the uniquely hybrid identity of Cubanidad while at the same time assuming the a priori cultural purity of the different elements that constitute national identity and culture.[1] Furthermore, as will be discussed below, Cuban scholars have categorically denied both the continued existence of populations of indigenous descent on the island, and any important contribution they may have made to national culture. Anthropologist Peter Wade (2005) makes an interesting point regarding hybrid people and cultures, and how discourse about them paradoxically tends to invoke "racial origins and primordial encounters." He states, "Mestizo-ness is not simply opposed to blackness and indigenousness; rather, blackness and indigenousness are actively reconstructed by mestizo-ness. This can be thought of in terms of the persistence of a symbolics of origins which exists alongside a symbolics of mixture. Instead of disappearing in a homogenous fusion, losing their identity, the original elements of the mixture retain their presence in the imagination of the cultural and racial panorama" (Wade 2005, 245).

The work of nationalist composer Emilio Grenet (1939) offers a clear example of a racialized taxonomy of Cuban music, but there are also hints of it in the works of Cuba's celebrated scholar and folklorist Fernando Ortiz ([1950] 1998) and prominent musicologist Argeliers León (1952). Grenet categorized all Cuban popular music genres into three groups: "genres bordering on the Spanish," "genres of equitable black and white influence," and "genres bordering on the African" (Grenet 1939, 23, 30, 42). The three genres that have been most strongly linked to national identity—*contradanza* (whose popularity peaked in the mid-nineteenth century), *danzón* (an offshoot of contradanza featuring Afro-Cuban rhythmic elements more prominently, and considered to be Cuba's national dance), and *son* (which has from the 1920s been considered Cuba's quintessential music genre)—were classified by Grenet as equally European and African. Rumba, on the other hand was placed into the category of heavy African influence. He presented a distorted and rather elitist description of rumba song, stating that it consisted of a refrain that lasts eight measures and "is repeated indefinitely," and that "the melody is almost always a pretext for the rhythm which is everything in this popular genre. Thus, the greatest number of rumbas are written with absurd text which generally is a result of the rhythmical impulse" (Grenet 1939, 47). Like Grenet, who characterized Cuban music in general as "the Spanish melodies and the African rhythm" (Grenet 1939, 10), Fernando Ortiz took for granted this racialized binary, explaining in a manner reminiscent of Alan Lomax's Cantometrics project that these differences may have been due to the divergent types of societies found in Europe (hierarchical, individualistic) and Africa (egalitarian, cooperative), respectively (Ortiz [1950] 1998, 177).

While clearly not denying musical hybridity, it is problematic to assume that European—particularly Spanish—cultural elements were "pure" before the encounter with African-derived musics in the Americas. As various musicologists have noted (see, for example, Pasmanick 1997; Acosta 2004; Manuel 2009b), there was a long-standing presence of Africans (mainly from North Africa) in Spain between the seventh and fifteenth centuries, which certainly brought non-European music making into contact with the Spanish before Columbus's journeys to the Americas. In an article on rumba song, Philip Pasmanick critiques the discursive Africanization of rumba that tends to deny or minimize Spanish and European elements of the practice, finding that Fernando Ortiz and other proponents of the African contribution to Cuban culture viewed *décima* (a Spanish poetic form that was often used in early rumba song) as "too Spanish, too colonial, too white" (Pasmanick 1997, 269). Pasmanick states, "Rumberos themselves are quick to cite the Spanish influence in their singing, and it takes away nothing from the African roots and esthetic values of rumba to celebrate and explore the Spanish textual and melodic heritage" (269). In addition, he refutes the type of thinking, exemplified by the aforementioned Grenet quotations, that simplifies rumba song and lyrics as simply a "pretext" for rhythm, noting "a tendency to dismiss singing, and texts particularly, as secondary to drumming in rumba." He continues, "However . . . I have seen rumberos stop a rumba in great disgust when the singing is inadequate" (269). Furthermore, as will be discussed in chapter 6, there has been a tendency to compartmentalize the various Cuban popular genres and to "ghettoize" rumba from son, when in reality the two genres have had a long and complex relationship with each other. Cuban musicologist Leonardo Acosta has recently challenged the tendency to view rumba as more African-derived in every sense, asserting that son is a more polyrhythmic music than rumba (Acosta 2004, 54). Finally, as noted by ethnomusicologist Benjamin Lapidus (2008), the Guantánamo-based genre changüí is another casualty of this racialized taxonomy within Cuban musicology: because it is primarily practiced by rural blacks, it is distinguished from *música campesina* ("country" music, racialized as white), even though practitioners find many musical similarities with the latter. Furthermore, changüí is characterized as "funky mountain music" (Lapidus 2008, 121), with the word "funky" clearly reinforcing an association with blackness.

In his revisionist consideration of a number of issues relating to Cuban popular music, Acosta asserts that the most naturalized and repeated myth in all of Cuban musicology "is that which attributes to all Cuban music 'African and Spanish' roots" (Acosta 2004, 21; my translation). Acosta elucidates several reasons for debunking the exclusively biracial notion of Cuban identity and culture. These include a simple semantic critique that a nation's culture (Spain) should not be understood as equivalent to that of a continent (Africa), for there were specific African ethnic groups—Yoruba, Bantu, and so on—that were brought to Cuba as slaves and whose cultural influence is evident in the island's music. Acosta also specifies that even using the adjective "Spanish" is problematic in that it both lumps together diverse regional influences—from Andalusia, the Canary Islands, Galicia, and other provinces—and ignores the non-Spanish European influences on Cuban culture that came directly from France and central Europe. Finally, and perhaps most importantly, Acosta highlights the historical negation of indigenous influence on national culture, stemming from the oft-reified assertion that Cuba's original inhabitants, primarily Taínos and Ciboneys,[2] were basically exterminated by the end of the sixteenth century. While the denial of indigenous survival is a complex issue that I cannot treat in depth, I don't think it irrelevant to note that the surviving communities are all generally thought to be in Oriente, while the large majority of researchers and research institutions are located in Havana.

A number of sources assert that by the mid-sixteenth century the indigenous population had been decimated from a peak of somewhere between 120,000 and 150,000 to just a few thousand, concentrated in isolated rural communities primarily in Oriente, and that consequently their influence on national culture was marginal (Comité Estatal de Estadísticas 1979; Guanche 1996; Louis Pérez 2006).[3] The *Atlas demográfico de Cuba*, compiled by the State Committee on Statistics in 1979, notes that more than half of the population at the time of Spanish conquest lived in the region corresponding to modern-day Oriente (Comité Estatal de Estadísticas 1979, 9), and Louis Pérez states that over 90 percent of them belonged to the Sub-Taíno group (2006, 14). Notwithstanding the discourse of extinction that is often employed when discussing Cuba's indigenous population, Cuban ethnographer Martha Esquenazi Pérez asserts that in the mountainous regions of Santiago, Guantánamo, and Granma, there were, as of 2001, over a thousand people referred to as *indios* (Indians), with physical characteristics suggesting that they were descendants of Taínos (2001, 31). The municipality of Yateras in Guantánamo Province has a particularly high number of indigenous descendants, who formed a community called Caridad de los Indios, possibly in the nineteenth century. Esquenazi Pérez asserts that they still practice endogamy and conserve foods, traditions, and some indigenous words and archaic Spanish words from the colonial period (31–32).[4] In fact, I interviewed a folkloric dancer from Guantánamo, Isaias Rojas, who claimed to have indigenous relatives on one side of his family who are originally from Yateras (pers. comm. 2011). He asserted that changüí emerged in Yateras, which suggests the possibility of indigenous influence on this traditional genre.

Esquenazi Pérez elucidates the difficulty in accurately calculating the indigenous population during the colonial period: first, later descendants were often counted as white in census figures, and second, they were concentrated in rural mountainous areas, and the lack of transportation to get to these communities until fairly recently made it difficult to count them (2001, 23). She discusses the musical instruments used by indigenous Cubans, including the quintessentially "Latin" maracas, and their principal musical tradition, called *areíto*, which she believes was used for both festive and religious occasions. She also presents possible links between areíto and the musical, dance, and religious traditions of rural eastern areas, most notably in the hybrid sacred practice called *Espiritismo de cordón*: she cites the beliefs of many informants in Granma Province who believe that the tradition was inherited from Indians, and she also notes that the form of worshipping in a circle while holding hands is similar to the practice of areíto. In fact, Esquenazi Pérez suggests that this style of Espiritismo is likely composed of Spanish, African, indigenous, and Kardecian spiritism, making it one of the most hybrid religious practices in Cuba (39).[5] Ethnomusicologist Nolan Warden discusses the possibility of a relationship between indigenous and Bantu/Congo spirits in most forms of Espiritismo throughout the African diaspora, noting that many practitioners place statues of Plains Indians on their altars (Warden 2006, 30). I discuss the various forms of Espiritismo in further depth below.

Leonardo Acosta explains the negation of indigenous influence with reference to the now infamous debates about national cultural identity that took place in the 1920s and 1930s primarily between Fernando Ortiz—representing the ideologies of the *afrocubanismo* movement, which promoted the importance of African contributions to national culture—and composer Eduardo Sánchez de Fuentes, head of the *ciboneísta* or *indigenista* movement, which celebrated indigenous influence ostensibly in order to deny the African influences.[6] Robin Moore notes that one of the main focuses of the debates related to a folk song called "Areíto de Anacaona," which Sánchez de Fuentes attributed to the Ciboney Indians and which Ortiz (correctly, Moore suggests) asserted was a vodou song from Haiti (R. Moore 1997, 261, n. 21).[7] Moore writes, "Reimagining the past and their relationship to it, advocates of musical *indigenismo* generated a considerable body of work inspired by historical figures such as Hatuey, Anacaona, and Yumurí. . . . [T]hey ascribed indigenous origins to numerous instruments and musical forms developed by Afrocubans and Hispanics" (128).[8] However, Moore also problematizes the notion that the afrocubanistas were interested in promoting African-derived culture primarily for the purposes of advancing racial equality: he notes that they championed and created art music that incorporated particular Afro-Cuban elements, but that the music was largely European-derived and the composers were still hostile to Afro-Cuban traditions themselves, such as rumba and son. He suggests that their main agenda was to promote a unique brand of Cuban nationalism, stating, "To Roig [Emilio Roig de Leuschenging, a prominent intellectual of the 1920s and 1930s] and like-minded individuals, syncretic Afrocuban forms had the potential to serve as a barrier to national disintegration and the possibility of cultural subsumption by the United States" (127).

Acosta critiques the extremist positions that were taken on both sides of the afrocubanista-indigenista debate, but he ultimately defends Ortiz against accusations of being "anti-indigenous" by noting that Ortiz and his intellectual cohorts (such as Alejo Carpentier and Argeliers León) were merely fighting against attempts to obscure African influences. He asserts that their responses must be considered in light of the very racist context of the early twentieth century, which included the campaigns of blanqueamiento (see the introduction) and the racist backlash against the Partido Independiente de Color (see chapter 1), in addition to the antiblack premises of the indigenista movement. Rather than blaming Ortiz for the devaluation of indigenous people as "backward" and "taparrabos" (a word that literally means "loin-cloth," but that was used to signal their savage, uncivilized nature)—which he finds to be pervasive in contemporary Cuban society—Acosta suggests that anti-indigenous and antiblack racism come from the same roots and have the same objectives, which is to elevate the Hispanic elements of Cuban culture (2004, 27).

The denial of indigenous cultural survivals in intellectual discourse during the early twentieth century is somewhat understandable, given the ulterior motives of indigenistas. Nevertheless, because Ortiz was (and still is) Cuba's preeminent scholar, his negation of any indigenous influence was extremely influential for later folklorists, and ultimately his vision of the Cuban nation was accepted as the "truth." Esquenazi Pérez's critique of Ortiz is relevant here: "This absolute negation of Cuban aborigines, on the part of Ortiz and his contemporaries who were at the forefront of the defense of black cultural contributions, has wide-ranging repercussions into the present and it impedes us from objectively analyzing the musical traditions of the descendants of *taínos* that still live in the mountains of Yateras and Baracoa, and that call for in-depth research" (2001, 31; my translation). I similarly believe that, almost a century later, there is a need to reconsider the narrative about the country's racial composition, not in order to downplay the enormous significance of the African contribution to Cuban culture, a fact that is by now unanimously accepted, but rather to understand that indigenous elements and survivals have been marginalized in the promotion of a biracial national identity. My goal is to understand this negation in light of the politics of place and to suggest that western Cuba's hegemony (Havana's in particular) in all arenas—political, economic, and cultural—is a major factor. In other words, the tendency to take western Cuban culture as representative of the island as a whole has resulted in a disregard for the cultural specificity of Oriente, where the primary indigenous survivals are historically and currently found. Furthermore, this western-centric perspective has obscured an even more influential cultural influence than the indigenous one: the impact of other Caribbean, particularly Franco-Haitian, populations on the development of folklore oriental, which presents marked cultural distinctions from the folkloric music of western Cuba.

The Racialization and Regionalization of Folkloric Traditions

In tandem with the trend toward racial taxonomization in Cuban folklore and music studies, researchers have consistently sought to identify the specific cultural attributes of different regions, documenting the predominance of African and European ethnic groups, respectively, in each province. The most recent publication dedicated to the systematic categorization of musical instruments on the island, *Atlas de los instrumentos de la música folclórico-popular de Cuba* (Atlas of folkloric and popular musical instruments in Cuba; Elí Rodríguez 1997), was a monumental project conducted by dozens of music researchers over a period of a decade and constitutes a treasure trove of ethnographic data. It includes detailed maps illustrating the incidence of different instruments and folkloric and popular musical traditions in each province.[9] While the goal of seeking out the unique cultural attributes of each region seems to present an incongruous juxtaposition to the unifying rhetoric characteristic of the revolution and of Cuban nationalism more generally, the two discursive tendencies have gone hand in hand to function as a sort of "unity-in-diversity" discourse. Far from constituting a phenomenon unique to Cuba, this nationalist promotion of the cultural distinctiveness of particular regions—and the related linking of genres with particular regions or cities—has been pervasive during periods of nation building throughout Latin America, as evidenced by ethnographic research conducted in Colombia (Wade 2000) and Venezuela (Guss 2000). In this vein, Cuban folklore research has consistently linked rumba to the cities of Havana and Matanzas, son to Santiago, changüí to Guantánamo, *punto guajiro* (Spanish-derived "country music") to the countryside (often Pinar del Río), and danzón to Matanzas. Thus, despite the state's objective of promulgating a sense of national unity within the population, state-funded ethnographers have been simultaneously employed in "locating" cultural traditions and ethnic groups in particular regions of the country.

This project of highlighting the cultural distinctiveness of each region has resulted in a rich body of folklore research in Cuba, particularly as compared to other Latin American countries; in short, Cuba has long been a leader in Latin America in its support of documenting and preserving the nation's regional cultural practices.[10] However, while the state cultural apparatus acknowledges regional differences, I also believe that the unifying nationalist discourse that accompanies this recognition tends to obscure the privileging of certain regions and cities that are constructed as sites of racial and cultural authenticity.[11] For example, while both Matanzas and Santiago are coded within popular discourse as sources of blackness, the former's designation as "the cradle of Afro-Cuban culture" functions to authenticate the types of blackness associated with Matanzas. Conversely, orientales are associated with a criminal blackness, as I discussed in chapter 1, evidenced by the racial and regional profiling they are subjected to by state police on the streets of Havana. As a result, when people talk about Matanzas's racial identity, they are primarily referring to a cultural blackness—represented by rumba and Santería—and not to the racial blackness of the population. In contrast, social/racial blackness is projected onto all of Oriente and its population regardless of skin color as a way of implying inherent inferiority, poverty, and/or criminality. I discuss this issue in more depth in chapter 6.

In terms of cultural representations of blackness, the Afro-Cuban religious and musical practices that enjoy the most national and international scholarly attention—including Santería, Abakuá, and rumba—have been the traditions associated with western Cuba. Their cultural counterparts that hail from Oriente—including Afro-Haitian sacred and secular musical practices such as *Vodú* (as the Cuban manifestation of the Haitian religion is spelled) and *tumba francesa*, and various religious practices included under the umbrella term Espiritismo—are not celebrated to the same extent, nor are they discussed as representing the nation as a whole. In fact, despite the fact that they have been practiced in Cuba since the nineteenth century,

Franco-Haitian musical and religious practices are still not considered to be part of national culture, as illustrated by the fact that they are still referred to as "Franco-Haitian" or "Afro-Haitian." Furthermore, the Franco-Haitian influence on the formation of a national Cuban culture tends to be ignored or diminished, a point highlighted by Benjamin Lapidus (2008) in his research on changüí.[12] Even less is known and published about the Jamaican and British West Indian traditions brought to the island by contract laborers during the early decades of the twentieth century, although they arrived in smaller numbers and their impact on Cuban culture is much less significant than that of Haitians.[13] Perhaps because these traditions were "always already" hybrid when they arrived in Cuba, in contrast to the "pure" African traditions that reached western Cuba with the slaves, they do not fit into the binary formulation of Cubanidad that is composed of *lo afro* (the African ancestry) and *lo español* (the Spanish ancestry). Furthermore, whiteness is so marginal in Haiti that the mainly African ancestry of Haitian immigrants in Cuba jeopardizes the "perfect" racial mixture (i.e., the ratio of white/Spanish and black/African) contained within Cubanidad. In other words, I would argue that the Haitian element of eastern Cuban ancestry threatens to upset the racial balance and tip the scales in favor of blackness. Needless to say, the long history of prejudice against Haitians in Cuba and the racialized threat they were thought to represent both before and after independence has contributed to the marginalization of their cultural and religious traditions. Unlike rumba and Santería, Afro-Haitian traditions have never been incorporated fully into national culture but instead have continued to be ghettoized and largely confined to Camagüey and the eastern provinces.

Folklore Oriental: The Status of Published Research in National and Regional Contexts

Eastern Cuban folkloric traditions are underrepresented in academic publications that aspire to discuss the nation's traditions in a comprehensive fashion, which is not to say that they have not been studied at the regional level (see below). In sources considered to be authoritative for Cuban musicology—such as various works by Argeliers León (1984; [1982] 1998) and Olavo Alén Rodríguez's entry for "Cuba" in *The Garland Encyclopedia of World Music* (1998)—the only Afro-Cuban folkloric tradition that is discussed as distinctly eastern Cuban is tumba francesa. Although *conga*, or eastern Cuban carnival music, is often briefly discussed in these types of publications, there is no specification of regional differences in terms of rhythms, instrumentation, or methods of parading, which is a lacuna, considering the distinct nature of Santiago's conga tradition. In addition, nothing is discussed about the various dances and rhythms encompassed under the Vodú tradition, leaving readers to assume that the only tradition introduced by the various waves of Franco-Haitian migration is tumba francesa. This tradition has in fact been fairly well studied at the national level, largely due to the efforts of Alén Rodríguez (1986; 1995). It has also gained more recent attention due to its designation in 2008 (originally proclaimed in 2003) as one of the roughly two hundred traditions on UNESCO's Representative List of the Intangible Cultural Heritage of Humanity.[14] Nonetheless, as Alén Rodríguez notes, tumba francesa is no longer even practiced in a regular or spontaneous manner by the population but is rather kept alive by folkloric groups and the two societies that are still extant, in Santiago and Guantánamo (1998, 826).[15]

In succinct terms, tumba francesa, which translates to "French drum/dance," is a doubly creolized (first in Haiti, then in Cuba) dance genre that belongs to the family of Caribbean contredanse traditions that drew from the European salon dances of the seventeenth and eighteenth centuries.[16] Tumba francesa was basically a slave imitation of the masters' social dances, at least in terms of the dance figures and formations. However, it was accompanied by a range of African-derived percussion instruments (membranophones and idiophones) with no melodic instruments, and an Africanized song form featuring call and response. In his book on the tumba francesa, Alén discusses two main dances, *masón* and *yubá*, noting that the latter is likely a synthesis of various dances that were combined at some point, and that there were originally other dances that are no longer practiced (1986, 43). He notes that the first tumba francesa festivities were held in the rural *cafetales* (coffee plantations) among slaves who had been brought to the island by their masters fleeing the Haitian Revolution in the early nineteenth century, and that the formal societies only developed later, after emancipation and the migration of former slaves to urban areas (16–17).[17] The postemancipation societies operated much as *cabildos de nación*, mutual aid societies formed in the late eighteenth and nineteenth centuries by Africans and their descendants along ethnic lines. Mutual aid societies were important institutions for newly freed blacks—as they were suddenly tasked with finding paid employment—and they also functioned to preserve cultural practices, religious traditions, and, in the case of descendants of Franco-Haitian immigrants, the Creole language (Alén 1986, 16–17). In addition, José Millet and Rafael Brea (1989, 33) assert that the Santiago-based tumba francesa society—originally founded with the French name "Lafayette" in 1862 but changed to "La Caridad" in 1905—had important links to the independence struggle: Antonio Maceo held meetings there, and Guillermón Moncada and Quintín Bandera formed part of the society.

Tumba francesa societies flourished primarily from the late nineteenth to the early twentieth centuries, maintained by descendants of the first wave of Franco-Haitian immigrants. By the time of the 1959 revolution, the societies were in decline, but Alén asserts that the Ministry of Culture understood the importance of preserving them and attempted to revive the two societies in Santiago and Guantánamo. At the time the book was published, he wrote that these efforts—constituted primarily by a push to incorporate new, younger members—hadn't been very successful and that the societies were in grave danger of extinction (Alén 1986, 20–21); this prediction now seems like a miscalculation, as they are still engaged in folkloric performance. In a perfect display of the double-edged sword of "authenticity," Alén stated that while he personally viewed the Guantánamo-based society La Pompadú as maintaining tumba francesa in a more "pure" state than that of the Santiago-based society La Caridad, the reason for this preservation was probably due to the Guantánamo society's lack of success in attracting new members (21).

In work published fifteen years later, Martha Esquenazi Pérez also stated that La Caridad was in the process of disappearing despite the efforts of younger members, and that the other two societies were being maintained by elders (2001, 157). However, in my limited experience—I have only attended one tumba francesa rehearsal at La Caridad, in June 2011—it appears that the society, while not flourishing, is still active at least during a portion of the year. The cultural tourism industry certainly has helped, as many tourists who travel to Santiago are likely to have read about La Caridad. When I spoke to the director in 2011, he told me they do occasional performances for tourist groups and also open their regular rehearsals to the public, hoping to solicit donations from foreign visitors. In addition, La Caridad always performs in Santiago's July carnival, a major cultural event and tourist draw to the city, which provides the society with a reason to continue rehearsing. The rehearsal that I attended included members—both percussionists and dancers—of various ages, with the younger members tending to be male; of the four dance pairs performing that evening, one of the male dancers was a boy who could not have been older than ten. It's possible, then, that the UNESCO designation and the cultural tourism industry have been successful in attracting younger members. I do not know the situation of the Guantánamo society, La Pompadú, but can only assume that it is not receiving the same amount of attention that La Caridad has, primarily because Guantánamo does not receive many tourists.[18]

Regional Folklore Research and the Casa del Caribe

The choice of tumba francesa as the national representative of folklore oriental is somewhat odd, given the fact that it is a languishing tradition. This
stands in contrast to the relative lack of academic attention given to *conga
santiaguera* (Santiago-style conga), which is extremely popular with large
segments of Santiago's population.[19] In fact, tumba francesa is thought to have
had an important influence on conga, as illustrated by the fact that La conga
de Los Hoyos, Santiago's most famous conga group, was founded by former
slaves of both Spanish and French masters and is often referred to as "the sons
of El Cocoyé" (Millet, Brea, and Ruiz Vila 1997, 8); now defunct, El Cocoyé,
based in the neighborhood of Los Hoyos, was the most important and famous
tumba francesa society in nineteenth-century Cuba, and its melodies were
known even in Havana.[20] One of the three primary rhythms played in conga
santiaguera, the *masón*, is taken from tumba francesa, and it is said to be particularly popular with the parading public (Millet, Brea, and Ruiz Vila 1997).
Conga is a both a musical practice and a particular type of mobile percussion
ensemble within the Cuban carnival tradition that is associated specifically
with Santiago. Although the term *comparsa* has been used to refer to Cuban
carnival music in general (see R. Moore 1997, for example), it more accurately
refers to a more formalized carnival ensemble that includes music, choreographed dances, and costumes, and that engages in formal competitions with
other groups. Comparsas are more elaborate and stylized presentations than
the more working class and unruly congas, which in contemporary Santiago
include mass participation by neighborhood residents. Every year in July, in
preparation for Santiago's carnival (the most historic and prominent one on
the island), thousands of santiagueros pour out into the street to *arrollar*, or
parade in front of, behind, and encircling their favorite conga.[21] Particularly
popular with santiagueros is *la invasión*, "the invasion," an event held in the
weeks leading up to carnival in which La conga de Los Hoyos visits the five
other conga groups in Santiago, engaging in a sonic battle with them that is
witnessed by and includes the participation of thousands of spectators (see
figure 3.1).[22] Folklorist Odilio Urfé captured the sentiment of Santiago's congas when he compared them to the carnival celebrations in the capital thus:
"While in Havana the people are merely spectators, they participate actively
in the Santiago Carnival" (Urfé [1977] 1984, 185).[23] As detailed by Lani Milstein
(2013), the conga ensemble is constituted by a group of musicians playing a
wide range of portable percussion instruments. These include drums of different sizes, various idiophones—such as the *llanta*, or brake drum of a car
(see figure 3.2), which plays the timeline—and the emblematic *corneta china*

Figure 3.1: *La invasión* in Santiago, July 2005. Avenida Trocha is packed from sidewalk to sidewalk, and the throng of participants goes on for blocks.

Figure 3.2: *Llantas* and various drums used in the conga ensemble. Percussionists attach a string to the drums and tie it around their necks in order to play while parading.

Figure 3.3: Well-known corneta china player parading in *la invasión*, July 2005. It's common for police officers to surround musicians during *la invasión* in order to protect them from getting swept up in the crowd.

(literally, "Chinese cornet"), a double-reed aerophone (similar to an oboe) originally brought to the island by Chinese immigrants.[24] Often the corneta china (see figure 3.3) acts as the soloist of the ensemble, playing the melody of the choral refrain, which is then repeated in sung call-and-response form by the parading public, and thereafter improvising and adorning the melody.[25]

As Santiago-based researchers José Millet, Rafael Brea, and Manuel Ruiz Vila repeatedly foreground in their sociological study of the relationship between the historic Santiago barrio of Los Hoyos and its representative conga, also called Los Hoyos, this tradition is one of the primary cultural markers of Santiago identity. They state, "life here is rooted and essentially tied to carnival. Carnival and the people form one indissoluble unity" (Millet, Brea, and Ruiz Vila 1997, 19; my translation), and reproduce a quotation from an informant stating that the conga "is the soul of Santiago's people" (51;

my translation).[26] The barrio of Los Hoyos is historically black and mulato—almost 70 percent, according to the surveys conducted by Millet, Brea, and Ruiz Vila (31)—and yet their data suggests similar levels of identification with the conga and carnival across race, including 66 percent of whites who live in the neighborhood (37). They note that this figure debunks cultural stereotypes that paint carnival and conga as *una cosa de negros* (a black thing), and confirms its cross-racial acceptance within this neighborhood and, arguably, Santiago more generally. Similarly, Milstein states, "While the phenomenon does not necessarily break down racial borders, conga is considered a *cosa de santiagueros* before being considered a *cosa de negros*, meaning that conga is a *santiaguero* 'thing' before it is a black 'thing'" (2013, 249, n. 2). I believe that this cross-racial embrace of what is generally understood to be an Afro-Cuban tradition presents a contrast to the situation in Havana and western Cuba in general, where similar practices (such as rumba) are supported largely by blacks and mulatos, and less so by whites. This is also likely linked to the different racial configurations of society in the eastern and western parts of the island that I discussed in chapter 1, as the latter is generally characterized by more social segregation between whites and nonwhites and a lower level of race mixture.

The study conducted by Millet, Brea, and Ruiz Vila is a thorough and multifaceted examination of the culture of the conga in Santiago and its meaning to santiagueros. It presents several firsthand testimonies from a variety of people linked not only to La conga de Los Hoyos but to other conga/comparsa groups in the city and to carnival officials.[27] The authors are part of a collective of researchers organized under the Casa del Caribe, an institution that has supported the study of popular culture and religion in Oriente for three decades. The Casa del Caribe, whose name ("House of the Caribbean") references the close relationship between Santiago and its Caribbean neighbors, is a prominent regional institution whose goal of promoting the study of Oriente's history and culture is sorely needed, given the hegemonic status of Havana and its research institutions, which tend to ignore eastern Cuban phenomena. Anthropologist Grete Viddal states, "It is an institution with a twofold mission: engaging both in cultural production and academic research. That is, the Casa del Caribe produces festivals and events that feed on research by the institution and vice versa. This emphasis on performance shaped the spread of non-institutional religions, including Vodú, into the Cuban public space" (Viddal 2012, 216). The journal published by the Casa del Caribe since 1983, *Del Caribe*, has consistently provided a space for eastern Cuban researchers to publish their work on a variety of topics and has also included publications by scholars from other Caribbean countries and even the United States. The

Casa del Caribe has also sponsored an important annual cultural event since 1981, the Festival del Caribe or Fiesta del Fuego, in which music and dance groups from all over the Caribbean and Latin America are invited to perform for a week in Santiago; the festival is dedicated to a different Latin American or Caribbean country each year. An academic conference is held during the Festival del Caribe in which scholars from all over the region are invited to present papers.

Founding director of the Casa del Caribe and former editor of its journal, Joel James Figarola was a prolific writer and researcher who contributed an unprecedented body of work—along with José Millet—on understudied cultural traditions in Oriente, particularly religious practices such as the Bantu-derived *Regla de Palo* and the practice of Vodú in Cuba.[28] Despite the fact that he was one of modern Cuba's most productive scholars, his work has been marginalized within the national context and its recognition confined largely to eastern Cuba. While studying for my doctoral exams, I scoured the archives in an attempt to gain comprehensive knowledge about Cuban popular and folkloric music and never came across James's work or mention of him until I traveled to Santiago to conduct research. Cuban scholar María Nelsa Trincado Fontán asserts that, considering the body and volume of his work, James has never been recognized to the extent that other Cuban scholars have, particularly in Havana. She states, "He has been an unknown, not by those who truly know history, but because of the silence that has been built up around his books, and because he is very controversial, no one wants to get involved in his work" (Trincado Fontán 2007, 96; my translation). She also suggests that although his work lacks national recognition, she has come across instances of scholars who cite his work without giving him credit. James, Millet, and Alexis Alarcón published the first work on Vodú in Cuba, a religious practice that Trincado Fontán notes was overlooked by the most esteemed Cuban folklorists of religion, Fernando Ortiz and Lydia Cabrera, no doubt because they did not conduct much (or any) research in the eastern region.

The cultural events and academic work sponsored by the Casa del Caribe reveal a very different conception of Cubanidad as compared to the dominant one found across much of the island: santiagueros define themselves not only as Cuban but also as Caribbean. As Joel James, José Millet, and Alexis Alarcón note, the southeastern part of the island has since the nineteenth century developed a "conciencia de caribeñidad" or "Caribbean consciousness" (2007, 27) that is not found in other parts of Cuba. They also underline Cuba's importance within the Caribbean, which was one of the reasons it was a destination for immigrants in the early twentieth century. One experience alerted me to this unique regional identity and understanding of Cuba's place in the

Caribbean: while attending the Sunday rumba event at the Casa del Caribe in June 2011, I noticed that, between sets, the DJ played a variety of Caribbean genres—I heard both zouk and Jamaican dancehall—which caught my attention because I could not recall ever having heard music with lyrics in a language other than Spanish at a rumba event anywhere else in Cuba. It showed me in a very banal way how Santiago sees itself as culturally distinct from other places on the island, and it also signaled a lesser tendency toward ethnocentrism, which Cubans are famous for throughout Latin America.

Sacred Traditions within Folklore Oriental

Afro-Cuban sacred musics have been the subject of many studies by both Cuban and foreign scholars. While the most well-studied topic by far has been the Yoruba-derived religion known as Santería or *La Regla de Ocha,* Abakuá and other sacred practices historically concentrated in the provinces of Havana and Matanzas have also received a fair amount of attention.[29] In contrast, eastern Cuban religious practices such as Vodú and Espiritismo are often obscured in the discussions of Afro-Cuban sacred traditions. Furthermore, regional research suggests that, although associated primarily with western Cuba, Santería was established in the east almost a century ago, much earlier than is assumed in much of the literature. Based on extensive ethnographic research on religious practices in Santiago, José Millet asserts that both Santería and Palo were brought to Oriente in the first decades of the twentieth century by religious practitioners from Havana and Matanzas (2000, 110–11). He suggests that, before that time, religious practice in Oriente was centered around "muerterismo," or sacred rituals honoring dead ancestors, and that in Santiago specifically the reigning belief systems were Catholicism and a form of Espiritismo distinct from the *cordón* type (110–11). The work of the Casa del Caribe under Joel James's direction has made major inroads into the study of religious practices in Oriente, exemplified by the book he cowrote with José Millet and Alexis Alarcón, *El vodú en Cuba* (2007).[30] This was the result of state-funded fieldwork initiated in 1983 and designed to conduct research with Haitian communities in the province of Santiago, an area of research that James recognized as fundamental to the mission of the Casa del Caribe. In line with this goal of recognizing the Haitian roots of eastern Cuban identity, Santiago historian Jorge Berenguer Cala published a short book on the *gagá* tradition, as practiced by the descendants of Haitian migrants in the rural community of Barrancas in Santiago Province. Gagá is derived from the Haitian carnival tradition *rara,* consisting of parades and competition between carnival groups during Lent.[31] Like rara, gagá has both religious and secular components and objectives, although Berenguer Cala (2006) asserts that much of the sacred meaning of the tradition was lost with the death of the first generation of Haitian immigrants (those who arrived in the twentieth century).[32]

While Vodú and gagá as performed in their original contexts (i.e., not in folkloric representations) are fairly marginal practices in Cuba, as they have not spread much beyond the communities of Haitians and their descendants who are concentrated in the rural areas of Oriente and Camagüey,[33] some Cubans and scholars believe that Espiritismo is the most widely practiced religion on the island (Warden 2006, 25–26). Espiritismo is a religious movement stemming from traditional Christianity that emerged in the mid-nineteenth century, and it is practiced widely not only in Cuba but also in other parts of the Spanish Caribbean. It is based on the idea of communicating with the souls/spirits of the dead through a medium, similar to what we might call, in American popular culture, a séance. Espiritismo has various worship styles, some of which are regionally defined. In his master's thesis on the *cajón de muerto*, a ceremony associated with a very popular style of the religion called *Espiritismo cruzado*, ethnomusicologist Nolan Warden states, "The forms of Espiritismo in Cuba are almost impossible to delineate, partly due to their localized, non-institutional existence" (2006, 28). Nonetheless, in my experience and drawing from existing research on the subject—most of which has been conducted by eastern Cuban scholars—many associate the practice with Oriente. A well-respected folkloric musician and religious elder in Matanzas once told me that the best *brujos* (literally, "witches" or "sorcerers," but taken to mean practitioners of Espiritismo) come from Guantánamo.

Much of the published work on Espiritismo has been initiated by researchers associated with the Casa del Caribe, such as José Millet (1996) and Ángel Lago Vieito (1996, 2001). While the practice is gaining more recent attention, there is still relatively little published work on the topic, either from prominent national scholars or from foreign researchers. I suspect that this lacuna is due at least in part to the highly hybrid nature of the practice, and the fact that—like Franco-Haitian traditions—it does not easily fit into the neat binary formulation of Cubanidad discussed above. Although the origins of Cuban Espiritismo are sometimes attributed to a French academic, Allan Kardec (for example, see Van Nispen 2003), Warden and most of the Cuban researchers note that what Kardec called "Spiritism" was actually a codification of a practice called Spiritualism that developed in upstate New York in 1848 (Warden 2006, 22). Lago Vieito asserts that the practice had spread to Europe by 1852, when Allen Kardec formalized the doctrines, but that it was introduced to Cuba directly from the United States in 1856 (Lago Vieito 2001,

72). Millet's book *El espiritismo: variantes cubanas* (1996) is the most in-depth study of the Cuban manifestations of the practice, and discusses the most widely practiced styles: Espiritismo cruzado ("crossed" or mixed Espiritismo, which borrows rituals and objects from various African-derived religions, especially Palo and, to a lesser extent, Santería); and Espiritismo de cordón (in which participants worship in a cordón, a cord or circle configuration). Espiritismo de cordón was the first Cuban manifestation of the practice to emerge, and it has always been practiced almost exclusively in Oriente. Both Lago Vieito and José Sánchez Lussón (1996) discuss the emergence of cordón, also known as *cordón de orilé*, in the Cauto Valley area in the province of Granma, noting its links with the Cuban independence movement and asserting that many *mambises* (insurgents) practiced it.[34] Lago Vieito (2001) produces documents showing that by the 1870s the Spanish colonial authorities were alarmed by the quick spread of cordón, because it had penetrated the highest levels of Cuban society, and by its possible links to masonry and pro-independence activity and thought.[35] He thus debunks Fernando Ortiz's claim that cordón was established in the twentieth century (Ortiz's assertion that it had no indigenous influences, a critique also made by Martha Esquenazi Pérez).

There is a wide range of musical accompaniment utilized in the different variants of Cuban Espiritismo. Nolan Warden notes that Kardecian spiritism (called *Espiritismo de mesa* or "scientific Spiritism" in Cuba) includes no music, and that it was in the cordón style that music—some original compositions and some songs from the Catholic *Altar de Cruz* tradition—began to be used for worship (2006, 28). Esquenazi Pérez, on the other hand, suggests that cordón is a highly hybrid practice and that its songs have a wide range of influence, including not only the Altar de Cruz repertoire but also the imprints of Protestant hymns, African-derived song forms (like call and response), indigenous practices like areíto, and even Mexican *rancheras* (2001, 33–39). The most popular ceremony within the cordón practice is the *misa espiritual*, "spiritualist mass," which is hosted by someone who wants to remember a loved one who has died and which often takes place around the anniversary of the death. This ceremony is dominated by sung *plegarias*, prayers based on Catholic liturgy, and does not contain African-derived songs or drumming as in the ceremonies of Espiritismo cruzado. In fact, Millet notes that *cordoneros*, as practitioners of this version are called, routinely deny that their practice includes any African elements (despite evidence that suggests otherwise) and look suspiciously on Palo, Santería, and Espiritismo cruzado as engaging in "trabajos sucios" (roughly translated, black magic, such as casting spells on enemies or doing religious work aimed at material gain) (1996, 22–23).

While Espiritismo de cordón is practiced primarily in Oriente, Espiritismo cruzado, the more Africanized tradition that is mixed with Palo and sometimes Santería, is found throughout the island and is thus thought to be the most widely practiced form of Espiritismo. The cajón de muerto is the most popular ceremony associated with this style and is usually held to honor and communicate with a dead ancestor or to pay tribute to an *orisha* or *santo*, the Yoruba-derived deities worshipped in Santería.[36] I have attended several of these ceremonies in Havana and Matanzas and would characterize them in musical and liturgical terms as a mix between Espiritismo de cordón and Palo, often including elements of Santería as well. Generally, the ceremony begins with the Catholic plegarias and gradually moves toward the African-derived Palo songs, which are sung in *bozal*, an Africanized form of Spanish associated with slaves and mixed with Bantu words.[37] Once the Palo songs start, there in an overall increase in the rhythmic density of the drumming, and, partly because of the heavily repetitive nature of Palo drumming, it is not uncommon for several people to "get mounted" or possessed. Interestingly, all the songs, no matter the provenance, are accompanied by a secular drumming tradition, *rumba de cajón*, a style of rumba played on *cajones* (wooden boxes of various sizes that constituted the early instrumental format of rumba in the late nineteenth and early twentieth centuries). A variety of rhythms are used in different parts of the ceremony, which are discussed in depth in Nolan Warden's thesis (2006).

Pablo, a Santiago-based musician, discussed the very different functions and objectives of the cajón de muerto, as compared to the misa espiritual, foregrounding important differences between these two most popular styles of Cuban Espiritismo.[38] He described the former (associated with Espiritismo cruzado) as a "party for the santos" where orishas come down and mount a worshipper in order to speak with the other participants (pers. comm. 2011). He added that practitioners can also get mounted by non-orisha spirits, either their familial ancestors or unknown African slaves. The misa espiritual (associated with Espiritismo de cordón), in contrast, is centered on the remembrance of the host's ancestor or loved one, and, although it can include possession, it does not include any animal sacrifices, drumming, or African-derived singing. Pablo described it as a ceremony designed to allow the living to communicate with the spirit of their loved one, or their *angel de la guardia* ("guardian angel"), and to reincarnate the spirit (through the body of an experienced medium) so that he or she can give the living relatives "strength and clarity." José Millet's comparison of the visual representations of the two practices is also useful: he states that cordoneros use an "economy of means"—represented by very simple altars often adorned only with photos of the deceased loved one, glasses of water, and flowers—as compared to the more elaborate and heterogeneous altars in Espiritismo cruzado, which include ritual elements borrowed from Palo and Santería (Millet 1996, 27).

Although I have not conducted research on these ceremonies in Santiago or other locations in Oriente, I believe that the cajón de muerto, or at least the term, is a primarily western Cuban phenomenon, and that the *bembé de sao* is the corresponding eastern Cuban ceremony. I do not yet have sufficient ethnographic experience attending bembé de sao ceremonies to confirm this hypothesis, but Pablo's descriptions of it contained notable similarities to the cajón de muerto ceremonies I have attended in Havana and Matanzas. In fact, he discussed the latter as a reinterpretation of the bembé de sao (pers. comm. 2011), which seems plausible, given the fact that Espiritismo emerged in Oriente and later spread to western Cuba. Millet also discusses bembé de sao as an antecedent for Espiritismo cruzado, the practice with which the cajón de muerto is associated. He notes that the former was a more rural practice—thus the use of the term *sao*, a Portuguese-derived word that refers to a "bush" or backwoods (Viddal 2012, 226)—which displayed heavy hybridizing in its songs, mixing elements of Spanish, French, Haitian Creole, and Yoruba- and Bantu-derived languages (Millet 1996, 45). One difference that Pablo noted between the two was that in bembé de sao, despite the fact that there is drumming, the songs are all Catholic plegarias sung in Spanish, as opposed to the mixing of languages and song styles that characterizes the cajón de muerto. Although I would have to gain more experience with bembé de sao ceremonies to confirm this assertion, his statement concurs with Esquenazi Pérez's description (2001, 149) of the practice.

In general, the increased presence of Spanish Catholic liturgy in what are otherwise more African-derived religious ceremonies likely relates to regional differences in terms of the retention of African-based languages: there has been less preservation in Oriente due to the large amount of mixing and the fact that the slaves who arrived the latest (i.e., the mid-nineteenth century) went primarily to western Cuba. Thus, as noted by Esquenazi Pérez, Santería ceremonies in Oriente tend to conform less to "orthodox" or African-derived elements and to be more heterogeneous: songs use more Spanish and less Lucumí (the Yoruba-derived language), Yoruba-derived elements are mixed with Palo, Vodú, and/or Espiritismo, and the instrumentation tends away from the use of culturally specific drums, such as the *batá*, substituting them with conga drums or other nonconsecrated instruments (2001, 146–48).[39] Two of the eastern Cuban musicians I interviewed also discussed the more hybrid style of Santería practiced in Oriente. Guantánamo-born dancer Isaias Rojas asserted that the religion can be traced back to the nineteenth century in Oriente but was practiced in a very different way than what is considered the norm (i.e., western Cuban Santería) (pers. comm. 2011). He stated that ceremonies were often played in the style of bembé, where conical drums with sticks were used rather than the consecrated double-headed batá drums that are so intimately associated with Santería worship. Thus, it is perhaps more accurate to say that it is not Yoruba-derived worship that is new to eastern Cuba, but that it is a certain style and particular norms of Santería, appropriated from western Cuba, that are currently so *en vogue* in Oriente.

While the bulk of literature on Espiritismo and eastern Cuban religious traditions has been conducted by researchers from Oriente and written in Spanish, the Casa del Caribe has proved quite open to working with foreign scholars, resulting in the very recent publication in English of research on these sacred practices. Grete Viddal (2010, 2012) has conducted extensive research with folkloric groups and religious leaders in various rural and urban locales in Oriente, focusing specifically on the folklorization of Haitian-derived cultural and religious practices under the revolutionary government and arguing that these traditions have become key markers of eastern Cuban identity. A recent book by sociologist Jualynne Dodson and her research team, *Sacred Spaces and Religious Traditions in Oriente Cuba* (2008), also provides more visibility for these regional religious traditions. Unfortunately, while Dodson's book provides in-depth details about the four "indigenous" religions practiced in Oriente—Palo, Vodú, Espiritismo, and "*Muertera Bembé de Sao*"[40]—in an explicit attempt to fill a research lacuna, there are some major problems with the work. To begin, her chapter on Espiritismo seems to replicate whole sections of Millet's 1996 book on the subject (albeit in English rather than in Spanish), adding little new information or ethnographic perspectives and not even bothering to cite Millet. In fact, although the book asserts that the research and writing was conducted "in collaboration with" Millet and the Casa del Caribe, Millet has publicly denounced Dodson and accused her of academic fraud, specifically of withholding proper credit to him as the book's coauthor.[41]

Also troubling is a basic premise underlying Dodson's book, the assumption that Oriente is an autonomous region that has since early colonial times been completely isolated from events and cultural phenomena in western Cuba. Although my book argues that eastern Cuba has a distinct cultural history that is often ignored in national accounts, Dodson's work takes an extreme and myopic perspective that ignores anything outside of Oriente, including the mutual cultural exchanges between east and west that have greatly influenced national culture, and music especially (see, for example, chapter 2 on the history of contemporary dance music and chapter 6 on the relationship between rumba and son). She states, "The relative isolation ensured that developing transculturated behaviors would be authenticated by Oriente influences rather than rely upon affirmations from populations in other parts of the island. The region's ritual practices were self-referring" (Dodson 2008, 163). Putting aside the problems with her use of the notion of "authenticity" to discuss inherently hybrid practices, this statement constitutes a denial of cross-regional influences within religious practice in Cuba. It is an even more egregious notion when one considers that, in the chapter on Palo, she presents information that contradicts her own assertion that Oriente is a completely separate cultural entity from the west. She cites an expert on Cuban religion, David Brown, thus: "As an organized and coherent set of ritual behaviors, Palo Monte/Palo Mayombe arrived in Oriente at the turn of the twentieth century with migrants from western Cuba's Matanzas area" (84). Thus, although Bantu-derived slaves were the first to arrive to Cuba in the sixteenth century via Oriente and exerted a significant influence on African-derived culture in eastern Cuba, the specific rituals practiced today by Palo initiates in Oriente (not to mention the folkloric representations of these rituals) show undeniable influence from western Cuba, a point also made by Millet (2000) and some of the musicians I interviewed. In other words, the research that Dodson cites is clearly incompatible with one of the fundamental theoretical frameworks of her project, namely Oriente's complete cultural exceptionalism. In sum, while constituting an admirable goal, *Sacred Spaces and Religious Traditions in Oriente Cuba* is a conceptually flawed research project that, in its apparent attempt to overturn the hegemony of western Cuba, presents a distorted view of contemporary religious practice in eastern Cuba. Considering the large waves of eastern migration to Havana and western Cuba since the Special Period that I discussed in chapter 1—including the eastern Cuban folkloric groups now residing in Havana (see below)—cross-regional hybridity within religious practices on the island is arguably at its peak.

The Current Status of *Folklore Oriental* beyond Oriente

I began conducting research in Santiago with the assumption that local folkloric musicians would view the performance of folklore oriental as underrepresented in the national sphere. One of the examples of the hegemony of western Cuban folklore is the disproportionate amount of attention in Cuban and foreign scholarship given to the Conjunto Folklórico Nacional (National Folkloric Troupe, or the CFN), as compared with the equivalent large folkloric dance troupes in Oriente, the Ballet Folklórico Cutumba (often referred to simply as "Cutumba") and the Ballet Folklórico de Oriente, both of which are based in Santiago. I was surprised to learn that both of these groups were founded in the first year of the revolution, 1959, a full three years *before* the CFN; I doubt that this is a widely known fact outside of Santiago. Despite my assumptions about how eastern Cuban folkloric musicians might view the status of their region's traditions, most felt that folklore oriental has been gaining visibility and exposure in other parts of the island, particularly in Havana, where some folkloric groups include representations of Vodú, tumba francesa, or *merengue haitiano*. There are several possible explanations for this increase in visibility, which I gather has begun in the past two decades. One has to do with the increased presence of eastern folkloric groups in Havana; most of these were established in eastern cities and later relocated to the capital. The second factor relates to the perceived desire of audiences to see more varied *espectáculos*, or folkloric shows.[42] During my extended research on rumba and folkloric groups in Havana and Matanzas, I came to view espectáculos as quite formulaic in terms of repertoire: generally the first set consists of a representation of Afro-Cuban sacred traditions (usually orisha dances, with an Abakuá or, more rarely, a Palo dance thrown in for variety), followed by a second set composed of rumba. It was always refreshing to see something new, such as rumba group Clave y Guaguancó performing a few songs from the merengue haitiano repertoire. The audience always responded with great enthusiasm and dancing, and at times even requested that the group play merengue haitiano. In a similar vein, as one Santiago-based musician pointed out, the CFN sometimes performs eastern Cuban traditions such as *tajona* and *chancleta*.[43] According to an interview Grete Viddal conducted with veteran folklorist and choreographer Antonio Pérez, the performance of folklore oriental in the capital can be traced back to 1972, the year of the Ballet Folklórico de Oriente's first performance in Havana, when the group performed gagá and chancleta to great excitement and acclaim (2012, 213).[44]

A third reason for the increased visibility of folklore oriental may have to do with a recognition on the part of folkloric groups that there are many orientales in Havana, and in their audiences. There is a good representation of eastern Cuban musicians in these groups, and they act as cultural "informants" who can teach the other members how to play the rhythms and sing the songs, many of which are sung in a Cubanized version of Haitian Creole. Finally, Viddal offers a provocative suggestion regarding the spread of Vodú in Havana: "Cosmopolitan practitioners of Santería in the capital have begun to study Haitian religion, perhaps as the final frontier of exotica available in a country where travel abroad is restricted" (2012, 207). Thus, perhaps like in the folkloric context, where both musicians and audiences are hungry to play and see something other than the ubiquitous orisha and Abakuá dances, Afro-Cuban religious practitioners are searching for something more taboo, more African, in the post-Soviet era of official religious tolerance and what Katherine Hagedorn (2001) referred to as *santurismo* (Santería-related tourism).[45]

The Performance of Folklore Oriental in Havana: Two Case Studies

Before discussing the perspectives of eastern Cuban musicians regarding the status of folklore oriental, I would like to briefly present two case studies of this phenomenon, one detailing a genre commonly associated with folklore oriental and one highlighting the history and repertoire of an eastern Cuban folkloric group now residing in Havana.

Merengue Haitiano

Merengue haitiano is presumably (because of its name) an eastern Cuban manifestation of the influential Haitian popular genre *meringue*. Nonetheless, despite its apparent popularity within performances of folklore oriental, I have rarely seen anything in print about this tradition and thus think it worthwhile to say a few words about it.[46] Alberto Pedro's ethnographic article (1967) detailing the celebration of Semana Santa (Holy Week) among Haitians and their descendants in Camagüey and Oriente mentions merengue as a dance and song genre linked to rara, the main Haitian tradition associated with carnival. He notes that it is characterized by call-and-response singing in Haitian Creole and that its lyrics have a "picaresque" character that is seemingly at odds with the religious intentions of Holy Week (Pedro 1967, 54). In a book documenting the various folkloric groups in Santiago, José Millet and Rafael Brea also mention the genre briefly, describing the dance as *fuerte* (strong or vigorous), requiring excellent physical preparation, and as possessing an "erotic" character and "contagious rhythm" (1989, 114). Beyond a few passing comments in other sources, these seem to be the only published descriptions of the tradition, and none of them discuss its history in Cuba or its musical and dance characteristics in detail.[47] I have seen and heard performances of merengue haitiano by four different groups: the Havana rumba group Clave y Guaguancó, Siete Potencias (a Guantánamo-based group now residing in Havana), and the two major folkloric groups in Santiago, the Ballet Folklórico de Oriente (BFO) and Cutumba.[48]

When I compared the Cuban performances to the Haitian genre called meringue, there were a number of obvious sonic differences between the two, although both are sung in Creole. Meringue, which emerged after the Haitian Revolution, combines the music of European figure dances, such as contredanse, with Bantu-derived secular dances, and makes use of melodic instruments (Averill 1997). The conga drum and bell patterns (featuring the three-beat rhythm called *tresillo*) used in the Cuban merengue haitiano recordings sound very similar to those used in the Haitian meringue recordings I listened to. Thus, it is the use of melodic instruments in the latter, particularly guitar and accordion, that accounts for the obvious sonic difference; the Cuban version utilizes only percussion and song.[49] The result is that merengue haitiano as performed in Cuba sounds to my ears like other Afro-Cuban secular drumming and song traditions, and has particular similarities with the Bantu-derived *makuta*.

In terms of comparing the four performances of merengue haitiano by Cuban groups, I found the major point of continuity to be related to the song element: although all of the groups included more than one song within the merengue haitiano piece, they all referenced a particular song at some point. In addition, two of the performances—by Clave y Guaguancó and the BFO— used the same song progression for much of the piece: the first two songs were presented in the same order, and the performances diverged only on the third song. Although this suggests that Havana groups perform eastern Cuban folkloric genres quite faithfully, there was one major difference I found between the Clave y Guaguancó version as compared to those performed by the eastern Cuban groups: the tempo in the former was much slower and "funkier" compared to the faster pace of the latter three versions. The Siete Potencias version displayed the most variation in dynamics and tempo throughout the piece and also seemed to include a rhythmic change in the percussion, something not found in the other recordings. Finally, the BFO's version introduced a non-traditional element in their performance, the use of a melodic instrument—a flute—which served alternately as melodic accompaniment and as a substitute for the singers within the call-and-response format.

One last difference between the performance of Clave y Guaguancó and those of the two eastern Cuban folkloric groups (Siete Potencias and the BFO) that I recorded live, was that the latter two included a choreographed group dance. Apart from the possibility that the standardized choreography for merengue haitiano may not be familiar to many within the Havana folkloric scene, this difference also relates to the fact that Clave y Guaguancó is primarily known as a rumba group, not a full-fledged folkloric troupe, and does not have the large corps of dancers needed to stage a choreographed group dance. I was able to video-record the performance of merengue haitiano as performed by the BFO, thus affording me the opportunity to analyze the dance. Choreographically, the dance appeared to be secular, alluding to both functional tasks—the women danced with baskets and the men with hoes—and to the erotic dynamics of heterosexual relationships—there was a point where the dancers paired off and performed sexualized hip rolling while facing each other. All in all, merengue haitiano is a playful, infectious music and dance genre that warrants in-depth study, especially because it seems to be an oft-performed style within folklore oriental. It would be particularly productive to explore the reasons for its name and to understand its specific connections to Haitian meringue.

Ban Rarrá: An Eastern Cuban Group Living in Havana

Although there are instances of Havana folkloric groups performing repertoire from Oriente, these tend to constitute isolated cases more than the norm. The primary representations of folklore oriental are still coming from groups such as Ban Rarrá and Siete Potencias—both originally from Guantánamo and now residing in Havana. I believe that these groups constitute a sort of niche market in the capital, as their drawing power comes from the fact that they offer a different repertoire than one can get from the major Havana-based folkloric groups such as the CFN. I will focus my discussion of eastern folkloric groups living in the capital on Ban Rarrá, as it is the most prominent group of its kind.

Isaias Rojas, director of the group, asserted that Ban Rarrá was the first to introduce folklore oriental to the capital, in 1994, when it relocated to Havana only a month after being founded in Guantánamo.[50] He noted that, along with the rise in eastern migration to the capital after the onset of the Special Period in 1991, several folkloric groups of Franco-Haitian descent came to Havana. He made a distinction between the groups composed of culture bearers (i.e., ancestors of Haitian immigrants) who perform only Haitian-derived traditions, and his own group, which has a wider repertoire and is composed of musicians and dancers who are not necessarily descendants of Haitians.[51] Nonetheless, the group's name, Ban Rarrá, is taken directly from Creole and references a Haitian musical practice—*ban rara* are the parading groups who play and sing rara during Haiti's carnival season—thus making a clear statement about the Haitian influence on eastern Cuban culture and identity. Isaias described his decision to move the group to Havana as a concerted effort to disseminate folklore oriental to the rest of the country, and the capital in particular. In our interview, he stated, "Guantánamo has an extraordinary [cultural] richness that no other province has," and repeatedly spoke of wanting to increase the breadth of knowledge about these traditions on the island, including not only the Haitian-derived genres but also changüí.

Ban Rarrá's repertoire is currently quite wide ranging, including traditions from both eastern and western Cuba. Isaias, also the group's choreographer, described the group's dance style as a sort of fusion between "pure" representations and nontraditional elements, which might include elements of modern and classical dance.[52] Although he admitted to using elements of "theatricalization" so that his group is not considered a *museo* ("museum," or nonliving entity), he described his choreography as fairly conservative. In the early years, Ban Rarrá performed mainly folklore oriental, focusing on Haitian traditions, but they have expanded more recently into the domain of popular dance genres—such as mambo, cha-cha-cha, and *rueda de casino*[53]—as well as western Cuban folklore. Isaias stated that the group started performing orisha dances around 2000 and incorporated Abakuá a few years later. This raises an interesting issue that I address in more depth below: why do eastern Cuban folkloric groups feel compelled to perform western Cuban traditions, which already receive a disproportionate amount of attention, in addition to the less represented eastern genres? While not necessarily a related issue, Ban Rarrá's membership has changed over the years since the group moved to Havana and currently includes a good proportion of performers (primarily dancers) from the capital. This suggests that there is now a diverse combination of regional identities represented in eastern Cuban folkloric groups who reside in Havana, as has been the case in Havana folkloric groups for some time now.

One distinct aspect of Ban Rarrá's repertoire concerns the prominence of changüí and related genres that feature the use of *tres*, the Cuban guitar with three sets of double strings, in addition to percussion instruments. In my experience there is generally a line drawn in Cuban musicology and cultural parlance between "folkloric" groups, which focus on repertoire dominated by percussion and song ensembles, and "traditional" or "traditional popular" groups, which employ a son-like ensemble featuring European-derived melodic instruments (such as tres, guitar, and trumpet) in addition to percussion and song.[54] Thus, whether in Havana, Matanzas, or Santiago—and independently of the tradition represented (whether rumba, conga, or a variety of African-derived religious musics)—most "folkloric" ensembles do not utilize "melodic" instruments.[55] Nonetheless, it was clear in my interview with Isaias that he considers changüí and other rural eastern Cuban variants of son that feature a combination of string and percussion instruments—such as *nengón* and *kiribá*—to be an essential part of Ban Rarrá's repertoire that needs more exposure beyond Oriente.[56] The prominence of changüí within the group's repertoire is doubtless informed by Isaias's own family history and the fact that he descends from a long line of *changüíseros* (changüí musicians) from the town of Yateras in Guantánamo Province, often thought to be the "cradle of changüí" (Lapidus 2008, 42).[57] This repertoire focus is also reflected on Ban Rarrá's only commercially recorded CD, *Con Sabor al Guaso* (2002), which features eight tracks representing "traditional popular" genres such as changüí, son, and cha-cha-cha, and only four "folkloric" music tracks (three of which are Franco-Haitian and one "Oriente-style" conga). One other explanation for the prominence of changüí in the group's repertoire is the possibility advanced by Benjamin Lapidus that the genre itself has direct musical influences from Franco-Haitian genres, including tumba francesa and Vodú drumming. In this vein, he asserts that the most prominent changüí musicians are of Haitian descent (2008, 124). Thus, in some senses changüí could be viewed as part of the spectrum of Haitian-derived music in Cuba.

Ban Rarrá began performing a weekly *peña* (folkloric show) at the Asociación Cultural Yoruba (Yoruba Cultural Association)—one of the most prominent state-sponsored institutions of Afro-Cuban religion and a venue for rumba and folkloric performance—in 2011.[58] While I am not sure if this peña is still active (see Bodenheimer 2013 for a discussion of the instability of contemporary rumba performance), the fact that an eastern Cuban group would be offered a regular gig at such a renowned cultural institution is a positive sign for the visibility and popularization of folklore oriental beyond Oriente.

The Perspectives of Eastern Cuban Musicians on the Status of Folklore Oriental

While folklore oriental has been gaining visibility in the arena of performance outside of Oriente, my interview with Isaias confirmed that nationwide scholarly interest has only been very recent. He noted that he has worked with several university students at the Instituto Superior del Arte in Havana (ISA, Cuba's primary institution of higher learning for the visual and performing arts) who are conducting research on these traditions. Unsurprisingly, many of them are from Oriente. Published research in this area is still lagging behind that of western Cuban folkloric practices, although publication is difficult for any scholar on the island. In his capacity as a dance instructor at the ISA, Isaias claimed to be the first person to introduce teaching methods for eastern Cuban traditions beyond tumba francesa, which was already established (pers. comm. 2011). He asserted that the relocation of Ban Rarrá to Havana had a direct correlation with the decision to begin teaching Franco-Haitian folklore not only at the ISA but also at the Escuela Nacional de Arte (ENA, the National Art School, a prestigious and internationally recognized training program for high school students).[59] One assumption underlying Isaias's desire to disseminate knowledge about folklore oriental to Havana was evidenced in his statement that the capital city has historically been nourished by the culture of other provinces on the island, including not only Oriente but also western provinces such as Matanzas and Pinar del Río. As will be evident in chapter 4 in relation to Matanzas musicians' views on Havana-style rumba and folkloric practices in general, the notion that the capital is a repository for cultural knowledge that has originated elsewhere is not limited to musicians from the east. Furthermore, it is often accompanied by a sense of frustration, and at times resentment, that Havana groups enjoy more international acclaim and institutional support—and thus financial gain—for representing traditions that don't "belong" to them.

Ramón Márquez, the current musical director of the prominent Santiago-based Cutumba and a professor of Cuban percussion at the ISA in Santiago, asserted that even in the capital of Oriente there are not adequate methods for teaching folklore oriental at the ISA or the ENA.[60] This statement is echoed in Benjamin Lapidus's assertion (2008, 11) that, despite being the musical practice most associated with the province, changüí is not part of the curriculum even in the Guantánamo branch of the ENA. Ramón attributed this lacuna to the cultural hegemony of Havana, noting that Cutumba's significance has been obscured when compared to the prestige enjoyed by the capital's corresponding group, the Conjunto Folklórico Nacional, partly because Cutumba suffers from a lack of TV and radio promotion. Because media attention is geared toward Havana groups, Ramón added, Cutumba's opportunities for lucrative foreign tours are diminished. He foregrounded the symbolic importance of the name of Havana's premier folkloric group, the *National* Folkloric Troupe, suggesting that this was a misnomer because, in reality, the group represents the capital city and perhaps the western region but not the nation as a whole. In other words, folkloric groups located in other provinces are defined in regional terms—the Ballet Folklórico de Oriente or the Ballet Folklórico de Camagüey—while Havana's troupe is put forth as a national representative, even though it does not often perform other region's traditions.

Ramón also partly blamed local cultural officials in Santiago for the marginalization of local folkloric groups, stating that eastern troupes sometimes relocate to Havana because they do not enjoy financial or institutional support in Oriente. Like Isaias, however, he noted that when he was invited to impart classes on eastern traditions at the main site of the ISA in Havana, he saw a growing interest on the part of students in this repertoire. Furthermore, he characterized Santiago's culture as *un archivo*, an archive that has yet to be discovered by folklorists and scholars of culture. He spoke of western Cuban culture—such as rumba and Santería—as almost passé, an already traversed terrain of cultural knowledge, stating: "El Occidente no tiene más nada que brindar" (The west has nothing left to offer). He saw eastern Cuban culture, on the other hand, as a new frontier, noting that there was still much to be uncovered about Haitian and Dahomey-derived traditions and that the repertoire was much broader than what is currently represented, even by professional folkloric groups in Oriente.

Regionalist Sentiment among Eastern Cuban Musicians

One assertion that consistently came up in my discussions with folkloric musicians in Santiago was that the repertoire of folklore oriental is "richer" and that eastern Cuban musicians are more *completo* (literally "complete," or well rounded) than their western Cuban counterparts in terms of their folkloric knowledge.[61] I found it particularly interesting that when I asked the musicians about regionalist sentiment, several of them asserted that it was less apparent within the world of folkloric music than it was in Cuban society overall. As I noted in chapter 1, the musicians viewed themselves as artists and thus able to see beyond the petty regionalist antagonisms that are regularly played out in other arenas of social life, such as baseball. Despite this disavowal of regionalist sentiment, however, several musicians explicitly characterized folklore oriental as richer—perhaps in part because it is less studied—and "mas amplio" (broader, or more diverse) than western Cuban folklore. Ramón attributed the "richer" folkloric tradition in eastern Cuba to the region's racial and ethnic diversity, thus suggesting that the history of Antillean migration contributed in positive, rather than negative, ways to Oriente's cultural development.

Several musicians insisted that eastern Cuban musicians were more complete musicians because, as Ramón stated, "dominan todo" (they are able to play in all styles, both eastern and western). Mario "Mayito" Seguí, a Santiago percussionist who played with the rumba group Kokoyé for many years, offered Ronald González Coba, lead singer of the Havana rumba group Yoruba Andabo, as a perfect example of this phenomenon: a Santiago native, Ronald is a gifted singer in a large variety of styles, including Yoruba, rumba, Palo, and various genres within folklore oriental, and thus, in Mayito's view, the most "complete singer on the island."[62] In fact, Ronald's career trajectory is extraordinary in that he has been a member of elite folkloric groups in Santiago (Cutumba), Matanzas (Los Muñequitos de Matanzas), and Havana (Yoruba Andabo) (see chapter 4 for more on Ronald's career). Similarly, Isaias asserted that percussionists from Oriente, and specifically Guantánamo, are particularly sought out by rumba groups in Havana because their training

Figure 3.4: Mario "Mayito" Seguí, Santiago percussionist.

in Franco-Haitian repertoire is thought to contribute greatly to their skill. He stated that Franco-Haitian song style is particularly "melodious," and he attributed the decision of Havana-based groups like Clave y Guaguancó to include merengue haitiano in their repertoire to this aesthetic superiority.

Folkloric singer Pablo issued a slightly different place-based discourse of authenticity that conforms to the comments made to me by many Matanzas-based musicians concerning the origins of cultural traditions (see chapter 4). He stated, "En el Oriente hay religiosos de verdad. Es el campo. Todo eso nace aquí en el campo y se populariza en las ciudades" (In Oriente there are true religious believers. It's the countryside. All of that [religion] is born here in the countryside and then popularized in the cities. Pers. comm. 2011). He stressed that further research was necessary on traditions from el campo, as these were the sites of large concentrations of slaves, where the *cimarrones* (escaped slaves) fled in order to practice their own religions and traditions. Although Pablo conceded that not all religion emerged from the eastern half of the island—he reiterated the common belief that Santería was born in the province of Matanzas—his statements were clearly designed to authenticate el campo and the cultural and religious traditions associated with it. As discussed in chapter 2, the term *el campo* has both a general meaning, "the countryside," and a more specific connotation that habaneros associate with people from anywhere outside of the capital and take to mean "backward." Nonetheless, as suggested by Pablo's statement, people from el campo, including large cities like Santiago, have appropriated this designation to speak about themselves and their traditions in a positive manner—as more authentic, sincere, and down to earth than those of habaneros.

The fact that all the eastern Cuban musicians I interviewed independently characterized (with no prompting from me) eastern Cuban traditions as "richer" and/or oriental musicians as more versatile and perhaps more skillful than western Cuban folkloric musicians, leads me to believe that this is a commonly held perspective. In addition, two of the musicians went a step further in their assertions, stating that western Cuban musicians themselves recognize the superiority of their eastern counterparts. While I cannot take these musicians' views to be the final word on the subject, and in fact do not believe that western Cuban musicians would assert their own inferiority, establishing the truth of these claims is not my goal. My main point is to posit the importance of regional identity on one's artistic identity and opinions, whether musicians actively recognize this or not. Given the history of regional tensions on the island and the distinct development of the eastern half of the island, it is perhaps not remarkable that local musicians would issue aesthetic judgments that appear to be deeply influenced by their regional identity; after all, as will be detailed in depth in chapters 4 and 5, these divisions are seen even among western Cuban musicians who hail from different cities, such as Havana and Matanzas. Nonetheless, what is more interesting is the extent to which musicians sometimes deny the impact of their regional identities on their aesthetic preferences. The reason for this inconsistency may lie in the hegemony of the Cuban nationalist discourse, specifically the disciplining of Cuban citizens by the state to believe that they are "one people," indivisible by differences of region, race, gender, or other axes of identity. However, when even a celebrated folklorist and supporter of the revolution, Rogelio Martínez Furé (2000), critiques the "homogenizing" cultural discourse that posits a singular Cuban identity, perhaps this narrative is showing signs of decay.

Another common theme emerging from the statements made by eastern Cuban folkloric musicians concerns the origins of national cultural practices, an issue inevitably entangled with tropes of authenticity. In addition to the comments made by Pablo (stressing the eastern origins of much of the island's religious culture) and Isaias (who discussed how the culture of the capital was nourished by eastern Cuban practices), Ramón was insistent that Oriente gave birth to traditions that have defined Cuba's artistic identity;

he mentioned both antecedents of son—changüí and nengón—and a more recent innovation in Cuban dance music, a rhythm called *pilón*.[63] These assertions echo the critique made by Cándido Fabré in his song "Soy Cubano y Soy de Oriente," discussed in chapter 2. All of these musicians are presumably attempting to combat anti-oriental prejudice by foregrounding the centrality of eastern Cuban traditions to national culture. However, what is at stake is much more than proving the origins of Cuban music; more importantly, eastern Cubans are staking a claim to national identity, weaving a counternarrative to the popular discourse (particularly in Havana) and written histories that leave them out.

Finally, I want to address one other issue that arose in my interviews: if eastern Cuban musicians consider folklore oriental to be more rich and varied than western Cuban traditions, why do folkloric groups in and from Oriente feel the need to perform established genres such as orisha dances and Abakuá in addition to their own regional genres? As mentioned above, Ban Rarrá eventually decided to incorporate western Cuban folklore into their repertoire. In addition, during a research trip to Santiago in summer 2011, I attended a performance by the Ballet Folklórico de Oriente in which they performed both orisha dances and Franco-Haitian repertoire. While I was not able to attend a recent performance by Cutumba, the other large folkloric troupe in Santiago, promotional materials on the Internet and my conversations with musicians in the group indicate that orisha dances are a standard part of their repertoire as well. Writing in 1989, Millet and Brea (1989, 101–2) do not list Yoruba-derived traditions as part of Cutumba's repertoire, suggesting that this may be a recent addition, as in the case of Ban Rarrá. The fact that Cutumba's recent commercially released album (2007) is dedicated exclusively to orisha songs also suggests that this has been a larger focus of their repertoire in the past decade.[64] Finally, although there is an extremely long history of Bantu presence in Oriente, several musicians pointed out that the folkloric traditions representing this African metaethnic group that are performed by Santiago-based groups, specifically Palo, were borrowed primarily from Havana and Matanzas.[65] Thus, there seems to be a desire on the part of musicians and dancers, and/or pressure from local *empresas* (state-run artistic agencies) and cultural officials, to perform the best-known representations of Afro-Cuban folklore on the island. Western Cuban traditions have become so hegemonic that they have been established as the national standard for defining what constitutes a good folkloric group. However, other important factors that determine repertoire decisions relate to the cultural tourism industry—including international tours—and to audience desires to see varied performances. In other words, it would be inconceivable for a Cuban folkloric group to conduct an international tour in which Yoruba-derived repertoire was not included, precisely because this particular tradition has been constructed as the most representative of Afro-Cuban folklore. In terms of audience desires, it also seems relevant that knowledge about Yoruba traditions and initiation into Santería has been a growing trend in eastern Cuba in recent decades.

For Pablo, the primary explanation for why eastern musicians and groups feel the need to "do it all," or be proficient in traditions from both regions, relates to the privileged status of western Cuba in all aspects of social life. In comments that echoed his previous statements concerning how traditions from el campo are appropriated and disseminated in the city (specifically the capital), Pablo stated that eastern musicians feel obliged to imitate the style of western folkloric musicians because it represents *la onda*, or the trend of the moment (pers. comm. 2011). He offered a specific example: when he sings a song in the *columbia* style of rumba, which displays a strong Bantu influence, he is often taken to task by the audience for not inserting a Yoruba-derived chant, an inclusion not traditionally used in columbia but one that is now fashionable. In other words, although not a traditional element of columbia, the incorporation of Santería refrains has become trendy, particularly in the capital, and this innovation informs the performance of the genre across the island because of Havana's cultural dominance. Interestingly, Pablo noted that even traditions known to originate in Oriente that were later appropriated and popularized in western Cuba often undergo a second, reverse process of dispersion, back to the east, only to be imitated by the originators. Thus, his comments echoed the lyrics of Cándido Fabré (discussed in chapter 2) regarding the tendency of Havana-based musicians to appropriate music that emerged in Oriente and then to refashion it and "sell it back" to orientales. To clarify, I am not arguing that Pablo's perception reflects the reality of cultural exchange between eastern and western Cuba; instead, I am reproducing comments by eastern Cuban musicians that display a certain resentment regarding what they perceive to be their marginalized status and that of Oriente's musical traditions, as well as a lack of recognition for eastern Cuban creativity more generally.

Rumba in Santiago

Given the fact that rumba is a tradition that originated in western Cuba, it is interesting to consider the defense of a traditional style of rumba performance by Pablo, a santiaguero who—if using a regionalist logic—cannot lay claim to ownership of a practice that is not historically associated with his city or region. Nonetheless, one could argue that rumba is a special case in that it has become nationalized—I argue in fact that it is the most important black-identified secular practice on the island (Bodenheimer 2013)—and has thus lost its regional connotations. The popularity of rumba has been steadily growing beyond Havana and Matanzas since the revolution, and there are now important rumba scenes and nationally recognized groups in Santiago, Camagüey, Cienfuegos, and other cities. Thus, I want to briefly discuss the contemporary rumba scene in Santiago, as it constitutes an interesting case study in relation to chapter 4's discussion of the polarized discourse surrounding Havana- and Matanzas-style rumba.

Santiago percussionist Mayito asserted that rumba is currently enjoying a boom in the eastern capital, at least in part owing to the success of Kokoyé, a local group that, while including various traditions in their repertoire, has long been thought of as the pillar of Santiago-based rumba. Founded in 1989 with the objective of playing for the tourism sector in Santiago, Kokoyé has always been associated with a less traditional, more fusion-based style of rumba (Seguí Correoso, pers. comm. 2011), especially as compared with the performances of Cutumba and the Ballet Folklórico de Oriente. Until recently, the group served as the house band for the only well-established rumba event in Santiago, held on Sundays at the Casa del Caribe.[66] Kokoyé has played a major role in maintaining and promoting rumba performance in Santiago since then. In 2009, the group was given a permanent locale in which to rehearse, and it subsequently established a new rumba event on Saturday evenings in the Distrito José Martí neighborhood. Although the band often amasses a sizable crowd for its shows, the event's location is not central or easy to access by public transportation and thus cannot serve a large segment of the rumba aficionado population in Santiago. Furthermore, Mayito noted that while rumba performance has become more visible and popular in recent years, more institutional support by local cultural officials is needed. Ramón Márquez echoed this assertion, indicating that local rumba performance faced substantial challenges. He stated that, similar to the situation in Havana, local cultural officials have often displayed prejudicial attitudes toward rumba due to its perceived associations with blackness and criminality, and that his attempts to organize community rumba events have not been very successful (pers. comm. 2011).

When asked how Santiago-style rumba differs from the styles of other cities, the musicians I interviewed were hard pressed to offer a specific description of the musical distinctions. However, notwithstanding the style of Kokoyé—a group that self-consciously employs a fusion strategy based upon the Havana guarapachangueo style (see chapter 5)—Ramón felt that

Santiago-style rumba conforms more to the sound of Matanzas rumba—more traditional and slower—than to that of Havana. My observations, based on a performance by the group that currently plays on Sundays at the Casa del Caribe, Rumbaché, concurred with his assessment. Further buttressing this idea was a statement by Santiago-born Ronald González Coba, who stated that as an aspiring rumba singer he used to imitate the style of Los Muñequitos de Matanzas and sing many of their songs (pers. comm. 2007). The legendary rumba group later recruited him, he asserted, precisely because they liked his sound and felt that it would fit well with their style. Another point of convergence between rumba musicians from Santiago and Matanzas was the display of a more traditionalist, conservative mindset vis-à-vis innovation and fusion in rumba. While I cannot take one musician's views to be representative of all Santiago rumberos, Pablo issued a sharp critique of certain contemporary trends in rumba performance that are coming mainly from Havana, including not only the aforementioned insertion of Yoruba refrains into columbia but the popularization of the guarapachangueo style and the incorporation of reggaetón choruses into rumba songs (see chapter 5). He spoke of these innovations, and of the tendency to mix rumba with other genres, as a threat to the identity of the practice, noting also that many rumba performers are conflating the three major styles—*yambú*, guaguancó, and columbia—by, for example, singing *puyas* (verbal battles between singers) in guaguancó when the goal of this style is to narrate a story and not to engage in a war of words (pers. comm. 2011).[67] He stated, "At the end of the day you don't know if you're Chinese, or if you're Cuban, or if you're French, or if you're in summer or if it rained . . . you don't know if you're in autumn. You don't know what season it is, because you don't even respect that and you dress however, just to be trendy" (pers. comm. 2011).[68] Pablo ended our conversation by singing a rumba song he had composed that condemns the loss of traditional elements in both the song and percussion style; needless to say, it was reminiscent of many of the critiques Matanzas-based folkloric musicians make about Havana-style rumba.[69]

Conclusion

Both Ramón Márquez and Isaias Rojas attributed what they deemed to be the "richer" folkloric tradition in eastern Cuba to the region's ethnic diversity, thus suggesting that the history of Antillean migration and influence contributed in positive ways to Oriente's cultural development. This perspective stands in contrast to the hegemonic narratives regarding the relationship of the island to the rest of the Caribbean. At various moments throughout the past two centuries, Haitians in Cuba have been demonized as too black, too rebellious, too poor, and/or too illiterate, and yet a century ago as migrant agricultural workers they faced conditions often compared to slavery. Under the revolution, Cuba has provided a great deal of humanitarian assistance to its eastern neighbor—in fact, the Cuban doctors already in Haiti were able to respond immediately after the devastating 2010 earthquake—and Cuba has helped Haiti become more self-sufficient by offering free medical training to aspiring Haitian doctors at the Escuela Latinoamericana de Medicina (Latin American School of Medicine). Nonetheless, many Cubans still view Haiti as a "charity case" and thus display a rather paternalistic stance toward Haitians. In the realm of folklore, there have been deliberate attempts recently to recognize the Haitian roots of national culture in Cuba, and folklore oriental has correspondingly gained visibility. Some, like Grete Viddal, view the situation with optimism: "In eastern Cuba, members of a historically marginalized and denigrated population are using folkloric performance to challenge marginalization, build cultural capital, and cultivate regional pride" (2010, 93).

In a piece entitled "Multicubanidad" (translated roughly as "multi-Cubanness"), anthropologist Ariana Hernandez-Reguant discusses the shift in notions about Cubanidad since the Special Period, noting a rise in Cuban identification with "ethnic minorities" such as the Chinese and Jewish communities. She states, "Slowly but surely, Cuba's ethnic communities (in plural) were helping to shape a sort of revolutionary multiculturalism in line with similar trends in the United States, Canada, Australia, and other countries" (2009, 80). The growing popularity and visibility of folklore oriental, and its strong associations with Haitian and Caribbean influences, could be interpreted as corresponding to this phenomenon. It seems that the global trend of multiculturalism is gaining steam on the island, which may create room not only for the recognition of Cuba's Caribbean connection but also for a larger redefinition of Cubanidad. Perhaps the next generation of Cuban folklore research will reflect this more inclusive concept of national identity by presenting a more regionally balanced portrait of the island's traditions.

Chapter Four

Racialized Discourses of Place and Rethinking the "Cradle of Afro-Cuban Culture"

My conceptualization of the politics of place consists of several distinct yet related discursive formations. The first, which was detailed in previous chapters, concerns contemporary regionalist sentiment within Cuba, which is manifested in various ways: in everyday social relations among Cubans from different provinces (especially in Havana), in the lyrics of Cuban dance music and rumba songs, and in musicians' aesthetic opinions. In many ways, this chapter constitutes a continuation of my analysis in chapter 3 of how musicians' local identities inform their artistic perspectives. However, my primary goal here is to examine a separate discursive formation that elaborates the politics of place through race and musical traditions, what I refer to as racialized discourses of place. By this, I mean the ways that certain locales in Cuba are linked with particular racial and cultural attributes in both popular and academic arenas. Specifically, I explore the racialized tropes of place attached to Havana and Matanzas, the two cities with the longest and most influential histories of rumba performance, and examine how these discourses relate to the different rumba styles. I argue that these cities are inserted into a polarized cultural discourse in which Havana is represented as the center of contemporary innovation and hybridity, and Matanzas as the heartland of Afro-Cuban tradition and "authentic" blackness. The latter's reputation as "la cuna de la cultura afrocubana" (the cradle of Afro-Cuban culture) exemplifies these racialized tropes of place, which, as I have already discussed, are also pervasive in notions about other locales on the island. My focus in this chapter (and the next) on the cities of Havana and Matanzas also allows me to narrow my discussion of regionalism from a national perspective (i.e., the regionalist antagonisms between eastern and western Cuba) to a more region-specific analysis. In other words, exploring the differences in playing styles and racialized notions about tradition and innovation in Havana and Matanzas (two western cities) elucidates a more localized and complex portrait of the politics of place on the island. Interestingly, as will be evident, the notions that *matanceros* (people from Matanzas) hold about *habaneros* are quite similar to those expressed by musicians from Santiago.

Drawing on my fieldwork with rumba and folkloric groups in Havana and Matanzas, I posit that these polarized tropes of place are problematic in their essentialization of the two cities' cultural identities. I follow anthropologist Donald Moore in his suggestion that places are hybrid: "Place emerges as a distinctive mixture, not an enduring essence, a nodal point where the translocal influences intermesh with practices and meanings previously sedimented in the local landscape" (2005, 20). Notwithstanding this hybridity of place, it is important not to dismiss the effects of essentializing discourses of place, for they have strongly informed the choices of folkloric musicians about how to represent themselves musically. The government's investment in cultural tourism centered on Afro-Cuban music and dance since the Special Period has significantly raised the stakes for folkloric musicians in terms of representing themselves as "authentic." Competition for cultural tourism, mainly in the form of music and dance lessons, presents a very concrete example of the impact of these discourses of place on the economic landscapes of folkloric musicians. Thus, this chapter also explores how cultural politics and racialized discourses are entangled with material realities in contemporary Cuba.

In her ethnography on racial formation in Liverpool, Jacqueline Nassy Brown discusses the ways in which the northern English city is constructed discursively, particularly in relation to London and southern England more generally. She notes that with deindustrialization and the decline of Liverpool's importance as an international port city, "[t]he North and South were increasingly recognized as two nations, separate and unequal" (Brown 2005, 16). She also notes "the North's abject working classness . . . Liverpool itself is depicted as death" (17). Later, she analyzes the discussion of Liverpool by Caribbean British author Caryl Phillips: "Liverpool is also beyond the pale of any known civilization. . . . In contrast to Britain, evoked through the magical white cliffs of Dover, Liverpool's physicality is satanic (perhaps like its people?). Liverpool is a place apart. It has nothing to do with Britain, the North, or Phillips himself" (130). Brown asserts that Liverpool is viewed by black Britons as the most racist place in Britain, largely because of its role in the transatlantic slave trade. Meanwhile, London is juxtaposed to Liverpool and constructed as racially progressive. Highlighting the fact that no one discusses London's past as a large slave port, she states, "London existed either as Liverpool's eternal nemesis or as the vanguard of racial politics, the site where civilizing, liberal, antiracist discourses had triumphed. . . . [M]ost slavery discourse shows London forging boldly ahead, while Liverpool remains hopelessly out of step, mired in the backward, 'traditional' ideology inherited from its 'unique' slave-trading past" (178–79). I have quoted Brown at length here precisely because I see so many parallels between the discourses of place she describes, and the ones with which I am concerned in Cuba. First, like northern England, Oriente is criminalized and associated with backwardness and poverty. Second, like Liverpool, Camagüey is singled out as the most racist place in the country, allowing people to disavow racism in other places, like Havana or Santiago. Finally, as with Liverpool, Matanzas is defined by its slave past. Brown states, "Place acts—and it always does so first. Place *explains*. 'Liverpool was a slave port and therefore . . .'" (249). Matanzas could easily be substituted for Liverpool in this sentence; as I will show below, the discourse of place attached to Matanzas is almost always explained in terms of its slave past.

In chapter 1, I cited Peter Wade's work (1993) on the "racialization of region" in Colombia, where the Atlantic coast is associated with blackness. A more recent Wade article (2005) reproduces comments by Colombians speaking about particular foods and musical forms as belonging to certain racial and regional groups. He states, "Territory, people and musical culture were thought of as a unified whole. . . . Each region had its music and its food and its people. All of these had their racial associations: the highlands, with its food, music and people, were non-black, the coast black. People from the latter region could not play the music of the former. But the comment still held out the possibility of transformation: by eating the right food in the right milieu, one could (theoretically at least) acquire the correct bodily and mental dispositions required to play the music properly" (2005, 246–47). In fact, Wade ultimately identifies a tension in his informants' perspectives between nature-based arguments—essentialist notions exemplified by the common saying "it's in the blood"—and nurture-based arguments, which emphasize the impact of the surrounding environment. This chapter similarly explores the ways that race is regionalized and region is racialized in the polarized notions about Havana and Matanzas and their different styles of rumba, and in the ways that musical traditions are conceived of more generally as "belonging to" a particular region.

In addition to elucidating the discursive links between race and place as they pertain to musical style, this chapter foregrounds the authenticating discourses that are often embedded within racialized tropes of place. Scholars from different disciplines have problematized place-based discourses of authenticity. Similar to Wade, anthropologists Akhil Gupta and James Ferguson (1992) and Liisa Malkki (1997) have critiqued the long-held assumption within their discipline of an isomorphic link between cultural groups, seen as unitary and homogeneous, and the territories they inhabit. Instead of reifying these essentialized discourses, Gupta and Ferguson call for attention to ethnographers' *production* of spatialized difference, insightfully stating, "The special challenge here is to use a focus on the way space is imagined (but not *imaginary!*). . . . How are spatial meanings established? Who has the power to make places of spaces? Who contests this? What is at stake?" (Gupta and Ferguson 1992, 11).[1] In terms of my own concerns, I intend to explore the questions, How, why, and by whom has Matanzas been constructed as the "cradle of Afro-Cuban culture"? Who benefits from the reification of this notion, and who, if anyone, is attempting to contest this claim? Finally, it is important to ask what is at stake in the reproduction of these tropes, particularly in the context of post-Soviet Cuba and the expansion of the tourism industry over the past two decades.

While it is necessary to recognize ethnographers' production of spatialized difference, it is also crucial to examine how and why musicians invoke place-based discourses of authenticity. Here I draw upon cultural geographer Michael Watts's discussion of the "cultural politics of territoriality," contained in an article about development discourses and alternatives in which he critically examines indigenous political movements and land reclamations. He states, "A community, then, typically involves a territorialization of history ('this is our land and resources which can be traced in relation to these founding events') and a naturalized history ('history becomes the history of my people and not of our relations to others'). Communities fabricate, and refabricate through their unique histories, the claims which they take to be naturally and self-evidently their own" (Watts 2003, 446). Watts goes on to note the inherent heterogeneity of and internal power struggles within marginalized communities, which, however, must be glossed over and sublimated (at least temporarily) in order to attain a specific political goal. In this chapter, the cultural politics of territoriality involve a struggle not to reclaim land but rather to reclaim, or hold onto, ownership of a musical tradition. Lastly, Watts's interrogation of indigenity refers to it as "an invented space of authenticity" (447), a productive notion for examining the place-based discourses of authenticity attached to Matanzas that are repeatedly invoked by local folkloric musicians.

In another example of place-based discourses of authenticity, Murray Forman's study of space and place in hip-hop asserts that rappers invoke racialized regional identities to prove their "ghetto authenticity" (2002, 5). This chapter's focus on place-based discourses of authenticity within a musical practice that is also mapped as black (rumba) presents a clear parallel to Forman's work on hip-hop. Whereas New York is recognized as the birthplace of hip-hop, a fact frequently employed by New York artists in asserting their authenticity, Matanzas occupies this position in rumba and folkloric discourse within Cuba. Forman, a mass communications scholar, examines discourses of authenticity through song texts and written media. Following Donald Moore's call for "ethnographic attention to the *spatiality* of power relations and the politics of positioning" (2005, 9; his emphasis), this chapter entails an ethnographic exploration of how notions of racialized local authenticity make a crucial difference in the lives of folkloric musicians in both Havana and Matanzas. To accomplish this, I draw on a variety of sources that link race, place, and cultural expression, including published scholarship, the opinions of folkloric musicians, commercial recordings, and live performances.

The religious, musical, and social histories of the city and province of Matanzas constitute convincing evidence for accepting the "cradle" notion without further investigation. Ethnomusicologist Jocelyne Guilbault touches on a similar discourse, stating, "In both popular and academic discourses, invocations of Trinidad's organic relation to calypso are often taken as self-evident truths" (2007, 21). Instead of accepting this discourse at face value, Guilbault elucidates both the historically specific factors that resulted in this association of calypso with Trinidad, and the ways in which calypso's hybrid, transnational musical formation was disavowed once it was claimed as "national" music. In the same vein, I hope to interrogate the racialized discourse of tradition attached to Matanzas in several ways. My interventions include highlighting some of the inconsistencies within the scholarship, critically analyzing opinions expressed to me by folkloric musicians, and presenting historical evidence that complicates the trope of origins associated with Matanzas. Finally, I will offer a few examples of Matanzas-based groups engaging in musical fusion, which challenges the implied fixity and antimodernness of the "cradle" notion. In the last section of the chapter I address the "spatiality of power relations and the politics of positioning" (D. Moore 2005, 9) by discussing some of the material effects of racialized discourses of place and related claims of authenticity.

Racialized Discourses of Place

The "Cradle of Afro-Cuban Culture"

The city of Matanzas has been famously dubbed the "cradle of Afro-Cuban culture," a nickname that evokes notions of "authentic" blackness tied to tradition. This epithet is usually explained by referencing Matanzas Province's deep entanglement with plantation slavery: it boasted the largest and most productive sugar plantations and greatest concentration of slaves in nineteenth-century Cuba. In contrast to the Anglophone Caribbean, where the slave trade was outlawed in the first half of the nineteenth century, Cuba saw a growth in the importation of African slaves during the middle of that century after the island became the world's leading sugar producer. The increased importance of sugar production after the Haitian Revolution explains not only why the island became the focal point and crowning jewel of waning Spanish colonialism,[2] but also why the abolition of slavery came so late to the island, in 1886. The province of Matanzas became a hub for the growth of slavery in the nineteenth century, as the enslaved population grew at three times the rate of the rest of the nation (Bretos 2010, 57). Matanzas historian Raúl R. Ruiz (2001) posits that by 1826, 57 percent of the population in the province of Matanzas was made up of slaves, a figure that rose to 62 percent by 1841. Historian Rebecca Scott notes that in 1862, 46 percent of Cuba's overall slave population was concentrated in Matanzas and the central Cuban province of Santa Clara, a figure that rose to 57 percent by 1877 (2000, 88).[3] Matanzas-born historian Miguel Bretos states, "the modern Cuban barracón [slave barracks] was perfected, if not altogether invented, in Matanzas" (2010, 59). By 1840, Matanzas Province had become a leader in the mechanization of sugar production and other technological advances, and boasted the largest, most modern, and most profitable sugar plantations in Cuba. By 1857, sugar from Matanzas came to represent almost 56 percent of the island's total production (Scott 2000, 88). Bretos states, "Sugar catapulted Matanzas from an obscure coastal settlement to Cuba's third largest city in population and, arguably, second in importance by 1850" (2010, 54). Rebecca Scott breaks down the number of fully mechanized sugar plantations in 1860 by province: Matanzas had forty-four, Santa Clara had ten, La Habana (the province, not the city) had four, and Santiago had none (2000, 22). Incidentally, the fact that Santiago had 109 more sugar mills than La Habana Province, none of which were fully mechanized, is a testament to the historical (and ongoing) regional inequalities within Cuba with respect to technological advances and modernization more generally.

Scholars have generally used Matanzas's slave plantation history as a principal explanation for the "cradle" nickname, taking this notion as self-evident fact (Cabrera 1973; Vinueza 1986; Delgado 2001). For example, ethnomusicologist Kevin Delgado states, "The reason Matanzas is the capital of Afro-Cuban culture is simple and sad—it was once the capital of slavery" (2001, 16). Beyond the slavery explanation, many scholars also refer to Matanzas's particularly strong tradition of Afro-Cuban religious worship (Vinueza 1986;

Vélez 2000; Delgado 2001; Hagedorn 2003; Bretos 2010). In addition to the ongoing practice of sacred traditions not found anywhere else in contemporary Cuba—namely *Iyesá, Arará, Bríkamo,* and *Olokún*[4]—many religious practitioners are initiates of two or more Afro-Cuban religions.[5]

Matanzas is also considered to be "la mata de la rumba" (the "tree" or birthplace of rumba). Ethnomusicologist María Teresa Vélez even asserts that rumba has "made this region [Matanzas] famous" (2000, 36). Legendary rumba singer Hortensio "Virulilla" Alfonso, founder of Los Muñequitos de Matanzas and one half of the most famous vocal duet in rumba history, stated, "I don't want anyone to be offended by my response, but they have to realize that the cradle is here, in Matanzas, in Cuba, where any kid can play a great rumba or *quinto* [improvising rumba drum] before even learning to walk. . . . Not to mention [the Matanzas tradition of rumba] singing!" (Diago Urfé 1997, 28; my translation). In fact, if a poll were taken among both Cubans and foreigners to determine the group most closely associated with rumba (both historically and currently), Los Muñequitos de Matanzas would certainly win. The majority of Cuban scholarship concurs that two of the three traditional styles of rumba still performed today, yambú and columbia, emerged in Matanzas Province around the mid-nineteenth century (León 1984; Urfé [1977] 1984; Grasso González 1989). However, there is a long-standing debate regarding whether the third and most popular style of rumba, guaguancó, emerged in urban Matanzas or Havana.[6] Some scholars, including the pioneering Cuban musicologist Argeliers León (1984), simply acknowledge the fact that guaguancó's site of emergence is disputed, without coming down on one side of the debate. Scholars engaged in Matanzas-based research, however, tend to view the province as the unequivocal birthplace of all three styles of rumba (for example, Martínez Rodríguez and González 1977; Grasso González 1989; Vélez 2000), which suggests that the debate may be colored by regionalist sentiment, even when the scholar does not hail from Matanzas. The city's reputation as the birthplace of rumba is also well known outside of Cuba, as illustrated by a rumba compilation CD called *¡La Rumba Está Buena!* (1994). The CD includes eleven tracks, nine of which are performed by Matanzas-based groups and two of which feature the Santiago folkloric group Cutumba, an interesting choice given that the eastern city is not historically associated with rumba performance.[7] In other words, not one of the tracks includes a Havana-based rumba group, despite the fact that the capital boasts the largest number of rumba groups on the island by far.

Musical odes to Matanzas as the birthplace of rumba and various Afro-Cuban religious practices are another illustration of the ways that the city is discursively constructed as the "cradle of Afro-Cuban culture." Los Van Van has a song entitled "De La Habana a Matanzas" (From Havana to Matanzas), which is an homage to Matanzas's rich tradition of Afro-Cuban culture that begins with a rumba clave rhythm and rumba-style vocals punctuated by guitar harmonics.[8] The song chronicles a trip from the capital to Matanzas and the narrator's intention of investigating the origins of rumba, presumed to reside there. The opening verse states, "Quería saber del guaguancó, de la rumba, de la columbia" (I wanted to learn about the guaguancó, about rumba, about the columbia). In the montuno (call-and-response) section, the lead singer mentions the most famous singing duo in rumba history, Saldiguera and Virulilla, founding members of Los Muñequitos de Matanzas in the 1950s. A more recent timba song that reifies the "cradle" discourse is "La Habana Me Llama" by Manolito y Su Trabuco.[9] The song begins by naming virtually all the Cuban provinces and praising them for their unique qualities, which, in the case of Matanzas, is "su rumba y su religion" (its rumba and religion).

Although modern-day Matanzas is internationally renowned for its Afro-Cuban religious and musical practices, the "cradle of Afro-Cuban culture" was not always known as such. In 1860, the city was given a very different moniker during the inauguration of Matanzas's first *liceo* (high school dedicated to the study of arts and literature): the "Athens of Cuba" (Ruiz 2003). The linking of Matanzas to the ancient center of Western civilization was precipitated by the flourishing European-derived art scene that began to develop in Matanzas in the 1830s as the region and city acquired wealth from the slave-driven sugar industry. Theater, literary mediums, and classical music were all institutionalized during this time, creating the conditions under which intellectuals and artists gravitated to the city (Ruiz 2001). As noted by Miguel Bretos, Matanzas was the hometown of Cuba's first historian and the nation's first public library (1833), and the place where Cuban baseball was established (Bretos 2010, 103). Matanzas reached its height of European-derived cultural splendor during the 1850s and 1860s, exemplified in the construction of the Teatro Sauto, a neoclassical theater in the city center that still functions as the main performing arts venue in Matanzas. The city was also the birthplace of Cuba's most important nineteenth-century musical genre, danzón, which is still considered by some to be the country's national dance. The first danzón, "Las Alturas de Simpson," was composed by Matanzas native Miguel Faílde in 1879.[10] Miguel Bretos discusses the intentions behind naming Matanzas the "Athens of Cuba," noting that the original idea came from a group of boosters affiliated with the new liceo. He states, "The proponents of the idea may have been naïve and provincial but they were not foolish. Rather, calling their city 'Athens' implied a program for the future to be achieved, not necessarily a description of the present. . . . In all likelihood the inspiration for 'the Athens of Cuba' came down from New England, like the hard granite cobblestones that paved the streets" (Bretos 2010, 102, 115–16). He goes on to note that in addition to Boston, Nashville and Bogotá had also been likened to the ancient Greek city, all before the boosters suggested it for Matanzas. By the 1880s, Matanzas's sugar industry was in decline due to various global forces, like the growth of beet sugar, and Bretos concludes of the "Athens" nickname, "What had been a credible boast in the halcyon days of prosperity became a slightly ridiculous provincial conceit" (119).

The fact that Matanzas was known as the "Athens of Cuba" highlights the very different attitudes toward Afro-Cuban people and culture in the colonial era, as compared with the valorization and "nationalization of blackness" (R. Moore 1997) that began in the late 1920s and intensified after the 1959 Cuban Revolution. Cuban musicologists Raúl Martínez Rodríguez and Pedro de la Hoz González (1977) present historical documents showing that the wealthy white occupants of the "Athens of Cuba" were horrified by parties held in the late nineteenth century that included public drumming, dancing, and singing, and blacks were often fined or arrested for having rumba parties. Although danzón is a European-derived, literate genre that bears little resemblance to the more African-sounding rumba, its emergence in 1879 resulted in a racist backlash. White intellectuals pointed to danzón's African-derived ostinato, the *cinquillo* rhythm, as evidence that black Cubans were trying to "Africanize" Cuban culture and would eventually start a race war in the vein of the Haitian Revolution.[11] Although African-derived culture began to be valorized as it was discursively linked to a nationalist agenda, Afro-Cuban religious drummers and practitioners in Matanzas continued to be persecuted and harassed by the authorities throughout the nation-building decades of the 1920s and 1930s and even after the revolution (Vélez 2000; Delgado 2001).

In addition to the "Athens of Cuba," Raúl Ruiz presents a number of other nicknames that have been given to Matanzas since the nineteenth century, including "la ciudad de los ríos" (the city of rivers), "la ciudad de los puentes" (the city of bridges), "el Nápoles de América" (the Naples of America), "la Venecia cubana" (the Cuban Venice, precisely because of its many bridges), "la ciudad de los poetas" (the city of poets), and finally "la ciudad dormida" (the sleeping city, alluding to the decline of commercial and artistic activity in the city during the twentieth century) (Ruiz 2003, 86–87).[12] In 1961, one Cuban writer jokingly came to conclusion that, rather than deciding among the many epithets attached to the city, Matanzas should be known as "la ciudad cubana de los sobrenombres" (the Cuban city of nicknames) (Ruiz 2003, 86–87). Curiously, Ruiz does not mention the "cradle of Afro-Cuban culture" when discussing Matanzas's various nicknames, although he does consider

Matanzas to be one of most important sites for the preservation of African culture in the Americas due to the diversity of African ethnic groups brought to work on sugar plantations (27–28). Furthermore, Miguel Bretos notes that Matanzas could have well been called "the Ilé-Ifé of Cuba"—a reference to the ancient center of the Yoruba people and culture in Nigeria—stating, "At the end of the day, Matanzas as the Ilé-Ifé of Cuba makes so much more sense than Athens" (2010, 125).

Although I have not been able to ascertain exactly when the "cradle" notion became widespread in popular and academic discourse, I believe that its appearance is correlated with the shift in the Castro regime's racial politics away from the segregationist policies that were widespread in prerevolutionary Cuba. Since the early 1960s, there has been a discursive valorization of African-derived culture by state officials, and the government has supported the creation of institutions dedicated to researching and performing Afro-Cuban music, dance, and religious traditions.[13] My fieldwork in Matanzas indicates that the two nicknames (the "Athens of Cuba" and the "cradle of Afro-Cuban culture") currently coexist, which is interesting, considering that each represents a racial extreme. The "Athens of Cuba" effectively likens Matanzas to the birthplace of European civilization and foregrounds colonial influences in Cuba. On the other hand, the "cradle of Afro-Cuban culture" constructs Matanzas as the principal site of the preservation of African-derived musical and religious practices and emphasizes the African presence on the island. Thus, rather than emphasizing *mestizaje* (racial mixture), the cornerstone of Cuba's nationalist discourse, the tropes of place associated with Matanzas actually underscore racial *difference*. Furthermore, while the "Athens" nickname implies European-style cosmopolitanism and a certain level of engagement with culture beyond the island, the "cradle" trope is inevitably entangled with a discourse of purity and preservation, in which "outside" cultural influences tend to be minimized or even denied. Interestingly, both nicknames are tied to premodern societies and thus link Matanzas with the past, whether African or European. As I discuss below, this association with antimodernity is not always beneficial for local folkloric musicians' livelihoods.

While conducting fieldwork in Matanzas, I heard the folkloric group Afrocuba de Matanzas perform a rumba song dedicated to its native city that provides an interesting example of these racially polarized, rather than hybrid, discursive representations of Matanzas.[14] The song extols the virtues of the city's and province's natural beauty, mentioning the Valle de Yumurí (Yumurí Valley), the Cuevas de Bellamar (Bellamar Caves), and Varadero's incomparable beach. The lyrics also reference Matanzas's importance within the political history of the Cuban Revolution as a site of the creation of important Communist Party institutions. In terms of the two prevailing nicknames associated with the city, the song explicitly refers to Matanzas as "el Atenas de Cuba" (the Athens of Cuba) and recalls the city's rich legacy of European-derived poetry. However, like the Los Van Van song, the lyrics also mention Saldiguera and Virulilla as *rumberos* (rumba musicians) from Matanzas and salute the city's two principal rumba groups—Afrocuba itself and Los Muñequitos de Matanzas—thereby making an implicit assertion regarding the city's reputation as the birthplace of rumba. Ironically, within the montuno section, Afrocuba appropriates the melody for the choral refrain from a traditional rumba refrain dedicated to the capital city. While the original lyrics are "O La Habana, O La Habana," in Afrocuba's version "La Habana" is substituted by "Matanzas." Although not intended by the musicians to allude to the racialized discourses of place attached to these two cities, I believe that the appropriation by a Matanzas group of a refrain associated with Havana problematizes the notion that the former is the originator of all Afro-Cuban culture, which is then appropriated and commercialized by Havana musicians.

Havana as the Geographic Representation of National Hybridity

While Matanzas is represented as the principal site of Afro-Cuban tradition, I would argue that Havana is constructed as the cosmopolitan capital where Cuban modernity is located and where musical innovation and fusion take place.[15] Contemporary Havana has in fact been the locus for the creative appropriation of jazz, rock, hip-hop, and other musical practices in the Americas, as well as the site of important innovations within rumba performance. In terms of discourses of place, Havana is often associated with racial hybridity, a trope undergirded by several historical factors: the capital was both the seat of the Spanish colonial authority and a major site for the concentration of free people of color.[16] This presents a contrast with the history of Matanzas, which in 1877 was the only province in Cuba in which the slave population outnumbered the free population of color (Scott 2000, 261). Historian Louis Pérez highlights the relative prosperity of free people of color in mid-nineteenth-century Havana, noting that they could be found in almost every occupational category in the professions and skilled trades (2006, 70). After emancipation, former slaves migrated en masse to the cities, particularly Havana, which resulted in even greater racial hybridity among the population.

In terms of the national imaginary, Havana—as the capital—is assumed to represent Cuba in many ways. Assertions of racial and cultural hybridity have been the cornerstone of nationalist discourse throughout the twentieth century irrespective of the distinct political orientations of different governments, and Havana's demographic makeup is generally thought to mirror these notions of national race mixture. Whereas other provinces of the country are often racially coded as black (Matanzas, Santiago) or white (Camagüey, Pinar del Río), Havana stands in for the racially hybrid nation.[17] While the capital is able to resist binary racial classification, the constituent elements that make up the hybrid nation must also be emplaced and "come from" somewhere within the country. As the primary locus for Cuba's slave-driven sugar economy, Matanzas represents Cuba's "pure" African past—as opposed to Oriente, which is also discursively blackened but linked to a more hybrid blackness due to the historical presence not only of various African groups but of Afro-Caribbean and indigenous peoples.[18] Conversely, Cuba's Spanish past is often discursively emplaced in the rural province of Pinar del Río, even though, as discussed in previous chapters, there are substantial white populations in other regions and a relatively high proportion of blacks (not including mulatos) in Pinar del Río.[19] This discursive mapping of Cuba's racial ancestry onto different regions of the country leads me to suggest that while Havana's identity as the racially hybrid capital allows it to escape rigid categorization, the rest of the country tends to be essentialized in racial, cultural, and/or class terms.

"Para Gozar, La Habana," the song by Havana rumba group Clave y Guaguancó that was discussed in chapter 2 in relation to its assertions of regionalist sentiment, provides a good illustration of the discourses of place that help construct Havana as the seat of racial and cultural hybridity. Following is the first verse of the song's canto (narrative) section.[20]

La Habana tiene un sabor muy difícil de igualar (2x)	Havana has a flavor that can't be matched (2x)
Es una mezcla Yoruba, del Congo, del Abakuá,	It's a mix of Yoruba, Congo, Abakuá,[21]
del Andaluz, del Gitano y de	of Andalusian,[22] Gypsy and
varias mezclas más (2x)	various other mixtures (2x)
Para gozar, La Habana	To have fun, Havana
Para disfrutar, La Habana	To enjoy yourself, Havana

This ode to Havana references the capital city as the main site of racial mixture on the island, asserting that it is primarily in this way that the capital distinguishes itself from other Cuban cities (and, for that matter, from other cities internationally). The song provides an interesting contrast to the homage to Matanzas discussed above: while the Afrocuba song alludes to both the city's European- and African-derived cultural histories as sources of pride, thus emphasizing two presumably opposite poles on the racial spectrum, the Clave y Guaguancó song celebrates Havana's racial hybridity. I believe that these two songs are representative of the polarized discourses of place that circulate about Havana and Matanzas, respectively. Now I turn to an examination of these racialized tropes of place in music scholarship and within popular discourse among Cuban musicians.

Discourses of Place within Music Scholarship

Lydia Cabrera, the famed Cuban folklorist who made important field recordings in the rural areas of the Matanzas and La Habana Provinces during the 1950s, was instrumental in constructing the polarized discourses of place about Havana and Matanzas. Her work is a clear example of Akhil Gupta and James Ferguson's assertions regarding the ways that ethnographers produce spatialized difference. Cabrera considered Matanzas Province to be the most fruitful for her research and stated, "In no other place as in Matanzas were our inquiries so easy, the African gods that we searched for more accessible, nor in plain light and at all hours were they found so close to man. Going from Havana to Matanzas was for us, in little more than an hour by highway . . . like passing from the 20th century . . . to the 19th century, and feeling like we were more in Cuba than in the capital, naïvely sophisticated with its North American disguises" (Cabrera 1973, 7; my translation). Invoking a discourse of racialized authenticity, Cabrera's ode to Matanzas views Havana as a breeding ground for the introduction of foreign elements and the corruption of an authentic national culture that originates and is maintained in the Matanzas countryside. However, it also sets the stage for the conception of Matanzas as antimodern and irrevocably tied to the past, a trope often invoked by Havana musicians that has certain negative consequences for Matanzas folkloric musicians that I will detail later.

While Cuban scholars (Martínez Rodríguez and González 1977; Vinueza 1986; Ruiz 2003) have been the most strident in upholding the notion that Matanzas is the "cradle of Afro-Cuban culture," foreign scholars have also tended to reify this racialized discourse of tradition and to discuss Havana and Matanzas in binary cultural terms. In *Rumba: Dance and Social Change in Contemporary Cuba* (1995), Yvonne Daniel characterizes Matanzas-style rumba as more "participatory" and "spontaneous" (8) and Havana-based rumba performance as having a more institutional, "prepared" character.[23]

I believe that Daniel's methodological choice to work with the Conjunto Folklórico Nacional (CFN) in Havana, which probably has the most rigid performance criteria of any folkloric group in Cuba, may have led to her distinction between Havana-style rumba as "institutional" and Matanzas-style rumba as "spontaneous."[24] This dichotomy does not accurately depict the current, diverse rumba scenes in Havana and Matanzas. Afrocuba de Matanzas, for example, performs at least as often as most Havana rumba groups in official, state-sponsored venues and has quite a prescribed repertoire. Furthermore, in my experience, common descriptions by musicians about the different sounds of Havana- versus Matanzas-style rumba do not coincide with the polarized characterization offered by Daniel. Matanzas-style rumba is often critiqued by Havana musicians as a conservative style that sounds repetitive as compared with the more improvisatory (or spontaneous) and lively Havana style. Many musicians who prefer the Matanzas style, on the other hand, describe the rhythm, tempo, and dance as *cadencioso* (lilting) or *asentado* (grounded), which they juxtapose with the *corriendo* (running, or too-fast) style of Havana. As evidenced in the previous chapter with respect to rumba in Santiago, this critique of Havana-style rumba is not limited to Matanzas folkloric musicians.

In a brief article addressing racialized discourses of place, ethnomusicologist Katherine Hagedorn analyzes the ways that ritual drummers speak about the respective styles of Yoruba-derived batá drumming in Havana and Matanzas. She does not conceptualize these notions in the terms I use, as racialized discourses of place, but hers is one of the very few academic explorations of discourses of place in relation to different styles of one musical practice.[25] Hagedorn insightfully posits, "Talk about music reveals not only aesthetic preferences and norms of performance practice, but deeply embedded ideologies about identity and territoriality" (2003, 95). Similar to the descriptions I presented above, Hagedorn juxtaposes Matanzas-style ritual drumming— discussed as "laid back and funky" (97)—with the Havana style, characterized as more fast-paced and hybrid in terms of its influence from popular musical styles. Furthermore, she links this "drum talk" to notions of race by highlighting how the slower tempos used in the Matanzas style are taken as evidence of "blacker" and more "authentic" traditions (100). This is a clear example of how musical style in Matanzas comes to discursively represent a closer connection with Africa. Hagedorn thus touches on the discourse of racialized authenticity attached to Matanzas, although her focus is not on interrogating this notion or addressing how the city's racial identity is juxtaposed with that of Havana. My research with rumba and folkloric groups in both Havana and Matanzas leads me to argue for problematizing this discourse of racialized authenticity and for unsettling widely held assumptions about where tradition is "located" and where hybridity "takes place" in Cuba. Whereas Hagedorn identifies these polarized racial tropes, I go a step further in actively challenging them, as I believe that their reification obfuscates the diversity that characterizes the folkloric scenes in both cities.

Discourses of Place within the Popular Domain: Folkloric Musicians' Perspectives

Folkloric musicians in Matanzas and Havana broached several distinct issues related to racialized discourses of place in my interviews and conversations with them. These included questions of rumba's origin and its relation to identity formation, both the cities' discursive identities and individuals' local identities; different attitudes regarding innovation in the two places; place-based ownership of cultural practices; issues of authenticity related to musical style; and the notion that musicians' abilities and limitations are determined (or not) by their place of birth. As my interview questions were not standardized, musicians interpreted this issue in their own way, which revealed a variety of concerns that elucidate the importance of place-based identifications in relation to cultural practices.

I began to conduct research in Matanzas in July 2004 with the explicit goal of working with Afrocuba de Matanzas, an internationally renowned folkloric group famous both for its wide-ranging repertoire in Afro-Cuban sacred and secular practices and for its creation of the rumba hybrid *batarumba*, an innovation that I believe challenges the discourse of tradition surrounding the city. During my interviews and conversations with various members of Afrocuba between 2005 and 2007, I broached the subject of Matanzas's reputation as the "cradle of Afro-Cuban culture." Not surprisingly, all of the musicians felt strongly that the city deserved this distinction, and many referred to the city as the *cuna* (cradle) or *mata* (tree) of many Afro-Cuban religious and musical traditions such as Santería and rumba. Afrocuba founder and longtime director Francisco Zamora Chirino, known to everyone in Cuba's folkloric world as "Minini," commented that Matanzas was the only place in Cuba where several rare African-derived traditions are still conserved, an assertion that is frequently used—by academics as well as musicians—to buttress the "cradle" discourse and notions of racialized authenticity.[26] He further asserted that the group's mission has been to "rescue" African-derived traditions from Matanzas that were being lost. In fact, several scholars—including one of Cuba's most prominent musicologists, María Elena Vinueza—consider

Figure 4.1: Francisco "Minini" Zamora, director of Afrocuba de Matanzas.

Minini to be one of the leading actors in reviving the Arará tradition in Matanzas, which had been "dying out" due to the passing of elders. Minini noted that the primary reason for the loss of rarer traditions was not necessarily a lack of interest on the part of younger generations, but the fact that culture bearers were hesitant to pass on religious secrets to people outside their immediate family. He asserted that the history of persecution by government authorities during much of the twentieth century had created widespread distrust on the part of religious elders, resulting in a culture of secrecy that was hard to penetrate even for Minini, now considered one of Matanzas's best-known cultural ambassadors and tradition bearers.

When we spoke about Matanzas- and Havana-style rumba, Minini seemed to view them as two parallel traditions, that is, with very different styles of performance, and he was careful not to issue an explicit value judgment. However, he also stated that because Havana is the capital and receives more tourists than Matanzas, Havana musicians are more inclined to *inventar*, or make things up, an opinion that is extremely common among Matanzas folkloric musicians.[27] He recounted that whenever Afrocuba performed in Havana, people would come up to him and tell him they had just witnessed "real" rumba. While it is possible to interpret this comment as a way of shifting the responsibility for reinforcing the discourse of authenticity from himself to other people, it is also true that many Cuban rumba aficionados outside Matanzas believe firmly in this "origin story," in part due to the long-standing fame of Los Muñequitos de Matanzas and their role in popularizing rumba in the 1950s. Minini directed explicit critiques not at Havana musicians but at the newer generation of Matanzas rumberos who he feels are trying to imitate Havana-style playing. Then he injected a very suggestive proverb into the conversation, borrowed from José Martí: "Nuestro vino es agrio, pero es *nuestro* vino" (Our wine is sour, but it's *our* wine). I believe that this commentary functioned as a claim of local ownership of cultural practices and a veiled critique of musicians who overstep the limits of place-based identity in performance. Minini reiterated this stance with the phrase "lo mio es lo mio" (what's mine is mine), suggesting that a musician should not attempt to play in a style associated with a different place from where he was born.

One of the most strident arguments for reinforcing the "cradle" notion came from Reinaldo Alfonso García, known as "Wichichi," a well-respected religious elder, percussionist, and veteran member of Afrocuba. During our interview, he attributed the Matanzas "cradle" notion to the province's unique history of slavery and to the breadth of African-derived traditions found there.[28] He expressed the opinion that most folklore practiced in Havana emerged from other provinces, principally Matanzas. Similar to Lydia Cabrera's narrative, Wichichi painted Havana's traditions as culturally derivative, noting that bembé and Arará music could only be "imitations" in Havana since they had not existed there "originally."[29] Alluding to issues of authenticity and revealing his own regionalist-oriented stance (despite his claims to the contrary) vis-à-vis the different styles of rumba played in Matanzas and Havana, Wichichi felt that an objective comparison of the two styles would invariably lead to the conclusion that the latter is a "richer" tradition. He stated:

> It's not because I'm from Matanzas, which I am very proud of, nor because I'm a *regionalista* [roughly translated as someone displaying strong regionalist sentiment], nor because I am very pretentious or think we are the best, and least of all because I'm smug. But he who has the opportunity to listen to what they play in Havana and what they play in Matanzas, even if he is not a knowledgeable listener, will realize that what they play here in Matanzas is richer, is more, how can I explain to you, more pleasing to listen to and to see. . . . Because in Havana they play very fast, running, as if they're in a rush, and many things [in the percussion] cannot be distinguished. And they dance the same way, they dance with the same intensity with which they play and sing. Nevertheless, here in Matanzas we play in a more grounded [slow] way, we sing in a more grounded way, we dance in a more grounded way, the music can be distinguished better, and the rhythm is different.[30]

Figure 4.2: Reinaldo "Wichichi" Alfonso, Afrocuba de Matanzas percussionist.

Finally, like Minini, Wichichi used a metaphor to police the bounds of local identity, asserting, "If we dedicated ourselves to cultivating a style of folkloric music, something that is not ours, we would identify ourselves as habaneros, not as matanceros, we would lose our identity as such."[31] This statement articulates the belief that it is important for matanceros to conserve their identity as separate and distinct from that of Havana, that musical traditions are absolutely constitutive of local identity formation, and that they are owned and should be practiced only by particular people.

Wichichi's statements present a parallel to the assertions made by eastern Cuban musicians and discussed in the previous chapter: in both cases, the non-Havana musicians characterized the capital's folkloric culture as derivative, as nourished by traditions from el campo. Musicians from both places also presented what I view to be aesthetic opinions informed by their regional/local identities, even while disavowing the impact of their place-based affiliations. Wichichi took pains to discursively distance himself from a "regionalist" mindset, all the while arguing that the Matanzas style of playing was "objectively better"; this statement is reminiscent of the assertions made by eastern Cuban musicians about the "richer" nature of folklore oriental. Incidentally, in many ways, these comments conform to a more generalized dichotomy that is often posited between rural and urban musical styles.

As noted by Benjamin Lapidus, this polarized discourse can be found even within one province, Guantánamo: "City dwellers characterize rural changüí performers as less polished and criticize them for being out of tune. Similarly, rurally based performers contend that urban changüiseros play too fast, all of the bongoceros sound the same, and that changüí really comes from the mountains of Yateras and other areas outside the city" (Lapidus 2008, 104). Lapidus's characterization is quite close to the various critiques Havana musicians make about Matanzas-style rumba and vice versa.

Dolores Pérez Herrera, a veteran singer and dancer who retired from Afrocuba in 2004 after thirty-seven years with the group, is part of a large and prestigious family in Matanzas known for its Afro-Cuban religious and cultural knowledge, particularly in the domain of Santería worship. Several members of the family have been core members of Afrocuba and/or Los Muñequitos de Matanzas since the 1970s. When I discussed the "cradle" notion with Dolores, she recalled that during her childhood, "se formaban las rumbas" (rumba parties were started up) for any reason, not necessarily for a special occasion, and people would compose songs spontaneously about the most banal idea or event.[32] Dolores thus felt that her city deserved the distinction of being named the "cradle of Afro-Cuban culture" primarily because of Matanzas's history of spontaneous rumba performance and its ubiquity within the city during the mid-twentieth century. While she conceded that these spontaneous rumbas were a less common occurrence now, she recounted that on special days— such as the eve of December 17, San Lázaro's day[33]—one can still happen upon a rumba party that lasts well into the early hours of the morning. She asserted that in Havana this type of rumba performance does not occur and that habaneros are much more likely to play recorded music at parties, particularly reggaetón, than to play live rumba. Here, Dolores clearly reinforced the binary discourse that characterizes discussions of Havana and Matanzas: habaneros are portrayed as being interested only in the latest popular musical trend, and not in preserving traditional musical practices, while matanceros are represented as traditionalists.

Dolores's husband, Juan García Fernández, is a prominent Havana choreographer who was drawn from the CFN to become Afrocuba's artistic director at a key moment in the group's history, when they were making the transition from rumba group to full-fledged folkloric group in 1980.[34] During my interview with Dolores, Juan entered the house and was eager to offer his perspective on the matter. Although he is from Havana, Juan has spent many years going back and forth between the capital and Matanzas, working with both Afrocuba and the CFN. Like Wichichi, he expressed the opinion that much of Havana's folkloric knowledge is a result of what he termed *préstamos culturales* (cultural loans) from Matanzas. As an example, he stated that celebrated Havana folkloric singer Lázaro Ros—founder of the CFN and considered to be the most important tradition bearer of Yoruba-derived religious song until his death in 2005—came to Matanzas in the 1950s to learn songs from elders knowledgeable in the Santería and Iyesá repertoires. Juan noted, however, that due to the inherently unstable nature of oral transmission, some of the songs' characteristics were changed when Ros returned to Havana and began to perform them. He also talked about the historical cultural and musical exchanges between Havana and Matanzas, stating that men from Matanzas often went to Havana for work in the early twentieth century and that habaneros came to Matanzas and took rumba back to the capital. Thus, he clearly viewed Matanzas as the unequivocal site of origins for rumba and many Afro-Cuban sacred practices, a perspective that might seem "out of place" for a habanero.

One interpretation of Juan's comments is that he prefers to forge a symbolic alliance with Matanzas as a way of representing himself as more authentically black, both in terms of his racial/social identity and his cultural/artistic identity. In other words, Juan may be identifying himself not only with a particular place but with blackness and more broadly with Africa, which are emplaced discursively in Matanzas. It is also possible that Juan's identification with Matanzas-based cultural traditions is evidence that habaneros' allegiances are more flexible, and that there exists a broader difference in identity formation between Havana and Matanzas: while matanceros' views on folkloric music may be more tied to their place of birth and the notions circulating about it, habaneros may feel the freedom to associate themselves with other places and styles at strategic moments and not feel that this entails a loss of identity. I believe that this hypothesis is borne out by certain comments made by Havana-based musicians reproduced below, and that this difference in place-based identity formation may be linked to the spatiality of power relations on the island, an issue I elaborate toward the end of this chapter.

Although there were some divergences among Matanzas-based musicians' perspectives, Havana-based folkloric musicians displayed a wider variety of opinions on the "cradle" notion. Some well-respected Havana rumberos, such as my song and percussion teacher Daniel Rodríguez Morales, agreed wholeheartedly with the notion that Matanzas is the "cradle of Afro-Cuban culture."[35] Daniel attributed much of his musical and religious knowledge to his experiences in Matanzas, and foregrounded not the differences between the cities' traditions but the many connections between the two. Despite the fact that he was one of the few *habaneros puros* (pure-bred Havana natives) that either he or I knew, he did not display a great deal of regionalist sentiment.[36]

Figure 4.3: Daniel Rodríguez, director of Los Ibellis.

He felt that Matanzas deserved the "cradle" title, particularly in relation to rumba and Abakuá, and critiqued the widespread egocentrism, lack of discipline, and tendency to *inventar* in the Havana folkloric scene. Thus, like Juan, despite his identity as a habanero, Daniel felt a certain cultural allegiance to Matanzas, although not to the same extent as Juan. He also reified the common dichotomy that Matanzas-style rumba is about conserving tradition while the Havana style is about drawing from diverse styles and mixing them. However, when speaking about the differences in batá drumming, although Daniel located the origins of the musical practice in Matanzas, he stated that he prefers the Havana style. He made a gendered critique of the Matanzas style, noting that the musicians there often use the bottom of a wooden sandal instead of their fingers to play the *chachá* (the smaller end of the double-headed batá drum), thus displaying a lack of endurance for pain. The Havana style, in other words, represented a more "hard-core," masculine way of playing.

Another Havana musician I interviewed, Gerardo de Arma Sarria, had spent periods of his career in Matanzas performing with rumba and folkloric groups in the resort town of Varadero. He professed deep admiration for Matanzas's folkloric history and cultural identity, stating that his time there had constituted his "schooling" in folklore.[37] Although he expressed his

Figure 4.4: Amado Dedeu, director of Clave y Guaguancó.

preference for Matanzas-style rumba, much like Daniel, he found fault with the Matanzas batá drumming tradition, stating—similar to the descriptions reproduced in Hagedorn's article (2003)—that the musicians played too slowly and took too long to get through the *toques* (rhythms) for the different orishas. These sorts of opinions suggest that the labeling of one style as "original" or "more traditional" does not necessarily translate into greater aesthetic appeal.

Despite the overall respect Havana musicians have for Matanzas folkloric traditions, there were some who disputed the "cradle" trope and the origin stories linking Matanzas with Afro-Cuban culture. Amado Dedeu, longtime director of rumba group Clave y Guaguancó, asserted that this notion was not "historically justified" for a number of reasons relating to the history of slavery in Cuba.[38] He listed several reasons for considering Havana's connections to slavery and colonial African–derived culture to be just as strong as those of Matanzas, including the fact that many African slaves entered Cuba via the port of Havana rather than that of Matanzas and that Havana had a long history of *Día de los Reyes* celebrations.[39] He noted that the majority of the surface area that constitutes the modern city of Havana was *monte* (countryside)

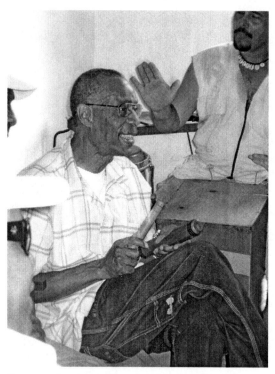

Figure 4.5: Geovani del Pino, director of Yoruba Andabo.

during the nineteenth century and was a sugar zone just like Matanzas. He also offered a challenge to the common perception of a unidirectional flow of cultural influence from Matanzas to Havana, stating that many songs from the *coro de clave* tradition had originated in Havana and were subsequently appropriated by Matanzas-based rumba groups.[40] In general, Amado was hesitant to attribute the origins of Afro-Cuban culture to just one province of the country, noting that Pinar del Río and the eastern provinces also have long-standing African-derived traditions. He asserted that the "cradle" notion is not an official one and was probably invented by a writer or journalist, after which people began to reproduce it. He likened it to a "slogan," utilized as an authenticating marketing term (possibly to attract a foreign audience), rather than a notion based on historical truth.

Geovani del Pino Rodríguez, director of the popular Havana rumba group Yoruba Andabo, offered a different, more philosophical perspective than the other musicians I interviewed regarding the "cradle" notion and all its implications. He acknowledged differences in playing style between Havana- and Matanzas-style rumba and, like Amado, asserted that each region has its own distinctive traditions.[41] He stated, "La cuna de la cultura cubana es Cuba" (The cradle of Cuban culture is Cuba) and, much like an ethnomusicologist, questioned the need to assert ownership over Afro-Cuban cultural traditions. He also called into question the common perception that Matanzas groups are still playing traditional rumba, noting that even Los Muñequitos de Matanzas do not play rumba in the same style as before, an issue I address in more detail below. However, notwithstanding Geovani's rather neutral views concerning the "cradle" notion and the discursive polarization of Havana and Matanzas, a regionalist perspective surfaced when he discussed the difference between Afro-Cuban folklore in western and eastern Cuba. He asserted that western Cuba possesses a more "developed" and "conserved" Afro-Cuban culture, while eastern Cuban African-derived traditions display more influences from other parts of the Caribbean such as Haiti, France, and Jamaica, and were thus "already hybrid." What Geovani ultimately seemed to be positing was a binary cultural discourse not between Havana and Matanzas, but between western and eastern Cuba; western Cuba, instead of Matanzas, was the "cradle of Afro-Cuban culture," as compared to the more hybrid expressive practices deriving from Oriente.

Finally, an interesting perspective was offered during my interview with Ronald González, one of the most popular and well-known rumba singers of the new millennium. As mentioned in chapter 3, Ronald occupies a unique position for the following reasons: he was a member for three years of Los Muñequitos de Matanzas; he is currently a member of Yoruba Andabo, one of the two rumba groups that most embodies Havana-style rumba; and he hails from neither city, but from Santiago, not considered to be an important place for rumba performance. Because Ronald's regional identity was not linked to either Havana or Matanzas, he had no emotional attachment to the debate concerning the origins of rumba or the virtues of its different styles, and he felt that he could provide a more neutral perspective.[42] He asserted that he felt comfortable performing both styles of rumba and could see both the merits and the weaknesses of the different regionally influenced critiques: while matanceros often felt that habaneros were always *inventando*, habaneros often expressed the opinion that Matanzas-style rumba was boring because they always played *lo mismo* (the same thing). Considering the widespread marginalization of eastern Cubans in Havana and other western Cuban cities generally, I find it interesting that Ronald has come to occupy the middle ground in this debate. Furthermore, he is a santiaguero who has proven himself to be a versatile musician, able both to sing well enough in the Matanzas style to be invited to join Los Muñequitos de Matanzas—a prestigious honor and a rare occurrence for an eastern Cuban—and to have enough creative insight to be invited to join Yoruba Andabo, where he has helped forge a new, more hybrid style of rumba singing that is intimately associated with Havana.[43]

Although Ronald recognized the merits of both habaneros' and matanceros' perspectives, like many of the musicians I interviewed, his comments buttressed the "cradle" trope and the polarized cultural discourses attached to both cities. He asserted that Matanzas respects its traditions and that matanceros are not even capable of straying far from traditional playing styles. This essentialist statement illustrates the widespread belief that tradition can actually be found "in the blood" of matanceros and that innovation and change are antithetical to their character. In contrast, he characterized Havana musicians as predisposed to engage in hybridity and fusion practices and to "recoger todo lo que está en el ambiente" (roughly, to soak up everything in their environment). Thus, like Daniel, not only did Ronald posit an essential and fixed difference between musicians from Havana and Matanzas, he also suggested that the former usually engage in an indiscriminate sort of fusion, an issue I address in chapter 5.

There were some clear differences among Havana musicians regarding the "cradle" notion, the question of where rumba originated, personal preferences in playing style, notions of authenticity, and the relationship of cultural practices to local identity formation. Juan seemed to overwhelmingly prefer Matanzas playing styles, which he felt were closer to African antecedents and thus more authentic; he fully endorsed the "cradle" discourse. Daniel and Gerardo also buttressed this racialized discourse of authenticity, presenting Matanzas as a sort of "school" of folklore; however, they did not prefer all Matanzas playing styles over those of Havana, which suggests that sometimes personal preference has more to do with the style with which musicians are familiar. Amado was the only musician I interviewed who rejected the validity of the "cradle" discourse and all its implications regarding authenticity, and who offered antiessentialist rebuttals to these notions. Geovani offered a neutral perspective, in that he neither endorsed nor critiqued the "cradle" notion, although he replaced the polarized Matanzas-Havana discourse with a dichotomy between eastern and western Cuban traditions. Given the diversity of these perspectives, I cannot generalize much about them. What I can suggest, related to my aforementioned hypothesis, is that Havana musicians display a certain flexibility in terms of their identifications with and opinions about particular playing styles. However, while this flexibility may indicate that Havana musicians are less bound by their local identity vis-à-vis their musical preferences than Matanzas musicians, this lack of rigidity may in fact be very much related to their local identity and the privilege they have, as musicians from the capital, that allows them to "dabble" in different styles.[44]

Rethinking the "Cradle" Trope and Polarized Discourses of Place

The Relationship between Racialized Discourses of Place and Claims of Authenticity

In many cases, the perspectives and opinions expressed to me about the "cradle" trope are illustrative of Michael Watts's notion of a "territorialization of history"—in this case, a "territorialization" of expressive practices—where the linking of a particular place (Matanzas) with various musical traditions (rumba, bembé, Arará) serves to authenticate the specific performance style with which that person aligns him or herself. While the Matanzas musicians asserted a more obvious and uniform discursive territorialization through the reification of the "cradle" trope and the claims that Havana's traditions are culturally derivative, this type of authenticating discourse can also be detected in the claims of many of the Havana musicians. While two Havana musicians issued gendered critiques of the Matanzas style of batá drumming in order to posit the superiority of the Havana style, another musician, Amado, attempted a "reverse" territorialization discourse by highlighting the historical existence of slaves and African-derived culture in the capital. In much the same way that Matanzas-based musicians and scholars invoked the history of plantation slavery as an explanation for its preservation of African-derived culture, he linked Havana's cultural identity to its social history. This tendency suggests that, like Murray Forman's "ghetto authenticity," assertions of regional/local identity are often entangled with the desire or need to claim authenticity in some arena, especially in the realm of expressive practice.

The construction of Matanzas as the "cradle of Afro-Cuban culture" is not only an example of the pervasiveness of racialized tropes of place in Cuba (and elsewhere). This discursive identity also constitutes a claim about the unparalleled cultural authenticity of the city and province of Matanzas within the country. Here I examine the articulation, in Stuart Hall's sense,[45] of two discursive formations embedded in the "cradle" notion: racialized tropes of place and assertions of cultural authenticity. The "cradle" notion is illustrative of the fact that in the minds of many Cubans, foreigners, and scholars, Matanzas is synonymous not only with blackness but with "authentic" blackness. In the article discussed earlier, Katherine Hagedorn states, "Even as late as the 1980s, Matanzas has been coded as more 'African' than Havana" (2003, 99). In fact, I would argue that this association of Matanzas with authentic African-derived culture still enjoys widespread currency in the twenty-first century both in academic scholarship and popular discourse. Owing to this discursive "Africanization" of Matanzas, the city and province have been constructed within the national imaginary as the main site of racially defined tradition. The cultural capital bestowed upon Matanzas musicians owing to the racialized associations of the city is evident in their frequent assertions that Havana musicians are always making things up and introducing foreign elements into Afro-Cuban traditional practices, claims that function to deauthenticate all cultural production from Havana and present it as impure. As will be discussed in chapter 6, the discourse of authentic blackness attached to Matanzas can also be juxtaposed to common racialized perceptions about Oriente, often considered the "blackest" region of the country. The last section of this chapter will explore how these notions of racialized authenticity inform material realities for Matanzas folkloric musicians.

Challenging the "Cradle" Discourse

There are historical explanations that underlie the polarizing cultural discourses circulating about Havana and Matanzas, and that make a good argument for accepting these notions as self-evident truths. Matanzas Province had the largest number of sugar mills, the largest number of slaves on the plantations, and the most diverse combination of African ethnic groups in nineteenth-century Cuba. Given this history, it is logical that the province became the focal point for African-derived religious and musical traditions. Conversely, Havana's population boasted the highest number of free people of color per capita and was the seat of the Spanish colonial administration. Thus, there was bound to be more racial and cultural mixing than in other parts of the country.[46] Furthermore, as the capital, Havana has always been not only the locus of interaction between Cubans and foreigners but also the primary meeting ground for Cubans from different provinces. Notwithstanding these social histories, my fieldwork has alerted me to the many ways that these racialized discourses of place essentialize and fix the cultural identities of these two cities, and how they fail to account for the diverse nature of rumba and folkloric performance in both Havana and Matanzas. I have come across several examples, both in the performance and repertoire of rumba and folkloric groups, and within the literature discussing the histories of different Afro-Cuban cultural practices, that have prompted me to scrutinize these discourses of place.

To begin, many folkloric groups in Havana are actively engaged in the preservation of traditional Afro-Cuban music and dance practices. Yvonne Daniel (1995) states that the Conjunto Folklórico Nacional is prohibited from engaging explicitly in hybridizing practices, a constraint not faced by folkloric groups like Afrocuba de Matanzas that were formed independently of the government.[47] It is precisely my research with Afrocuba that leads me to argue that tradition-bearing activities and hybridizing practices are not mutually exclusive, and consequently that viewing Matanzas and Havana as two poles on the tradition-innovation spectrum constitutes a false dichotomy. Furthermore, as alluded to by Clave y Guaguancó director Amado Dedeu, the capital has a long history of African-derived religious and musical practice that calls into question the notion that Matanzas is the unequivocal source of Afro-Cuban traditions.

Referring to research conducted by Fernando Ortiz, María Teresa Vélez asserts that the first known set of batá drums was manufactured in Havana in 1830 (2000, 53); this fact suggests that the Yoruba-derived drumming tradition was being performed in Havana at least as early as it was being practiced in Matanzas, and possibly earlier.[48] Similarly, while many Cubans consider Matanzas to be the birthplace and center of Abakuá religious practice, it is well documented that Regla, an outlying municipality of Havana, was the site in 1836 of the first Cross River secret society to be formed in Cuba; from there it spread to other parts of the capital and to the port cities of Matanzas and Cárdenas (Vélez 2000; Miller 2009).[49] One further piece of evidence that complicates the notion that Matanzas is the "cradle of Afro-Cuban culture" concerns the history of the religious practice called Arará, which derives from the ancient kingdom of Dahomey in modern-day Benin.[50] It is commonly accepted in Cuban and foreign scholarship that the Arará religion was first practiced in Matanzas Province, and it is currently retained only in a few locales there (Martínez Furé 1979; Vinueza 1989; Delgado 2001). Nonetheless, Rogelio Martínez Furé cites Ortiz's research that found evidence of an Arará cabildo[51] in Havana as early as 1691 (1979, 123), which again suggests that the religion and related musical practice may have just as long a history in the capital as in Matanzas. These three examples of historical research indicate that Matanzas is not *the* "cradle of Afro-Cuban culture" (although it certainly holds a privileged position with respect to the variety and preservation of African-derived traditions), but rather *a* "cradle of Afro-Cuban culture." Instead of continuing to reify this discourse of place, I believe it is more productive to explore why Matanzas has been singled out for this particular distinction and why Matanzas-based musicians might be invested in upholding this notion.

Although it is a discourse that affirms the uniqueness of a particular place, the "cradle" notion also constructs a discursive barrier around the city's creative expression and fails to take into account the multifaceted nature of its musical identity. Innovation is not confined to the city of Havana, a point that is exemplified in fusions such as the Afrocuba creation batarumba. Broadly defined, batarumba is a hybrid practice that fuses rumba rhythms and percussion instruments with rhythms taken from batá drumming.[52] Batarumba was created by various members of Afrocuba in 1973 and since that time has been not only a staple of the group's repertoire but also one of the key musical signifiers of the group's identity. However, the "cradle" notion discursively charges Matanzas with the burden of safeguarding Afro-Cuban sacred and secular traditions, a duty that involves discouraging fusions of any kind. Thus, this trope of place is inherently at odds with, and cannot accommodate, the type of fusion embodied in batarumba.

Batarumba is not the only example of fusion found in Matanzas. One of the sons of well-respected rumbera and Santería priestess Ana Pérez Herrera,[53] with whom I became very close during my fieldwork, is a percussionist working in a professional modern dance company, Danza Espiral. The company's pieces mix diverse genres, utilizing a combination of recorded instrumental music and live Afro-Cuban drumming as accompaniment for modern dance choreography. In addition to the innovative spirit that is perhaps as native to Matanzas as it is to Havana, it is important to note that the former is not a hermetically sealed locale severed from the current trends within popular music that have taken hold across the island. Afro-Cuban folkloric music and dance is not the only form of creative expression performed or enjoyed by matanceros. As in every other city and town in Cuba, people of all ages love listening and dancing to timba, and the youth love reggaetón. In fact, several of the younger members of Los Muñequitos de Matanzas have founded a group in recent years called Rumba Timba, in which they mix rumba singing and percussion with musical elements from timba and reggaetón. This phenomenon indicates that rumba performance is being influenced by elements of popular music and style, and that rumba and timba are being reciprocally nourished by each other.

A recent interview with Rogelio Martínez Furé, a matancero by birth, constitutes yet another challenge to the purity discourse entailed in the "cradle" notion. Martínez Furé was asked on the fortieth anniversary of the establishment of the CFN (an institution he helped found), how his identity as a Matanzas native had influenced his formation as a folklorist. Surprisingly, he spoke of his native city not as the "cradle of Afro-Cuban culture" but as a cosmopolitan and racially hybrid place, asserting that all the major ethnic components that make up Cuban identity were represented in Matanzas. In addition to the four major African ethnic groups brought to Cuba during slavery (Yoruba, Bantu, Calabar, and Dahomey), Martínez Furé listed many non-African ethnic groups who coexisted in Matanzas during his childhood—Galicians, Dominicans, Chinese, Mexicans, Catalans, Jamaicans, other Caribbeans, and North Americans (2004, 179).[54] Martínez Furé noted that his own ancestry included Mandinga, French, Spanish, Chinese, and probably some sort of indigenous blood if one looked back many generations, stating, "I neither came from Spain, nor was I brought from Africa, but rather I am a native Cuban just like the royal palms" (2004, 179; my translation). He summed up with a description of his native city that is reminiscent of ways that Havana is often discussed: "Matanzas's culture is a perfect example of national identity, 'many and one' as Aimé Césaire would say, original and one of a kind, where the erudite and the popular . . . have been fused into a synthesis, which has permitted us to always be open to the world without forgetting where we came from, and above all, fully accepting who we already are" (2004, 179; my translation).

As a final illustration of the problematic nature of the "cradle" trope, I present a brief discussion of Los Muñequitos de Matanzas, a group that has functioned as the international emblem for *rumba matancera* (Matanzas-style rumba), and has represented Cuban rumba in general, for over fifty years. Given the group's universally acknowledged status as the embodiment of traditional rumba, it is useful to explore the opinions of Matanzas and Havana folkloric musicians regarding Los Muñequitos' current playing style. Specifically, I aim to question whether the discourse of tradition surrounding this emblematic group does justice to, or even accurately describes, the music they presently perform. In our interview, former Afrocuba artistic director Juan García asserted that Los Muñequitos have never actually played in the traditional style, even when they emerged and became popular in the 1950s. He stated that the group has always had its own signature style that differs in many ways from traditional rumba matancera, which he feels has been more faithfully represented by Afrocuba. Juan's comments could be viewed as biased, given his long-standing artistic association with Afrocuba and as evidence of a certain level of competition that does in fact exist between the two famed Matanzas groups, despite their many familial connections. However, if I compare recent rumba performances by both Matanzas-based groups, I would agree that Afrocuba plays rumba in a more traditional style, partially owing to recent stylistic changes by Los Muñequitos that I describe below.

Further problematizing the association of Los Muñequitos with traditional rumba matancera, Cuban musicologist Nancy Grasso González (1989) presents biographical information about the group suggesting that the original intentions in founding Los Muñequitos had as much to do with commercial interests as with preserving and/or representing a traditional practice. She asserts that the group was actually founded by a businessman/producer along with one of the founding members in 1952, and that its main objective was to record albums and radio programs. The amusing name Los Muñequitos de

Matanzas, which translates to "the Comic Strips from Matanzas," was not even self-ascribed: the group's original name was Guaguancó Matancero (Matanzas-style Guaguancó), but it was unofficially renamed by the Havana public after their song "Los Muñequitos de Matanzas" gained widespread popularity in the 1950s.[55] Thereafter, the group adopted this name (Grasso González 1989, 44). These biographical details illustrate that, despite the discourse of tradition that circulates widely about Los Muñequitos, the group's initial success was mediated by their ties to commercial actors and the opportunities they were given in terms of dissemination through recordings and the radio.

Turning to the issue of musical style, despite the normative narratives within published scholarship and tourist-oriented publicity accounts, it is widely believed in both Havana and Matanzas that Los Muñequitos are no longer playing like they used to. Many believe that they are shedding the "essence" of their signature style, particularly with regard to singing. The legendary duo of Esteban Lantriz and Hortensio Alfonso, famously known as "Saldiguera" and "Virulilla," respectively, revolutionized rumba vocals in the 1950s,[56] creating an unmistakable style that split up the soloist role into three parts: one vocalist would sing the introductory *diana* section, two different vocalists would sing the *canto* section (the body or narrative of the song) in a harmonized duet, and the first singer would return as the improvising soloist for the *montuno* (call-and-response) section.[57] This singing format is still largely retained not only in Los Muñequitos' performances but also in the majority of Afrocuba de Matanzas's rumba songs and even some of Havana-based Yoruba Andabo's songs. Nevertheless, in recent years younger singers have joined Los Muñequitos and seem eager to integrate elements of popular music into their style; the formation of the aforementioned fusion group Rumba Timba illustrates this desire for innovation. Incidentally, former Los Muñequitos singer Ronald González stated in our interview that traditionally the group never had young singers; the younger members were either percussionists or dancers, but it was always *los mayores* (the elders) who sang (pers. comm. 2007).

Judging from the group's performances I witnessed between 2006 and 2008, the percussion style is changing as well. While often starting songs in a more "traditional" style, during the montuno section Los Muñequitos engages in several "breakdowns" or stop-time sections during which the conga drums drop out, leaving only the singers and idiophones (*claves*, *catá*, and *shékere*),[58] and the musicians encourage audience participation through clapping. I had an opportunity to witness further changes when the group toured the United States in 2011 (their first US tour since 2002). The show included not only rumba and Santería numbers but also an extended rumba–tap dance fusion in which an American tap dancer joined two younger Los Muñequitos dancers onstage. In addition, Jon Pareles's review of the concert states that the singers "paid tribute to New York City, briefly singing the hook of [rapper] Jay-Z's 'Empire State of Mind'" (*New York Times*, May 8, 2011). All these musical changes suggest that Los Muñequitos' recent style has been influenced by a number of popular trends in the United States and Cuba: tap dance, hip-hop, and innovations associated with the contemporary Havana style of rumba percussion called guarapachangueo, which I discuss in detail in chapter 5.

These anecdotes, taken from published scholarship and my fieldwork, suggest that the "cradle" notion should be taken with a grain of salt and understood more as a strategic deployment of a discourse of authenticity by various actors for various reasons, rather than as an accurate reflection of the current musical/cultural scene in Matanzas.

Racialized Discourses of Place, the Politics of Location, and Strategic Essentialism

Throughout this chapter I have been alluding to the material effects of discursive formations such as the "cradle of Afro-Cuban culture." Taking my cue from Donald Moore's analysis of spatiality and power relations in Zimbabwe and Jacqueline Nassy Brown's discussion of place as an axis of power in Liverpool, here I discuss the ways that the "cradle" trope may constitute an attempt by Matanzas musicians to position themselves at the center of a cultural tourism industry focused on Afro-Cuban music, dance, and religious practice. I believe that it is crucial for local musicians to assert the cultural significance of their city in the face of its lack of visibility within the national tourism industry.

Matanzas is a small city, presenting a major contrast to the sprawling and seemingly endless geography of Havana. In addition, the city has almost no tourism infrastructure to speak of, which negatively impacts cultural performance and musicians' livelihoods. For most foreigners, Matanzas city is merely a stop on the bus line from Havana to Varadero, the island's most famous beach resort, located twenty-two miles northeast of Matanzas. The city is currently characterized by a rather depressing restaurant and nightlife scene and a striking lack of tourist-oriented amenities; for example, during the three months I spent conducting research there in early 2007, both of the city's hotels were closed for repairs and only one of them has since reopened. While Matanzas's folkloric scene is internationally renowned and foreigners come somewhat regularly for religious purposes or to take lessons with members of Afrocuba or Los Muñequitos, local musicians often experience periods of tourist drought and, consequently, economic hardship. Some musicians have suggested that Matanzas's lack of restaurants and entertainment venues is related to its proximity to Varadero; they feel that the state has made a decision not to invest in Matanzas, preferring to focus its energy and resources on the nearby beach resort. Historian Miguel Bretos's analysis of the city's economic decline in the twentieth century also foregrounds location, noting that the city is "[c]lose enough to Havana to preclude its becoming an important regional hub" (2010, 194). In my experience, matanceros enjoy a better standard of living than many Havana residents due to the relative lack of overcrowding, pollution, and crime. Nevertheless, a better standard of living does not necessarily translate into more material wealth. Even the musicians and dancers of Afrocuba de Matanzas, who during my fieldwork period performed a bimonthly gig in one of the Varadero hotels for which they were paid in dollars, rarely had more than a few dollars in their pockets at any given time.

Jacqueline Nassy Brown discusses how place can be an axis of power relations, and her analysis works well for examining the situation of Matanzas in the era of cultural tourism. She states, "Why does place matter? What is Liverpool remote from? Liverpool's marginality owes not to its geographic location—for example, as a seaport that lost its competitive edge to other ports. Rather, that marginality owes to Liverpool's *historical* dislocation. The postcolonial subjectivity expressed in Liverpool autobiographies refers to the insuperable loss of the city's stature as the producer of global, nay imperial, economic relationships" (2005, 133). Matanzas is close to Havana—a little over an hour by car—and thus, like Liverpool, does not really suffer from geographical dislocation. Rather, it too has been historically/temporally dislocated: the riches produced from plantation slavery built Matanzas into one of the most important cities on the island, but it has been steadily declining for more than a century.

It seems apparent when considering the opinions of the musicians I interviewed that Matanzas-based folkloric musicians are more invested in reinforcing the racialized discourse of place attached to their city than are Havana-based musicians in overturning it. I believe that there is much at stake for Matanzas-based musicians in maintaining their identity as the "originators" of Afro-Cuban religious and musical practices via the "cradle" trope, for it is in many ways the only thing that sets Matanzas apart and draws tourists to the city. Havana rumba musicians are in constant contact with foreigners and tourists, many of whom do not travel beyond the capital. Matanzas, in contrast, has a weak tourism infrastructure that does not offer much to foreigners beyond those who go there specifically for religious purposes or to take percussion or dance lessons. Without a steady stream of tourists traveling to Matanzas, local musicians have less opportunity than their Havana counterparts to earn supplemental income in *divisa* (hard currency, namely dollars) and often experience periods of economic drought. One effect of the lack of a tourism industry is that, as I have discussed elsewhere (Bodenheimer 2013), despite Matanzas's reputation as "la mata de la rumba" (the birthplace of rumba), there are currently no regularly occurring rumba events in the city. This presents a major contrast to the situation in Havana, where one can attend rumba shows in various venues several times a week. Thus, provincial cultural officials are not even exploiting the treasure trove of folkloric resources living in Matanzas; if rumba were presented more often, it is likely that more tourists would travel to the city. Matanzas musicians, then, fall victim to the politics of location vis-à-vis the tourism industry because of the geographically uneven ways in which the state has invested in this sector.

My previous discussion of the flexibility of Havana musicians' allegiances and musical tastes also relates to this relative disempowerment of Matanzas-based musicians. Because Havana occupies a hegemonic status on the island, specifically in terms of the tourism industry, its musicians may feel that they can take more license and experiment with different styles. Musicians from smaller locales do not have this option, as their local traditions are the primary signifiers that allow them to claim a distinctive cultural identity. In other words, musicians from Havana likely do not feel obliged to "defend" a cultural heritage that already has much influence throughout Cuba and abroad. On the other hand, the stakes are higher for Matanzas musicians in terms of reinforcing the "cradle" notion, as it provides them with a unique local identity. Furthermore, it is not improbable that local musicians are engaging in tactics of strategic essentialism in the hopes of attracting foreign students to their city to supplement their meager state salaries. In other words, I don't believe most Matanzas musicians would care to be thought of in limited, essentialized terms as merely traditionalists, but the strategic deployment of this cultural capital could translate into much-needed economic capital.

Conclusion

In *Nationalists, Cosmopolitans, and Popular Music in Zimbabwe*, ethnomusicologist Thomas Turino states, "The tension here between the financial benefits of translocalism versus the artistic value of being rooted in a place and its lifeways provides a concrete microcosm of tensions defining Zimbabwean identities and music much more broadly" (2000, 92). In a similar vein, I view the "historical dislocation" and economic isolation of Matanzas as the hidden side of the double-edged sword that is entailed in being known as "the cradle of Afro-Cuban culture." As I discussed above, Havana musicians tend to consider their "country cousins in Matanzas" (Hagedorn 2003, 101) to be conservative and even "boring" in their approach to music making. This statement perfectly elucidates the ways that carrying the label of "traditional" or "authentic" does not result in uniformly enhanced social power, and sometimes translates into economic marginalization. At a time when the national expansion of the tourism industry has created competition for foreign dollars among cultural workers, racialized discourses of place and related claims of authenticity heavily impact the livelihoods of folkloric musicians in different ways. They can lead to more opportunities for Matanzas musicians through the reification of the notion that in order to gain true, deep knowledge of an Afro-Cuban religious or musical tradition, foreigners must study with Matanzas musicians. At the same time, foreigners interested in Afro-Cuban music and religion are a small minority of those who travel to the island. The orientation of the "cradle" trope toward an imagined African past—or, for that matter, an imagined European-derived past glory via the "Athens" nickname—rather than a hybrid present and future (represented by Havana), threatens to render Matanzas and its expressive practices obsolete. Furthermore, the lack of any systematic tourist infrastructure in Matanzas—working hotels and a wealth of dining and entertainment options—means that foreigners' visits will continue to be few and far between.

Beyond the material implications of racialized discourses of place, I want to emphasize that my intention in problematizing the naturalized link between Matanzas and racially defined tradition has not been to completely overturn the "cradle" notion or to suggest that it is not based on real, historical phenomena. Instead, my aim has been to illustrate how it essentializes the cultural identity of a city that in fact has a history of musical innovation within diverse genres, and to counter the assumption that one cannot find "authentic" Afro-Cuban folkloric representations in other places on the island. Matanzas *was* a focal point for plantation slavery and the preservation of various African-derived practices in the nineteenth century, and this history has left a strong cultural legacy. However, as evidenced by the flowering of European culture in the mid-nineteenth century, this is not Matanzas's only cultural legacy. Furthermore, as illustrated by the anecdotes about Havana's history, Matanzas is not the only place with a long history of Afro-Cuban cultural expression.

Finally, notwithstanding the important impacts of cultural tourism, representing their city as the "cradle of Afro-Cuban culture" is not only an economic concern for Matanzas musicians. As they suggested in their interviews, their city and province's identity as the birthplace of many African-derived cultural traditions is profoundly intertwined with their own sense of self and their desire to proclaim a distinct local and provincial identity within Cuba. The "spatiality of identity" (Mitchell 2000) is a powerful force that is often entangled with discourses of authenticity. As I mentioned in chapter 1, matanceros often distinguish themselves from habaneros in terms that allude to authenticity: they see themselves as more "genuine" and "down to earth" and not as interested in material consumption and external appearances. Seen in this light, the "cradle" notion and racialized tropes of authenticity attached to Matanzas can be viewed as an extension of the musicians' individual and community identity formation. As such, it is unlikely that local musicians will disavow this discourse of place anytime in the foreseeable future.

Chapter Five

Localizing Hybridity

In the preceding chapters, I have elucidated the politics of place in detail, highlighting the pervasive influence of regionalism on social relations among Cubans and on Cuban popular music. I have also examined the ways that racialized discourses of place both impact folkloric musicians' material realities, and are in many ways constitutive of regional and/or local identity formation. This chapter constitutes another exploration of the ways that discourses of place and local identity inform musical performance, here focusing on the issue of innovation in rumba performance. I detail two important rumba hybridizing practices that have emerged in the past three decades, one associated with Matanzas and the other linked to Havana.[1] The first hybridizing practice I investigate is the creation of a rumba fusion called *batarumba* by the folkloric group Afrocuba de Matanzas. Batarumba fuses Yoruba-derived batá drumming with secular rumba rhythms, creating an especially dense polyrhythmic texture. The second hybridizing practice is an innovation in rumba percussion and performance style called *guarapachangueo*, which was created during the 1970s on the outskirts of Havana and disseminated in the capital in the following decade. This relatively free-form approach to percussion playing has revolutionized Havana-style rumba, particularly rumba guaguancó, to such an extent that it is now rare to hear local groups playing the traditional interlocking conga drum rhythm that has functioned for so long as rumba's primary sonic signifier. While the chapter focuses on batarumba and guarapachangueo, I will also briefly discuss other rumba hybridizing practices in both cities.[2]

In speaking about hybridizing practices, I wish to problematize the acritical celebrations of hybridity that have been hegemonic in Caribbean and Latin American nationalist discourses since the nineteenth century, and that have become fashionable in Euro-American academic and popular arenas since the explosion of the "world music" phenomenon in the early 1990s. Thus, my analysis of the particular, locally defined musical hybridizations emerging respectively from Havana and Matanzas employs Stuart Hall's notion of *situated hybridity*, which views hybrid identities as anchored in a particular place and time. I argue that the rumba innovations are specific—in the sense that musicians make particular choices about which genres to fuse—and situated, in the sense that they are informed strongly by the social and cultural histories of the locales from which they emerge. Furthermore, I view batarumba and guarapachangueo as illustrative of the different approaches toward rumba-based fusion in Havana and Matanzas, respectively, and will elucidate how the racialized discourses of place discussed in chapter 4 inform local hybridizing practices.

As I discussed in the introduction, mestizaje (or racial mixture) has been the conceptual centerpiece of Latin American nationalist discourses—in different forms and to different degrees—since the nineteenth century. I detailed the problematic celebration of hybridity within Cuban nationalist discourse throughout the nation's history, noting in particular the gap between the rhetoric of racial equality and the reality of inequality that Afro-Cubans still face in contemporary Cuba. In sum, while the goal of the nationalist hybridity discourse (at least as imagined by José Martí) was to present a more inclusive conception of Cubanidad, it has also functioned to maintain certain colonial structural conditions in the postcolonial context by denying the racialization of access to political power, and to economic and land resources.[3] Given this history, to reify a depoliticized and celebratory conceptualization of hybridity would be, in my mind, to endorse the use of nationalist hybridity discourses to deny the material effects that racialized notions of difference have had on Cubans of African descent. The current situation of Afro-Cuban folkloric music exemplifies the tension inherent in the gap between the discursive celebration of hybridity as racial equality, and the lived realities of inequality that black citizens confront in contemporary Cuba. For example, rumba is still a highly racialized practice that, despite its incorporation into the nation's "folklore," is marginalized due to its continuing association with blackness and el bajo mundo (the "underworld") (Bodenheimer 2013).

Ethnomusicologist Timothy Taylor scrutinizes the use of the term "hybridity" as found in discussions of the world music phenomenon of the past few decades, particularly as it has been utilized by the music industry to categorize music recorded by non-Western artists. He states, "Thus hybridity has become a marketing term, a way of identifying, commodifying, and selling what on the surface is a new form of difference, but one that reproduces old prejudices and hegemonies. . . . [N]onwestern musicians who make world musics are still consigned to the Other, 'savage slot' [while their Western collaborators like Paul Simon and Peter Gabriel are marketed as rock]" (Taylor 2007, 143). Taylor also discusses the ways that perceptions of authenticity have shifted in the wake of the world music phenomenon, such that hybrid world musics are now understood as "authentic" (as long as they do not incorporate too much Western influence) rather than impure or tainted by contact with the West: "World musicians may not be expected to be authentic anymore in the sense of being untouched by the sounds of the West; now it is their very hybridity that allows them to be constructed as authentic" (144). In fact, as Taylor notes, it is not the most "unadulterated" forms of non-Western music that are commercially successful—after all, field recordings and the like are purchased only by a limited number of aficionados and/or scholars—but rather, precisely those hybrids that can be intelligible and aesthetically pleasing to substantial numbers of Western listeners. Paradoxically, then, discourses of hybridity can often function as discourses of authenticity in disguise, a phenomenon that, as will be evident in this chapter, I have also come across in my research on rumba hybrids.

Donald Moore borrows postcolonial scholar Dipesh Chakrabarty's notion of "provincializing Europe"—which critiques the assumption that European modernity has a natural claim to "Universal History and Reason"—for his own metaphor of "provincializing governmentality." Moore's Foucaultian notion "suggests a spatial mode of analysis—an emphasis on the production of scale, of a politics of location, of power geometries and geographical imaginaries" (D. Moore 2005, 12). Following Chakrabarty and Moore, my study aims to "provincialize" hybridity by foregrounding how rumba musicians in Havana and Matanzas engage in fusion practices in distinct and locally specific ways. To accomplish this, my analysis of rumba hybridizing practices draws on Stuart Hall's alternative theorization of hybridity: "I think cultural identity is not fixed, it's always hybrid. But this is precisely because it comes out of very specific historical formations, out of very specific histories and cultural repertoires of enunciation, that it can constitute a 'positionality,' which we call, provisionally, identity. It's not just anything" (Chen 1996, 502). Jocelyne Guilbault makes a similar point in the context of the French Caribbean, stating, "*Métissage* [creolization], I want to stress, happens selectively. It is precisely what is being combined and how a so-called hybridized music like *zouk* maintains itself as a signifying system that makes a fusion process and product unique" (1994, 175). I hope to illustrate that recent innovations in rumba performance constitute precisely this type of situated, specific hybridity, in that they are informed greatly by the cultural histories of and racialized discourses attached to the locales from which they emerge. I thus argue that rumba fusions are illustrative of the entangled relationship between local identity formation, racialized discourses of place, and musical hybridizing practices.

Hybridizing Practices in Matanzas-Style Rumba

Batarumba

One of the most influential innovations to come out of the Matanzas rumba scene since the revolution is batarumba, a hybrid created by Afrocuba de Matanzas in 1973, sixteen years after the group's emergence. Batarumba marked the group's identity to such an extent that it inspired a temporary name change to Afrocuba con su Ritmo Batarumba (Afrocuba with its Batarumba Rhythm). In concise terms, batarumba is a fusion of rumba percussion and rhythms, particularly rumba guaguancó, with Yoruba-derived batá drumming, used to accompany worship in the Lucumí religion (popularly known as Santería). Afrocuba director Francisco "Minini" Zamora described the combination as "revolutionary" because, until this innovation, batá drums had only been used in ceremonial contexts (pers. comm. 2007).[4] Although there have been other rumba groups who have performed and recorded fusions under the name batarumba, it is commonly acknowledged that Afrocuba had the original idea, and the style is uniquely associated with the group.[5] Minini asserted that batarumba emerged from the musicians' desire to create a new sound within rumba performance, and to differentiate their style from that of other rumba groups in Matanzas. The oft-quoted definition of batarumba in the few published sources in which it is mentioned describes it as a rhythmic innovation that fuses the guaguancó rhythm with the most popular and "all-purpose" batá drum *toque* (rhythm) in the Lucumí pantheon, *chachalokofún*.[6] Unlike most batá rhythms, this one can be utilized in Santería ceremonies to play for every orisha, and it is often placed at the end of a song due to its upbeat and infectious rhythmic matrix that impels worshippers to dance and the orishas to "come down" and mount a practitioner. Katherine Hagedorn states of the rhythm, "The *chachalokofún* rhythm can be played for any *oricha* as a 'breakout' dance section (imagine that a *toque* is becoming too stayed, too reserved, and that the drummers want more audience participation—*chachalokofún* is the rhythm that makes people get up and dance)" (2001, 124).

The aforementioned definition of batarumba has circulated widely, particularly in places like the United States where the innovation might be taught to a student of rumba. For example, Kenneth Schweitzer states, "In this style, a *batá* toque like chachalekefon is juxtaposed over the tres golpes rhythm that defines the medium-tempo rumba, guaguancó" (2003, 157). Nonetheless, through my extensive fieldwork with Afrocuba, I have come to believe that a more nuanced definition is needed to describe this complex innovation. Batarumba does not necessarily entail a particular combination of rumba

Figure 5.1: Afrocuba de Matanzas *batarumba* ensemble. The percussionists playing the conga drums usually sit behind the *batá* drummers. The *campana* can be partially seen at the far left of this image, and the *bombo* drum is not visible.

and batá rhythms, for in many of Afrocuba's songs, either the guaguancó or chachalokofún rhythms, or both, are replaced by other rhythms, some of which have been invented by Afrocuba percussionists. In his explanations during Afrocuba performances, Minini has often stated that batarumba is basically the union of batá drums with *tumbadoras* (conga drums), thus defining it as a particular instrumental ensemble (see figure 5.1)[7] rather than a particular rhythm; as will be evident in the musical analysis below, some of these rhythms are even borrowed from other (non-Yoruba) Afro-Cuban religious traditions. Furthermore, batarumba also involves percussion instruments from other genres, specifically the *bombo* drum (roughly corresponding to the bass or tom-tom in a standard drum set) and *campana* (cowbell), both of which are used in *comparsa* (carnival music). Finally, several batarumba songs are appropriated from the repertoire of "the queen of salsa," Celia Cruz, an issue I address later in the chapter.

Pedro "Pello" Tápanes, a founder of Guaguancó Neopoblano (Afrocuba's original name) who retired in 2003, is the percussionist most closely associated with the creation of batarumba. Although most people attribute the innovation to him, Pello credited Hector Alfonso, a founder of the group and former dancer, with the idea of uniting rumba and batá percussion and rhythms (pers. comm. 2007). In fact, Pello asserted that he originally doubted whether this innovation would be successful and worried that introducing the batá drums into a secular genre might be viewed by religious elders as profaning the Lucumí religion. Nonetheless, the group began to experiment with different rhythmic combinations, the first of which was indeed the fusion of guaguancó with chachalokofún, and with the Iyesá rhythm. Like chachalokofún, Iyesá is a highly danceable rhythm originating from the Iyesá culture and religion, a subgroup of the Yoruba/Lucumí whose traditions are currently maintained only in Matanzas.[8] Pello stated that while guaguancó was used in most songs, the batá rhythm varied according to the song. Dolores Pérez, a veteran Afrocuba singer who retired in 2004, is also associated strongly with batarumba, because her songs have been most prominently featured on commercial recordings.[9] She added that it is not only the batá rhythms that vary from song to song but also the point in the song where the guaguancó rhythm is introduced, which is not always at the beginning (pers. comm. 2007). Finally, Afrocuba percussionist Reinaldo "Wichichi" Alfonso described the process of creating batarumbas as "una ensalada mixta" (a mixed salad), in which the percussionists look for different polyrhythmic combinations that fit well together for each song (pers. comm. 2007).

Afrocuba director Minini characterized the original batarumba rhythm as "rudimentary" in that it was basically the fusion of guaguancó with chachalokofún (introduced in the montuno or call-and-response section); this combination was meant to encourage the audience to dance. However, he emphasized that batarumba kept evolving and becoming more complex throughout the 1970s and 1980s, to the point that the pieces came to be like "compositions": specific rhythms were inserted to fit with the particular songs, and different rhythms—such as those for the orishas Obbatalá, Changó, or Ochún—were used in different sections of any one song. As an indication of the variety that characterizes the group's batarumba repertoire, Minini noted that songs can begin with a certain batá rhythm, a traditional guaguancó, or a rhythm that the group has invented, which he characterized as *bolereado* (bolero-derived) or *soneado* (son-derived).[10] While he stressed that each batarumba has a distinct rhythmic configuration, he generalized that all have *cierres* (stop-time sections) and that chachalokofún is generally played at some point in the song but that guaguancó was not a feature of all songs. Thus, Minini's characterization of the general rhythmic features of batarumba was not entirely consistent with the descriptions given by other veteran members of Afrocuba, specifically Pello. However, all of them presented the innovation as more complex than the simplified notion that it is the combination of chachalokofún and guaguancó.

The cierres feature two additional percussion instruments—the bombo (bass) drum and campanas (cowbells)—and prescribe that some of the percussionists switch instruments and rhythmic patterns: the conga drums often drop out and those drummers pick up the campanas. The original three idiophones used to accompany the two sets of drums (congas and batá) were a campana and the standard rumba idiophones: claves (which play the clave rhythm, the timeline for the ensemble) and catá (a hollowed-out piece of sugarcane against which drumsticks are beat to play a rhythm that is complementary to the clave). Later, the group added another cowbell, in line with the comparsa tradition of *campanas jimaguas* ("twin" cowbells that play an interlocking rhythm). The final addition to the batarumba ensemble in the early 1990s was the bombo drum, also taken from the comparsa ensemble. These additions illustrate that batarumba currently entails a fusion of rumba not only with a sacred Afro-Cuban practice but also with another secular Afro-Cuban tradition.[11] In fact, one batarumba song that Afrocuba regularly performs incorporates the instruments of comparsa—the cowbells and bombo—as well as its conga drum rhythms. In short, Afrocuba's batarumba songs are very elaborate and require rehearsal in order to get the timing right; Minini often counts the percussionists in and out of the stop-time sections.

All of the Afrocuba musicians I interviewed asserted that batarumba caught on very quickly, first with local audiences in Matanzas and then later in the 1970s when the group began to tour nationally. Batarumba gained widespread attention with the group's international tours, the first of which was to Angola and the Congo in 1987, and the second a trip to Washington, DC, in 1989 to perform at the Smithsonian Festival of American Folklife. With national and international success, however, came imitation, with some groups even claiming batarumba as their own creation. Wichichi explained that veteran musicians of the group are hesitant about providing rhythmic details because of this possibility of imitation by other groups; they see batarumba as their *plato fuerte* (main course) and their *arma estratégica* (strategic weapon), something that sets them apart.[12] He also asserted that it was due to batarumba's complex percussion and rhythmic configurations, which involve at least seven percussionists, that groups who have attempted to reproduce Afrocuba's innovation have been unsuccessful. It is interesting that Afrocuba defines itself so closely with this fusion, since its reputation as one of the best conservers of Afro-Cuban tradition on the island seemingly negates this association. I offer some possible explanations for this incongruity below.

Musical Analysis of Three Batarumba Songs

In order to showcase the variety entailed in this fusion, I provide here a musical analysis of three batarumba songs that have been recorded by Afrocuba. I do not provide transcriptions of the specific rhythmic elements of any bata-rumba song, in accordance with the aforementioned wishes of the group not to publish rhythmic details. I do, however, provide prose descriptions of the various rhythmic combinations and changes in each song, which is infor-mation that I gained both through musical analysis of commercial record-ings and my interviews with musicians. Because these three songs have been commercially recorded and released, unlike those that I recorded during fieldwork, I do not feel that it is unethical to discuss their general rhythmic combinations, as this information is not privileged or confidential. Regarding the information gleaned in my interviews, I was given consent by all the Afro-cuba musicians to reproduce their content. For his help with my analysis, I am particularly indebted to former Afrocuba percussionist Ramón García Pérez (known as "Sandy"), based in the San Francisco Bay Area since the late 1990s and recognized as one of the most knowledgeable Cuban ritual drummers in the United States.[13] He confirmed my analyses of the more straightforward rhythmic combinations and, as I have limited empirical knowledge about Matanzas-style batá drumming, was an invaluable source of information for the sections of the songs that feature more complex rhythmic matrices and/ or more obscure batá rhythms.

Before discussing the specific songs, I want to outline some of the gen-eral formal elements of Afrocuba's batarumba repertoire, based on my observation of various performances of thirteen different batarumba songs. I recorded live performances of most of these songs, including three that have been released commercially. Batarumba songs are based loosely on the tripartite rumba song form, which includes an introductory *diana* section characterized by the use of vocables to establish the song's tonal center, the *canto* or narrative section, and the *montuno* or call-and-response section, during which the tempo generally increases and the dancing starts. While many batarumbas include some sort of introductory section, they often do not involve the standard vocables of the diana, and some go straight into the canto section. Moreover, the montuno section in batarumba songs is usually introduced earlier than in a standard rumba song; most songs last from six to nine minutes, and the montuno section often comes in before the two-minute mark. The fact that the montuno section, in which all of the dancing takes place, is predominant in the majority of batarumba songs, correlates with the notion of their being "para guarachar" (to party), as Wichichi told me. Another common element is that the songs often maintain one coro (cho-ral refrain) throughout the montuno section, instead of changing the refrain two or three times, as is the case in Havana-style rumba. Seven of the thir-teen batarumbas I analyzed included only one coro in the montuno section.

Former Afrocuba singer Miguel Angel Dreke Reyes explained that the group prefers to maintain one coro throughout most of their rumba songs, but particularly in batarumbas, as this consistency in the vocals allows the audience to hear and focus on the rhythmic changes within the percussion section that constitute the essence of batarumba's novelty (pers. comm. 2006).

I was able to detect the guaguancó-chachalokofún rhythmic combination in the montuno section in eight out of the thirteen batarumba songs, meaning that it is indeed the most typical combination. In live performances there are usually two, and sometimes three, cierres in one batarumba song, always in the montuno section, although the number and placement of cierres in a song can vary from performance to performance. In most of the songs I analyzed, the first cierre involved the conga drums dropping out, regardless of whether they were playing guaguancó or not, leaving the batá drums, added campanas, catá, and clave. The subsequent cierre(s) most often involved all the drums dropping out, leaving only clave and handclapping to accompany the singing. The bombo drum, which is always played by Minini, is usually introduced in the second or third cierre.

"Tambor"

The first batarumba I will discuss is a song called "Tambor," recorded in Matanzas in 1985 and released on the album *¡La Rumba Está Buena!* (1994). The song's theme revolves around the harsh conditions of plantation slavery and, as suggested by its title, which is the generic word for "drum" in Spanish, alludes to the fact that slaves were generally prohibited from playing their drums. The song's rhythmic matrix is the simplest of the three batarumbas I analyzed—in the sense that there are relatively few changes in the percussion—and the montuno section features the common fusion of chachalokofún and guaguancó. However, neither of these rhythms is heard in the canto section, which features the batá rhythm for the orisha Ochosi and a conga drum rhythm that Sandy referred to as "Congo" (García Pérez, pers. comm. 2014).[14] He further noted that at least one of the conga drums, as well as the campanas, were doubling the rhythmic pattern of the *okónkolo* (the smallest of the three batá drums); this is presumably why the percussion in this section sounds so sparse and why it is difficult even to recognize that the conga drums are playing. As in many batarumbas, there is only one coro maintained throughout the montuno section. Following is a table displaying a chronological sequence of the song with rhythmic changes.[15]

Table 5.1: "Tambor"		
Time	**Song Sections and Lyrics**	**Percussion**
0:00	**Main coro:** "¿Adónde está mi tambor?" (Where is my drum?)[1]	Intro with drum rolls
0:10		Enter batá drums playing Ochosi rhythm, conga drums, and campanas playing "Congo" and doubling *okónkolo* rhythm (sparse percussion)
0:22	**Verse 1:** "Yo trabaja la mañana, yo trabaja mediodía, yo trabaja por la tarde, y por la noche . . ." (I work all morning, I work at midday, I work all afternoon, and at night . . .)	Same percussion
0:39	**Coro** (slightly altered from first coro): "Yo quiere bailar tambor" (I want to dance to the drum) (3x)	Same percussion
0:54	"Tambor" (Drum) (3x) and then coro "¿Adónde está mi tambor?" (Where is my drum?) (3x)	Same percussion
1:16	**Verse 2:** "Aquí no pagan dinero, látigo na' ma'" (Here they don't pay us money, they just whip us) (2x)	Same percussion
1:34	"Tambor" (3x), then coro, "Yo quiere bailar tambor" (I want to dance to the drum) (4x)	Same percussion
1:55	**Montuno section:** Coro continues, "Yo quiere bailar tambor"	Enter *chachalokofún* on batá drums and guaguancó on congas
2:44	Same coro	**Cierre:** congas drop out, extra campana added; congas play drum flourishes intermittently
3:12	Same coro	Drum flourish to signal congas' reentry with guaguancó
3:45	**END**	

1. The whole *canto* section is performed in call-and-response style, in which the chorus repeats or responds to each of the lead singer's phrases.

"Baila Mi Guaguancó"

"Baila Mi Guaguancó," released on Afrocuba's album *Raíces Africanas* (1998), chronicles the singer's love for rumba—guaguancó specifically—and in a larger sense expresses pride in her African roots. This is exemplified in the famous proverb sung right before the montuno section: "Él que no tiene de Congo, tiene de Carabalí" (He who doesn't have Bantu ancestry, has Calabar ancestry).[16] Like "Tambor," the montuno section in "Baila Mi Guaguancó" consists of chachalokofún and guaguancó, and the coro never changes. However, the rhythmic combinations in the canto section are much more complex in that there is a rhythmic change almost every time the song phrase changes (the phrases are so short that I don't consider them to be full verses). The opening rhythm, which sounds like drum flourishes with no specific rhythmic reference, is a batá rhythm for the orisha Inle. The rest of the canto section features several other rhythms, including the batá rhythm for Obbatalá, Abakuá drumming, and the well-known *tumbao* rhythm (the standard conga drum rhythm played in son; García Pérez, pers. comm. 2014).[17] These rhythms not only are derived from several distinct Afro-Cuban sacred and secular traditions, but they also entail a contrast in overall rhythmic feel: when the Abakuá and Obbatalá rhythms enter at 1:18 and then again at 1:59, there is a clear shift to a 6/8 feel, as compared with what comes immediately before it (guaguancó, felt in 4/4) and after it (tumbao rhythm, also in 4/4).

"Caridad"

The final batarumba I detail is "Caridad," which presented more of a challenge than the other two songs, partly because I analyzed two recorded versions of the song and found some rhythmic differences. The song's title alludes to La Virgen de la Caridad (the Virgin of Charity, patron saint of Cuba), who is syncretized with the orisha Ochún. The lyrics are centered around the process of a Santería initiate being assigned a patron orisha, with the choral refrain "Que santo le quiere dar?" (Which saint/orisha will they give her?).[18] While there is only one coro that is maintained throughout the montuno section, as in the other two batarumbas, this song does not feature the combination of chachalokofún and guaguancó; instead, it features various rhythms associated with the Iyesá tradition.

The first version was recorded in 1985 and released on the same album as "Tambor," while the second—which I present below—was released on the later 1998 album with "Baila Mi Guaguancó." Interestingly, the main difference between the two versions of the song is that, whereas in the first version

Table 5.2: "Baila Mi Guaguancó"		
Time	**Song Sections and Lyrics**	**Percussion**
0:00		Song begins with batá rhythm for Inle and invented polyrhythm on congas
0:20		Enter clave and *catá*; congas play guaguancó
0:25	**Intro phrase**: "Señores presente, oigan bién" (Ladies and gentlemen, listen up) (2x); "Soy cubana y me gusta el guaguancó" (I'm Cuban and I like the guaguancó) (2x)	Batá drums join the congas in playing guaguancó rhythm; *iyá* (largest batá drum) is heard punctuating the *bombo* (second beat of the clave rhythm)[1]
0:55	"¿Cómo me vas a decir, que es una cosa vulgar?" (How can you tell me that rumba is vulgar?) (2x)	Same percussion
1:18	"Si cuando pasa la conga detrás de la puerta, te pone a bailar" (When you hear the conga behind the door, it will make you dance) (2x)	Percussion changes to 6/8 feel: batá drums play Obbatalá rhythm, congas play Abakuá rhythm
1:31		Drums play clave rhythm; feels like transition to montuno section
1:33	"Yo te enseñaré un viejo refrán" (I'm going to teach you an old saying) (2x)	Percussion slows down and goes back to 4/4 feel: congas play *son tumbao* rhythm, batá drums play a related polyrhythm
1:59	Proverb: "Él que no tiene de Congo, tiene de Carabalí" (He who doesn't have Bantu ancestry, has Calabar ancestry) (2x)	Back to 6/8 feel and Obbatalá/Abakuá combination
2:18	**Montuno section**: Coro "Baila mi guaguancó" (Dance to my guaguancó)	Drums play clave rhythm, then *chachalokofún* on batá drums, guaguancó on congas (4/4 feel)
3:06	Same coro	**Cierre**: congas drop out and batá drums switch to guaguancó rhythm
3:50	Same coro	Drum flourish signaling congas' reentry with guaguancó; batá drums back to chachalokofún; gradual acceleration of percussion
4:54	Same coro	Percussion returns to opening combination: batá drums playing Inle and congas with polyrhythm; acceleration until end
5:12	**END**	

1. It is an interesting choice to have a rhythm so intimately associated with secular rumba percussion and its standard conga ensemble, be played by the sacred batá drums.

Table 5.3: "Caridad"		
Time	**Song Sections and Lyrics**	**Percussion**
0:00	"Changó, Yemayá, Hekua" (names of *orishas*)[1] (2x)	Intro with drum rolls
0:17	**Main coro**: "¿Qué le pasa a Caridad, qué santo le quiere dar?" (What's going on with Caridad, which *orisha* will they give her?) (2x)	Enter batá drums with rhythm for Ogún[2] and campana; no conga drums
0:28	**Verse 1**: "Todas las negritas se han de electriza'" (All the [black] girls have been electrified/ possessed) (2x) "La pasa la tiene dura, la bemba tá gurruña'"(Her [kinky] hair is standing on its end, her lips are puckered) (2x)[3] **Coro**: "¿Qué santo le quiere dar Caridad, qué santo le quiere dar?" (Which orisha will they give to Caridad, which orisha will they give her?)	Same percussion
0:48	**Verse 2**: "Amalia va uruque" (2x), "ina que ina la ma" (2x)[4] **Coro**: "¿Qué santo le quiere dar Caridad, qué santo le quiere dar?" (Which orisha will they give to Caridad, which orisha will they give her?)	Same percussion
1:00	**Montuno**: "Ay Caridad, ay Caridad" (Lead, Oh Caridad, oh Caridad), "¿Qué santo le quiere dar?" (Chorus, Which orisha will they give her?)	Batá drums shift to one style of *Iyesá* as played in Matanzas; congas play mix of son- and rumba-derived percussion and one conga doubles the *Iyesá* rhythm
2:13	Same coro	**First cierre**: congas drop out; batá drums switch to other, "traditional" Matanzas-style *Iyesá*; campanas play rhythm associated with *Iyesá* cabildo
2:59	Same coro	Conga flourish to signal reentry, play same mixture of rhythms that began montuno section
3:31	Same coro	**Second cierre**: congas drop out; batás continue playing traditional Matanzas-style *Iyesá*; campanas and bombo drum play *Iyesá cabildo* rhythm; noticeable acceleration
4:15	Same coro	Conga flourish to signal reentry, play same mixture that began montuno section
5:00	**END**	

1. The phrase "Hekua hey" is often used to salute the fierce female orisha Oyá, guardian of the winds and the cemetery.
2. Sandy noted that this rhythm can also be used in Matanzas to play for the orisha Osain.
3. This verse and the next were difficult to transcribe and translate because of their idiomatic nature, so there may be minor errors, although I did have Sandy check my transcription. What is fairly clear to me is that the lyrics of this verse are referencing images of women in a state of possession by an orisha.
4. I was not able to confidently translate this phrase, but I believe it is partly in Lucumí.

the Iyesá rhythm played on the congas can be heard in the montuno section, I could not clearly identify it in the second, more recent version. It is important to note here that the Iyesá rhythm played on the congas (which in folkloric contexts often substitute for the ethnically specific Iyesá drums because of the similarity in form and construction) is not the same as the Iyesá rhythm for the batá drums. Furthermore, as Sandy noted, there are two styles of Iyesá that can be played on the batá drums in Matanzas, and both are heard at different moments in this song.[19] While the conga drums do not play in the canto section (which lasts less than a minute), their rhythms in the montuno section are quite complex, involving a mix of son (the tumbao rhythm), rumba-style improvisations, and a doubling of the batá Iyesá rhythm. Finally, there is one additional detail of great interest in this song: this song borrows rhythms from the traditional context in which Iyesá is performed, the *cabildo* (a mutual-aid society formed in the nineteenth century along African ethnic lines), and mixes them with the Iyesá rhythms performed on the batá drums. While I assumed that the campanas were playing a comparsa rhythm in this song (as they usually do in batarumba), Sandy corrected me, noting that in the montuno section (heard specifically during the cierres) they are playing the traditional campana rhythm used in the Iyesá cabildo in Matanzas. In addition, the bombo (bass drum) rhythm heard in the second cierre at 3:31 is appropriated from the cabildo tradition. Thus, as in "Baila Mi Guaguancó" with its fusion of Lucumí and Abakuá traditions, this batarumba song entails an unusual mix of Afro-Cuban religious musical practices, this time Lucumí and Iyesá.[20]

As the various rhythmic combinations and sectional changes within these three batarumba songs make evident, Afrocuba de Matanzas's innovation is richly complex and involves much more than a simple fusion of chachalokofún and guaguancó. Instead, batarumba invokes rhythms from a variety of sacred (Lucumí, Iyesá, Congo, and Abakuá) and secular (rumba, son, and comparsa) Afro-Cuban traditions, and mixes them in innovative and unexpected ways. Now I turn to a discussion of batarumba song, which incorporates Cuban popular music and thus displays another layer of complexity and illustration of how Afrocuba's hybridizing practice engages with non-rumba elements.

Batarumba's Engagement with Cuban Popular Music

Despite its heavy reliance on what are considered to be "folkloric" practices—rumba, batá drumming, and comparsa[21]—batarumba also incorporates mass-mediated popular music, particularly the songs of Celia Cruz. In fact, from its inception, rumba repertoire has borrowed melodies from traditional popular Cuban genres—such as guaracha, son, bolero, and canción—as well as from sacred Yoruba-, Bantu-, and Calabar-derived repertoires (Grasso González 1989, 9).[22] Furthermore, the rumba groups with whom I worked have often adapted non-Cuban popular songs for rumba performance, such as an Afrocuba rumba song that draws from Venezuelan salsa star Oscar D'León's repertoire, and Havana rumba group Los Ibellis's adaptation of the song "La Media Vuelta," popularized by Mexican pop singer Luis Miguel. I have noticed that Afro-Cuban secular music is generally characterized by a large degree of recycling/quoting/borrowing among the various genres. For example, rumba coros often draw directly from the comparsa repertoire and vice versa, and both rumba and comparsa songs incorporate refrains from Santería, Palo, and Abakuá repertoires. During my fieldwork period, Havana rumba group Yoruba Andabo almost invariably opened their shows with a song from the Espiritismo repertoire adapted to guaguancó, the lyrics of which are taken from the standard Catholic liturgy used in cajón de muerto ceremonies.[23] A large proportion of the group's songs either incorporate Santería refrains in the montuno section or allude to common practices and rituals within the religion. Finally, the dance associated with batarumba is also highly hybrid and mirrors the musical fusion of rumba, Santería, and popular music, particularly son (Daniel 1995). During one Afrocuba rehearsal, for example, I observed a batarumba dance that included rumba steps, choreography associated with the orishas Obbatalá, Ogún, and Yemayá, and elements of son dance.

I have identified six songs within Afrocuba's batarumba repertoire that are adaptations of the recordings of Celia Cruz (1925–2003), the legendary black Cuban singer who would come to acquire the moniker "the queen of salsa." Cruz is an interesting choice for creative appropriation because she defected from the island in 1960, shortly after the triumph of the Cuban Revolution. She came to be considered one of most outspoken critics of the Castro regime in the United States, which is somewhat ironic given the overwhelmingly white composition and racist mentality of the early waves of Cuban immigrants. Cruz's songs were subsequently subjected to absolute censorship on the island, banned from radio and all media circulation. However, tapes of her music have been in constant clandestine circulation across the island since she defected, and she is held in high esteem by Cubans of all ages. My first trip to Cuba coincided with Cruz's death in July 2003, and the fact that the state-controlled press made almost no mention of it was an indication of the government's enduring inflexibility toward Cruz's political declarations and cultural production.[24]

Ultimately, Cruz was able to transcend her political identity as an anti-Castro Cuban exile in the sense that she is now recognized as a principal figure in the popularization of New York–based salsa, and its only female ambassador. In the 1970s and 1980s she recorded countless albums with Fania Records—a label that is inextricably tied to the birth and popularization of salsa—teaming up with some of its leading purveyors, such as Willie Colón and Johnny Pacheco. Nonetheless, before Cruz became "the queen of salsa" in the United States, she had established a very successful career in the 1950s with prominent group La Sonora Matancera, one of the oldest surviving Cuban dance bands.[25] Thus, although she was from Havana, her entire professional career in Cuba (from 1950 to 1960) was spent with the most prominent dance band to emerge from Matanzas; in fact, even after defecting to the United States, she stayed with La Sonora Matancera until 1965. In addition, of the six Cruz songs adapted by Afrocuba, five were originally recorded during her time with La Sonora Matancera: "Óyeme Agayú," "Chango ta' Veni," and "Lalle Lalle" from *Homenaje a Los Santos* (1994); "Rinkinkalla" from *Cruz & Colón: Only They Could Have Made This Album* (1977); and "Mata Siguaraya" from *Azucar! Caliente* (1993).[26] The only Cruz song recorded independently of La Sonora Matancera and adapted by Afrocuba was the well-known hit "Quimbara" from the album *Celia & Johnny* (1974). Although Afrocuba has not commercially recorded these batarumbas, I have heard four of them performed live by the group: "Quimbara," "Chango ta' Veni," "Lalle Lalle," and "Mata Siguaraya," indicating that these are the Cruz-derived batarumbas that are currently being performed. While I have never heard the batarumba version of "Óyeme Agayú," there is a commercial recording of Afrocuba's version of "Rinkinkalla," although it is not performed by the group. One of Afrocuba's former singers, Teresita Domé Pérez, currently lives in Los Angeles and has recorded this song with a local Afro-Cuban folkloric group called Ritmo y Canto on their self-titled album (2004).

In my dissertation, I hypothesized that Cruz's association with La Sonora Matancera (a Matanzas-identified group) may have influenced Afrocuba's decision to use her songs for inspiration instead of the many other Cuban popular songs they could have chosen that would have been less politically controversial (Bodenheimer 2010). However, I recently conducted a follow-up interview with Dolores Pérez in which I asked her directly why the group decided to use Cruz's songs. She stated that it had been her idea, and that she made the choice simply because she admired Cruz's singing style (pers. comm. 2013). Thus, I made an incorrect assumption about the primary reason for using Cruz's songs. Nonetheless, the link between Celia Cruz and a Matanzas-identified group may not be irrelevant or coincidental, especially because most of the songs chosen for adaptation were originally recorded with La Sonora Matancera. Perhaps, in addition to an aesthetic connection with Celia Cruz, Afrocuba musicians aimed to highlight Matanzas's long-standing importance in the history of Cuban popular music.[27]

Afrocuba's Mixed Toques

While batarumba is the main focus of my discussion of Matanzas-based hybridizing practices, I want to briefly discuss another innovation by Afrocuba de Matanzas, in the performance of sacred traditions. The Lucumí tradition boasts the most variety of all Afro-Cuban sacred practices in terms of the diverse instrumental ensembles used to accompany songs and ceremonies. These include the batá drums, the most revered Yoruba-derived instrumental ensemble; the *güiro* ensemble, characterized by the use of three shékeres (hollowed-out gourds covered in beads), a cowbell, and one or two conga drums; the bembé drums; and the Iyesá drums. In its folkloric shows, Afrocuba often performs orisha songs with at least two of these ensembles in order to showcase the musical variety of the Lucumí pantheon. However, the group has also employed two or three ensembles within one song, resulting in what are called *toques mezclados* (mixed rhythms), which might feature the batá drums and the güiro ensemble or some other combination of ensembles.

According to Dolores Pérez, it was her husband, former Afrocuba artistic director Juan García, who had the initial idea for the toques mezclados in the early 1980s (pers. comm. 2007). García, a habanero, had been brought in from the capital to choreograph Afro-Cuban sacred dances when the group transitioned from a rumba to a folkloric group in 1980. Group director Minini asserted that the toques mezclados emerged from a desire both to display the variety and richness of the Lucumí instrumental ensembles that can accompany an orisha song, and to experiment with the polyrhythms that were created by playing two different rhythmic matrices at the same time (Zamora Chirino, pers. comm. 2007). Afrocuba has also created set pieces like the Coro Folklórico, which mixes rhythms from two different Afro-Cuban religious practices, Santería and Palo. Their folkloric dance for the orisha Yemayá is perhaps their most innovative and timbrally rich toque mezclado in terms of its incorporation of different ensembles and rhythmic changes. The musical accompaniment begins with the batá drums, switches in the middle of the song to the bembé ensemble, then morphs into a combination of bembé and güiro, and finishes with a mix of bembé and batá accompaniment.[28] I have witnessed Havana rumba groups such as Clave y Guaguancó and Los Ibellis employ toques mezclados in their folkloric shows, but, considering the respective dates of professionalization of these groups as compared with that of Afrocuba, I believe it was the Matanzas group that first performed this innovation in a folkloric context.[29] Like batarumba, toques mezclados are evidence of the innovative spirit that resides in Matanzas, and constitute another challenge to the essentialist notions of the city (as *only* a site of preservation) that are embedded in the "cradle of Afro-Cuban culture" discourse.

Matanzas' Situated Hybridity

The main theoretical argument of this chapter is that rumba-based hybridizing practices are entangled with the politics of place, both in terms of musicians' local identities and the racialized discourses of place that I discussed in chapter 4. I want to suggest that the particular rumba innovations detailed here are delimited and defined in part by the musicians' understandings of the ways that their place-based identities are intertwined with their creative practices. In this case, I argue that the discourse of tradition attached to Matanzas, exemplified in the label "cradle of Afro-Cuban culture," informs the desire and sense of duty that many local folkloric musicians feel to preserve and faithfully represent the various traditions associated with their city and province. Many matancero musicians associate themselves with tradition and in turn disparage the tendency of habanero folkloric musicians to *inventar* (make things up, or stray from a traditional style). Alternatively, and in line with the various meanings of *inventar*—which can also mean to innovate or create something new—this might be viewed from a habanero perspective as a positive attribute. Nonetheless, the trope of place that ties Matanzas to racialized tradition is not simply a reflection of an already formed identity, for there is of course no one fixed matancero identity; in other words, I am not arguing that local musicians construct their city as the "cradle of Afro-Cuban culture" because their identity is inherently "traditional." However, I do believe that this discourse of place is constitutive of and reinforces a particular, locally situated notion of tradition in Matanzas that influences the identity formation of many of its musicians. Needless to say, other Matanzas musicians may not feel bound by tradition or feel an obligation to preserve an "authentic" style, just as some musicians in Havana *do* define their identity around tradition, despite the discourse of place that associates the capital with continual innovation and cultural hybridity.

In chapter 4 I alluded to batarumba as a hybrid creation that challenges the essentialization of Matanzas's identity as the "cradle of Afro-Cuban culture," a trope that cannot discursively accommodate fusion practices. Nonetheless, following the theorizing of Stuart Hall on hybridity, batarumba does not entail indiscriminate mixing. Afrocuba has drawn on musical practices—folkloric and popular, sacred and secular—that have historical foundations in their city, and the creation of batarumba is the result of specific artistic choices. In chapter 4 I discussed the intimate associations of Matanzas both with rumba (the city is considered to be rumba's birthplace) and with Afro-Cuban sacred practices, Santería being the most well known and widely practiced. Above, I suggested that Afrocuba's decision to adapt Celia Cruz's songs for the batarumba repertoire—while based primarily on an aesthetic preference—may have been in part due to the singer's connection with La Sonora Matancera. Ultimately, I find that the fusion of rumba percussion, form, and songs with sacred-derived batá drumming or other local religious practices (such as Iyesá), and the incorporation of popular music repertoire associated with a Matanzas-based band, illustrates a locally oriented approach toward hybridizing practices, and an excellent example of what Hall terms *situated hybridity*.

Beyond the hybridizing practices that have emerged from Matanzas, I also find that local conceptions of fusion tend to be more limited and tradition oriented than those of Havana. Not only do the musical elements of batarumba constitute an invocation of the local, but the larger conceptions of rumba-based fusion displayed by various Afrocuba musicians— particularly the importance they place on tradition—elucidate a process of situated hybridity. Minini told me that some people have suggested adding piano and/or bass to the group's instrumental ensemble, but he said that this would betray the essence of batarumba, which is to stay within the realm of Afro-Cuban folklore (Zamora Chirino, pers. comm. 2007). He felt that the sonic emphasis should be on the percussion and the polyrhythms created by the various instruments. In terms of the vocal elements, he stated that the arrangements should not include complex harmonies, as this was not in line with the folkloric tradition, and that the voices should not sound too trained or professionalized, but instead must maintain the nasal timbre and guttural techniques characteristic of Afro-Cuban folkloric song. Minini's declarations display a desire to reaffirm the notion that Matanzas is the "cradle of Afro-Cuban culture." For, even the fusions produced by the group are governed by certain principles that will not permit incorporating just anything. Veteran percussionist Wichichi went a step further in tying batarumba to tradition, discussing the innovation as "pure," despite its clear identity as a hybrid practice (Alfonso García, pers. comm. 2007). This comment suggested to me not a literal belief that batarumba is "pure" in terms of its musical elements but rather an attempt to discursively construct *every* cultural practice that emerges from Matanzas as "unpolluted," even those that are a conscious and direct result of fusion.

Hybridizing Practices in Havana-Style Rumba

Guarapachangueo

Guarapachangueo does not have a [rhythmic] pattern. Guarapachangueo is all about bomba, the "heart" or personal expression of the percussionist when he's inspired. Guarapachangueo means playing rumba on the cajón. Guarapachangueo is the bass tone pattern on the conga drum or cajón. Guarapachangueo is about "filling up" the empty spaces of the singer. Guarapachangueo is traditional rumba mixed with contemporary sounds. Guarapachangueo is mixing the sound of conga drums with the cajón. Guarapachangueo is a conversation between the quinto [high-pitched improvising drum] and the low-pitched conga or cajón. Guarapachangueo is like free jazz—the conga drum has no set rhythm, it's free. Guarapachangueo is any variation or improvisation performed on the low-range percussion instrument. Guarapachangueo is improvisation. Guarapachangueo is nothing and everything.

These are excerpts from some of the definitions of guarapachangueo provided to me by various Havana-based rumba musicians with whom I conducted fieldwork. As is evident, the term does not have any one meaning but rather is an exceptionally polysemic utterance that is difficult to define because there is so little consensus among its practitioners about what it is.[30] One of the only constants among the countless definitions I have heard relates to the particular instrument with which it is inextricably associated, the cajón (see figure 5.2), a wooden box fashioned into a percussion instrument. Cajones of various sizes served as rumba's main percussion instruments in the late nineteenth and early twentieth centuries, before the introduction of the conga drum to the rumba ensemble.[31] In his 2003 bachelor's thesis investigating the revitalization of the cajón in Havana, Dutch scholar Paul Van Nispen outlines the history of the instrument, concluding that it has reemerged as an important instrument in the late twentieth century in a variety of sacred and secular practices for several reasons. In terms of religious uses of the cajón, the most notable increase has been linked to the growing popularity of the cajón de muerto ceremony (see chapter 3), principally because it is less expensive than a tambor (the most formal ceremony within Santería worship), which features the three batá drums.[32] Referring to the revitalization of the cajón within rumba, Van Nispen opines that the deep (I would describe it as "boomy") sound of the cajón, as compared with the conga drum, provides a very strong, penetrating bass sound. He also adds that the cajón's capability to produce amplified volume makes it an ideal instrument for the guarapachangueo

Figure 5.2: Two *cajones* of different sizes seen at a rumba event at the home of *guara-pachangueo* creators Los Chinitos; at the center is the mid-range conical *cajón* and at the left is the *quinto cajón*, held between the percussionist's knees.

style, as one of its characteristics is an increase in improvisation in lower registers (Van Nispen 2003, 120).[33]

Returning to the problem of definition, most musicians seem to agree that, in contrast to rumba guaguancó, guarapachangueo does not refer to a specific rhythmic pattern. It is often characterized by a pattern of bass tones (known as *tukutukum*) performed with the palm of the hand in the middle of the mid- or low-range conga drum or cajón, which I present in a transcription below. However, this pattern (consisting of three or four notes, depending on whom you ask) cannot alone define guarapachangueo, because the bass tones are often inaudible in many live and recorded performances due to simultaneous improvisation on different drums. Some musicians characterized the innovation as a particular feeling, bomba, the improvisatory spirit emerging from the percussionist. A few musicians defined it in terms of its musical function within the rumba ensemble, namely to fill up the spaces left by the singer. Others defined it in terms of a mix of components—whether musical genres or percussion instruments. One definition of guarapachangueo viewed it as improvisation, absolute rhythmic freedom for the percussionist, while another delimited its meaning to improvisation on a percussion instrument of a particular range. Finally, guarapachangueo was defined in terms of the number of percussionists performing. Notwithstanding my belief that all of these definitions are valid and contribute to a constellation of meanings surrounding guarapachangueo, for the purposes of clarity I choose to discuss it as a style of percussion playing associated with contemporary rumba performance that generally involves four elements: the use of the cajón, either with other cajones and/or with congas; the tukutukum bass-tone pattern; increased rhythmic improvisation on the low-range conga or cajón; and a higher degree of simultaneous improvisation on different percussion instruments.

Guarapachangueo was invented by a group of brothers known as Los Chinitos (the little Chinese guys), which presumably refers to the physical markers of Chinese ancestry on both sides of their family, although they are racially mixed. Los Chinitos are four rumberos from the spatially and economically marginalized, primarily black municipality of San Miguel del Padrón, located on the outskirts of Havana, a place that has intimate associations with rumba. In my interview with the youngest of the four brothers, Irián López Rodríguez recalled that his father moved to the San Miguel del Padrón neighborhood of La Corea around the 1940s, when this part of Havana was *monte* (roughly, a backwoods area).[34] Contrary to the hopes of Irián's father that the area would become industrialized due to its proximity to the train station, it became another *barrio marginal* (marginalized neighborhood). Irián asserted that San Miguel del Padrón became a site for the migration of *delincuentes* (delinquents) and many Afro-Cuban religious practitioners. It was a particularly attractive destination for men initiated into the male secret society called Abakuá, who were fleeing the authorities and the criminalization of Afro-Cuban religious practice that accompanied the dogma of scientific atheism promoted by the revolutionary government.[35] This migration of poor, black, marginalized people contributed to the area's emerging reputation as a *barrio rumbero* (rumba-rich neighborhood).

This association of San Miguel del Padrón with particular racial, cultural, and social attributes—blackness, criminality, rumba performance, and Abakuá practice—constitutes another example of the racialized discourses of place that I discussed in chapter 4. This trope of place, however, highlights the micropractices of local identity formation within the sprawling and diverse geography of the Havana metropolitan area. Needless to say, each municipality and neighborhood in Havana has its own character and population, which is often discursively linked to race, class, and even religious practice. During my fieldwork, I had a conversation with my Havana percussion teacher, Daniel Rodríguez, in which he discussed the localized practice of different Afro-Cuban religions within Havana. For example, he asserted that whereas the municipality of Cerro had a strong Santería presence, Abakuá practice had particularly strong roots in Marianao, Pogolotti, and San Miguel del Padrón, which he also claimed had a strong presence of Palo (pers. comm. 2006). Some municipalities are associated with multiple Afro-Cuban religions, such as Guanabacoa, where Santería, Palo, Abakuá, and Espiritismo are all practiced widely.[36] Referring to the fact that San Miguel del Padrón had strong links with Abakuá and Palo, both considered to be very intense in terms of their ritual practices and associations with the dead, Daniel stated that the municipality was *tierra de mambises* (a land of rebels).[37] According to Irián, San Miguel del Padrón has never had a particularly high incidence of Santería worship, which is the main reason he and his brothers began playing the batá drums relatively late in their careers.

Irián was somewhat of a child prodigy on the conga drums, especially the quinto (improvising drum), although he and his brothers often played rumba on furniture drawers because they did not own congas before they became professional musicians in 1980. It was in this year that master folkloric dancer and member of the Conjunto Folklórico Nacional Juan de Dios Ramos asked them to join a new group that he was founding, the now highly revered Raíces Profundas. Los Chinitos were brought in as rumba specialists, while other percussionists were tapped to play the batá drums and other Afro-Cuban sacred traditions. Guarapachangueo emerged, however, while Los Chinitos were still amateur musicians, around 1973–1974. Irián described the very resourceful creation of the new style, which was first conceived using a makeshift cajón that was constructed from parts of a homemade wooden fan.[38] He attributed the very short rhythmic ostinato associated with guarapachangueo, called tukutukum and played with bass tones, to his older brother, Pedro López Rodríguez, and a cousin, Luis Ramón Zuleta López, stating "Sale ese ritmo, no se crea" (This rhythm simply emerged, it wasn't created). Figure 5.3 presents a transcription of the tukutukum rhythm as demonstrated to me by Irián, which I present in the context of the rumba clave rhythm.[39]

While the basic pattern is known as tukutukum, an onomatopoeia referring to the four notes of the bass tone pattern, Irián demonstrated that there are variations on the pattern, for instance three (*kutukum*) or two tones (*tukum*), with the accent always falling on the *kum* or last tone (see figure 5.4).

Irián stressed that the tukutukum pattern must be initiated in the middle of the clave cycle, between beats two and three (see figure 5.3), and not on the upbeat that leads into beat one or the start of the clave cycle. In fact, I have noticed that many rumba groups, including Yoruba Andabo and Los Ibellis, place the tukutukum pattern on the other, "wrong" side of the clave, leading into beat one, as seen in figure 5.5.

At the moment of its emergence, the new style created by Los Chinitos did not have a name, nor was the term "guarapachangueo" coined by them. Irián

Figure 5.3: Rumba clave rhythm and *tukutukum* pattern (bass tones of *guarapachangueo*).

Figure 5.4: Rumba clave and *tukutukum* variations #1 and #2.

Figure 5.5: Rumba clave and *tukutukum* on the "wrong" or "two" side of the clave.

recalled that it was a rumbero named El Llanero who came up with the name, which he used not positively but in a disdainful manner to assert that the guarapachangueo style represented neither traditional nor good rumba. Thus, as with innovations within musical practices around the world, this one was considered to be a degenerate version of the original before it became popularized. By 1975–1976, the term "guarapachangueo" had become widespread as a way of referring to Los Chinitos' new style, although there were (and still are) variations on the name, such as *guarapachanguero* and *guarapachanga*.[40]

Unsurprisingly, the style did not enjoy immediate success after its emergence. In fact, it was not until roughly ten years later, in the mid-1980s, that it gained acceptance and began to be disseminated widely within the Havana rumba scene. Irián asserted that rumberos were hesitant to associate themselves with this innovation, afraid that it might fail or was not traditional enough. He specified that musicians were wary about implementing the musical changes in rumba percussion that were intrinsic to guarapachangueo, such as the changing relationship of the quinto to the other percussion instruments. As Irián noted, the quinto loses some of its improvisational freedom;

"está esclavizado" (it becomes a slave) to the guarapachangueo because it has to respond to the improvisation on the low-range cajón or conga in order to have a "conversation," and thus has less space to solo. He recalled that Los Chinitos were playing at a rumba party where many master rumberos were in attendance (year unknown), and that it was not until a musician from Oriente got up to sing with them that big names in Havana's rumba scene—Luis "Aspirina" Chacón Mendivel, Gregorio "El Goyo" Hernández Rios, and Raíces Profundas founder Juan de Dios—took notice and began to view the new style as something to emulate. It was after El Goyo and Juan de Dios threw their support behind the style, and in part due to the increased attention for Los Chinitos after they joined Raíces Profundas, that guarapachangueo began to gain widespread acclaim.

Although guarapachangueo seems inextricably tied to the cajón (and to the instrument's revitalization within rumba), Irián described Los Chinitos' original instrumental ensemble as consisting only of conga drums. He asserted that it was only in the early 1980s, when Los Chinitos were playing with Raíces Profundas, that his brother Pedro came up with the idea to develop the guarapachangueo style on the cajón outside the context of their professional work. At this time they were playing rumba in a more traditional style in Raíces Profundas, and the only cajón they were using was the *cajón maleta* (literally, "suitcase cajón"), the largest and lowest-pitched cajón, on top of which the percussionist sits, executing his strokes on the front and side panels (see figure 5.7 below). Pedro adapted the cajón maleta to add more timbral variety, specifically to play guarapachangueo. In 1982, the Raíces Profundas ensemble downsized from thirty-odd performers to around eighteen. Four percussionists remained, so it became imperative to play in guarapachangueo style, which would have the maximum sonic effect with a minimum number of personnel. Irián stated that the style allowed them to play rumba with only four people: one percussionist playing the tres-dos (mid-range) conga drum, including the tukutukum bass tones; a second percussionist improvising on the quinto; a third percussionist playing the catá; and a singer playing the claves.

A few changes emerged within the guarapachangueo style in the late 1980s. First, a new cajón was developed around 1987–1988, the conical cajón, which was meant to be a substitute for the mid-range conga drum[41] and included extra protruding side panels that would allow for more timbral possibilities on the instrument (see figure 5.6).[42] In addition, Los Chinitos decided to add one tres-dos conga and one quinto to the ensemble, which before had employed only two cajones or congas. The added conga was placed in the middle of the two percussionists so that both the player of the lowest conga/cajón and the quinto player could have easy access to it. Thus, two percussionists would

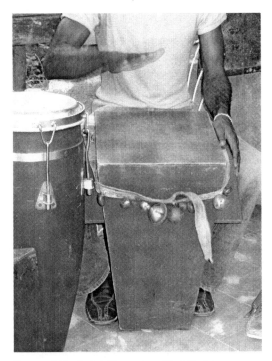

Figure 5.6: Conical *cajón*, as played by Irián López.

be playing four, instead of two, instruments. Regarding this reduced number of drummers, Irián stated that when other groups heard the recordings of rumba played in guarapachangueo style, they assumed that they were listening to four drummers, and this led many Havana rumba groups to play the style with more percussionists. He opined that many of the groups best known for playing guarapachangueo with three to five percussionists, including Yoruba Andabo and Clave y Guaguancó, are not technically playing guarapachangueo but instead "un gran poliritmo" (a great polyrhythm) with the bass tones characteristic of the style. Below I will outline a few instrumental configurations of guarapachangueo as interpreted by different rumba groups.

The Popularization of Guarapachangueo

Although guarapachangueo had not been the subject of an in-depth investigation until my dissertation (2010), most of the published mentions of the style speak not about Los Chinitos as its creators but of its intimate association with famed Yoruba Andabo founder and percussionist Francisco

Hernández Mora (1933–2005), known to all as Pancho Quinto.[43] For example, Kenneth Schweitzer states, "With the late 1980s emergence of another fusion genre, guarapachangüéo, Pancho Quinto positioned himself as a cutting edge musician. . . . In the guarapachangüéo, Pancho incorporates batá within rumba" (2003, 157–58).[44] Pancho Quinto, whose artistic name may have referenced his skills on the quinto, was a founder in 1961 of Guaguancó Marítimo Portuario, the group that would become Yoruba Andabo, and a key figure in the group's popular ascent in the mid- to late 1980s.[45] Like the majority of the group's founders, Quinto was a dockworker until the group transitioned from amateur to professional status. Cuban scholar Rosa Esther Álvarez Vergara (1989) asserts that in the period of the group's relative dormancy in the 1970s, Quinto became known as a master whom aspiring percussionists would approach to gain knowledge in cajón and batá playing techniques. In fact, when Los Chinitos decided to expand their knowledge to batá drums in the 1980s, they chose Quinto as their teacher. Alluding to Yoruba Andabo's creative adaptation in the face of a dearth of instruments before they attained professional status, Quinto is quoted as stating, "Yoruba, Arará, Palo, Abakuá, rumba . . . can all be played on three cajones" (Álvarez Vergara 1989, 23; my translation). Because of this unconventional philosophy, he is remembered as a percussionist who pushed the boundaries of rumba, particularly as concerns his role in the popularization of guarapachangueo.

Quinto and fellow Yoruba Andabo percussionist Jacinto Scull Castillo, known to all as El Chori, met and became friends with Los Chinitos in the mid-1970s at a rumba party; this was a relationship that would have long-standing repercussions for Havana-style rumba. Irián credited El Chori with helping establish Los Chinitos' guarapachangueo ensemble. They were playing with a standard rumba ensemble at the party—three conga drums of various sizes and functions—and El Chori suggested removing the mayor (lowest) drum and leaving the other two drums, with the tres-dos playing the bass tones of guarapachangueo. Yoruba Andabo was the first group to disseminate this new percussion style in the center of Havana, which is presumably why Los Chinitos have not received the recognition they deserve. Irián opined that people tend to speak more about Quinto because he established himself in *el arte* (the professional artistic world), and this is why many associate the style with professional rumba groups such as Yoruba Andabo and Clave y Guaguancó. I encountered one of the many examples of this misattribution of guarapachangueo's creation at a 2007 show in Havana's Teatro América called "Rumba del Nuevo Siglo" (Rumba in the New Century). The host dedicated the show explicitly to Pancho Quinto, referring to him as the "founder" of guarapachangueo and the current style of rumba being played in Havana at that time. In contrast to the widespread lack of awareness in the academic realm about Los Chinitos' role in the creation of this style, I was reassured by the fact that all the Havana musicians whom I interviewed mentioned them as the creators of guarapachangueo.

Far from viewing this misattribution as malicious intent on the part of Yoruba Andabo, Irián emphasized the close relationship between Los Chinitos and Pancho Quinto (and other members of Yoruba Andabo). During our interview, he stated, "No me interesa quién lo haya inventado, sino quién lo toca bien" (I don't care who invented it, only who plays it well). Similarly, Irián's brother Pedro credited Quinto and El Chori with helping facilitate widespread acceptance of guarapachangueo, and commented on their role in its popularization:

> Nevertheless Yoruba Andabo keeps going, with my brother Bertico, the oldest, who started to work with them, and was a founder of Yoruba Andabó with Pancho Quinto (in 1981?). And who brought the "kinpakin-pakin-patokotón" [the rumba guaguancó rhythm followed by the bass tones of guarapachangueo] was Bertico. Chori, and Julio "El Gordo" still do that. So it was Berto who kept that tradition of the guarapachangueo cajón, with Pancho Quinto and his invention with the spoon and the three batá, a very particular style. That was Pancho Quinto, that's lost already, the guarapachangueo format, that was Pancho Quinto's thing. But you see, the guarapachangueo comes from here, from la Corea [neighborhood in San Miguel del Padón]. (López 2007)

Thus, despite the obvious goodwill between Los Chinitos and Quinto, the end result, as Pedro implies in his statement, is that musicians from a fairly isolated municipality have been marginalized discursively, and, instead, a celebrated musician from the center of Havana has received most of the credit. This can be viewed as another example of the far-reaching implications of the politics of place vis-à-vis the historiography of a musical style, or the ways that being from a remote municipality within the Havana metropolitan area delimits musicians' conditions of possibility for widespread success and/or fame.

Another explanation for this misattribution relates to the privileged status of professional musicians within the state cultural apparatus and the related disregard of musicians who play *en la calle* ("in the street," earning their living illegally without state-sanctioned permission). While Los Chinitos were professional musicians for a number of years, beginning with their role as founders of Raíces Profundas, they made a decision sometime in the 1990s to leave el arte due to disillusionment with the state cultural bureaucracy regarding permission to travel and perform abroad. Irián expressed the opinion that an

Figure 5.7: Pancho Quinto playing *guarapachangueo* at La Peña Cultural Center in Berkeley, California, in 1998. Quinto is sitting on the *cajón maleta* with two *batá* drumheads partially visible in the left-hand corner of the photo. Photo by Sven Wiederholt.

official document stating that one had graduated from the Escuela Nacional de Arte (National School of Art), which has often been required to gain professional status, should not be the measure of a musician's talent. He spoke of the difference between el arte and la calle, noting that in artistic performances it was necessary to adhere to certain European-derived criteria of musical competence, such as singing in tune. However, en la calle, the definition of a good musician has more to do with one's bomba (heart, or ability to improvise). He concluded by asserting that musicians playing en la calle are condemned to eternal marginalization in the sense that "History" will never mention their names and their accomplishments. The fact that guarapachangueo did not enjoy widespread acceptance until after well-respected professional rumberos had endorsed it substantiates these claims about the marginalization of nonprofessional musicians.

As stated by Pedro, Pancho Quinto is known for his unique style of guarapachangueo, particularly his instrumental ensemble that features the batá drums. As is partially evident in figure 5.7, his configuration consisted of the three batá drums tied together, the cajón maleta (on which the percussionist sits and which he strikes with a spoon), and a cowbell, all of which were played by one percussionist (himself). Describing Quinto's way of interpreting guarapachangueo, Kenneth Schweitzer states:

Figure 5.8: Yoruba Andabo's current *guarapachangueo* ensemble.

Pancho plays all the drums by himself. This provides him the freedom to shape
and control the drum conversation and allows him to borrow rhythmic ideas
from the rumba genres—yambú, guaguancó, and columbia—as well as from the
batá repertoire. . . . Sitting on a *cajón* (Sp. wood box), he holds a spoon in his left
hand, which he alternately strikes against the front of the *cajón* and a cowbell that
is firmly held in place by his right foot. His right hand may strike any of the enú
[large] heads of the three *batá* that are stacked to his right, the side of the *cajón*,
or the conga that is laying [*sic*] on its side behind him, barely visible in this photo
(2003, 158).[46]

While Yoruba Andabo continues to use Pancho Quinto's guarapachangueo
format in most of their songs,[47] the three batá drums have now been replaced
by three conga drums tied together on their sides next to the percussionist
playing the cajón maleta (figure 5.8).[48] The group's percussion ensemble currently includes the following instrumental configuration: on the right side
(facing the stage) sits the percussionist playing guarapachangueo (cajón, congas on their sides, cowbell, and spoon); in the middle is the quinto player with
both a quinto cajón and quinto conga to allow him to switch back and forth;
and on the other side sits the percussionist playing both the tres-dos cajón
and tres-dos conga. This third percussionist is responsible for playing the

Figure 5.9: Clave and rumba *guaguancó* rhythms.

Figure 5.10: Composite of rumba *guaguancó* with the *tukutukum* (on the "two" side of the clave).

traditional tres-dos rhythm of rumba guaguancó on the conga. I present here a rhythmic composite of the guaguancó rhythm (which is itself traditionally played as a compound rhythm on the mayor and tres-dos congas; see figure 5.9) and the tukutukum bass-tone pattern in the context of clave (figure 5.10). As noted above, Yoruba Andabo plays the tukutukum on the "two" side of the clave, leading into beat one, which Irián deems to be an erroneous placement.

Pancho Quinto and Yoruba Andabo also altered the placement of guarapachangueo within the standard tripartite rumba form as performed by Los Chinitos. Originally, Los Chinitos would begin a song in a more traditional style and then switch to the more improvisatory guarapachangueo style in the montuno section. In contrast, Yoruba Andabo (and other groups) play in guarapachangueo style throughout the whole song, with the simultaneous improvisation increasing in the montuno section. In their recordings and live shows, the tukutukum bass tones are often all but inaudible due to the large degree of simultaneous improvisation.

Although there are some common denominators, each rumba group with whom I conducted research has its own particular format for playing guarapachangueo, most likely in order to differentiate themselves from other groups. Los Ibellis, for example, plays a style that Daniel Rodríguez calls "rumba ligada con guarapachangueo," rumba mixed with guarapachangueo (pers. comm. 2006). This style mixes elements of the traditional guaguancó rhythm with guarapachangueo rhythms and a variation on the guaguancó rhythm that is similar to that of rumba matancera (a style of rumba from Matanzas that is comparable to yambú, the slowest style of rumba). Los Ibellis's guarapachangueo format includes four percussionists playing the following instruments: one plays the mayor (the lowest conga drum), one plays the

Figure 5.11: Los Ibellis's *guarapachangueo* ensemble.

Figure 5.12: Clave y Guaguancó's *guarapachangueo* ensemble.

quinto (either the cajón or conga), another plays the tres-dos rhythm of guaguancó and the guarapachangueo bass tones utilizing both a tres-dos cajón
and a tres-dos conga (like Yoruba Andabo), and the fourth plays a rhythmic
variation on guaguancó using the tres-dos and mayor congas (see figure 5.11).
Daniel noted that the percussionist playing guarapachangueo uses the tres-
dos or conical cajón to play the bass tones, while the tres-dos conga is used to
play the open tones of guaguancó and to *lucir*, "shine" or improvise.

Clave y Guaguancó's guarapachangueo style is characterized by a heavy
presence of cajones, in which each of the percussionists has both a conga
and a cajón at his disposal (see figure 5.12). Rhythmically, the group's style is
quite free in the sense that it conforms less to a particular composite rhythmic pattern than the other groups. Group director Amado Dedeu asserted
that the only imperative for their style is that the mayor (lowest drum) play
the bass tones of guarapachangueo; beyond that rule, the percussionists are
free to improvise around the tones (pers. comm. 2006). The quinto then fills
the spaces left by the mayor. Clave y Guaguancó has also adopted the style of
Pancho Quinto in using the three batá drums tied together on their side for
added timbral variety (in figure 5.12 the largest batá drum can be seen peek-
ing out from behind the percussionist with the red visor).

Finally, the group's percussionists often perform short, prepared "routines"
in which all four of them play a thirty-second rhythm pattern simultaneously
at the beginning of a rumba song, a sort of showpiece of coordination.[49] While
favoring a relatively free guarapachangueo style, Amado recognized the haz-
ards of playing with such a large amount of improvisation, stating "se puede
formar una pelea de perros" (a dogfight can ensue). In other words, so much
simultaneous improvisation risks losing the "conversation" that should always
be maintained between the percussionists playing the mayor and the quinto,
respectively, and it could disintegrate into an excessive density of rhythms
that do not really "say anything." As is evident from the descriptions of the
various Havana rumba groups' configurations and adherence (or nonadher-
ence) to rhythmic patterns, there are many variations on and interpretations
of the guarapachangueo style, a phenomenon that correlates with the many
meanings attached to this nebulously defined innovation.

Reggaetón's Influence on Rumba Vocals

Certain changes in rumba singing have accompanied the popularization
of guarapachangueo in Havana, specifically the influence of reggaetón on
rumba's vocal style. I do not see these changes as necessarily linked to guarapachangueo, partly because they emerged two decades later (in the 2000s).
In fact, on Yoruba Andabo's celebrated first solo album, *El Callejón de los*

Figure 5.13: Ronald González, lead singer of Yoruba Andabo.

Rumberos (1993), the vocal configuration of most of the songs is fairly traditional in that it corresponds to the format introduced by the legendary duo of Los Muñequitos de Matanzas, Saldiguera and Virulilla, in the 1950s (see chapter 4). In other words, Yoruba Andabo retained a traditional vocal style despite the fact that their percussion style, guarapachangueo, was highly innovative. Notwithstanding, recent innovations in rumba song do seem to dovetail with the larger ideology of guarapachangueo, that is, to expand the boundaries of rumba by incorporating nontraditional musical elements. Thus, this innovation in vocal style has contributed, along with guarapachangueo, to a redefinition of the Havana rumba sound and demonstrates another example of place-based hybridizing practices.

Reggaetón is a highly hybrid popular music genre that emerged in the Spanish-speaking Caribbean in the early 1990s and that includes elements from US hip-hop, Jamaican dancehall, and various Latin American popular musics like merengue, salsa, and bachata.[50] It has become an international phenomenon in the new millennium and not only enjoys near universal appeal among Latin American and Latino youth but has also made major inroads in popular music markets oriented toward non-Latino American youth. Cuba's reggaetón profile has been rising in recent years, in terms of its local audience and artists and also in terms of scholarly attention to the practice (for example, Baker 2011).[51] Moreover, it has had a tremendous influence on a variety of Cuban music genres, most notably timba; many top-notch timba groups have recorded collaborations with reggaetón artists, and some have even sought out vocalists who can sing in both styles.

In the past several years, reggaetón refrains have been creeping into rumba performance in Havana, primarily in guaguancó songs, and the singer at the forefront of this movement is Ronald González (see figure 5.13), lead singer for Yoruba Andabo. He joined the group in late 2005 and began to introduce refrains from popular reggaetón songs that were circulating on the radio in order to "renovate" rumba (pers. comm. 2007), and presumably to expand rumba's audience to include younger Cubans by quoting lyrics from popular hits they might recognize.

Most often, Ronald inserts the reggaetón refrains in the montuno section of a rumba song, when the tempo of the song increases and couples come out to dance. The chorus of one of the biggest Cuban reggaetón hits of 2006, "Se Me Parte la Tuba en Dos" by Elvis Manuel, was frequently inserted by Ronald in Yoruba Andabo's performances in 2006 and 2007.[52] This sampling of popular reggaetón refrains has had precisely the desired affect of getting younger audience members to participate, both by singing along with the catchy, familiar refrains and by dancing. In addition to Ronald's keen sense of how to appeal to a young public, he also happens to be an extraordinary improviser. In his improvising "calls" he often manages to bring in references to current events—such as the 2007 national baseball championship that pitted the Havana-based Los Industriales against Santiago's team—and he even makes publicity announcements for Yoruba Andabo's future gigs.

In his book *Buena Vista in the Club* (2011), Geoffrey Baker briefly discusses the mutually influential relationship between rumba and reggaetón, mentioning Yoruba Andabo and other rumba groups who have incorporated the latter genre into their performances. Although he does not treat the subject at length (his book concerns the relationship between reggaetón and Cuban hip-hop), it is the only published recognition I am aware of, beyond my dissertation, of this trend. One of Baker's main arguments is that Cuban reggaetón artists have not been interested in "indigenizing" or localizing their style but have generally tended to imitate Puerto Rican reggaetón. He states of the rumba-reggaetón fusion, "It seems that Cuban [rumba] audiences are hearing even apparently nonlocalized reggaetón as distinctly Cuban, and it is among rumba musicians and audiences, in the processes of reception and recycling, that Cuban reggaetón's local connections may be observed" (Baker 2011, 130). Baker's analysis of Cuban reggaetón juxtaposes the notion of hybridization—which he uses to refer to reggaetón artists who are more oriented toward a globalized, largely Puerto Rican style and tend to have very open conceptions of fusion—with "indigenization" or "localization," meaning the incorporation of more obviously Cuban musical elements. Although Baker's book offers wonderful insights into the contemporary popular music scene in Havana, my analysis in this chapter has sought precisely to demonstrate how hybridization and localization—rather than being mutually exclusive—are employed in tandem in the rumba fusions emerging respectively from Havana and Matanzas. In fact, I believe that all fusion/hybridizing practices are localized, in that they are performed within a specific environment by actors whose identities are positioned in specific ways.

The Influence of Havana-Based Hybridizing Practices beyond the Capital

While Ronald's incorporation of reggaetón refrains into rumba songs is not an uncontroversial innovation—it is seen by some rumba elders as abandoning the practice's roots—his influence on contemporary rumba vocals cannot be denied. Not only has it become trendy in the past few years for other Havana rumba groups to quote reggaetón refrains in the montuno sections of their songs (and sometimes at the beginning of the songs, eschewing completely the traditional diana introduction), but this phenomenon has taken hold in other Cuban cities. Similarly, the guarapachangueo style has been disseminated to other provinces, influencing local rumba styles in Santiago, Matanzas, and other locales. Kokoyé, the Santiago rumba group discussed in chapter 3, plays in a guarapachangueo style, sometimes using cajones and batá drums (Seguí Correoso, pers. comm. 2011). In addition, I attended a 2008 performance in which the group inserted reggaetón choruses into their rumba songs. Rumbatá, a young and highly talented group from Camagüey that has gained national and international acclaim in the past few years, plays in guarapachangueo style. The group attributes its percussion and singing style largely to Clave y Guaguancó, whom the musicians refer to as their *padrinos* (godfathers). Rumbatá's cajones have a front panel added on, like those of Los Chinitos, in order to give the percussionist an extra surface with which to produce different timbres. In addition, the group performs with a set of batá drums tied together on their side and placed in between two percussionists, revealing an obvious influence from Pancho Quinto and Yoruba Andabo.

Perhaps most interesting are the appropriations of Havana hybridizing practices by groups from Matanzas. Despite its reputation as the primary site for the conservation of traditional rumba, I have witnessed several Matanzas groups play rumba in guarapachangueo style. The young rumba group Los Reyes del Tambor bases its playing style around guarapachangueo. I also observed an established rumba group from Cárdenas, Columbia del Puerto, play in guarapachangueo style at a folkloric festival in March 2007. In this performance, Columbia del Puerto introduced the popular reggaetón refrain

"Se me parte la tuba en dos," providing an example of how guarapachangueo is often linked performatively with reggaetón influence in rumba vocals. Even more surprising was an Afrocuba de Matanzas performance in Havana in which the group played a rumba song that included elements of both reggaetón and the Colombian popular genre *cumbia*.

Although this performance constituted an anomaly for a group whose stated goal is to preserve Matanzas's musical traditions,[53] Afrocuba director Minini expressed a surprisingly positive opinion of Havana-based rumba innovations. He professed admiration for guarapachangueo as a rhythmic and stylistic innovation, singling out the style of Pancho Quinto and Yoruba Andabo for praise (Zamora Chirino, pers. comm. 2007). However, he also stated that although Afrocuba might play guarapachangueo in an isolated performance, the group could never perform it as well as the "originators" in Havana because the latter were "cultivating it every day." This declaration suggested, yet again, that Minini sees musical practices as inherently tied to particular places and feels that one's local identity determines how well or not one can perform a given style. He viewed Afrocuba's focus on tradition as going against the current trend in rumba of adopting the guarapachangueo style in order to appeal to younger audiences; he thus framed tradition, paradoxically, as the exception instead of the norm. Nonetheless, he concluded his remarks with a fascinating comment, declaring that if a (foreign) producer approached Afrocuba to record a commercially oriented album and asked the group to play guarapachangueo, he would agree to it for the purposes of economic gain. That does not mean, he clarified, that he or the group would change the "essence" of their rumba style, only that he would be willing to perform guarapachangueo for an isolated project. Thus, financial opportunities—whether in the form of recordings or international tours—can and do inform creative decisions in the context of economic instability, and in some cases can lead a group to contradict its own artistic mission or expand beyond its place-based repertoire for the sake of earning much-needed supplementary income. Finally, Minini's assertions and the instances of guarapachangueo and reggaetón-influenced rumba vocals in places beyond the capital all illustrate the significant impact of Havana-based hybridizing practices across the island, and the cultural hegemony of Havana within Cuba more generally.

Havana's Situated Hybridity

The almost limitless improvisational potential of guarapachangueo and the incorporation of elements of reggaetón, a mass-mediated popular genre that is not generally associated with Cuba, into rumba songs suggest that Havana-based folkloric musicians have a much broader conception of fusion practices than their counterparts in Matanzas. The discourse of place that circulates about Havana constructs the capital as the locus of hybridity, the principal signifier for the hybrid nation's population and culture. Correspondingly, musicians from Havana are assumed to have less desire to perform Afro-Cuban music in a traditional style and to view Matanzas styles of playing as "too slow," "too repetitive," and too hostile to creative innovation. Although these assumptions do not accurately reflect the wide range of opinions regarding tradition and innovation among Havana musicians, my conversations with various rumberos from the capital suggest that they do tend to feel less obliged to preserve traditional styles of playing and to have less restricted conceptions about which genres can be mixed.

When speaking about guarapachangueo, Yoruba Andabo director Geovani del Pino displayed views on tradition and innovation that, while buttressing my argument about the influence of discourses of place on identity formation and hybridizing practices, were also somewhat unexpected in that they did not conform to the common tendency among older generations of musicians to police the boundaries of tradition.[54] Geovani stated:

> As a living genre rumba also has the right to evolve . . . and it does not stop being rumba. There are those who are tied to the idea that if it's not played like it was in the old days, it's not rumba. I don't agree with this standard of judgment. Because then we would have to say that what Adalberto Álvarez plays currently is not son. No one would dare tell Adalberto Álvarez that what he plays isn't son, just because he doesn't play like the Matamoros.[55] . . . No one would dare tell Arsenio Rodríguez that what he did later with son, to which he introduced piano, to which he introduced conga drums, to which he introduced trumpets, that what he was playing wasn't son. . . . There were those who thought it . . . but he prevailed. And "the new" will prevail, even if many old guys don't want it to happen . . . you know why? Because they don't have the technical ability to perform in the way that a young person can. And because they don't have the ability to do it, they don't want anything to change. But the youth prevail, and they always will. . . . Rumba hasn't died because of this, because it evolved, it changed with the times. (Del Pino Rodríguez, pers. comm. 2006)[56]

In line with these views on the necessity of rumba's adapting to its contemporary musical and cultural context, Geovani opined that rumba is linked to any Cuban genre that emerged after it because of the important role that the clave rhythm, a hallmark of rumba, plays in virtually all Cuban music. He stated that because the basis of rumba is clave and drums, rumba can be fused with basically anything; rumba fits into any style.

Los Ibellis director Daniel Rodríguez displayed a similar viewpoint, asserting that while Afro-Cuban tradition needs to be maintained, rumba should be a site of innovation, which implies that by "tradition" he is referring specifically to Afro-Cuban sacred music and that rumba innately constitutes a space of musical fusion (pers. comm. 2006). He also framed the discussion of tradition in terms not only of musical practice but also of reception. He considered his group to be "traditional" but added that they adapt their style to the specific audience that they have in front of them in any given venue; they perform in a more traditional style for older audiences, particularly ones that include many religious elders, and employ more "innovative" techniques for younger audiences, such as playing the batá at an increased tempo and inserting reggaetón refrains into rumba songs. This statement suggests that musicians' notions of tradition and innovation can be quite flexible according to the specific circumstances of any given performance. Furthermore, as exemplified in the repertoire of Clave y Guaguancó (see Bodenheimer 2010), rumba groups can include both "traditional" songs and guarapachangueo-influenced or fusion-based songs within any one performance.

Clave y Guaguancó's conception of rumba-based fusion is undoubtedly the least restricted of all the groups I have discussed. More than any other rumba group on the island, the group is associated with fusion, mixing rumba not only with other Afro-Cuban genres—such as batá drumming, timba, and *tonadas*[57]—but also with foreign genres such as rap, flamenco, and jazz. Each of the group's rumba hybrids has a specific name that refers to the genres being fused together. For example, the album they recorded with the late rumba singer Celeste Mendoza called *Noche de la Rumba* (1999) includes songs classified as *flameguanbatá* (a fusion of flamenco, guaguancó, and batá), *tonadaguaguancó* (tonada with guaguancó), and *bataguancó* (batá with guaguancó). Clave y Guaguancó's more recent album *La Rumba Que No Termina* (2006) takes rumba fusion to new heights, introducing elements from timba and incorporating melodic instruments such as trumpet, piano, bass, and tres. Some of these hybrids have names such as *guan-politimba* (suggesting guaguancó with elements of timba), *guan-polirritmo* (suggesting guaguancó with extra polyrhythms), *catumba-rap* (featuring Cuban female rapper Telmary),[58] *jazz-batá* (featuring Los Van Van vocalist Jenny Valdés), and *guan-batá* (which in addition to guaguancó and batá also features elements of comparsa). In addition to Clave y Guaguancó's recorded rumba hybrids, I have witnessed other fusions in live performance, such as a rumba-*lambada* fusion and another hybrid that combined comparsa rhythms with Brazilian *batucada* and sacred songs for the orisha Ochún.[59] In my interview with Clave y Guaguancó director Amado Dedeu, he stated, like the two other Havana rumba group directors, that rumba can be fused with any other genre of music. He asserted, "La nada, nada inspira," a proverb that translates roughly to "nothing (no musical creation) comes from/is inspired by nothing," adding "todo está hecho" (basically, everything has already been done). He suggested that the job of musicians now is not to create things from scratch but to recreate by mixing genres, and in his mind no musical practices were off-limits for creative appropriation.

It is particularly productive to highlight the contrasting perspectives on rumba-batá fusions expressed by the directors of Afrocuba de Matanzas and Clave y Guaguancó, respectively. While the former explicitly spoke about his opposition to introducing nonpercussion instruments and European-derived vocal aesthetics into the batarumba ensemble, Clave y Guaguancó's recent album features the use of several melodic instruments, and all of their albums feature elaborate vocal harmonies, both of which are elements that branch out beyond the domain of Afro-Cuban folkloric music. When I asked Amado whether Afrocuba's batarumba influenced his group's rumba-batá fusions, he denied any connection with Afrocuba's innovation, stating that although the instrumental format is basically the same, Clave y Guaguancó's fusions are not batarumbas as such. Instead, he asserted, each of the group's rumba-batá fusions has its own rhythmic basis and concept, which is what identifies them and inspires their specific names like *jazz-batá* or *flameguanbatá*. He contrasted this naming process with that of Afrocuba's, noting that the Matanzas group's name for its fusion, batarumba, denotes a generic complex (rumba) instead of specific rumba styles like guaguancó and columbia. He added that Afrocuba uses only a limited number of batá rhythms in their batarumbas— the most popular ones, namely chachalokofún, ñongo, and Iyesá. Clave y Guaguancó, he stated, aims to use more obscure and difficult batá rhythms as well as to incorporate the cajón for added timbral variety. Beyond displaying a conception of fusion that contrasts sharply with that of Minini in terms of its almost limitless approach, Amado's implication that Afrocuba's batarumba repertoire is fairly homogeneous and uniform—that their songs don't all have their own specific rhythmic combinations—reinforced the one-dimensional definition of batarumba that circulates so widely.

One last vignette constitutes an interesting illustration of the wide-ranging conceptions of hybridizing practices held by various musicians, especially when the fusions involve the incorporation of sacred instruments or songs. I saw Clave y Guaguancó perform a fusion in 2006 that invoked three separate Afro-Cuban traditions: rumba, Santería, and Abakuá music. The percussion involved a mix of the three drumming styles (with the rumba and Abakuá

Figure 5.14: Folkloric representation of the *Abakuá iremé*.

rhythms played on the congas and combined with batá drumming), and the vocals fused rumba song, chants for the orisha Oyá, and Abakuá refrains.[60] The song seemed to suggest a parallel between the traits of this particular orisha, who is known as the guardian of the cemetery and is thus associated with the dead, and the ritual principles on which Abakuá is centered, namely dead ancestors. During the performance, two dancers came out, one representing Oyá and the other as the *Abakuá iremé* or "little devil," the masked figure who embodies this practice (figure 5.14).

I was a bit bewildered by the choice to combine these two sacred practices and decided to consult other musicians about it. One Yoruba Andabo percussionist reacted with disparagement, stating that the Lucumí and Abakuá traditions should never be mixed, according to the religious precepts of the former. While Abakuá initiates can be subsequently initiated into Santería, the reverse cannot occur; people already initiated into Santería are forbidden from becoming initiates in Abakuá. Santería is considered to be the apex of Afro-Cuban religious practice; no other religion is valued more highly, and thus initiation into other religions—principally Palo and, for men, Abakuá—cannot come after one has "made santo." While Oyá is the orisha associated with the dead, and this was presumably the point of Clave y Guaguancó's fusion, the percussionist stated that the fusion was not appropriate in a religious sense. He then spoke about the close relationship between Abakuá and Palo; because both religions are centered on revering and establishing contact with dead ancestors, a fusion of the two could be justified. He concluded that the only Afro-Cuban genre that can truly be mixed with any of these religious practices is rumba. From his perspective, then, fusion has its limits, especially when it involves more than one Afro-Cuban religious practice. While my assessment of the fusion concerned aesthetic issues—it seemed to me like a hodgepodge of practices combined solely for the sake of fusion—this percussionist, like others, framed his critique in relation to religious precepts.[61]

Another folkloric musician concurred with this perspective, stating that Santería and Abakuá are two completely unrelated traditions and that fusing them profanes the former. He stated that while each Abakuá society has a patron orisha, an Abakuá iremé cannot come out to dance during the performance of a batá rhythm for an orisha. Furthermore, while the different religious traditions could be performed in a folkloric context alongside one another, they should not be mixed within any one piece. Thus, he too drew the fusion line at mixing religious representations. When I mentioned the fusion to a singer with Afrocuba de Matanzas, he wholeheartedly concurred with the two previous opinions, although he also offered a regionalist comment. He declared that this was just an example of how habaneros are always making things up in order to sell their culture to tourists, thus clearly homogenizing folkloric musicians from the capital who display distinct opinions on the matter. Ironically, as mentioned earlier in this chapter, one of Afrocuba's batarumba songs, "Baila Mi Guaguancó," mixes batá and Abakuá drumming in the montuno section; thus, much like Minini's comments about guarapachangueo, the singer's comments must be taken with a grain of salt.[62] This inconsistency also illustrates how aesthetic opinions are informed by the politics of place (for instance, a Matanzas musician linked this fusion to an essentialist narrative about Havana musicians, while he presumably found a similar fusion performed by Afrocuba to be acceptable), and can be very situationally specific.[63]

A third Havana-based musician reinforced the others' statements that the two traditions have nothing to do with each other but added that within the context of an *espectáculo* (folkloric show), it is a fusion that can be performed and does not constitute a bad idea conceptually. He alluded to the history of slavery, stating that Africans of different ethnic origins were thrown together on the plantations, and that not only were distinct traditions and religions practiced alongside each other but they also often adopted, whether consciously or not, certain ritual practices from one another. He distinguished between espectáculos and ritual contexts, asserting that while this fusion cannot occur within the latter, there was no reason not to do it in the former. Finally, he emphasized a further separation between these two contexts that makes this fusion permissible in a folkloric show: the batá drums used in espectáculos are not consecrated and, most often, the Abakuá songs are not even performed on Abakuá drums but rather on conga drums. Clearly this musician was in the minority in his endorsement of the Oyá-Abakuá fusion. However, my larger point is that this nuanced perspective is evidence of a wide range of views concerning the boundaries of hybridizing practices within rumba performance.

The portrait I have painted of Havana-based musicians' views on rumba fusion practices is not that of a neat and easily categorizable group of people who hold uniform notions about which genres can and cannot be mixed. Many musicians, most of whom practice one or more Afro-Cuban religions, do not feel that it is appropriate to mix different sacred traditions together within folkloric performance, even when both or all are being incorporated into a rumba context. Others feel that there are inherent and significant differences between ritual and folkloric contexts, such as the consecration or lack thereof of the percussion instruments and, as Katherine Hagedorn theorizes in her book *Divine Utterances* (2001), the different intents of the musicians in each context. In other words, they find that religious precepts governing ceremonies do not necessarily have to be adhered to in espectáculos. Notwithstanding these different perspectives, Havana musicians tend to feel less restricted in their hybridizing practices than Matanzas-based musicians, as illustrated by the formers' declarations that rumba can be mixed with anything. This observation leads back to my main objective in this chapter, which has been to elucidate the ways that musicians' conceptions of fusion, as exemplified by the two innovations I have discussed, are informed both by their local identities and by the discourses of place attached to their respective cities.

Conclusion

I want to emphasize that, as with all stereotypes and essentializing discursive formations, there is an element of truth in the notions that Havana is the locus of cultural and musical hybridity and that Matanzas is the principal site for the maintenance of Afro-Cuban tradition. These tropes of place reflect the social histories of each city in various ways. For example, the capital has long been what Mary Louise Pratt (1992) would term a "contact zone," a meeting ground for a variety of peoples from Europe, Africa, the Caribbean, and China, and thus more susceptible to racial and cultural mixing. Conversely, Matanzas Province was the site of the largest plantations and most numerous concentrations of African slaves and their descendants during the nineteenth century and thus has a historic connection with blackness. The histories of these places and the cultural discourses that circulate about them influence the formation of musicians' local identities and their notions about the limits or lack thereof in hybridizing practices. Furthermore, these discourses of place not only function negatively, to essentialize each city's cultural identities; they also function in a "productive" manner in the Foucaultian sense, by informing the creation of situated rumba innovations. Batarumba is a complex and fascinating hybrid whose specificity and situatedness derive from the particular histories of and racialized discourses about Matanzas that infuse the local identities of native musicians. If not for these notions about Matanzas, batarumba would likely be a completely different entity. Similarly, such a diversely conceived practice as guarapachangueo would likely not have been possible in a place where the majority of local musicians felt obliged to preserve traditional styles. It is precisely Havana musicians' propensity to "recoger todo lo que está en el ambiente" (soak up everything around them), as one musician told me, that sets the stage for the creation of innovations like guarapachangueo and the incorporation of foreign genres like reggaetón into their local practices.

It is my hope that this chapter has contributed a critical perspective on the notion of hybridity by viewing fusion practices as emanating from specific and situated positionalities vis-à-vis musicians' artistic choices. The process of situated hybridity is seen not only in terms of the racialized politics of place and musicians' local affiliations, as I have posited here, but also in terms of other axes of identity formation such as class, sexuality, religion, and generation. This way of conceptualizing hybridity thus seeks to highlight, rather than obscure, the inherently political nature of fusion practices, precisely because they are entangled with issues of representation and processes of identity formation.

Chapter Six

The Politics of Place and National Traditions: Race, Regionalism, and the Relationship between Rumba and *Son*

Rumba and son. These two musical practices have not only constituted the backbone of Cuban popular music for over a century, but they are also two of the most important creative forces responsible for the success of international tourism to the island since the early 1990s. Son has been revived since the Special Period in two major ways: first, by the reinterpretation of son-derived Cuban dance music through the emergence of timba, and second, through the neotraditional performance of the son in the global arena by the various producers and musicians associated with Wim Wenders's 1999 documentary *Buena Vista Social Club* and its related recording projects.[1] The latter instance is entangled with regimes of nostalgia, as it looks back to the "golden days" of Cuban popular music (the 1930s–1950s), not coincidentally also corresponding to the less politically controversial prerevolutionary era. In contrast, the timba phenomenon is unequivocally modern, with lyrics referencing the contemporary realities of the post-Soviet crisis in Cuban socialism and music that draws upon African American genres (funk, jazz) in addition to Cuban styles racialized as "black" (rumba, Santería music).[2]

Rumba performance has also enjoyed a renaissance since the 1990s, becoming increasingly visible and audible in the international arena owing to musical recordings and international tours in North America and Europe by big-name groups like Los Muñequitos de Matanzas, Yoruba Andabo, and Clave y Guaguancó. Rumba has been inserted into the cultural tourism narrative and presented as a particularly authentic Cuban cultural expression, the "heart and soul" of the people. Many foreigners travel to Cuba already proficient in playing rumba and/or other Afro-Cuban percussion genres, and in dancing rumba or *casino* (Cuban-style salsa). Even if they have no empirical experience with Afro-Cuban music and dance, most foreigners who travel to the island have consulted travel guides that tout rumba events in Havana, such as the Sunday rumba at the Callejón de Hamel and the Peña del Ambia at the Unión Nacional de Escritores y Artistas de Cuba (UNEAC), as the most authentic representations of Afro-Cuban culture.[3] While constituting important forces, the narratives of foreign journalists and Cuban tourism literature are only partially responsible for the growing relevance of rumba. Musicians from both rumba and mass-mediated popular genres such as timba and reggaetón have played an active role in increasing rumba's visibility by incorporating musical elements from each other's styles and thus highlighting both the historical and more recent entanglements between these musical spheres.

Given the historical and ongoing significance of these two national traditions, in this chapter I aim to tease out the ways that the relationship between rumba and son has been represented in scholarship by both Cuban and foreign music scholars, ultimately in order to argue that this literature constitutes another arena in which the politics of place are played out. Son, historically considered to have emerged from eastern Cuba, is often discussed as the quintessential musical representation of the island, a fact that seemingly contradicts my assertions regarding the hegemony of western Cuban traditions. However, there have been recent attempts to construct a revisionist history that reduces the significance of Oriente within the emergence and/or development of son. In addition, son's links to the east have been somewhat weakened through narratives concerning its relationship to rumba, in that they tend to focus almost exclusively on the latter's influence on the former. I have found that while rumba's impact on son and other mass-mediated popular genres has been well documented, the reverse flow of influence is rarely, if at all, acknowledged in scholarship. In my view this trend is related to the primary theoretical issues with which I am concerned in this book: race and place.

This chapter aims both to raise questions about racialized discourses of musical influence within academic literature and to continue foregrounding the politics of place as it relates to music making in contemporary Cuba. In terms of national discourses of race, I suggest that the asymmetrical narrative of musical influence involving rumba and son is entangled with notions of racialized authenticity and the ways that race is mapped onto musical practices in Cuba. I believe that rumba, more than any other secular genre of Cuban music, is articulated as the authentic, spontaneous expression of the national populace regardless of their race, even if the reality of rumba performance is quite distinct.[4] Given this discursive representation, rumba is often discussed as a major source of influence for son, timba, and other mass-mediated musics. I want to assert instead that the relationship between rumba and mass-mediated Cuban popular music is characterized by a bidirectional flow of influence, as evidenced by the rumba innovations I discussed in the previous chapter. I thus argue that rumba is a recipient of influence as well as a source of inspiration. Furthermore, I want to consider the ways that the long-standing regional inequalities on the island may inform scholars' discussions of rumba and son. As I discussed in chapter 3, the politically, economically, and culturally hegemonic status of the western region, particularly Havana, has often resulted in a disproportionate valorization of western Afro-Cuban culture and religious practices over their eastern Cuban counterparts. In this vein, I will discuss the distinct notions of blackness associated with Matanzas (considered to be the birthplace of rumba) and Santiago (known as "the cradle of son"). I will end the chapter with a final reconsideration of the racialized discourses of place attached to Oriente, emphasizing the significance of mestizaje in the identity formation of eastern Cubans.

Rumba and Son: the Traditional Narrative

Traditional narratives about the musical exchanges between these two incredibly influential Cuban genres generally begin the story a little over a century ago (1909), when son migrated to western Cuba and came into contact with rumba. There is no consensus among Cuban musicologists about who were the main agents that brought son to Havana and western Cuba. Odilio Urfé, as cited by Helio Orovio, asserts that eastern Cuban regiments of the Ejército Permanente (Permanent Army) brought son with them to Havana in 1909 (Orovio 1981).[5] Radamés Giro challenges the timing of this narrative, asserting that it was eastern Cuban musicians who had migrated to Havana and other western provinces *earlier* than 1909—and not members of the Permanent Army—who brought son with them ([1994] 1998). Jesús Gómez Cairo offers yet another version of the story: it was eastern Cuban migrant agricultural workers who brought son with them when they were forced to migrate to western Cuba for economic reasons; he does not mention a specific date ([1980] 1998). Finally, Benjamin Lapidus notes that, because the general trend within internal migration was from west to east until independence in 1898, and toward the center of the island in the following decades, it is unlikely that the main agents of transportation were eastern soldiers moving west at that time (2008, xvii). Below, I discuss some revisionist histories of son that further challenge the account of how son first encountered rumba.

While many scholars have recognized the intimate relationship between these two seminal Cuban genres, few have questioned their separation into two distinct "generic complexes," a system of categorization that became hegemonic after the revolution following the work of pioneering musicologist

Argeliers León. Leonardo Acosta has recently critiqued this "ghettoization" of genres, stating that "today they [the notion of generic complexes] weigh on rumba, *son*, and *danzón* like a prison sentence" (2004, 38; my translation). His main issue is that this method of categorization obscures the "fundamental unity" of Cuban dance music, particularly its common African roots, and severs it from its Caribbean cousins and siblings.[6] He also finds the methodology somewhat arbitrary, noting that within the son complex there is a mixing of "historical variants" with "regional variants" (i.e., some of the variants of son differ in historical era, while others are from different regions of the country).[7] In terms of the relationship specifically between rumba and son, Acosta states: "Today I conceive of them as two faces of the same coin" (2004, 54; my translation). Unfortunately, he does not expand upon this characterization, although one can infer that he aims to highlight the connections between the two genres. Notwithstanding his challenge to the categorical separation of rumba and son, Acosta's narrative reinforces the common tendency to present a unidirectional flow of influence from the former to the latter.

The overwhelming majority of scholarship about this relationship characterizes rumba as the source—never the recipient—of musical influence vis-à-vis son. This is significant given that the two are constructed as the musical symbols of the west and east, respectively. Ethnomusicologist James Robbins describes the early eastern Cuban manifestations of son as "an eastern counterpart to the rumba types that formed the basis of secular music among urban blacks in Havana" (1990, 184). Speaking about the changes applied to son once it took root in Havana, Ned Sublette states, "The son had been penetrated by the rumba, to the point that we can speak of a *son rumbeao*: a rumba-ized son, played by the same low elements of society that danced guaguancó and worked on the docks" (2004, 335). Similarly, Acosta states, "the rumba gave new life to the *son* when the latter reached Havana and Matanzas" ([1983] 1991, 67), and the late Canadian ethnomusicologist Lise Waxer asserts, "While *son* has provided the musical wellspring for Cuban music in the 20th century, it in turn has drawn continual nourishment from the *rumba*" (1994, 144). During the global "rumba craze" that began in 1930 with the performance of "El Manicero" by Don Azpiazu's orchestra in New York, son was essentially exported under the label "rumba," a mislabeling that had wide-ranging repercussions in terms of the creation of new popular musics, particularly in Africa.[8] In a case of reverse-diasporic flow, Cuban son (labeled as "rumba") was the primary influence on the emergence of Congolese rumba in the 1940s, a genre that included many musical elements of son; this style came to constitute the most influential popular music on the African continent.[9] Thus, while not necessarily the intention of the actors responsible for the mislabeling of son, the result was that rumba received undue credit for influencing musical styles that were really outgrowths of son.

Many scholars have discussed the structural similarities between rumba and son songs, noting in particular the adoption of rumba's montuno section as a crucial feature of son once it was established and formalized in Havana in the 1920s (Manuel 1985a; Manuel 1985b; León [1982] 1991; Waxer 1994; Gómez Cairo [1980] 1998; Averill 1999). Like the previous scholars quoted, ethnomusicologist Peter Manuel's statement is typical of the prevailing opinion concerning the flow of musical influence: "The son and its Puerto Rican— and New York–based derivative, salsa, generally retain the basic bipartite structure of the rumba (the diana generally being dispensed with or replaced by an instrumental introduction)" (1985a, 171). Lise Waxer characterizes son clave as a modified version of rumba clave (1994, 143), and both Waxer and Manuel discuss the "anticipated bass," a defining characteristic of son, as a reconfiguration of the rhythmic pattern played by the lowest-pitched conga drum in rumba guaguancó (Manual 1985b; Waxer 1994).[10] In terms of instrumental appropriations from rumba, the incorporation of *tumbadoras* (conga drums) into the son ensemble by black tres player Arsenio Rodríguez in the 1940s is considered by many scholars to be a "'rumbaization' of son" (Robbins 1990, 188).

The intimate relationship between the two genres is not surprising, given that many of the most influential Cuban *soneros* (son musicians) were also *rumberos*. Prominent examples include Ignacio Piñeiro—one of son's most prolific composers, who converted many rumba songs to the son format— and famed singer Beny Moré, both of whom incorporated specific aspects of rumba vocal style into son performance (Waxer 1994; Averill 1999). In fact, son lyrics provide clear evidence of rumba's influence, and there are numerous examples of son songs (not including those taken directly from rumba repertoire) that extol the virtues of rumba (R. Moore 1995). Robin Moore suggests that many musicians who started their careers as rumberos, including Piñeiro and Moré, formed son groups in response to commercial demand. Moore states, "An acceptance of Afrocuban performers as *soneros* but not as *rumberos* seems to have led to an increasing interpenetration of the two genres on the part of these musicians as they attempted to reconcile their personal musical experiences with the constraints of the international market and the biases of middle-class Cubans" (1995, 181).

In addition to its relationship with son, rumba's influence on Cuban dance music since the revolution has also been widely acknowledged. There were several rhythms/dance crazes that emerged in the 1960s and 1970s, such as *mozambique* and *pilón*, that were derived from combining rumba, comparsa, and Afro-Cuban sacred rhythms (Elí Rodríguez 1989; R. Moore 2006). In addition, Los Van Van debuted a polyrhythm called *songo* in the 1970s, invented by drummer José Luís "Changuito" Quintana, which helped set the stage for the emergence of timba in the late 1980s. Among the important innovations of songo were the adoption of the drum kit into the Cuban dance band ensemble and the transfer of rumba percussion patterns to this instrument (Perna 2005, 36). The jazz fusion band Irakere, led by pianist Chucho Valdés, was also a major innovator in the 1970s as it combined elements from jazz, rock, Afro-Cuban folkloric music, and rumba. In fact, timba scholar Vincenzo Perna states that Irakere's sound "represents the most direct antecedent of timba" (2005, 39), noting in particular the group's jazz-influenced phrasing and heavy reliance on rumba style and repertoire.

Drawing more heavily on rumba's rhythms and performance styles than any other contemporary genre is timba, which has a dense, polyrhythmic, syncopated texture and a more aggressive sound than its Caribbean cousin, New York Puerto Rican–style salsa. First, the shortening of the canto or narrative section of a song and the corresponding predominance of the montuno section can be viewed as an influence from rumba. Vincenzo Perna attributes this lengthening of the montuno section to José Luís "El Tosco" Cortés (2005, 64), a conservatory-trained flutist who honed his musical chops with both Los Van Van (1970–1980) and Irakere (1980–1988) before establishing his own pioneering timba band, NG La Banda, in 1988.[11] Second, many timba bands began to use the rumba clave rhythm, instead of the slightly less syncopated son clave rhythm, to structure the overall rhythmic texture of the ensemble. Moreover, as with son, many timba songs are odes to rumba and/or Afro-Cuban religions such as Santería. Finally, it seems that even the name for contemporary Cuban dance music—timba—has historical links to rumba. Both Perna and writer Philip Sweeney discuss the use of the term "timba" in traditional rumba songs, particularly those in the columbia style, and the fact that the terms "timba" and "timbero" were often used synonymously with rumba and rumbero (Sweeney 2001; Perna 2005).

Racialized Discourses of Influence

With so many connections between rumba and son-derived dance music, I find it curious that the source of influence is so unanimously attributed to rumba, especially considering that it is not necessarily an older tradition; the rural eastern Cuban antecedents of son are thought to have emerged in the mid- to late nineteenth century, roughly the same era in which the earliest instances of rumba were documented. I do not aim to contradict the significance of rumba's influence, particularly because I have often argued for more scholarly attention to contemporary rumba performance. Nonetheless, influence is rarely unidirectional in any musical exchange, and I believe that the literature's focus on only one side of the equation is what needs to be scrutinized. Acosta offers one possibility for the unbalanced nature of the scholarship: "If I have insisted on the importance of the rumba in our culture, it is because the rumba has been so disparaged, and at the same time so adulterated in deformed versions, especially, though not only, in commercial Yankee music" ([1983] 1991, 69). He is referring to the long-standing marginalization of rumba performance (and to the aforementioned "rumba" craze that resulted in the lumping together of many Latin American styles under that term), which even today is linked discursively to violence and excessive drinking, and considered disparagingly by some white and/or middle-class Cubans to be *una cosa de negros*, "a black thing."[12]

Notwithstanding the importance of a political reclamation of rumba such as the one issued by Acosta, I wonder if there are not deeper implications underlying these narratives of unidirectional influence. Specifically, I believe they are entangled with racialized discourses of authenticity. Much of the scholarship about these two practices discusses them in simplified racial terms: rumba is black, while son is mulato (a perfect blend of African and Spanish descent) and thus the quintessential national practice. For example, Fabio Betancur Álvarez (1993, 129) extends Fernando Ortiz's famous metaphor of "tobacco" and "sugar" as the roots of Cuban national culture to speak about the relationship between the two genres: he aligns rumba with the "liberatory" (and racialized) tobacco—cultivated with free labor—while son is linked to the dehumanizing system of slavery associated with sugar production.[13] These racialized associations are often invoked to imply that rumba is more authentic, because it is more "purely" African and thus more likely to influence other musics rather than be influenced itself by them. In this view, rumba represents the a priori "root" of national identity and culture, which forms one of the foundations (along with the Spanish elements) upon which the mixed-race Cuban citizen and the racially hybrid son are constructed.

Far from being the purview only of Cuban scholarship, this discourse of racialized authenticity is clear in the work of foreign scholars as well. In his book on timba, Vincenzo Perna (2005) argues that rumba has played a large part in the re-Africanization of Cuban dance music. He asserts that rumba has functioned as an authenticating mechanism for timba, partially through textual allusions to lower-class Afro-Cuban neighborhoods that are strongly associated with rumba performance. Regarding the relationship between the two genres, Perna states, "As a music and dance, timba is clearly and over-whelmingly black, but also because at a specific musical level timba is perme-ated by rumba rhythms and themes, by Afro-Cuban slang and references to life in the black neighbourhood. It is probably fair to say that timba re-inter-prets in modern times the rebel, anarchic and challenging spirit of rumba" (2005, 104). While Perna's work is in general an excellent study, I find his char-acterization of timba as unequivocally "black" to be somewhat reductionist, as the style displays a variety of influences and elements from hybrid genres such as jazz and rock.[14] More importantly, I disagree with his implication that rumba is a nonmodern practice from which timba has drawn its oppositional character. I would argue instead that rumba is a vibrant and contemporary genre that still has the currency to represent itself. Furthermore, the roman-ticized notion that rumba is a liberatory and rebellious performance practice that challenges the status quo oversimplifies the heterogeneous nature of con-temporary rumba performance across the island. This characterization also glosses over some of the more controversial aspects of rumba performance, such as its entanglements with the cultural tourism industry and "folkloric hustling,"[15] and its engagement with mass-mediated genres such as reggaetón. Perna's assertion also buttresses my thesis that it is precisely rumba's asso-ciation with blackness that informs the propensity to view it as exclusively a *source*, and not a *recipient*, of musical influence vis-à-vis Cuban popular musics. The problem with the construction of rumba as a unitary, bounded entity is that it denies the possibility of any musical influence permeating the practice, which simply does not correspond to the reality of rumba perfor-mance, especially (but not only) in the contemporary era.[16]

While the racialized discourses attached to rumba and son reduce the former to a strictly black, oppositional practice, they also disregard the his-tory of son's reception. As Robin Moore convincingly argues in *Nationalizing Blackness* (1997), son was not always considered the quintessential representa-tion of hybridized Cubanidad, what Argeliers León called the "Cuban musi-cal genre *par excellence*" ([1982] 1991, 21). As famously theorized by Michael Omi and Howard Winant (1986), racial formations and meanings are inher-ently unstable, and dependent upon changing historical and social contexts. Moore discusses how in the early decades of the twentieth century, son was subjected to similar types of discrimination and derision as rumba and also racialized as "black"; in fact, it was precisely because of this racialization that Cuban elites delighted in dancing to son, as they considered it to be "for-bidden" and "savage" music. Considering that son once occupied a discursive position similar to that of rumba, and that clearly there was much exchange going on between musicians of these two genres, it seems implausible that son did not exercise at least some influence on rumba. The rumba innovations I discussed in the previous chapter demonstrate clearly that rumba has been "penetrated" (to borrow Sublette's term) by son and other popular music traditions throughout its history, not only in the contemporary moment.

Revisionist Histories of Son and the Politics of Place

As I have argued throughout this book, racialized cultural discourses—both explicit and implicit—abound throughout the literature on Cuban music. I am certainly not the first scholar to recognize or write about this. My unique contribution lies in the articulation of these racialized notions with discourses of place, and my observations about how this relationship relates to various musical practices in contemporary Cuba. Thus, while I believe that the literature on the relationship between son and rumba has tended to view the latter as a source of musical influence for the former—often using racialized origin myths that stress rumba's connection to Africa and its oppositional, anticommercial character—I also want to suggest that the long-standing regional inequalities between eastern and western Cuba constitute another significant factor in how the two practices have been discussed. Quite simply, while rumba is perhaps "too black" to serve as the perfect musical representation for a nation that defines itself as racially mixed, paradoxically it is this association with blackness that confers upon the practice an authenticity that does not adhere to the more European-sounding son.[17] Although son is regularly proclaimed as Cuba's national music—a status that was reinforced with the success of the *Buena Vista Social Club* phenomenon and the birth of a neotraditional style of son—when it is discussed in relation to rumba, it is implicitly devalued as less original (because it has been a recipient of rumba's influence) and more commercialized, and thus less authentic. If rumba represents the west and son represents Oriente—in tandem with the fact that Afro-Cuban religious practices in Occidente are considered to be more "purely" African than their eastern Cuban counterparts (see chapter 3)—to put it crudely, the western region wins the battle of authenticity.

I have identified, in my archival and ethnographic research, two recent tendencies in discussions of Cuba's quintessential musical genre that shed light on how the politics of place manifest in academic scholarship. On one hand, there seems to be an attempt by various scholars to construct what amounts to a revisionist history of son, one that questions its links to Oriente and/ or reduces the importance of eastern Cuban traditions in the development of son. At the same time, there have also been recent attempts to strengthen son's connection to Oriente, principally by emphasizing the influence from changüí and Franco-Haitian traditions on the practice. While I will detail the perspectives associated with each trend, I believe that the first one is related to the cultural hegemony of Havana and its effects on the production of knowledge, which tends to disregard eastern Cuban musical creativity.

A Challenge to the Established Narrative about Son's Origins

Various scholars have recently published revisionist histories of son or highlighted the significance of western Cuban influences on the formation of the genre. These accounts have not necessarily debunked the narrative of how the practice arrived in Havana—although there is still no consensus on exactly how and when son migrated—but, more accurately, they have attempted to downplay the influence of rural eastern Cuban traditions historically thought to be son's predecessors. In other words, these scholars argue that the principal features that constitute son as a musical practice were not in place until it arrived in the capital, at which point various elements were added. While the scholars' goals are not necessarily related to the larger tensions between east and west—and I do not aim to impute bias to their projects—I nonetheless believe that their arguments reinforce the larger trend in Cuban music scholarship to view Havana and western Cuba as responsible for much of the musical creativity on the island.

Before discussing the new perspectives on son, I want to briefly outline the recent scholarship on contradanza, a musical practice that has also undergone a revisionist history in recent decades, as I believe it can illuminate this tendency to view musical creativity as primarily the purview of Havana. Cuban musicologist Zoila Lapique published an article in 1995 that traced the origins of contradanza, disputing the long-held notion advanced by earlier generations of music scholars—like Alejo Carpentier—that the European contredanse was brought to the island first by Franco-Haitian immigrants fleeing the Haitian Revolution in the 1790s. The crux of the debate relates to the *cinquillo* rhythm, often thought of as one of the main features that differentiates Cuban contradanza from its European predecessor. First, Carpentier's original argument:

> The "French blacks" would also play an important role in the formation of Cuban music—made from inherited and transformed elements—with a fundamental rhythmic element to be slowly incorporated into many of the island's folkloric genres: the *cinquillo*.... The *cinquillo* is of obvious African origin. It has the rhythmic regularity, the symmetry of certain percussive rituals of voodoo. Its

diffusion and persistence can be observed in regions of the Americas where blacks were the majority or a significant part of the population. . . . That it existed in Cuba before the arrival of the "French blacks" is quite likely. But it must have been confined to the slave barracks, since it passed into salon dancing in the days of the Haitian immigration. In the neighboring isle, its presence was so active that it was incorporated into the *contradanza*. (Carpentier 2001, 148–49)

He concludes that although contradanza may have been present in Havana before the mid-nineteenth century, it was more of a Europeanized, classical version, while the salon dance music in Santiago was more popular and African derived because the cinquillo had already been incorporated.

Lapique's argument firmly negates the notion that this altered musical practice took root first in the east and then moved westward, and that the Cubanization of the contredanse was due to the contributions of "French blacks." She instead asserts that the European salon dance arrived in Cuba via Spain (not Haiti) in the mid-eighteenth century and that it was black and mixed-race Cubans of Bantu origin—not French slaves and mulatos—who incorporated African-derived rhythms (such as the tango), thus Cubanizing the tradition (Lapique 1998).[18] She further states that the "French black" elements were not evident in the Cubanized contradanza until the mid-nineteenth century, when the French-derived *cocoyé* revitalized the contradanza via the incorporation of the cinquillo rhythm, first in Santiago, and then in the rest of the island. In sum, Lapique argues that the contredanse arrived to Cuba not secondhand, via Haiti, but directly from Europe (and directly to Havana), and that the localized version (the contradanza) had already taken form before the Franco-Haitian influence penetrated it.

Lapique's conclusions have been accepted by the majority of Cuban musicologists, and have in some cases been extended by them. While she maintains the link between the cinquillo rhythm and Franco-Haitian migrants, the recent consensus is that both contradanza and cinquillo were already present in western Cuba by the mid-eighteenth century, before the arrival of the first wave of migrants from Saint-Domingue. Both Cristóbal Díaz Ayala (2003) and Leonardo Acosta (2004) suggest that the cinquillo rhythm was already being used in the ritual music of Yoruba and Bantu slaves. However, it is Peter Manuel who most stridently challenges Carpentier's assertions regarding the provenance of the cinquillo as used in contradanza, and the notion that this element was a contribution of Franco-Haitian migrants. Manuel argues that, based on his extensive study of contradanza scores from Havana (and the few he could obtain from Santiago), the cinquillo did not in fact pervade the songs from either city, and that Santiago contradanzas showed no more preference for the rhythm than did those from the capital in the mid-nineteenth century (2009b, 198). He affirms that the cinquillo seems to have become hegemonic in the 1870s with the emergence of the more heavily Cubanized danzón. The wide-ranging acceptance and extension of Lapique's thesis that the contradanza became Cubanized in Havana before the arrival of Franco-Haitian immigrants means that the significance of eastern Cuban influence on a national genre has been diminished. However, while eastern Cubans do not necessarily have a deep connection with contradanza, they are very invested in the notion that son is from Oriente; thus an attempt to view son as having developed primarily in the capital is a more serious challenge to established narratives about the regional provenance of national cultural traditions.

Beyond his assertions about contradanza, Manuel's recent article—entitled "From Contradanza to Son: New Perspectives on the Prehistory of Cuban Popular Music"—is also a prominent example of the attempt to construct a revisionist history of son. Cognizant that he is presenting a serious challenge regarding the origins of Cuba's national genre, he states: "I further call into question the traditional invocation of rural Oriente as the son's cradle, suggesting that some of the genre's most basic structural features appear to have been absent in Oriente and probably derived from other sources—especially the creole vernacular song genres and salon dances of Havana of the 1850s–1860s. In particular, I present evidence suggesting a seminal role of the urban Cuban contradanza in the prehistory of the son" (Manuel 2009b, 185). Manuel attributes the narrative of son's eastern origins to the region's distinct racial composition and politics as compared with those of the west, noting that because Oriente was less racially polarized and had a longer history of miscegenation, it makes sense to view the eminently hybrid son as emerging from the east. He adds, "The natural assumption has been that the traditional son's relative popularity in Oriente derives from its having originated there— an assumption that I will call into question" (188).

Manuel's primary argument in challenging the traditional narrative is that the origins of son can better be located in the popular (as opposed to the "elite") versions of contradanza circulating in Havana in the second half of the nineteenth century. As he has asserted in previous scholarship, one of son's defining characteristics is an anticipated bass pattern, a syncopated feature usually thought to have its origins in rural eastern antecedents of the practice. In this article, he characterizes the anticipation found in eastern Cuban rural styles like changüí and nengón as "germinal and occasional rather than pervasive and structural" (Manuel 2009b, 206) and argues that this feature only became pervasive in son after it arrived in Havana. He states,

"Collectively, such evidence suggests that the son's characteristic anticipation evolved in Havana from the germination of a 'seed' brought from Oriente in the form of lightly anticipated tres and vocal patterns fertilized by compatible distinctive syncopations in Havana-based musics, as well as the ambience of a lively and dynamic urban popular music scene" (206–7). Manuel discusses most of the defining elements of son, concluding that the syncopated style of playing the tres is the only major feature that clearly derives from eastern Cuban antecedents.

Whether Manuel's article presents convincing evidence to overturn the narrative that son emerged in Oriente and was then introduced to Havana (where, no one disputes, it was formalized in terms of song structure and instrumentation), is a matter that perhaps can only be evaluated in the future. Furthermore, I should note that I am not a son expert, nor have I consulted primary sources on the genre, as Manuel has. Nonetheless, it is worth noting that there is one seminal feature of son that does not figure into his reconsideration of its origins: the *bongó*, the primary percussion instrument with which son has always been associated.[19] Early in his article, Manuel lists it as a defining characteristic that formed part of the "primordial" son ensemble brought from Oriente (2009b, 186–88), and he never challenges the narrative of the bongó's eastern provenance.[20] However, somewhere during the course of the article the instrument drops off his list of essential features, in that it is neither a focus of his revisionist arguments, nor is it mentioned in his summary of the elements he believes came from Oriente: "What was distinctive about the rural [eastern] son was the use of that term, the contrapuntal tres accompaniment style, and the subtle anticipation implicit in some tres and vocal patterns" (207). Whether or not this omission was an oversight on Manuel's part, I believe it contradicts his argument that most of son's primary features were introduced after it arrived in Havana. It seems clear that, at the very least, the styles of playing tres and bongó—the only two instruments that have remained part of the son ensemble throughout its evolution over the past century, and which are described by ethnomusicologist James Robbins as "the most '*sonero*' of instruments" (1990, 188)—were derived from Oriente.

Beyond the issue of the bongó, I found the tone of some of Manuel's statements about Oriente to be fairly dismissive. For example, he states that if his hypothesis were to be accepted, "there would be little need to seek the origins of the son in Oriente at all" (2009b, 203). Given the importance of the genre as a national symbol and its significance particularly to the cultural identity of eastern Cubans, this statement could be construed as rather harsh. In addition, Manuel seems to suggest that there is a hidden agenda behind the narrative that son is from Oriente, and he points to what he sees as a romanticization of rural over urban culture. His concluding paragraph sums up this argument nicely: "However, in Santiago that same 'traditional' son, rather than evolving directly from local heritage, was in some ways an import from Havana, where it had acquired septet instrumentation, clave-based rhythms, canto-montuno form, and more pronounced and distinctive forms of rhythmic anticipation. Many son refrains proclaimed a supposed origin in Oriente ('Son de Mayarí, Guantánamo' etc.), but such attributions were in some ways misleading and perhaps included an element of nostalgic idealization of eastern Cuba akin to the guajirismo with which many Havana-dwellers celebrated an imagined rural identity" (2009b, 209). As the reader might expect by now, I disagree with this interpretation. If capital dwellers ever romanticized rural life (which is definitely not the case in the contemporary moment), I do not believe it was the east that captured their nostalgic imaginings but more likely rural locales in the west like Pinar del Río and Matanzas.[21] Manuel's reading does not take into account the pervasiveness of regional tensions throughout the island's history, which began centuries before the emergence of son and which have only grown more antagonistic in post-Soviet Cuba.

Notwithstanding my reservations about some of Manuel's interpretations and statements, his article is also provocative for its assertions regarding the relationship between son and rumba. While he has in past publications highlighted the latter's influence on the former (which, again, I do not wish to contradict), here Manuel suggests that some of their common features may have come instead from contradanza or other popular genres of the mid-nineteenth century. For example, he asserts that two features supposedly taken from rumba—the clave rhythm and the bipartite canto-montuno song structure—could already be seen in contradanzas and urban popular songs of the 1850s. He states:

One might also hypothesize, however blasphemously, that even the rumba's canto-montuno form might have derived from the same [contradanza] tradition. While rumba is justifiably regarded as an Afro-Cuban genre, it should be kept in mind that some of its features are clearly of European derivation, including its language, the overwhelmingly tonal nature of guaguancó and yambú melodies, and the occasional use of the décima form. Similarly, while the rumba may have been the direct source of the clave pattern and structure as well as the clave sticks that became basic to the son, clave as a two-bar entity—although perhaps adapted from Afro-Cuban genres like rumba—was clearly a familiar feature of Havana popular song in the 1850s, as documented by contradanzas like "Cambujá." (Manuel 2009b, 204)

In fact, echoing this assertion, Acosta notes that the son clave rhythm—long thought to have derived from rumba clave—is implied in the cinquillo (2004, 48). Thus, Manuel not only suggests that rumba may not be the provenance of key features of son, but he goes a step further in positing that contradanza may have influenced rumba (as well as son) to a significant degree. He is not the first scholar to remind readers of the hybrid nature of rumba and to counter the discursive Africanization of the practice that misrepresents it as an unequivocally "black" genre: Philip Pasmanick (1997) emphasizes the importance of the European and Spanish elements of rumba song. Nonetheless, positing rumba's formal structure as an element possibly borrowed from contradanza is a new hypothesis, although unfortunately one that is nearly impossible to prove or disprove due to the fact that rumba is an oral tradition that emerged over 150 years ago. More importantly, this is a rare example of rumba being discussed as a *recipient* of influence from other, more European-derived practices. Interestingly, the "blasphemous" (as he puts it) element of Manuel's hypothesis involves rumba's racial connotations and the possibility that it could be discussed as something other than strictly "black." It is as if all of rumba's signifying power lies in its presumed blackness, and exposing its European influences threatens its claim to authenticity. I believe that Manuel's statement buttresses my interpretation of the underlying racial implications of academic discussions concerning the relationship between rumba and son.

Ivor Miller's book on the history of the Cross River secret society in Cuba known as Abakuá (2009) is another recent source that draws links between a western Cuban tradition and the development of son. Unlike Manuel, however, Miller is not attempting to rewrite the story of son's origins but rather aims to emphasize how Abakuá music, language, and terminology have infiltrated the ranks of Cuban popular music in general. He details the many son compositions from the crucial decade of the 1920s that incorporate Abakuá words, discussing how some of the most important innovators of the practice—most famously, Ignacio Piñeiro—were initiated into the secret society. While most of the connections he discusses relate to the evolution of son after it arrived in the capital, he offers one theory suggesting that Abakuá may have influenced son in its germinal stages in the east. This hypothesis relates to the bongó, which he argues may have been derived from an Abakuá word and drum, the Bongó Ékue (Miller 2009, 127). Since the Abakuá tradition never took root beyond the western provinces of Havana and Matanzas, Miller suggests that this influence may have come indirectly, as the result of an encounter between eastern and western Cubans imprisoned together in the Spanish penal colony of Ceuta (in Morocco) during the Cuban wars of independence. He states, "The exchange of ideas between an Abakuá leader from Havana like Felipe Villavicencio (Cara de gallo) and a Carabalí cabildo leader from Santiago like Baracoa would have influenced the practice of Carabalí-derived aesthetics upon their return. This might explain the relationship between two very different instruments, one used exclusively in western Cuba, the other developed in eastern Cuba, that have similar names and can produce similar sounds" (Miller 2009, 127).[22] While I take no issue with the notion that Abakuá drumming and song influenced the evolution of son in Havana in the 1920s and 1930s, Miller's theory about the birth of the bongó goes against the grain of existing research (for example, Elí Rodríguez 1997), in that this percussion instrument is considered to have Bantu, not Calabar (Cross River), origins. Moreover, although Miller's intention is not to rewrite the established narrative about the emergence of son, the linking of it to Abakuá (especially regarding the origins of the bongó) has a similar result: it ultimately helps to redefine son as a practice that is not really from Oriente and that took its true form only after its antecedents left the east. Incidentally, while conducting research on the island in June 2011, I was told in two interviews that there was a Havana-based scholar working on a book that would refute the notion that son emerged in the east and instead argue that it is from Havana and displays major influence from Abakuá. It seems, then, that this revisionist history of son is gaining steam within musicological circles in Havana and abroad.

Reaffirmations of Son's Identity as an Eastern Cuban Tradition

Counterbalancing the attempts to write a revisionist history of son's origins are accounts that seek to tie the practice even more strongly to Oriente. These arguments have centered around the significance of changüí as an antecedent to son. Isaias Rojas, director of the folkloric group Ban Rarrá (which specializes in eastern Cuban folklore and is discussed in chapter 3), vigorously opposed the notion of a strong Abakuá influence on son, refuting it largely by way of a discussion of the Franco-Haitian influence (pers. comm. 2011). He stressed that traditional son stems from a variety of eastern Cuban practices that go back to the nineteenth century but are not well studied, for instance changüí and its variants like nengón and kiribá. These traditions, he noted, were all heavily influenced by Franco-Haitian sacred and secular practices, a claim that he substantiated by listing specific parallels between son rhythms and dance and those used in Vodú and tumba francesa (see chapter 3 for details on these traditions). In addition, while conceding that son was influenced by rumba when it arrived in the capital, Isaias asserted that the manner of playing the bongó in changüí (and, by extension, son) was more reminiscent of the percussion style heard in tumba francesa than in rumba, in that the former is more heavily syncopated than the latter. This statement echoes Leonardo Acosta's statement that son's rhythmic components tend more toward syncopation than do rumba's (2004, 54–55), a surprising assertion given the general discursive Africanization of rumba. Isaias concluded by asserting that the richness of son's percussion is due to its provenance in Oriente, which nurtured the practice of heavily improvisatory Franco-Haitian practices like tumba francesa and Vodú.

Isaias's assertions regarding the Franco-Haitian musical impact on son via changüí are echoed by Benjamin Lapidus, whose research has centered on the history and contemporary performance practice of changüí. The main premise of his book on the Guantánamo-derived rural dance genre (2008) is that it should be categorized as its own generic complex and not considered a variant of son, as there are many divergences in playing style between the two.[23] Interestingly, Lapidus presents various parallels between changüí and rumba, asserting that the manner of interaction between musicians and dancers in the former more accurately resembles that of rumba rather than son (2008, 22). He critiques the traditional narrative of son thus: "This history attributes the son's pre-commercial development in Oriente to a faceless folk and considers changüí as part of a large and subsuming son complex. . . . [F]urthermore Oriente's importance as a crossroads between the Spanish, French, and English-Caribbean is ignored" (xviii). Lapidus also asserts the importance of regional variation in Cuban music, emphasizing the local nature of changüí lyrics and music.

In terms of his discussion of son as an eastern Cuban practice, Lapidus states on the first page of the book's introduction, "As the Mississippi Delta and the blues are to North American popular music, changüí and Oriente are to salsa" (2008, xv). Not mentioned, but implied, is the fact that son is widely considered to be the primary musical antecedent of salsa. He thus firmly places eastern Cuban creativity at the center of national musical tradition, countering the Havana-centric discourses and narratives that tend to keep Oriente on the periphery. Lapidus presents various pieces of evidence of the Franco-Haitian influence on changüí and son, and finds it hardly a coincidence that the most celebrated changüí musicians have been and still are of Haitian descent. Indeed, many of the musicians he discusses throughout the book have French surnames and are active in performing tumba francesa and/or practicing Vodú (124). Lapidus also mentions Guantanamo-based folkloric groups—such as Ban Rarrá—who frequently perform changüí styles alongside percussion-based Afro-Haitian genres like tumba francesa and gagá. He echoes Isaias's assertion of close similarities between bongó playing in changüí and the drumming in both tumba francesa and *petwo*, one of the two main styles of Haitian vodou (130–36). Finally, he discusses the similarity in dance between changüí and tumba francesa. He concludes, "Changüí and nengón come from the same rural coffee regions (Las Cidras, Yateras, etc.) where there were many people of Haitian descent and tumba francesa groups. There might be a relation between changüí and tumba francesa based on this evidence, but as of this writing it ... still remains hypothetical" (137). In presenting his evidence, Lapidus refers to Ivor Miller's hypothesis regarding the possibility that the bongó—both its playing style and name—is evidence of early Abakuá influence on son. He ultimately refutes Miller's argument, asserting that his own musical analysis suggests that the peculiar "howling or moaning sound" made by the glissando on the bongó (a sound also heard in Abakuá drumming) derives from Afro-Haitian sacred and secular percussion music (138). While I do not possess enough firsthand experience with these traditions to weigh in on this matter, I find Lapidus's explanation to be infinitely more feasible than Miller's. Notwithstanding the probability that Cubans from the east and west were in contact while imprisoned in Ceuta during the struggle for independence, it is less plausible that such specific information as Abakuá drumming technique—while it may have come up in conversation—was so influential on a musical practice, son, performed back on the island. Finally, the petwo lineage within Haitian vodou has Bantu/Congo antecedents (while the other principal lineage, *rada*, derives from Dahomeyan religious traditions), a fact that logically correlates with the established narratives concerning the origin of the bongó, namely that it is derived from Bantu drums; thus, a connection between vodou drumming and changüí/son bongó playing is not improbable.

One ideological current that runs throughout Lapidus's book is—similar to my own refrain—the hegemony of Havana-based scholarship and production of knowledge vis-à-vis the country's musical traditions. One of the principal contributions of this work is the presentation of the perspectives of local, Guantánamo-based music scholars on the history of changüí and son. Lapidus's last chapter recounts a tense scholarly exchange between Havana-based musicologists Olavo Alén Rodríguez and Ana Casanova on one hand and local scholars on the other during the annual changüí festival in 1998. He states, "In the face of assertions by non-local musicologists, local musicians feel their view of Cuban musical history is neglected. Locals feel that the non-local nationalist musical project—as expressed by Alén and Casanova—does not position changüí accurately, because the music does not fit into the established criteria for either black or white music or son. Changüíseros see their music as being both black and música campesina ['country music' associated with rural peasants and usually coded as 'white'], rural and urban, often even calling their music rumba. . . . [T]he racial categorization of folk music in Cuba is essentialist, outmoded, and denies local narratives of history" (2008, 157–58). Thus, local music scholars critique Havana-based musicologists not only for ignoring the specificities of changüí as a musical practice (as opposed to seeing it merely as an antecedent, and thus variant, of son), but also—as I discussed in chapter 3—for reifying racially essentialist taxonomies of Cuban music that have been dominant for almost a century.

I now turn to another genre that I believe is implicated in this discussion of the politics of place and music scholarship.

Reggaetón and Regionalism

Thus far, twenty-first-century Cuba has been accompanied by the musical soundtrack of reggaetón. The hybrid Latin American genre has become the favored music of Cuban youth, thus displacing the popularity of timba and redefining it as music for *tembas*, thirty- and forty-year-olds. As discussed in the previous chapter, reggaetón has been used by rumba (as well as timba) musicians to appeal to younger audiences. While it is a controversial musical practice that is much maligned by revolutionary cultural officials and defenders of socialist morality—for its "vulgarity," overt references to sex, and unabashed celebration of materialist consumption—no one can deny its mass appeal and impact in the past decade.[24] My interest in reggaetón lies in the roots of its introduction into Cuba—its national adoption began in Santiago—as I believe that it provides an interesting parallel to the regionally inflected debate about the origins of son.

As discussed in depth by Geoffrey Baker (2011), the majority of Cuban scholars view reggaetón as unworthy of research for myriad reasons, but primarily because it is a foreign genre whose Cuban proponents have thus far shown no interest in musical "indigenization," and because it celebrates a DIY approach that flouts the necessity for musical training that is so revered within the Cuban cultural apparatus.[25] Nevertheless, its adoption by Cuban youth and musicians has been recognized as a significant phenomenon by the nation's most prominent music research institution, the Center for the Research and Development of Cuban Music (CIDMUC). A 2008 paper presented by CIDMUC researchers Neris González Bello, Liliana Casanella Cué, and Grizel Hernández Baguer traces the history and features of reggaetón in Cuba (spelled *reguetón*), pinpointing its origins in the early years of this century and identifying Santiago rapper Candyman as the first proponent of the practice on the island. The fact that reggaetón initially enjoyed more popularity in Oriente makes sense, as it is a Caribbean-identified genre that draws heavily on Jamaican dancehall (as well as American hip-hop) and whose most popular artists have been Puerto Rican. González Bello, Casanella Cué, and Hernández Baguer (2008) note that Candyman's recordings never reached the level of success attained by later Cuban reggaetón artists, and that he has always been associated more with live shows, where his lyrics are not subjected to censorship. Interestingly, some of his more recognized songs have regionalist implications and reference his identity as an oriental. The song "El Pru" takes its title from a homemade fermented drink common in Oriente,[26] thus displaying a sense of pride in eastern roots. Another Candyman song discussed in the paper constitutes a social critique of the "regional profiling" I discussed in chapter 1: the rapper relates going to Havana and being harassed by a policeman who does not initially recognize him. When his friend tells the policeman that he is Candyman, the cop smiles and reveals that he's also from Oriente (González Bello et al. 2008).

In my interview with Cutumba percussionist Ramón Márquez, he mentioned the eastern roots of Cuban reggaetón, adding that Candyman—whom he referred to as "the father of reggaetón in Cuba"—was forced to move to Havana to advance his musical career because he faced marginalization by local cultural officials in Santiago (pers. comm. 2011). Ramón saw this as a common problem not only for reggaetón musicians but even for folkloric groups, who flee to the capital because they don't get institutional support from the local cultural infrastructure. These migrations then feed into and reinforce the hegemony of Havana as the only place on the island where musical creativity can truly flourish. For instance, although Cuban reggaetón emerged in Santiago, Havana-based artists like Cubanitos 20.02, Eddy K, and Gente de Zona have enjoyed more popularity and financial success; the only group from Oriente that enjoys a similar degree of recognition is Santiago's Kola Loca.

Geoffrey Baker's book *Buena Vista in the Club* discusses the reggaetón phenomenon in Havana, noting that in the early 2000s "reggaetón had been the music of bicycle-taxi drivers and poor immigrants from eastern Cuba" (2011, 141).[27] His concern is primarily with the tense and difficult relationship between Cuban hip-hop and reggaetón: "reggaetón's rise in Havana at the expense of hip hop . . . is sometimes characterized as the triumph of Caribbean music (filtered through Santiago) over African American music (filtered through Havana)" (171). While his book is strictly about the Havana reggaetón and hip-hop scenes (and not those of Santiago or other parts of the island),[28] he astutely interprets the rivalry between the two genres in terms of long-standing regionalist antagonisms, stating, "the musical innovation of eastern Cuba is viewed as both powerful yet potentially corrupting, hence the linguistic turns of Havana-based journalists, who described reggaetón as an invasion, avalanche, or epidemic" (172). Baker does not link this "invasion" directly to the more generalized hostilities of habaneros toward eastern migrants to the capital, but he clearly implies that these journalists are making that connection. He also notes—like Ramón—the dwarfing of Santiago reggaetón artists by those from the capital after Candyman introduced it to the island and it became popular in Havana, positing that the former have enjoyed much less media attention and financial success because the institutions created to support hip-hop and reggaetón artists are located in the capital. Finally, Baker asserts that a "stylistic lightening" of reggaetón took place once it took hold in Havana, where the blacker, more Jamaican aesthetic of Santiago reggaetón gave way to a more racially mixed Puerto Rican influence in Havana (172–73). Once again—as with the differences in rumba style between Havana and Matanzas—discussions of regional musical variations are shot through with racialized implications.

Given the regional origins of reggaetón's adoption in Cuba, it's not surprising that it was a santiaguero, Ronald González, who was responsible for incorporating it into rumba performance (as discussed in chapter 5). Ironically, though, because he did this as a member of Yoruba Andabo, this innovation is associated with Havana-based rumba. The incorporation of reggaetón refrains into rumba performance can thus be considered another case of eastern musical creativity influencing western traditions, and yet the agency of musicians from Oriente is overlooked or forgotten. Perhaps, as Cándido Fabré advocated for son (see chapter 2), there will eventually be a reclamation of reggaetón by eastern musicians, a nudge to "send it back home."

Rumba as Matanzas, Son as Santiago: Examining Distinct Discourses of Blackness

This chapter has been primarily concerned with the relationship between rumba and son, and the ways that academic discourse about the two relates to the politics of place. Here I want to return to an issue I have alluded to in previous chapters: the different discourses of blackness that circulate about Matanzas and Santiago, respectively. Because these are considered to be the respective birthplaces of rumba and son, a comparison of the two discursive formations can shed further light on the racialized, place-based associations of these musical practices. In chapter 1, I discussed the widespread racialized stereotypes about Oriente and the fact that it is often discussed as the "blackest" region of the country. In chapter 4, I examined the "cradle of Afro-Cuban culture" nickname, which emphasizes Matanzas's historic connections with blackness. I do not view these discursive formations as contradictory or mutually exclusive, but instead find that both places have been constructed as geographical signifiers of blackness. I want to argue, however, that each is associated with a very particular type of blackness. Peter Wade's discussion of the relationality of blackness within Colombia is relevant here. He states, "The Atlantic coastal region is 'black' in relation to the Andean interior, but 'not so black' in relation to the Pacific Coast. . . . [T]he former [is] not so black, poor, or peripheral as the latter" (1993, 64). While Wade is focused on relative degrees of blackness, here I want to distinguish between cultural blackness and social blackness.

I would argue that orientales are often subjected to a process of "social blackening," in which racial blackness is projected onto all eastern Cubans regardless of their race, with blackness standing in for poverty, underdevelopment, and/or criminality. Patricia Hill Collins theorizes social blackness and "honorary whiteness" in the current "color-blind" era of American politics, asserting that people are racialized in terms of their position in the social hierarchy in ways that do not necessarily relate to skin color. For example, undocumented Latino immigrants are socially blackened while middle/upper-class African Americans are considered to be "honorary whites." Hill Collins states,

> The best way to think about social blackness is to conceptualize it as a place to which people are assigned power in a hierarchy, not as an identity that people are born with. Within this conceptualization, rather than starting with a group of people who are assumed to be black and then studying the place that they occupy in a given society, one starts with the power relations that construct place itself . . . and then looks at which people are routinely assigned to those specific places. A socially black population refers to any group that is oppressed or "blackened" in a specific social context of racism as a system of power. . . . Social blackness is all about finding one's assigned place, and the place to which socially black people are assigned is one of poverty. Each society has its poor and disadvantaged groups who are black metaphorically, if not literally. (Hill Collins 2009, 140, 143)

I find this conceptualization of social blackness to be very productive for examining the specific discourse of race that adheres to Oriente. Orientales tend to be lumped together in the minds of western Cubans as poor, black, uneducated, and often immoral. As mentioned in chapter 1, the whole of eastern Cuba has been socially blackened despite large populations of whites in Holguín and Las Tunas. Southeastern Oriente—specifically the provinces of Santiago and Guantánamo—historically and currently has a rather small white population, although many people of color there would be considered mulato and not black. If I take the eastern Cuban musicians whom I interviewed in chapter 3 as representative of a larger oriental perspective, their tendency is to push against this social blackening and to posit their overwhelming hybridity, both racially and culturally. Perhaps this is their way of inserting themselves into the hegemonic formation of Cubanidad that privileges mestizaje. On the other hand, if, as Hill Collins suggests, the racial category "black" stands in for a position of powerlessness—which I believe it does—then perhaps orientales are also fighting for a more privileged place in the hierarchy of social and economic relations on the island.

Returning to a comparison of the tropes of blackness used to discuss Matanzas and Oriente, the former is constructed as the site of the most authentic and well-preserved African-derived traditions, which is a positive discourse that alludes primarily to the past and historical phenomena, particularly the importation of large numbers of African slaves in the late eighteenth and nineteenth centuries. On the other hand, the racialized tropes about Oriente are negative, in that easterners are often thought to represent a criminal, even foreign blackness. The "foreign" element is represented on one hand by the long history of Franco-Haitian/Haitian migration to Oriente and the ways that Afro-Haitian culture is still widely viewed as outside the limits of Cuban identity (see chapter 3). However, a connotation of foreignness is also constructed through the use of terms such as *indocumentado* (undocumented) to refer to orientales in Havana, which suggests that eastern Cubans are not really Cuban. In addition, this trope of foreign blackness is tied to contemporary social problems (as opposed to Cuba's slave past), exemplified in the idea that orientales' "illegal" migration upsets the stability of the capital and creates residential overcrowding. As should be evident, the discursive blackness that adheres to eastern Cuba is not "good" or celebratory like the one attached to Matanzas, which invokes tropes of purity vis-à-vis African-derived culture. Another way of interpreting the "cradle" trope and all its discursive implications is to emphasize the ways in which it constructs Matanzas as a museum of blackness. As I suggested in chapter 4, perhaps Afro-Cuban folkloric traditions are so important in Matanzas because they memorialize and conjure up the country's African past, and in doing so reaffirm a unique Matanzas identity. Unlike the social blackness projected onto orientales, this is a benign form of blackness that neither provokes social tensions among Cubans from different provinces nor threatens the hegemony of the nationalist hybridity discourse that disavows racial difference in the present moment.[29]

Alluding to Matanzas's other nickname, the "Athens of Cuba" (see chapter 4), Matanzas-born historian Miguel Bretos invokes both ancient European- and African-derived culture in an interesting comparison of Matanzas and Oriente: "Matanzas may be Cuba's Athens, but Oriente is Cuba's Sparta.... The legendary cradle of liberty is Ur-Cuba: an epic land of mountains, primeval forests, and wild shores. Sweet Ochún, the Afro-Cuban Venus, has her throne there amidst the hills, but it is Ogún, the Afro-Cuban Mars, who has the run of the place. Oriente is Ogún country, a land drenched in blood and testoster- one" (Bretos 2010, 177). In other words, while the shrine to Ochún[30] is located in the town of El Cobre on the outskirts of Santiago, Bretos likens Oriente to the male orisha Ogún because of his association with war and weaponry, and the fact that the wars of independence and the Cuban Revolution all began and took place principally in the east. In fact, the Yoruba-derived worship of orishas is historically associated with western, not eastern, Cuba, and Bretos's metaphor is thus somewhat incongruous. Furthermore, one could also see the figure of Ogún—who is said to live in el monte (the countryside/moun- tains)—as symbolic of nineteenth-century Matanzas, with its rural slave bar- racks and backbreaking work in the sugar fields; after all, the slaves' principal tool for cutting sugarcane, the machete, is also Ogún's primary instrument. In any case, I believe that Bretos's poetic characterization of the two places is emblematic of the different ways in which Matanzas and Oriente are discur- sively tied to blackness. While Bretos recognizes the strong legacy of African- derived culture and religion in Matanzas (2010, 125), in the above quotation he invokes the "Athens" nickname, thus choosing to portray Matanzas as the locus of European-derived civility, as compared with the violence and primitiveness of Oriente. Thus, Bretos's comparison of Matanzas and Oriente does not juxtapose two notions of blackness (but rather two places in ancient Greece, Athens and Sparta). Nonetheless, the overall feel is the same: Matan- zas represents a benign form of blackness that can be civilized, educated, and/ or controlled, whereas Oriente represents a savage, bellicose blackness.

Son and Mestizaje in Oriente

Given the very different associations with blackness of Matanzas and Ori- ente, I will now return to this chapter's main theme, the relationship between son and rumba, and issue a challenge to the social and discursive blacken- ing of Oriente. In national music scholarship, the two genres have long rep- resented the regional poles of the island, Oriente and Occidente. However, while there has been no debate regarding the western provenance of rumba,[31] the narrative of son's eastern origins has been recently contested. I have posited that this debate is deeply informed by the long-standing antagonism between eastern and western Cuba, and specifically the dominance of the capital and Havana-centric scholars in the production of knowledge. Thus my argument in chapter 3 details the ways that western Cuban folklore has been celebrated as national folklore, while eastern Cuban folklore has historically been marginalized or ignored. Beyond the question of the provenance of son, its historiography generally positions it in the middle of the racial musical spectrum, locating its authenticity in the rumba influence (the "black" part of son's mixed-race identity). The question is, how can we reconcile the notion that son is the perfect example of Cuban mestizaje (racial mixture), with the discourses of place that paint Oriente as the "blackest" place on the island? In turn, does the racialized representation of Havana as the center of racial and cultural hybridity (as I discussed in chapter 4) relate in any way to the attempts to revision son as emerging from the capital?

Racialized discourses of place are subjective and, like all racial forma-tions, ultimately unstable and likely to shift over time and space. Thus, while scholars and popular discourse emanating from Havana have consistently portrayed Oriente as the blackest region of the island, my interviews and conversations with eastern Cuban musicians and scholars produced a rather overwhelming narrative of hybridity. Several musicians contested the percep-tion that Oriente is "blacker" than the rest of the country and instead spoke of the region's high proportion of racial mixing, especially as compared with western Cuba, which they conceived of in more binary racial terms. Ramón Márquez noted the large numbers of blacks living in rural parts of the Matan-zas Province (the site of the largest sugar plantations during the nineteenth century), and the high proportion of whites in eastern provinces like Holguín and Las Tunas (pers. comm. 2011). Mario Seguí asserted that Oriente's black-ness was merely distinct from that of other regions because of the mixture with Afro-Haitians and other black Antilleans (pers. comm. 2011). Isaias Rojas mentioned the impact of *cabildos de nación*, or mutual aid societies formed in the nineteenth century by Africans and their descendants along ethnic/national lines: the greatest number of Africans were concentrated in central-western Cuba on the sugar plantations, and groups such as the Yoruba arrived in large numbers during this time, allowing them to segregate themselves to a certain extent from other African ethnic groups. In contrast, as Isaias noted, due to the smaller number of slaves in general in Oriente, there was more mixing between Africans, which in the current day is evidenced in the more hybrid religious practices found in eastern Cuba (Rojas Ramírez, pers. comm. 2011). These religions have also been discussed by scholars, such as Martha Esquenazi Pérez and José Millet, who emphasize the common mixing of elements of Santería, Palo, Vodú, and Espiritismo in Oriente (see chapter 3). Thus, in some cases the hybrid practices were constituted by mixing African-derived religious traditions from various sites of the diaspora (Africa, Cuba, and Haiti).

In my conversation with prominent Santiago historian Olga Portuondo, she strongly upheld the nationalist discourse of hybridity as well as the official state stance that racism is not pervasive in contemporary Cuban society (pers. comm. 2011). Like the musicians, she brought in a regional dimension, noting that mestizaje was so pervasive in Oriente that there was no need for a "black pride" movement, which she associated with Havana. She critiqued black intellectuals in Havana, whom she characterized as having "radical" views, asserting that they were unduly influenced by African-American conceptualizations of race and notions of racial inequality that could not be simply mapped onto the situation in Cuba.[32] As noted in the introduction, there have been recent recognitions by Cuban officials that racism was not simply eradicated as a by-product of the redistribution of wealth, and that in any case, there has been a reexacerbation of racialized class inequalities since the Special Period. Nonetheless, the fact that Cuban exile Carlos Moore, who is from a small town in Camagüey, is one of the leading critics of racism in revolutionary Cuba, suggests that, contrary to Portuondo's assertions, this is not an issue that is debated only by scholars from the capital. Furthermore, my conversation about the persistence of racism with Julio Corbea Calzado, current editor of the research journal *Del Caribe* based at Santiago's Casa del Caribe, is evidence of a more diverse set of opinions by eastern Cuban scholars on the matter (pers. comm. 2011). However, notwithstanding the fact that I understood Portuondo's argument as a defense of the nationalist hybridity discourse and a denial of the existence of institutionalized racism on the island, I also believe that local perceptions of Oriente's racial identity should be taken seriously.

Given the widespread identification with mestizaje by eastern Cuban musicians and scholars, it is not surprising that they also aim to reinforce the notion that son—the most hybrid of all national musics—is essentially an eastern Cuban practice; it makes sense according to racial logic. In addition, consider the fact that Africans (primarily Bantu) arrived early to Oriente but not in great numbers during the nineteenth century, and engaged in cultural exchanges with indigenous Cubans and Spaniards from the sixteenth century on. It follows that these slaves and their descendants became more acculturated to Spanish colonial culture and were less able to maintain their African languages and traditions than the Yoruba, for example, who arrived relatively late and in large numbers to western Cuba. Thus, emerging from Oriente was a more hybrid musical practice, son, that included a Spanish-derived stringed instrument (tres) and a Bantu-derived drum (bongó) at its core. In the meantime, western Cuba produced rumba, a more heavily African-derived genre that includes no melodic instruments and has clear African antecedents (e.g., yuka and makuta). If national scholarship tends to portray the most authentic African-derived practices—Santería, Abakuá, and rumba—as emerging from the west, then it should follow that Occidente was the location of the largest number of blacks. If Oriente—or, rather, southeastern Oriente—is demographically blacker than the rest of the country, it is paradoxically because of its hybridity, and the greater tendency for whites and blacks (as well as Haitian- and Cuban-born blacks) to marry and reproduce with each other. In other words, instead of more blacks in Oriente, it is more accurate to say that there are more nonwhites, more people of mixed racial descent (see chapter 1 for a discussion of census statistics on race).

Peter Wade, whom I have cited and quoted various times throughout this book, presents an interesting discussion of mestizaje and the various ways that it is invoked and inhabited in the lives of everyday people. After becoming famous for his astute critiques of Latin American nationalist celebrations of mestizaje (1993), Wade has more recently published a defense of mestizaje (2005)—not the discourse invoked by elites but rather mestizaje as lived by mixed-race people in Latin America. As Wade has elsewhere stressed, the nationalist discourse of mestizaje as utilized by governments throughout Latin America tends to be exclusionary, either by insisting that all citizens are of mixed race and thus disavowing people who identify in monoracial terms, or by engaging in strategies of "whitening," such as encouraging European immigration in an attempt to dilute the ancestry of future generations of Africans and indigenous people. However, what he is discussing here is a very different engagement with mestizaje: "Mestizaje provides the possibility for exclusiveness, by emphasising one racial origin—often whiteness, but also indigenousness or blackness—at the expense of others, yet it also provides the possibility of inclusion, and this may be at the level of the body itself. Mestizaje is physically lived through a tension between sameness and difference" (Wade 2005, 250). One of Wade's examples involves a Brazilian woman who might be viewed by society as black but who self-identifies as racially mixed. He states, "For this woman, and others like her, being mixed meant maintaining simultaneous identifications, rather than fusing everything into a homogeneous new whole in which origins lose their meaning. . . . Mestizaje was not just an 'all-inclusive ideology of exclusion,' a matter of elite discourses, but an everyday practice in which inclusion was not just rhetoric, but a lived reality" (253). Wade is referring to a more personal experience of mestizaje, one that relates to ancestry and kinship rather than nationalist ideologies, and a conceptualization that I find very useful for thinking about Oriente's racial identity.

For the musicians and scholars from Oriente who view themselves and/or their local culture as racially hybrid, their goal is not to uphold a nationalist discourse that has often glossed over racial inequalities—and in many cases resulted in their own marginalization—but to express their own lived experience of mestizaje. They feel that their culture is particularly hybrid, and the region's history backs up their claims. In a similar fashion, we could consider son's history and trajectory as an example of lived mestizaje. If the practice has been consistently molded in academic discourse to fit the contours of hybridized Cubanidad—often ignoring the fact that in its early days it faced racialized marginalization—the fact is, son is in musical terms a particularly potent example of Ortiz's notion of transculturation, the merging of several distinct traditions to form a new one. Its unique form of musicking seems to be particularly receptive to hybridizing and fusion practices, and this process of mestizaje did not stop once son was formalized as a distinct genre in the 1920s.

When son encountered rumba, new elements—such as claves—were incorporated, and a new formal structure took hold. Throughout the 1920s and 1930s the son ensemble grew, adding various instruments and taking on features of American big band jazz. Then in the 1940s, another major transformation occurred—defined by some as a "re-Africanization"—when tres player Arsenio Rodríguez added conga drums, incorporated Afro-Cuban religious lyrics and themes, and lengthened the montuno section of the song. New York Puerto Rican salsa and Cuban timba, as outgrowths of son, have continued this process of hybridization, bringing in influences ranging from American funk and rap to rock. In the meantime, a neotraditional form of son was born in the 1990s stemming from the success of the *Buena Vista Social Club* project. We can compare this to the trajectory of rumba in the twentieth century, which has undergone much less transformation. I do not want to argue that this is an innate feature of rumba, because, as I discussed in the previous chapter, hybrids such as batarumba and guarapachangueo are evidence of significant innovations in rumba performance. However, son has been in a constant state of adaptation and change since its formation because it has enjoyed substantially more global media dissemination, greater contact with foreign traditions, and stronger institutional support than rumba. Perhaps all of this is because son is recognized as a hybrid genre, which makes it easily appealing to all sectors of the national population; it is not considered, like rumba, to be just "a black thing."[33] Thus, just like Wade's notion of lived mestizaje and the personal identifications with racial mixture among many eastern Cubans, son inhabits mestizaje in its everyday practices, and there is no expectation that it should "preserve" the African roots of national culture, as there is among some rumba practitioners.

Conclusion

Recently, Cuban bandleader Adalberto Álvarez released a song called "Entre el Son y la Rumba,"[34] which translates roughly to "[the relationship] between son and rumba." The song is a collaboration between Álvarez's group—a dance band that is often classified as timba but whose songs have a relatively heavy presence of elements from traditional son—and rumba group Rumbatá. It is an ode to the city of Camagüey, of which both the Rumbatá musicians and Álvarez are natives, and repeatedly references one of its primary symbols, the *tinajón*, a large clay jug used since the colonial period to collect and store rainwater. The song's instrumentation shifts several times between a rumba and salsa format. It begins in rumba format, featuring percussion and Rumbatá's excellent vocal harmonies, and transitions into full salsa orchestration at almost exactly the midpoint of the song, 2:46. The rumba section returns from 3:30 to 4:37, followed by a brief salsa section, another return to rumba instrumentation at 4:54, and finally the reentry of the full orchestra at 5:15 until the close of the song. It seems relevant to mention that Rumbatá is one of the most innovative rumba groups on the island: not only does the group play in guarapachangueo style, but one of their regular members is a rapper who doubles on trumpet, and their songs often include rapped vocals and/or trumpet riffs. During the first rumba section of this song, there is a thirty-second rhythmic shift in the percussion accompanied by rapped vocals (from 1:54 to 2:22), and the rapper returns in the second rumba section, from 3:35 to 3:59. This is certainly not the first rumba-salsa fusion to be recorded. There are countless examples from the past fifty years, including the Los Van Van song "De la Habana a Matanzas," which I discussed in chapter 4, and Celia Cruz's hit "Quimbara." However, this recent song exemplifies the deep and enduring connection between these two seminal Cuban genres.[35] Furthermore, "Entre el Son y la Rumba" is evidence, I believe, of the mutually influential relationship between the traditions, and the ways that both have been penetrated by foreign musical elements (in this case, rap).

The variety of perspectives presented in this chapter regarding the origins of son suggests that there is still much to be learned about the tradition's relationship to both eastern and western Cuban musical antecedents. It is likely that we will never know exactly how the practice that came to be called son arrived in Havana, nor in what form it arrived (i.e., with which musical features already present). However, I would argue that rumba historiography suffers from similar imprecision and conjecture; after all, both are oral traditions whose earliest instances and first encounters with each other were not recorded. If we could travel back in time to the early twentieth century, we might learn that rumba took as much from son as son from rumba. One might ask why we need to revisit son's origins at all, especially because rumba's identity as a western Cuban tradition has never been questioned. The idea that one of the major roots of Cuban popular music came from the east and the other came from the west presents a balanced (and to my mind, more credible) portrait of musical creation across the island. I cannot assume that scholars are actively attempting to diminish the significance of eastern Cuban creativity, but I do believe it is necessary to emphasize how long-standing regional inequalities might impact the production of knowledge, and to advocate for a counterweight to Havana's hegemony, especially because there is still so much to be known about cultural practices from other Cuban provinces. The capital enjoys the vast amount of research attention from both Cuban and foreign scholars, and until this imbalance is addressed, music scholars are only working with partial information about the history of the island's traditions.

Conclusion

This study has aimed to examine contemporary Cuban music making through the analytical lens of place and race. My exploration of place has broached a variety of distinct issues, including regionalism—both at the interregional level (between the eastern and western regions) and the intraregional level (the relationship between Havana and Matanzas)—racialized discourses of place, localized notions of tradition and innovation, and the ways that historical regional inequalities have informed the production of knowledge about Cuban music. With respect to race, my primary goal has been to build on the important body of literature scrutinizing and critiquing the apolitical celebration of mestizaje, or hybridity, in Cuba (and Latin America more generally), and to suggest that a more specific, localized notion of hybridity is warranted when discussing cultural practices. I have also sought to reframe the racialized discourse of place associated with Oriente, by offering evidence that rather than the "blackest" place on the island, it would be more accurate to characterize the east as the most racially mixed region. Finally, I have explored the intersections between race and place in Cuba and elucidated the ways that these two issues both inform and are informed by specific practices of music making on the island. Rather than rehash the specific arguments laid out in previous chapters, here I want to allude to some of the broader implications of my study by discussing possible directions for further research on issues with which I have engaged.

Ethnographic Studies of Place

Since the 1990s, there has been a wealth of literature published on the relationship between music and place. Nonetheless, as I discussed in my introduction, the vast majority has been written by cultural geographers, communications scholars, and popular music scholars, most of whom do not employ ethnographic methods. Anthropologists have made important inroads into expanding the field of ethnographic studies of place, but their work—for example, Donald Moore (2005) and Jacqueline Nassy Brown (2005)—does not generally center around music making. Ethnomusicologist Martin Stokes's anthology *Ethnicity, Identity, and Music: The Musical Construction of Place* (1994) is a notable exception, and yet it is now two decades old. In the early 1990s theoretical work on space and place was only beginning to blossom; now it has become a major concern in a variety of fields—ethnomusicology, anthropology, sociology, cultural geography, cultural studies, and more. Thus, it is time for music scholars who rely heavily on ethnography—whether ethnomusicologists, historical musicologists, anthropologists, or others—to engage seriously with issues of space and place to explore their impact on identity formation and music making. The specific issues I explored in my interviews with musicians and my examination of musical performance in Cuba concerned regionalist sentiment, racialized discourses of place, and localized notions of hybridity. However, there are myriad theoretical issues around which to orient ethnographic studies of music and place; the larger point is to undertake them.

While not related to music, I believe that Brown's ethnography *Dropping Anchor, Setting Sail* (2005) is an excellent model of a study that theorizes place and its intersection with racial identity formation. As I discussed in previous chapters, what stands out most about her framework is the primacy she gives to place in its relationship with race: she argues that place essentially makes race, and that "Liverpool-born black" is a specific, very localized category of racial identity that could have only been formulated in relation to that city's unique history. This was exactly my point in juxtaposing the distinct, respective notions of blackness associated with Matanzas and Santiago. It is, of course, not only notions of blackness that change depending on place, but also whiteness and mixed-raceness, a point made by Peter Wade (1993) when he discussed the regionalization of blackness and mestizaje in Colombia. I believe that one of the most important implications of examining the ways that racial identity differs from place to place is the prospect of moving away from homogenized notions of race that, despite their disavowal in academia, are still very pervasive in daily life.[1] As is widely recognized, there are different ways of being racialized based on one's gender, sexual orientation, religion, and class (to name just a few of the intersections). Perhaps one way that we can truly start to "get past" race is to recognize the ways that it is informed by other axes of identity and to thus emphasize its provisionality, specificity, and situatedness. To clarify, I don't believe we can discount the material, structural effects of long-standing notions of racial difference—the correlation between blackness or indigeneity and poverty throughout the world is devastatingly clear—but I do believe we should continue to work on deconstructing essentialized ideas about whiteness, blackness, Latino-ness, Asian-ness, indigeneity, and Arab/Muslim-ness (not to mention notions of gender and sexuality). Examining racialized discourses and identities in tandem with other axes of identity—and thus highlighting their situated, provisional nature—is one way to accomplish this.

Hybridity in Latin America and the Caribbean

Another broad theme within my study has been the examination of notions of mestizaje, both in relation to hybrid musical practices and in relation to identity formation, specifically in Oriente. Scholars have constructed an impressive body of literature critiquing the overly triumphant notion of hybridity that tends to be central to nationalist discourses in Latin America and the Caribbean. This literature has been incredibly formative for my work, and I firmly believe that an oversimplified celebration of hybridity is still evident in political and public discourse in Cuba, Brazil, and throughout the Americas (including the Anglophone and Francophone Caribbean). Latin American nationalist discourses are still used to argue that countries with large or majority populations of mixed-race descent are inherently antiracist. This notion is of course patently false and relies on the faulty logic that non-whites cannot hold racist views or be involved in the perpetuation of racialized power inequalities. Nonetheless, following the important intervention by Peter Wade (2005) and discussed in chapter 6, I think it might be time to return to a serious consideration of mestizaje and the ways that Latin Americans and Caribbeans engage with notions of mixed race-ness on the ground and in their daily lives.

The question is, can we recognize the importance of mestizaje in the identity formation of many people in the Americas (including the United States!) and thus renounce the black/white binary that still structures racial discourse in the United States, while at the same time recognizing and counteracting the unequal material effects of notions of racial difference? Some critiques of mestizaje by US scholars tend to reject or downplay the important distinction made in Latin America between blacks and mulatos, which ultimately reifies a racial binary system of categorization. This move has, in turn, prompted Latin American scholars to accuse US scholars of ethnocentrism in attempting to impose a US-specific racial analysis onto the situation in Latin America; this counterclaim is then used by Latin American academics to rationalize their denials of racism in the region. I would like to second Wade's suggestion that, precisely because the notion of hybridity holds so much importance for many Latin Americans in terms of their individual and collective identity formation, we need to recognize the specificity of Latin American racial formation.[2] This means not discounting or rejecting mestizaje just because elites and politicians have utilized this notion to deny the existence of racism and gloss over the racialized inequalities within their countries. Instead, it is the job of scholars to distinguish between the manipulation of the notion of mestizaje by those in power in order to conceal societal inequalities, and its utilization by ordinary people who do not feel that categories like "white," "black," or "Indian" authentically represent their identities. Furthermore, as I hope I demonstrated in chapter 5, the notion of hybridity is crucial in the analysis of music and cannot simply be discarded; music scholars must come up with an analytically rigorous way of discussing musical fusion. Thus, the specific conditions of musical hybridizing should be elucidated, including a consideration of whether or not musicians place limits on the amount or type of fusion they engage in.

Cuban (Music) Studies

The third implication of my study relates to a more delimited field of research: Cuba studies in general and Cuban music studies in particular. With regard to ethnographies and other research projects conducted on the island, I have been quite clear in advocating for more studies to be based outside of Havana. I am heartened by the fact that since the 2000s there has been an increase in foreign scholars conducting and publishing research based in Oriente,[3] but there are other regions of the country that have been similarly neglected, such as central Cuba and Pinar del Río. In a small country such as Cuba, the capital city understandably enjoys disproportionate attention. However, while Havana is an incredibly important locus of expressive practices on the island and a crucial "contact zone" (Pratt 1992) for Cubans of different regional provenances, it is home to only two million of Cuba's more than eleven million people. Cubans who live elsewhere often define themselves in opposition to habaneros, and—leaving aside the problems with this type of polarized thinking—it is worth exploring their histories, daily realities, and cultural practices. There are, of course, regional scholars (particularly historians) who have published work on places outside the capital, but there is still relatively little written in English.

Finally, I want to say a word about Cuban music studies. No one could legitimately argue that Cuban music has been underexamined, and I would argue that, given the disproportionately high level of influence Cuba has had on musics around the world, the amount of scholarly attention is not unwarranted.

However, Cuban music has tended to be discussed in a vacuum, with foreign influences beyond the colonial period generally downplayed. Leonardo Acosta (2004) has been one the few Cuban musicologists to consistently recognize this tendency and to critique the ethnocentricity of much of the literature on Cuban music, arguing that it should be studied in comparison with similar musical practices from other sites in the Caribbean. I, too, believe that Cuban music studies should take on a more transnational approach, taking into account not just the influence it has had on traditions in the Americas and beyond but also the continual nourishment it has drawn from foreign musical sources. The case of reggaetón promises to be an interesting one for future scholarship, as it is an example of a foreign genre that has become dominant all over the island and that has, to a large extent, displaced "homegrown" popular genres like timba, to the consternation of many Cuban music scholars. Furthermore, as Cuban communities have begun to crystallize in places beyond the United States in the post-Soviet era—particularly in Spain and other parts of Europe—the island's music has taken on a more transnational character, owing to collaborations both between Cuban and foreign musicians, and between Cubans who live on the island and those residing abroad.

In what will perhaps become a future research project, I would specifically like to advocate for greater attention to the bidirectional influence of Cuban and contemporary African musical styles. While quite a bit has been written on the relationship between Cuban and other Latin American, Caribbean, and US musics, I think it's time to look beyond the Western Hemisphere, particularly to Africa, to explore the "reverse migration" of cultural influence. The African roots of Cuban music are widely acknowledged, but Cuban music has also been a primary inspiration for the creation of contemporary African popular styles, particularly in the two Congos. Congolese popular music, originally called "Congolese rumba" when it emerged in the 1940s and later called soukous, drew heavily from son (labeled as rumba), which was disseminated via recordings and radio to all corners of the globe beginning in the 1930s.[4] Congolese popular music, in turn, has been incredibly influential for the creation of local popular styles all over the continent, particularly in East Africa (i.e., Kenya and Tanzania) and as far south as Zimbabwe, with the popular style called *sungura*. Just as I've argued that son and rumba have a mutually influential relationship with each other, so have Cuban and African (specifically Congolese) musical styles, but only one side of this exchange has been explored. It would be interesting to conduct research in Kinshasa or Brazzaville, for example, to investigate the question of why Cuban dance music was so appealing to Congolese musicians in the mid-twentieth century, especially because it was not sung in the colonial language, French.

The unique transnational history of Cuban music leads me to believe that the island's musical legacy is almost unparalleled among small nations in the world, although some would also make a case for the heavy global influence of Jamaican popular music (which emerged from a much smaller island). I truly hope my research has contributed to a more critical way of thinking about Cuban music that moves beyond the celebratory discourses that often accompany literature on this subject. It is undoubtedly true that Cuban music is infectious, lyrical, and rhythmically exhilarating, and that it inspires an almost obsessive following by people of all ethnicities. Nonetheless, this is precisely because of some of its contradictory and antagonistic features—like denigrating a whole region of people while in the same song advocating national unity, reinforcing racist notions (often veiled as jokes) while insisting that racism is nonexistent, celebrating materialist consumption and the accumulation of wealth within the context of a socialist society, and reifying sexist, patriarchal ideas (often in the form of double entendres) while at the same time promoting a degree of sexual freedom that is unparalleled in Latin America; and this is all accomplished employing an endlessly inventive wellspring of local slang. Cuban music is not always progressive, but it is deeply addictive.

Glossary

Abakuá: Cuban term for the male secret society originating in the Calabar/Cross River region of southeastern Nigeria and southwestern Cameroon.

Arará: Cuban term for the slaves and religion originating in the ancient kingdom of Dahomey, present-day Benin.

Bantu/Congo: Metaethnic category used to refer to various ethnic groups from the area of the present-day two Congos and northern Angola; *Congo* is the Cuban term for people, culture, or religion of Bantu descent.

Batá drums: Trio of double-headed, hourglass-shaped membranophones used to accompany orisha worship in the Yoruba-derived Regla de Ocha religion, also known as Lucumí or Santería.

Batarumba: Rumba hybrid fusing Yoruba-derived batá drumming with rumba percussion.

Bembé: Type of Lucumí ceremony practiced primarily in Matanzas and the central provinces; also denotes an ensemble and a group of drums.

Blanqueamiento: Literally, "whitening," or the policy of encouraging European migration to Latin America in the late nineteenth and early twentieth centuries.

Bombo: Large bass drum used in comparsa and batarumba; also refers to the second beat of the clave rhythm.

Bongó: Bantu-derived percussion instrument that includes two drumheads (one larger, one smaller) attached to each other with a wooden bridge and open at the bottom; thought to have originated in Oriente and associated with changüí and son.

Cabildos de nación: Mutual aid societies formed in the late eighteenth and nineteenth centuries by African slaves and their descendants, formed principally along ethnic lines; for instance, Africans of Lucumí, Congo, Carabalí, and Arará descent each had their own respective cabildos.

Cajón(es): Wooden box(es) used as rumba's original percussion instruments in late nineteenth and early twentieth centuries; now associated with the guarapachangueo style and cajón de muerto ceremonies.

Cajón de muerto: Ceremony within Espiritismo cruzado (see below) that honors dead ancestors and mixes Catholic liturgy with Bantu-derived Palo songs and rhythms; musical accompaniment consists of cajón-based rumba.

Campana: Cowbell, used in various Afro-Cuban folkloric genres and in batarumba.

Canto: Narrative or body section of a rumba song; follows the introductory diana and precedes the montuno.

Carabalí: Cuban term used to refer to various African ethnic groups from the region of Calabar, the Cross River region of southeastern Nigeria and southwestern Cameroon; Abakuá is a specific tradition within Carabalí culture in Cuba.

Catá: Instrument used in the rumba ensemble; a hollowed-out piece of sugarcane against which drumsticks are beat to play a complementary rhythm with the clave.

Chachalokofún: Most popular batá drum rhythm in the Lucumí pantheon that can be used to play for all orishas; the most common batá rhythm found in batarumba.

Changüí: Traditional dance music genre from the eastern Cuban province of Guantánamo; performed mainly by Afro-Cubans (many of whom have Haitian ancestry) and believed to be one of the rural antecedents of son.

Cierre: Stop-time section or rhythmic break, used in batarumba.

Clave: Rhythmic timeline around which most Afro-Cuban musics are structured; also refers to an idiophone—two wooden sticks beat against each other to produce the clave rhythm.

Columbia: The fastest style of rumba, featuring solo male dancing.

Comparsa: A generic term to denote Cuban carnival music; also refers to a specific carnival ensemble that includes music, choreographed dance, and costumes, and that engages in competition with other groups.

Conga santiaguera: A specific genre and type of mobile percussion ensemble within the Cuban carnival tradition that is associated with the city of Santiago and includes mass community participation.

Contradanza: Cuba's first social dance genre; emerged in the early nineteenth century and was derived from the French contredanse, which was introduced to Cuba via Spain and Franco-Haitian migrants fleeing the Haitian Revolution.

Coro: Chorus or refrain, most often used in the montuno section of a song; can also refer to the backup singers who alternate with the solista (lead singer) in call-and-response form.

Cubanidad: Cubanness, or what it means to be Cuban.

Danzón: A more Cubanized (Africanized) version of the contradanza that emerged in the latter part of the nineteenth century; still considered by some to be Cuba's national dance.

Diana: Introductory section of a rumba song in which the lead singer uses vocables to establish the song's tonal center.

El campo: Literally, "the countryside"; term used by Havana natives to refer to every place beyond the capital, and sometimes used to refer to someone perceived to be backward and/ or poor.

Espectáculo: Folkloric show, in which a variety of Afro-Cuban sacred and secular practices are represented.

Especular/ando: Literally "speculating" or "showing off"; used in contemporary popular discourse to refer to someone displaying conspicuous signs of wealth, such as cell phones or gold chains.

Espiritismo: The Cuban manifestation of Spiritism, a hybrid religious movement stemming from traditional Christianity that emerged in the United States in the mid-nineteenth century and spread to Cuba and other parts of the Spanish Caribbean soon after; based on the idea of communicating with the souls of the dead through a medium; most popular variants are Espiritismo de cordón (practiced primarily in Oriente) and Espiritismo cruzado (practiced all over the island and mixed with African-derived religions, principally Palo).

Folklore oriental: Eastern Cuban folklore, which encompasses various sacred and secular traditions such as tumba francesa, Vodú, merengue haitiano, and gagá.

Guaguancó: The most popular of the three styles of rumba still performed today; has a medium tempo in relation to the other two styles; couples dance characterized by the vacunao (see below).

Guarapachangueo: Havana-based innovation in rumba percussion and performance style involving the heavy use of cajones and a characteristic bass tone pattern called tukutukum (see below).

Güiro: A more informal ceremony within the Lucumí pantheon featuring musical accompaniment by three shékeres (hollowed-out gourds covered with beads) and one or two conga drums.

Habanero: Native of the city of Havana.

Inventar: Literally, "to invent"; has various meanings both negative and positive, such as to make things up or stray from a traditional style, or to innovate or create something new.

Itótole: Middle-sized drum of the batá ensemble; often engages in improvisatory "conversations" with iyá.

Iyá: "Mother" or largest drum of the batá ensemble; has a lead role and does most of the improvising.

Iyesá: Subethnic group of the Yoruba; also denotes a religious practice, a corresponding musical tradition, and a rhythm.

Jinetero/a: Hustler (male or female), broadly conceived; someone who attempts to establish relationships with foreigners for purposes of financial gain, which can (but does not always) involve a sexual relationship.

Makuta: Bantu-derived secular dance symbolizing an erotic game between a rooster and a hen; possible predecessor of rumba guaguancó.

Matancero: Native of the city of Matanzas.

Mayor: Low-pitched drum of a rumba ensemble that plays an interlocking rhythmic pattern with the tres-dos (middle-range drum); also known as a tumbador.

Merengue haitiano: Secular music and dance tradition presumably derived from the Haitian meringue; original performance context is linked to carnival celebrations within Haitian-descendant communities in Oriente.

Mestizaje: Roughly, "racial mixture"; a central notion of Latin American and Caribbean nationalist discourses.

Montuno: Call-and-response section of a rumba, son, or timba song.

Mulato: Racial term designating someone of mixed Spanish and African ancestry.

Música campesina: Literally, "country music"; Spanish-derived music associated with rural areas of the island.

Occidente: Western Cuba, constituted by the provinces of La Habana, Mayabeque, Artemisa, Matanzas, Pinar del Río, and Isla de la Juventud.

Okónkolo: Smallest drum of the batá ensemble; does not engage in improvising.

Oriental(es): Person/people from the region of Oriente.

Oriente: Eastern Cuba, constituted by five provinces: Santiago de Cuba, Guantánamo, Holguín, Las Tunas, and Granma.

Orishas: Yoruba-derived deities/spirits that act as intermediaries between humans and the supreme deity or "God," Olodumare; each orisha "owns" a specific element of the natural world and each Santería initiate is assigned a guardian orisha; also referred to as santos.

Palo/Regla de Palo: Primary Bantu-derived religion still practiced in Cuba; centered around the relationship between the living and the dead.

Palestino: Literally, "Palestinian"; a derogatory term used primarily in Havana to refer to eastern Cubans.

Partido Independiente de Color: The Independents of Color Party, or PIC; formed in 1908 by Afro-Cuban political leaders (mainly from Oriente) as a response to the continuing inequalities faced by blacks and mulatos after independence in 1898, and effectively destroyed when government forces and white militias massacred thousands of PIC leaders and sympathizers in 1912.

Peña de rumba: Rumba event or gathering.

Período especial: Literally, "Special Period"; the period of extreme economic crisis in Cuba beginning in 1990, following the fall of the Soviet Union, and ending in the late 1990s.

Quinto: High-pitched improvising drum of a rumba ensemble.

Rumba: Afro-Cuban secular music and dance genre involving percussion and song; encompasses several genres (principally, yambú, guaguancó, and columbia).

Rumba de cajón/rumba de tiempo España: Rumba played with cajones/rumba "in the time of Spain," or during the colonial era.

Rumba habanera: Havana-style rumba.

Rumba matancera: Matanzas-style rumba.

Rumberos: Rumba participants, whom I conceive of in a broad sense as not only musicians and dancers but, in some cases, spectators.

Santería/Regla de Ocha: Yoruba-derived religion centered around orisha worship; also known as Lucumí.

Santiaguero: Native of the city of Santiago.

Solista: Lead singer.

Son: Traditional popular dance music, considered to be Cuba's national musical practice because of its "equal" synthesis of African and Spanish elements; the foundation of both New York Puerto Rican salsa and contemporary Cuban dance music.

Tambor: The most revered and formal type of Lucumí ceremony, in which the batá drum ensemble accompanies the singing for the orishas; also known as toque de santo.

Timba: A contemporary style of Cuban dance music that emerged in the late 1980s and is characterized by a dense, polyrhythmic texture, a longer montuno section, multiple coros, and lyrics that reference the economic crisis and social upheavals of the Special Period.

Toque: Literally, "rhythm"; used specifically to refer to batá drum rhythms.

Tres: Cuban guitar that features three sets of double strings; primary melodic instrument in son and changüí.

Tres-dos: Middle-range drum of a rumba ensemble that plays an interlocking rhythmic pattern with the mayor (low-pitched drum); also known as a segundo (second).

Tukutukum: The bass tones played on the cajón or conga drum associated with guarapachangueo.

Tumbadora: Conga drum.

Tumba francesa: Literally, "French drum/dance"; an African-derived imitation of the contredanse performed by slaves who were brought to eastern Cuba by French planters fleeing the Haitian Revolution.

Vacunao: Characteristic dance move of guaguancó; involves the male dancer thrusting his groin and other appendages toward the groin area of the female dancer in attempts at symbolic sexual possession.

Vodú: The Cuban variant of the Haitian religion called vodou; practiced principally in eastern Cuba among descendants of Haitian immigrants.

Yambú: The slowest and oldest style of rumba; a couples dance with no overtly sexualized gestures, as opposed to guaguancó.

Yoruba/Lucumí: Metaethnic category used to refer to various ethnic groups from Yorubaland, encompassing modern-day southwestern Nigeria, Benin, and parts of Togo; also denotes a religion; Lucumí is the Cuban term for the people, culture, or religion of Yoruba descent.

Yuka: Bantu-derived secular music and dance tradition considered to be the primary antecedent of rumba.

Notes

Introduction

1. This should not be taken to mean that Cuba's current economic system can be defined as strictly "socialist." There have been a number of measures taken since the 1990s that have opened up the island to Western tourism, foreign investment, and private enterprise. In the context of the 2008 global economic crisis, Raúl Castro's government has pushed for even less reliance on a centralized state and urged citizens to engage in private enterprise. See Domínguez et al. 2004 for details on the economic changes in Cuba's economy since the so-called Special Period.

2. Music has been a particularly potent symbol of Cuban identity since the nineteenth-century dissemination to Europe of the *habanera* rhythm, which was incorporated into Georges Bizet's celebrated opera *Carmen*. The "rumba craze" of the 1930s in the United States was another key moment of global representation for Cuban music. Finally, Wim Wenders's 1999 documentary film *Buena Vista Social Club* and its related recording projects thrust Cuban music once again into the international spotlight.

3. The most significant distinction is between the countries that retained large indigenous populations—like Peru, Bolivia, Mexico, and Guatemala—and those located in the circum-Caribbean area where native populations were decimated within one century of the arrival of the Spanish. In the former group, *mestizos* (people with mixed indigenous and Spanish blood) are generally held up as the national ideal, while in the Spanish Caribbean it is often *mulatos* (people with mixed African and Spanish blood) who discursively represent the nation. I should note that the "ideal" hybrid citizen refers to a very specific mixture of white and indigenous or white and black ancestry, and does not necessarily include people who are of East Indian and black (but not white) ancestry, a common mixture in Trinidad and Guyana. I thank Peter Manuel (pers. comm. 2014) for this comment.

4. Haiti's nationalist discourse, for example, departs from this trend in the country's self-identification as a black republic immediately following independence in 1804. In contrast, the Dominican Republic (located on the same island) has long denied the existence of blackness within its conceptualization of national identity, an ideology that is in many ways a reaction to the Haitian Revolution and has had tragic consequences for Haitian migrants.

5. Again, I want to qualify this statement by pointing out that not all Latin American countries promoted mestizaje immediately after independence and that each country has its own historical trajectory vis-à-vis its changing conceptualization of national identity.

6. Caribbeanist scholar Percy Hintzen suggests that the desire for whiteness is in fact inherent in the conception of Caribbean Creole (hybrid) identity (Hintzen 2002).

7. The redefinition of Cubanidad as "Latin-African" is exemplified in Cuban writer Roberto Fernández Retamar's 1971 essay "Caliban: Notes toward a Discussion of Culture in Our America" ([1971] 1989). He uses Shakespeare's play *The Tempest* as a metaphor, arguing that the enslaved Caliban (often discussed as being of African descent) can be viewed as a symbol of Latin American identity and its historic oppression by European colonizers, which are represented by the character Prospero.

8. The "Special Period" was a term coined by Fidel Castro to refer to the period of severe rationing and shortages in food, gas, electricity, medicine, and other products in the early 1990s after the fall of the Soviet bloc, when Cuba's economy contracted by 35–40 percent (de la Fuente 2001).

9. See http://afrocubaweb.com/actingonourconscience.htm for the declaration organized by Carlos Moore and issued on November 30, 2009; and http://www.lajiribilla.cu/2009/n447_11/447_29.html for the response on December 3, 2009, by Cuban intellectuals published in the weekly cultural magazine *La Jiribilla*.

10. See Roberto Zurbano, "For Blacks in Cuba, the Revolution Hasn't Begun," *New York Times*, March 23, 2013. Much of the controversy surrounding this editorial was due to its title, suggesting that the revolution hadn't yet *begun* to address racial inequality. Zurbano subsequently asserted that the *New York Times* changed the original title of his piece, which translated directly to "The Country to Come: And My Black Cuba?," and argued that the revolution was not yet *complete* for blacks in Cuba. Thus, the *New York Times* title implied that no progress had been made, which distorted Zurbano's argument that while certain goals had been achieved, there was still progress to be made. For more details on Zurbano's demotion and the fallout from the editorial, see http://www.afrocubaweb.com/zurbano-changes-jobs.html.

11. Anthropologists, on the other hand, have produced a number of ethnographic studies framed by issues of space and place. See, for example, Peter Wade (1993), Steven Gregory (1999), Donald Moore (2005), and Jacqueline Nassy Brown (2005).

12. It is also true that Cuba is more unified ethnically and linguistically than many other Latin American countries, in the sense that it is a monolingual nation without marked ethnic divisions (unlike Peru, for example). However, it is precisely because of this apparent national cohesiveness that the regional divisions on the island deserve to be explored.

13. While "Oriente" is the term used in Cuba to refer to the easternmost provinces, and was once the name of a much larger province that has since been divided into five smaller ones (see chapter 1), it is not found on contemporary maps of the island.

14. Unless otherwise indicated, all the musicians whose opinions and/or comments I reproduce in this study have given their consent for their real names to be used, and thus I have not anonymized them except in cases where a sensitive topic was broached. I do not use a uniform manner of referring to them (for example, by first or last name), preferring instead to use the names by which they are commonly known in musical/professional contexts. Thus, while some are called by their first or last name, many are known by nicknames they have acquired either within their family or in musical arenas.

15. For example, my interest in the politics of place was inspired partly by discussions with my percussion/song teachers in both Havana and Matanzas about the different styles and attitudes toward rumba performance in each city; their comments led me to observe how the two cities are constructed as sites of innovation and tradition, respectively.

16. Cuban race scholar Tomás Fernández Robaina offers quite a different reason for why Cubans don't tend to use the term to refer to themselves, stating: "Within all Cubans, and deeply within blacks and mulattoes, is embedded Martí's view that to be Cuban is to be more than white, more than black, more than mulatto; or [independence hero Antonio] Maceo's dictum not to ask for anything as a black but for everything as a Cuban" (2005, 173). This assertion clearly points to the hegemony of the nationalist hybridity discourse, which eschews racial difference, and is at odds with my experiences of how Cubans identify themselves and others racially.

17. Conducting research during the George W. Bush administration constituted a particularly difficult challenge, since between 2003 and 2009 much harsher restrictions were imposed on Cuban Americans and immigrants traveling back to Cuba. These included limits on the frequency of travel and the amount of money that could be sent to relatives, and a redefinition of "relatives" as immediate family members only. One of the first acts of the Barack Obama administration was to repeal the Bush administration's additional restrictions, including those related to family remittances and family travel between the two countries. Regarding the recent restoration of diplomatic ties, this policy change was made possible by the negotiation of a high-profile prisoner swap. Former subcontractor for the USAID program and American citizen Alan Gross—who was arrested on the island in 2009 while dispersing cell phones and laptops to the local Jewish community and accused of engaging in subversive activities designed to destabilize the government—was returned to the United States. In exchange, the remaining three jailed Cuban operatives who were part of the group known as "The Five Heroes" because of their infiltration in Miami of various anti-Castro exile groups and who had been sentenced to long prison terms for espionage, were sent home to Cuba; the other two had already been released. More importantly, the restoration of diplomatic ties includes an economic component that makes certain financial and trade transactions between the United States and Cuba possible despite the official continuation of the economic embargo. Only Congress can officially repeal the Helms-Burton Act that codified the embargo within United States law, and despite the fact that many in Congress view it as ineffective and anachronistic, there is still opposition to repealing the law, notably by Cuban-American senators Robert Menendez and Marco Rubio. The law sanctions not only any American individual or company who trades with the island, but also any other nation that does business with Cuba. Notwithstanding the fact that the embargo is still in effect, the Obama administration's actions have effectively crippled the law's effectiveness and ability to be enforced.

18. Many dissertations and even books on Cuban topics are based on only a few months of continuous fieldwork, or on several short fieldwork trips.

19. In 2013 the Cuban government announced an imminent end to the dual currency system: the Cuban convertible peso (CUC) will be eliminated, and the country will return to operating with just one currency, the Cuban peso (CUP). Details have not been released

about how the gap between the value of the CUC and CUP (the rate of exchange is 1:24) will be reconciled.

20. Economic difference in Cuba does not necessarily translate to class difference, as we tend to assume in the United States, because Cuban professionals and intellectuals are not compensated much better than their working-class compatriots. In fact, it is commonly acknowledged that waiters in large hotels and taxi drivers earn more than doctors, professors, and engineers because of their proximity to tourist dollars.

21. In addition, Cuba's consistent solidarity with other nations in the "global South" in their liberation struggles, and its dedication to aiding these countries, was strikingly evident in the aftermath of the catastrophic earthquake in Haiti in January 2010. The four hundred Cuban doctors already in Haiti immediately set up field hospitals and were the first to begin treating earthquake victims, and since then Cuba has sent hundreds more medical professionals who were trained at Havana's Escuela Latinoamericano de Medicina (Latin American School of Medicine, which offers low-cost or free medical training to citizens of many countries, including the United States); many of these doctors are Haitian. Again in 2014, Cuba took the lead in responding to a global humanitarian crisis, the Ebola outbreak in West Africa, by sending hundreds of doctors to treat patients and train local medical practitioners.

22. See journalist Ann Louise Bardach's excellent book *Cuba Confidential: Love and Vengeance in Miami and Havana* (2002) for an in-depth exploration of the mafia-style tactics of the Miami exile power structure. Here I am not including the third wave (the so-called *Marielitos* of the early 1980s) or fourth wave (the *balseros* of the mid-1990s) of Cuban immigrants, because their racial and class composition was noticeably different from that of the first two waves and because they tend to have more nuanced, less extreme views of the revolution. While the early waves were constituted of many landowning whites fleeing the socialist redistribution of land and nationalization of economic resources, the later immigrants included much larger proportions of poor, black, and mixed-race Cubans. In addition, many of the Marielitos were people deemed by the Castro regime to be *indeseables* (undesirables) or *escoria* (scum), including felons, gay men, and people with mental illnesses.

23. The repression of LGBT people and *creyentes* (religious adherents) has seen a sharp decline since the early 1990s. The Castro regime's declaration in 1992 that Cuba was no longer an "atheist," but "secular" state constituted a major policy change vis-à-vis tolerance for religious practice. LGBT movements have more recently gained visibility and strength, largely due to the initiatives of Raúl Castro's daughter, Mariela Castro, director of the Cuban National Center for Sex Education (CENESEX), a government organization that successfully lobbied to grant transgender Cubans the right to free sexual reassignment surgeries and that has recently conducted publicity campaigns to encourage tolerance for sexual diversity.

Chapter 1

1. Unless otherwise noted, all information in this paragraph is taken from the January 1, 2011, print edition of *Granma* (Cuba's national newspaper).

2. Pérez asserts that by the mid-nineteenth century, western Cuban mills accounted for almost 91 percent of the island's total sugar production (Louis Pérez 2006, 60).

3. In general, Cuba had the highest percentage of free people of color of all Caribbean slaveholding societies: Pérez asserts that they made up between 18 and 20 percent of the island's population in the late eighteenth century, and more than 40 percent of the total population of color (Louis Pérez 2006, 49). This was primarily due to the high incidence of manumission, whereby slaves could buy their freedom from their masters.

4. The three wars that constituted the Cuban struggle for independence were the Ten Years' War (1868–1878), the Guerra Chiquita (Little War, 1879–1880), and the final War of Independence (1895–1898).

5. The Grito de Yara is considered to be not only the beginning of the struggle for independence from Spain but also a significant event in the abolition movement, and October 10 is a national holiday.

6. James, Millet, and Alarcón (2007, 87–88) assert that during this time there were basically two Cubas, one at war and one at peace.

7. Mulato is a recognized racial category in Cuba, and the term does not carry the pejorative connotations of its English-language equivalent.

8. This characterization of Bantu/Congo slaves is at odds with much literature on slavery, as well as popular discourse in Cuba. Many of the musicians I conducted research with describe Bantu culture and religion as extremely "fuerte" (strong, powerful), and even brutish as compared with the more "refined" Yoruba culture.

9. Spain has a centuries-long history of interregional conflict that is still very pervasive today, as evidenced by the hostile relations between Madrid and independence-minded regions such as the Basque country and Cataluña, where it is more common to hear the regional languages—Basque and Catalan, respectively—than Castilian (standard) Spanish.

10. The *Atlas demográfico de Cuba* provides maps from 1970 showing that the urban population constituted 60.5 percent while the rural constituted 39.5 percent of the population (Comité Estatal de Estadísticas 1979, 23). In terms of population density, the rural population was significantly denser in the eastern provinces and Pinar del Río (30).

11. The following discussion of the contemporary manifestations of regionalism in Havana is based upon my own observations since 2004 and personal communication with many Cubans from both Havana and the outer provinces. I would like to particularly acknowledge my husband, Lázaro Moncada Merencio, whose experiences as a *santiaguero* (Santiago native) in Havana have deeply informed my observations and knowledge about the subject and who has provided me with a unique lens through which to view this issue.

12. Alejandro de la Fuente reports that an estimated fifty thousand Cubans migrated to Havana in 1996 and that ninety-two thousand people attempted to legalize their residential status in the city in early 1997, thus prompting the government to ban migration to the capital in spring 1997 (de la Fuente 2001, 328).

13. Various Cubans with whom I spoke about the term approximated that it came to have this connotation sometime in the 1990s, with the surge of eastern Cuban migration to Havana. I have come across only a few published mentions of the term (de la Fuente 2001; Rodríguez Ruiz and Estévez Mezquía 2006). Ethnomusicologist Ben Brinner reminded me

that this time period coincided with the end of the first Palestinian uprising and the forging of the Oslo accords between Israel and the Palestine Liberation Organization, and therefore that the conflict was receiving much media attention at this time, which could account partly for the use of this term in response to large-scale migration from Oriente (pers. comm. 2009).

14. See Sawyer 2006 and Blue 2007 for a discussion of the racial dynamics of remittances in the post-Soviet context.

15. These neighborhoods also boast disproportionately high numbers of black and mulato residents and consequently have a heavy police presence (de la Fuente 2001, 313–14).

16. This view is substantiated in de la Fuente's book and in an article written by Genevieve Howe in *Z Magazine*. Howe interviewed one Cuban academic who asserted that even Fidel Castro characterized Old Havana as full of delinquents from Oriente (Howe 1998, 37).

17. Another joking commentary I've heard is that when orientales travel, they go to Havana, but when habaneros travel, they go to *el yuma*. The assumption with both is that wherever they go, they will stay. Incidentally, this term originally referred to the United States, but its meaning has evolved to include European countries.

18. Non-Havana residents must have a "legitimate" reason to be in the capital, such as visiting a family member or working there temporarily through the auspices of a state agency, and must register with the local police for a finite period of time.

19. Genevieve Howe summarizes Decree 217 thus: "This law requires that people get government permission before moving to Havana. Inspectors must verify that the new lodging in Havana affords adequate sanitary conditions and at least ten square meters of space per person. Violation of the law brings a fine of 300 pesos [roughly US$12 or an average monthly salary] and the requirement to return immediately to the place of origin" (Howe 1998, 37). Recent articles that I found while conducting an Internet search suggest that the law is still in effect. For example, see http://www.cnn.com/2010/WORLD/americas/05/19/cuba.illegal/, accessed February 2014.

20. Racial profiling is also in effect, given that more black Cubans than white Cubans are routinely stopped.

21. Howe asserts that government officials have denied rumors of mass deportations of orientales back to their provinces of origin in the 1990s, but she also reproduces statements contradicting this assertion (1998, 37).

22. Some Cubans view the recruitment of police officers from outside the capital as a strategic move by the government to create a sense of division between habaneros and orientales, thereby helping maintain control over the population and preventing cross-regional dissent.

23. "La gente de Occidente siempre tratan de ver al oriental más chiquito que ellos." Unless otherwise noted, all translations of musicians' statements are my own.

24. See chapter 2, which analyzes a rumba song by the Havana group Clave y Guaguancó that presents an incendiary imitation of an oriental accent.

25. Here he was referring to the overflowing mountains of garbage that pile up daily on the streets of Centro Habana and Habana Vieja, as local officials do not seem to be responding to the need to empty the communal containers several times a day instead of just once.

26. I am using a pseudonym for this musician, as he preferred to remain anonymous in published work.

27. I should note that I have heard this comment not only from habaneros but from Cubans of other regions as well.

28. "El habanero habla muy diferente del matancero, y hablamos español. . . . Hasta en eso, el habanero se diferencia del matancero, la forma de ser, la forma de andar, la forma de manifestarse, en todo."

29. While I also find that Matanzas is constructed as "black" in certain ways, chapter 6 elaborates on the differing notions of blackness, I propose, that adhere to the two provinces.

30. My observations regarding the discourse of whiteness associated with Camagüey are confirmed by published scholarship (de la Fuente 2001, 278).

31. Ethnographer Jesús Guanche cites the number of slaves imported during this period as 1,137,300, which includes Africans who were brought to Cuba illegally, after the abolition of the slave trade in 1820 (1996, 47). Louis Pérez states that 90,000 slaves were imported only between 1856 and 1860, one of the largest numbers for a five-year period in the history of the slave trade (2006, 83). The *Atlas demográfico de Cuba* states that a total of 1,310,000 Africans were brought to the island from the sixteenth through the middle of the nineteenth centuries (Comité Estatal de Estadísticas 1979, 69). In addition, the total number of Chinese "coolies" brought between 1848 and 1874 is estimated to be 150,000 (69).

32. In addition to the Franco-Haitians, around four thousand Dominicans arrived in Cuba in the early nineteenth century as a result of the upheavals related to the Haitian Revolution that had repercussions across the entire island of Hispaniola (Álvarez Estévez and Guzmán Pascual 2008, 167).

33. In referring to this specific publication by Olavo Alén Rodríguez I use only his first surname (Alén), as this corresponds to the manner in which the author's name appears on the cover of and in the book. His other publications use both of his surnames.

34. Coffee cultivation did not remain confined to eastern Cuba but spread throughout the island. In 1827, the Havana region accounted for 58 percent of the island's production (Bergad et al. 1995, 82).

35. Many Cuban sources refer to the period 1902–1958 as the "neocolonial republic," as Cubans, finally independent and free of American occupation (1898–1902), were still excluded from land ownership: in 1905, an estimated 60 percent of rural property was owned by either individuals or corporations from the United States (Louis Pérez 2006, 151).

36. In addition, illegal immigration of Antilleans likely continued into the 1940s (de la Fuente 2001, 105).

37. As first-person testimonies from descendants of Haitian immigrants evidence, many Haitians also planned to return to their homeland eventually (Corbea Calzado 2004; Berenguer Cala 2006).

38. This number would not include descendants of the first wave of Franco-Haitian immigrants. James makes his estimation from census numbers indicating that around 250,000 Antilleans stayed permanently in Cuba, and that for every person who stayed, another four had come and gone. He does not indicate where he obtained this information or how he made his calculation.

39. These immigrants were composed of 190,255 Haitians (56 percent), 121,520 Jamaicans (36 percent), and smaller numbers of Puerto Ricans, Dominicans, and Antilleans of non-specified nationalities (Álvarez Estévez and Guzmán Pascual 2008, 34).

40. The Rural Guard was a national police force established by the American occupation government in 1898, which was stationed in the Cuban interior primarily to protect American agricultural interests.

41. Notwithstanding the horrible treatment of Haitians during this period, James, Millet, and Alarcón also present testimonies by Cuban Rural Guardsmen who asserted that some Cuban farmers hid and protected Haitians from deportation. Although this was often for selfish reasons—for instance, the planters did not want to lose their source of cheap labor—the narrative also presents these acts as representative of cross-national intimacy (James et al. 2007, 60–71).

42. Despite the overall nativist atmosphere of the 1930s, de la Fuente discusses cross-racial and cross-national labor organizing efforts by the Cuban Communist Party, which attempted to forge bonds among laborers of all nationalities, including Spanish, Chinese, Antillean, and eastern European immigrants.

43. This census predated the twentieth-century waves of Antillean migration to the island, which would result in a drastic change in demographics specifically in the province of Puerto Príncipe.

44. While it is generally understood that Cuba has three main racial categories—black, white, and mulato—it is possible that the economic, political, and cultural influence of the United States on Cuba in the first half of the twentieth century led to more binary racial thinking on the island during this period and a discussion of race in white/nonwhite terms.

45. Unfortunately, none of these articles distinguish between blacks and mulatos, using only the term "black" to speak about what I assume more precisely to be "people of color."

46. Robin Sheriff (2001) conducted an in-depth ethnography on racial identification in Brazil, showing that people often "whiten" themselves in official surveys.

47. Although the more recent waves of migration (since 1980) have included much larger numbers of nonwhites, white Cubans continue to constitute the majority of émigrés, as they tend to have the resources necessary to emigrate, in part because of the financial support of family members already living and working abroad.

48. Gramsci's analytics seem particularly appropriate for my discussion of regionalism, as his work was thoroughly informed by his own regional identity as a Sardinian. Sardinia is one of the most marginalized provinces in Italy, both spatially—it is an island off the country's western coast—and within the Italian national imaginary. When I lived in Italy I heard more than one person characterize Sardinians as uneducated "sheep-shaggers."

49. As is discussed by many Cuba scholars, the post–Special Period economy has been a hybrid one, mixing socialist and capitalist models.

Chapter 2

1. The transcription of the Spanish lyrics was taken from the liner notes of the group's 2006 album *La Rumba Que No Termina* (2006). The translations are my own.

2. Both songs can be found on the album *En la Calle* (1992).

3. Although the decision to examine songs from two different musical practices—Cuban dance music and rumba—may not constitute an obvious methodological choice, the emergence of the Cuban salsa style called *timba* has highlighted and intensified the intimate and long-standing connections between these two genres. As discussed in detail by Vincenzo Perna (2005), contemporary Cuban dance music has borrowed from rumba music in many ways, an issue that will be broached in chapter 6.

4. In this chapter I use the term "Cuban dance music" to refer to what is sometimes known as Cuban-style salsa, following the practice of scholars who differentiate Cuban salsa from the style of salsa that emerged in New York in the 1960s. While the latter style is strongly associated with New York Puerto Ricans and is a major symbol of Puerto Rican identity both on the island and abroad, other regional styles influenced by New York–style salsa emerged throughout Latin America beginning in the 1970s, notably in Colombia and Venezuela. Although there have been musical exchanges between New York– and Cuban-style salsa, many features differentiate them. I use the commonly accepted term *timba* to speak about Cuban dance music from 1990 on, as it refers to specific stylistic and thematic differences from earlier styles of Cuban dance music. For details on the development of timba and its principal musical features, see Perna 2005 and R. Moore 2006.

5. The career trajectory, musical innovations, and overall significance of Los Van Van to Cuban dance music have been chronicled extensively in literature from both Cuba and the United States, including Perna 2005, R. Moore 2006, articles in the Cuban popular music journals *Clave* and *Salsa Cubana*, and many Internet sources.

6. Although "La Habana No Aguanta Más" has been mentioned in publications discussing the social relevance of Los Van Van's lyrics, it is usually interpreted in a more literal way as addressing housing shortages in the capital (Perna 2005; R. Moore 2006) and has not been examined through the lens of regionalism in Cuba.

7. This song can be found on the compilation album *The Legendary Los Van Van: 30 Years of Cuba's Greatest Dance Band* (1999). Lyrics and translations of the verse section of the song are taken from the album's liner notes, although I have made minor changes where I felt a better translation was warranted. The translation of the *montuno* section lyrics are my own.

8. In this chapter, when there is a *coro* (choral refrain) that alternates with a *solista* (lead singer) repeatedly, I present the coro lyrics once, and in subsequent instances I provide only the solista's lines with a dash before each one to denote the repetition of the coro that is sung between each solo line. When the coro changes or is shortened, I present the full lyrics and then proceed with dashes before the solista's lines.

9. Coppelia is the name of Cuba's national brand of ice cream, established after the revolution. There are Coppelia ice cream parlors in every major city on the island.

10. La Jata is a neighborhood in the Guanabacoa municipality of La Habana, the province representing the greater Havana metropolitan area, which is divided into fifteen

municipalities. *Doce plantas*, literally a "twelve-story building," refers to the drab, Soviet-style apartment buildings built by the government to fill housing needs in the 1970s and 1980s.

11. Calvo left Los Van Van in 2000 and currently has his own dance band, Pedro Calvo y La Justicia. He still makes occasional guest appearances with Los Van Van for high-profile performances.

12. The band is currently under the direction of Revé's son, Elio Revé Jr., or "Elito." Although Revé relocated to Havana in 1955 before forming his group, Orquesta Revé has always been associated with eastern Cuba, in part due to its musical style and in part due to lyrical references to Guantánamo and its traditions.

13. By "extensive use of coros," Perna is referring to the predominance of choral refrains and the montuno (call-and-response) section as compared with the verses of Cuban dance music songs; he argues that the coros constitute the heart and soul of the song. In addition, it should be noted that Cuban dance music tends to use multiple coros within a song rather than using one refrain throughout, as is the case in American popular music and other styles of salsa. Many view this focus on the coro as evidence of influence from rumba and other Afro-Cuban folkloric genres.

14. Kevin Moore, creator of the website Timba.com (which has served as an invaluable source of information on timba's genealogy), asserts that most timba groups can trace their roots back to the Orquesta Revé.

15. Despite its name, which translates to "French *charanga*," the ensemble does not have any obvious French influences but rather appears to have been an attempt to link the ensemble with a more sophisticated (i.e., French) sound (Madrid and Moore 2013, 51).

16. *Changüí*, believed to be one of the rural eastern Cuban antecedents of son, is almost universally associated with the province of Guantánamo. See chapter 3 and Lapidus 2008 for more on the genre. While tangential to my own concerns, Lapidus makes an interesting point regarding the reception of Revé's music by traditional changüí practitioners, who don't really consider his music to be changüí: "Elio Revé's music is a good example of how genre, generic identifiers, and geographic origin are conflated. The end result is good popular Cuban dance music that really bears none of the social and musical characteristics of traditional changüí. Revé, born and raised in Guantánamo, labels his music changüí and is perceived by non-Guantanameros to be a changüisero because of his connection to Guantánamo" (Lapidus 2008, 175).

17. Pedroso's rhythmic innovations on the piano have been essential to the development of timba. He left Los Van Van in 2001 in order to form his own band, Pupy y Los Que Son Son, which has had tremendous success and is currently one of Cuba's most popular dance bands.

18. I thank Lázaro Moncada for alerting me to the existence of this song (which seems to have been buried in the vaults of Cuban popular music history) and for providing meaningful insight concerning my reading of the text.

19. This song can be found on the Cuban salsa compilation *Cuban Gold: Que Se Sepa, ¡Yo Soy de La Habana!* (1993). Transcription and translation of the lyrics are my own.

20. The *malecón*, a quintessential symbol of Havana, is a long boardwalk that runs for miles along the sea in the city's center. It is also a primary site of nocturnal entertainment

for Cubans of all ages, classes, races, and sexual orientations—who sit on top of the seawall, socializing and drinking with friends and loved ones—and for tourists.

21. Orquesta Aragón is a highly esteemed dance band founded in 1939 in the city of Cienfuegos. The band gained widespread popularity after relocating to Havana in the early 1950s and is still performing today.

22. The "trenches" allude to the rhetoric of the revolution emphasizing the importance of national defense in every corner of the island. Fidel Castro often used the expression *trincheras de ideas* (ideological trenches) in his speeches.

23. I have translated *monte adentro* (literally, "mountain inside") as "boondocks," since it is a vernacular expression used in Cuba to refer to the middle of nowhere, a rural location very far from an urban center.

24. The Sierra Maestra is a large mountain range in Oriente that extends through the provinces of Santiago and Granma and is famed for being the base of operations for Fidel Castro and the guerrillas during the revolution.

25. The Moncada Barracks is a former military site (currently a school) in the city of Santiago where Castro staged his first (failed) attack on Cuban government forces in 1953. Gran Piedra is, as its name suggests, a famous "large rock" that sits atop a mountain in the Sierra Maestra. Caney is a beach town near Santiago where some of the best mangoes in Cuba are grown. The Granjita Siboney is a farm located near Siboney Beach just outside of Santiago, where Castro hid after his failed assault on the Moncada Barracks and where the authorities caught and arrested him. Bayamo is one of Cuba's oldest cities and is famous for its colonial-style charm. The Glorieta, located in the city of Manzanillo, is a unique architectural monument in terms of its strong Moorish influence and its design reminiscent of the Alhambra in Granada, Spain.

26. It's not entirely clear in the song whether, by "there," Fabré is referring to Havana or to going back home, i.e., Oriente.

27. Majaguabo is a small town in the rural part of Santiago Province.

28. Santiago is known throughout Cuba as *la tierra caliente* (the hot land) for its extreme heat and humidity as compared with Havana and the northern coast of Cuba. However, this sobriquet also has a symbolic meaning, alluding to the hospitality and openness of santiagueros and their penchant for partying.

29. This argument may have held true in the mid-1980s, but in the context of the Special Period and ongoing economic crisis since the 1990s, it is doubtful that many eastern migrants would willingly return to the even worse situation in Oriente.

30. Chapter 6 delves into the scholarly debates surrounding the origins of son.

31. Robin Moore's *Nationalizing Blackness* (1997) elaborates a similar argument, although he focuses on the racial politics of the nationalist appropriation of son rather than the regional politics.

32. "Alguien tiene que quedarse en esta región para seguir representando desde aquí al oriente que es seguir representando a un solo país que se llama Cuba."

33. *Puyas* are most often associated with the rumba style called *columbia*, where two singers engage in a war of words/wit.

34. A Google search conducted on "Soy Cubano y Soy de Oriente" in March 2008 resulted in only four hits, three of which were track listings for the song on compilation albums; the fourth was a brief encyclopedia entry on Cándido Fabré listing his most famous compositions.

35. I am grateful to León, a researcher at the Santiago-based Casa del Caribe, for telling me about Alonso's analysis and attaining a digital copy for me. I attempted to contact Alonso, who no longer lives on the island, but was unsuccessful.

36. Biographical and professional information about Adalberto Álvarez was drawn from his website, http://www.adalbertoalvarez.cult.cu, accessed January 2008. The website now appears to be defunct.

37. On *Mi Linda Habanera* (2005) Álvarez rereleased one of his most popular songs from the early 1990s, "Y Qué Tú Quieres Que Te Den" (And What Do You Want Them [the *orishas*] To Give You?), and its resurgent popularity has cemented his band's current popularity in the timba era. During my fieldwork period in 2006–2007, it was almost impossible to go to a rumba or dance music event in which the song was *not* played during an intermission. The song, which includes rapped lyrics in addition to the insertion of Yoruba-derived choruses for various *orishas*, is one of the most prominent timba odes to Santería worship. When first released in the 1990s, it helped inspire countless dance songs extolling the virtues of Afro-Cuban religious practice.

38. Recent songs in this vein include "El Melón"—literally "The Melon," a Cuban slang term for money—and "Tu Falta de Ortografía" (Your Spelling Errors), a humorous commentary on a common problem among Cubans, from his album *El Son de Altura* (2010); and "La Canción de los Gorditos" (The Song about the Chubby Guys), which lists various famous singers who could benefit from some weight loss, from his album *Respeto pa' los Mayores* (2013).

39. The transcription and translation of all lyrics are my own.

40. *Especulando*, literally "speculating" or "showing off," is used in popular discourse to mean displaying conspicuous signs of wealth, such as a cell phone or gold chain. In this song it also refers specifically to people from the outer provinces passing themselves off as *habaneros*.

41. Santa Fe is a Havana neighborhood. To "make santo" means to be initiated into Santería.

42. Baracoa is a city located at the eastern tip of Cuba. It was the first city founded by the Spaniards in 1511 and the island's first capital.

43. Niquero is a town in the province of Granma.

44. Found on the group's 2008 album *Control*, the song (meaning "Havana Is Calling Me") begins by naming virtually all the Cuban provinces and praising them for their unique qualities, and then moves on to pay homage to Havana.

45. Pianist/composer Manolito Simonet, from Camagüey, currently leads one of the most popular timba bands since the mid-1990s, Manolito y Su Trabuco. Flutist José Luís Cortés, known as "El Tosco" (the coarse guy), is the bandleader of the pioneering timba band NG La Banda and is from the central Cuban province of Santa Clara. Before starting his own band, Cortés played with both Los Van Van and legendary jazz/fusion group Irakere. Singer Isaac

Delgado, born in Havana but presumably with parents from el campo, was an original member of NG La Banda who launched his own group in 1992. Pachito Alonso is the current director of Pachito Alonso y Sus Kini Kini, a dance band begun by his father Pacho Alonso, a Santiago native and bandleader who began his career during the 1940s.

46. In fact, there is a popular saying about Fabré among orientales: "La gente amanece con Cándido" (People "wake up," or party until dawn, with Cándido).

47. *Guaguancó* is the most popular of the three main styles of rumba performed in contemporary Cuba.

48. This song can be found on the album *Congo Yambumba* (1994).

49. The transcription of the second verse lyrics is taken from the liner notes of the group's 2006 album *La Rumba Que No Termina*, and the English translation is my own. For the montuno section, I was responsible for both the transcription of the Spanish lyrics and the English translation.

50. The Spanish adjective *popular* has multiple meanings, and is a false cognate in some senses. In this case it is used to mean something belonging or corresponding to "the people" or "the masses." Thus, I have translated it here to "down-home" to give a connotation of something associated with working-class or poor people. In Cuba, an *ambiente popular* would imply activities such as drinking, dancing, and/or playing dominos.

51. *Barbacoa*, coming from the Spanish word for "barbecue," is a Cuban vernacular term referring to "a platform or mezzanine constructed in the interior of an already existing space. It is composed of wood beams that serve as a frame for planks of diverse materials, providing a surface or floor on which to stand" (Del Real and Scarpaci 2011, 63). In other words, it is a housing solution that basically converts one floor into two. This trend is associated with eastern migrants in Havana trying to create more living space but is now quite common among habaneros as well.

52. Lázaro was an invaluable help in transcribing the spoken interlude, which is not included in the Spanish lyrics in the CD's liner notes. Nonetheless, there were a few phrases that proved impossible to discern because of the exaggerated accent, and there may be a few errors in my transcription.

53. *Babalaos* are the diviners within Santería, high priests revered for their ability to advise practitioners on how to proceed with various life decisions. Anyone can be initiated into Santería, but only men can become initiated into Ifá, the Yoruba-derived practice associated with divination.

54. *Jabao* is a racial category in Cuba used to describe a light-skinned person of mixed race. For example, the child of a mulato person and a white person might be described as jabao.

55. This phrase is quite perplexing in that I haven't been able to make sense of the meaning of the word *dibujo* (drawing) here. There was an Argentine television series in the 1990s called *Mi Familia Es Un Dibujo* that mixed live acting and animation (the "drawing" in the title refers to an animated character), and it was shown in Cuba. However, the phrase seems to have taken on a localized meaning in Cuba that I haven't been able to decipher.

56. De la Fuente (2001) and Sawyer (2006) also make reference to the pervasiveness of racialized/racist humor in Cuba.

57. Of course, a rumba song like this one would not have received even a fraction of the media dissemination of the Los Van Van or Fabré songs.

58. Some habaneros might even consider him to be one of their own, as the capital has been his home for years.

Chapter 3

1. Peter Wade (2000) has also identified this contradictory tendency in Colombia's mestizaje discourse.

2. The *Atlas demográfico de Cuba* (Comité Estatal de Estadísticas 1979, 11–12) displays a map showing Ciboneys as predominant in western Cuba, especially Pinar del Río, while the group referred to as Sub-Taínos (part of the larger Arawak group from South America) covers a large area on the map, from Cienfuegos in central Cuba all the way to Guantánamo. Fernando Ortiz asserts that the Ciboneys were the first people in Cuba, corresponding to the Paleolithic age, and that they were eventually conquered and dominated by the Taínos, more advanced Neolithic peoples who brought agriculture and a more hierarchical social organization ([1940] 1999, 81). Historian Louis Pérez notes that Cuban archaeologists have in recent decades found evidence of a third indigenous group, the Mayarí, who inhabited north-central Oriente (2006, 12).

3. All of these sources note that it is very difficult to correctly estimate the number of Indians in Cuba when the Spanish arrived, but that the number could be closer to five hundred thousand.

4. José Barreiro (1989) provides another account of this community and indigenous descendants in Cuba.

5. Fernando Ortiz, on the other hand, lists the influences on Espiritismo as traditional Christianity (both Catholic and Protestant traditions), Kardecian spiritism, Bantu religions, and vodou (Ortiz 1965, 457–59).

6. See Robin Moore's *Nationalizing Blackness* (1997) for an in-depth discussion of the competing discourses of nationalism in the early decades of the twentieth century, including afrocubanismo, indigenismo, and *guajirismo* (the promotion of the rural Spanish-derived, or white, peasant as the symbol of national identity).

7. See the first section of Ortiz's *La africanía de la música folklórica de Cuba* ([1950] 1998) for a withering critique of Sánchez de Fuentes's theories on indigenous influence.

8. Hatuey was a militant Indian chief from Hispaniola who traveled to Cuba and warned the local indigenous population about the invading Spaniards, and who was eventually burned at the stake. Anacaona was a female Indian leader from Hispaniola at the time of the conquest, also killed by the Spaniards, and Yumurí was an Indian princess from Cuba who became involved in a love triangle with a Spanish conquistador.

9. The *Atlas etnográfico de Cuba* (Centro de Investigación y Desarrollo de la Cultura Cubana Juan Marinello 1999) constitutes a similar study conducted by ethnologists at the Center of Anthropology from the late 1970s to 1990; they collected data on oral traditions, popular music, and dance throughout the country.

10. Examples of this support include state sponsorship of local cultural and musical festivals, like the changüí festival in Guantánamo, and of groups classified as *portadores*, or tradition bearer groups.

11. Caribbeanist scholars have emphasized, in a parallel argument, that hybridity discourses often mask the privileging of whiteness (Hintzen 2002; Puri 2004).

12. One exception to this tendency is the ample scholarship discussing the early Haitian influences on nineteenth-century Cuban social dance genres (Averill 1989, 1997; Hill 1998; Carpentier 2001; Sublette 2004; Lapidus 2005). In the early nineteenth century, a creolized version of the French contredanse (country dance) was introduced by French planters and their slaves fleeing to eastern Cuba after the Haitian Revolution. A Cubanized version, contradanza, emerged soon after, which in turn spawned habanera (Cuba's first musical export in the mid-nineteenth century), danza, and danzón, which came to be considered Cuba's national dance. Notwithstanding this recognition, the Haitian influences on Cuban music tend to be discussed only in historical terms, while the post-nineteenth-century, more contemporary influences are overlooked. In addition, recent research suggests that the introduction of contredanse to Cuba predated the first Franco-Haitian migration and in fact appeared in Havana (not eastern Cuba), imported directly from Spain (Lapique 1998; Manuel 2009b), thus implying that the early Haitian musical influence had less of an impact than originally thought. In contrast, Benjamin Lapidus (2008) asserts that there have been important Afro-Haitian contributions to the development of son (via changüí) that have been ignored, which is interesting considering the fact that son is widely discussed as being the island's quintessential musical representation due to its "perfect" synthesis of African and Spanish elements. I discuss this issue in further depth in chapter 6.

13. Some Cuban sources discuss what is thought to be the only extant community of Jamaican descendants, located in Baraguá in the province of Ciego de Ávila, where a group of culture bearers still carries on the tradition of the *cinta* or May Pole dance. They celebrate festivities on August 1, emancipation day in Jamaica (Esquenazi Pérez 2001; Álvarez Estévez and Guzmán Pascual 2008). In addition, Benjamin Lapidus (2008, 7) mentions an Anglophone Caribbean performing group in Guantánamo called Jagüey.

14. For more information, see http://www.unesco.org/culture/ich/index.php?lg=en&pg=00011&RL=00052, accessed August 2011.

15. Martha Esquenazi Pérez asserts that there are three extant societies—the two mentioned above and a "tumba de monte" (rural tumba francesa society) in the municipality of Sagua de Tánamo in Holguín Province (2001, 157). While conducting research in Santiago in June 2011, I visited the tumba francesa society La Caridad and was also told by the members of an existing society in Sagua de Tánamo. From information provided by the *Atlas etnográfico de Cuba* (Centro de Investigación y Desarrollo de la Cultura Cubana Juan Marinello 1999), it appears that the Sagua de Tánamo society was an institution that was defunct and later was revived.

16. See Peter Manuel's *Creolizing Contradance in the Caribbean* (2009a) for an in-depth comparative discussion of various Caribbean forms of the French contredanse, including Haitian contredanse, Cuban contradanza, and the quadrilles of various Francophone islands.

17. Nonetheless, Rolando Álvarez Estévez and Marta Guzmán Pascual (2008, 96) assert that the Santiago-based society La Caridad emerged in 1862, thus predating both the onset of the Ten Years' War (1868) and emancipation (1886).

18. Guantánamo may be gaining a foothold in the Cuban tourism industry, according to Benjamin Lapidus, who discusses a recently organized excursion in which foreigners can travel to the town of Yateras and pay to attend "authentic" changüí parties (2008, 1). He also asserts that tumba francesa is currently enjoying a boom in Guantánamo among younger musicians and dancers.

19. Ethnomusicologist Lani Milstein's recent English-language article on Santiago's conga tradition (2013) is a hopeful sign that the status of the research on this genre is changing. See also the various contributions in Bettelheim 2001 for work published in English on conga and Santiago's carnival.

20. Although many people (including Santiago natives) assume that La conga de Los Hoyos and El Cocoyé are one and the same (i.e., that Los Hoyos was an outgrowth of the tumba francesa society), Lani Milstein details the differences between the two and the ways that the conga group came to be associated with El Cocoyé (2013, 232–33).

21. Lani Milstein describes the movement thus: "While the basic step of arrollando is a march, the word refers quite specifically to a type of movement. Most of this movement occurs in the hips, which tend to move in a circular motion, in a figure eight, or side to side" (2013, 247).

22. See Milstein 2013 for details regarding the musical differences between the six conga groups in Santiago. Los Hoyos is widely considered to have the most "traditional" style and slowest rhythm of all the congas.

23. It is important to specify that Santiago's carnival activities include both the participatory congas in the streets and the more formal, organized comparsas and *paseos* (floats) that parade in front of judges. In other words, while comparsas are not necessarily specific to one region, congas are explicitly linked to Santiago. See Milstein 2013 for more information on the differences between paseos, comparsas, and congas within Santiago's carnival tradition.

24. The large majority of the roughly 150,000 Chinese contract laborers who were brought to the island to work on sugar plantations in the mid- to late nineteenth century arrived to and stayed in Havana and/or western Cuba. Millet and Brea (1989, 45) assert that the corneta china was transported to Oriente by members of the Permanent Army around 1912, when troops from the west were stationed in the east and vice versa. Milstein (2013, 243) states that two soldiers from Santiago who had been stationed in Matanzas brought the instrument back to the eastern city.

25. The most celebrated performer of the corneta china, who plays with La conga de Los Hoyos, asserts that other cities have begun to incorporate the instrument into their carnival music (Millet, Brea, and Ruiz Vila 1997, 130).

26. In 2005 Sur Caribe, a popular dance band from Santiago, released a tribute to the conga called "Añoranza por la conga" (Egrem, 2005) and featuring La conga de Los Hoyos, which became a huge hit all over the island and reinforced the discursive link between the city and its carnival tradition.

27. Another book coauthored by Millet and Rafael Brea (1989) provides a comprehensive look at all of Santiago's conga and comparsa groups, in addition to detailing the history and repertoire of the local folkloric groups.

28. James died in 2006, and *Del Caribe* issues 48 and 49 (2007) were dedicated to honoring his memory and scholarship.

29. Santería is practiced widely not only in Cuba but also in Latin America and, in recent decades, among Europeans and non-Latino Americans. Abakuá is an all-male secret society derived from the Cross River region of southeastern Nigeria and southwestern Cameroon. There is debate as to whether it can be called a "religion," but many refer to it as such, and it certainly contains many ritual elements that can only be known by its initiates. In his book on Abakuá, Ivor Miller refers to it as a "mutual aid society" and "male initiation society" (2009, 3).

30. Originally published in the Dominican Republic in 1992, the first Cuban edition was published in 1998.

31. See Elizabeth McAlister's *Rara! Vodou, Power, and Performance in Haiti and Its Diaspora* (2002) for an in-depth discussion of rara. Grete Viddal (2010) has a brief description of the folkloric version of the gagá dance, probably the only information published in English on the topic.

32. As I discussed in chapter 1, the first wave of immigrants from the island of Haiti, those who arrived during the Haitian Revolution, referred to themselves and were seen as "French"; a distinctly Haitian conception of identity had not yet been formed. Thus, this first wave is often referred to as "Franco-Haitian," while the second wave, arriving more than a century later, is referred to as "Haitian."

33. Viddal (2012) argues that this situation is changing. She asserts that the practice of Vodú is spreading to urban centers, notably Havana, among practitioners of other Afro-Cuban religions, and has become an important symbol of eastern Cuban identity.

34. Sánchez Lussón asserts that the first house of worship was established in 1878 in the city of Manzanillo.

35. Miguel Bretos (2010, 191) notes that the first Kardecian spiritualist organization to be founded in Matanzas was in 1882, suggesting that the practice spread quickly to western Cuba.

36. *Orisha* is the Lucumí or Yoruba-derived word used to refer to these deities, while *santo* is the correlating Spanish word for them. The two words are used interchangeably among practitioners. Sometimes Santería practitioners are instructed by the orishas themselves (via a human medium) to give a cajón in their honor.

37. Bantu or Congo slaves arrived early and throughout the colonial period and were widely dispersed across the island, rather than arriving in large waves in a relatively short period of time like the Yoruba slaves in the nineteenth century. Thus the Cuban version of the Bantu language is much more hybridized with Spanish and has not been as well conserved as Lucumí, the Yoruba-derived language.

38. All information is drawn from an interview that took place on June 14, 2011, in Santiago. I am using a pseudonym for this musician, as he requested that I not use his real name in published accounts.

39. Rather than constituting a conscious choice to engage in cultural mixing, the substitution of nontraditional language and instrumentation in eastern Cuban Santería probably relates to the fact that Yoruba slaves never arrived in large numbers to Oriente. Although Santería has been practiced in the east for at least a century, knowledge of Lucumí, traditional chants, and the construction of consecrated batá drums are more recent phenomena in cities like Santiago and Guantánamo.

40. She made a conscious decision to omit Santería from her discussion because it already enjoys a disproportionate amount of research attention.

41. Millet's 2010 denunciation can be found at https://nepabuleici.wordpress.com/2010/09/01/jose-millet-fundador-de-la-casa-del-caribe-acusa-de-fraude-a-libro-sobre-el-caribe-publicado-en-estados-unidos/, accessed July 2012.

42. For a discussion of the increase in espectáculos in the past few decades, especially by rumba groups, see chapter 5 of my dissertation (Bodenheimer 2010).

43. *Tajona* is a rural comparsa, or carnival dance, that originated during Holy Week among the slaves working on French-owned coffee plantations in eastern Cuba. Like tumba francesa, it is currently only performed in folkloric contexts, by groups like Cutumba and La Caridad, the tumba francesa society in Santiago. For more information, see Viddal 2010. Grete Viddal states that the *chancleta* (the Spanish word for flip-flop) is "a dance of Iberian origin featuring wooden sandals that clack against the floor" (Viddal 2012, 213, n. 11).

44. The 1970s, as Viddal discusses, saw the penetration of institutional folklore into rural parts of Oriente, including Haitian descendant communities, and the formation of many amateur folkloric groups. It was during this time that professional folklorists and groups traveled to these isolated communities to learn about Haitian traditions and incorporate them into their repertoire, in a stylized manner. However, *portador* or culture bearer groups—also referred to by Viddal as "heritage performers"—were also being formed by the descendants of Haitians themselves. Petit Dansé in Las Tunas is one such group.

45. In 1991, the Cuban Communist Party decriminalized religious practice, a policy that reversed the revolution's decades-old dogma of "scientific atheism" and resulted in an increased tolerance and relevance of the sacred domain in the public sphere. See Hagedorn 2001 for more on the state's sponsoring of religious tourism.

46. As noted in note 12 above, there has been little scholarship on twentieth-century Haitian musical influences in Cuba, particularly the introduction of the Haitian meringue into folklore oriental. According to ethnomusicologist Gage Averill, Haitian singer Martha Jean-Claude was the main agent in bringing meringue to Cuba when she left Haiti in 1954 and settled in eastern Cuba for the rest of her life (Averill, pers. comm. 2009). She recorded several albums in Cuba featuring Haitian meringues. Nonetheless, there are major sonic differences between Haitian meringue and what is known in Cuba as merengue haitiano, and a deeper investigation into the topic is warranted.

47. The *Atlas de los instrumentos de la música folclórico-popular de Cuba* (Elí Rodríguez 1997) has a few passing references to merengue in relation to the gagá (rara) festivities celebrated by Haitian communities in Cuba. Grete Viddal describes it in generic terms as "a

couple dance for festive occasions" (2010, 92). Benjamin Lapidus has a passing reference to the genre in a list of traditions Haitians in Guantánamo perform (2008, 131).

48. The first three examples were live performances that I recorded, while the Cutumba example is taken from a commercial recording (Ballet Folklórico Cutumba 2005a). The first two live performances were audio recordings taken during my fieldwork period in 2006 and 2007, while the BFO performance was video recorded in June 2011.

49. It's worth noting that meringue is considered to be Haiti's national genre, and as such it is an expansive practice that can be represented by a variety of ensembles.

50. All information is drawn from an interview that took place on June 26, 2011, at Isaias's home in Havana.

51. Culture bearers of Haitian traditions are not all located in Oriente but also in Camagüey, home of the group Caidije (see Guanche and Moreno 1988), and Ciego de Ávila. See Viddal 2012 for more on Haitian-Cuban portador (culture bearer) groups.

52. This type of stylization is quite common among folkloric groups across the island, including the CFN and the BFO, although the discourse surrounding their styles may deny the nontraditional elements.

53. *Rueda de casino* is a type of Cuban salsa dance (or *casino*) that is danced in a circle with numerous couples who switch partners throughout a song, while simultaneously executing complicated turns.

54. Clearly this brings up the issue of the construction of genre categories, and why certain types of ensembles and/or musical practices are categorized as "folkloric" or "traditional." While I cannot address this issue at present, it is a problematic distinction that deserves scrutiny.

55. My use of scare quotes is meant to suggest that, while traditionally placed in the category of "rhythm," drums can also be considered melodic instruments; I have heard many percussionists speak of drum "melodies" that are created by interlocking patterns of drums tuned to different pitches.

56. As discussed in depth by Lapidus (2008), changüí is traditionally categorized as a variant or antecedent of son and thus discussed as part of the son complex, but he argues that it contains enough musical distinctions that it should be considered its own complex with variations.

57. As will be evidenced in my discussion in chapter 4 with respect to rumba, the "cradle" metaphor is a popular one for speaking about musical origins. Another discursive formation noted by Lapidus in relation to changüí is the dichotomy that is constructed between rural and urban styles of playing (2008, 104), something I have observed in my research on the differences between Havana- and Matanzas-style rumba.

58. Every January the Asociación Cultural Yoruba releases their highly anticipated *letra del año*, "letter of the year," which features predictions made by *babalaos* and other Santería elders about the year to come and particular challenges Cubans will face.

59. The ENA has regional sites throughout the country, possibly in every province. The ISA has four additional locations outside Havana—two in Holguín, one in Camagüey, and one in Santiago—although the location in the capital is the primary institution.

60. All information is drawn from an interview that took place on June 17, 2011, at Cutumba's rehearsal site in Santiago.

61. I would have liked to reproduce photos of the three musicians whose comments I discuss in this chapter who didn't wish to remain anonymous, but unfortunately the only one I photographed was Mayito.

62. All information is drawn from an interview that took place on June 14, 2011, at Mayito's home in Santiago. Incidentally, the reason that Mayito is no longer playing with Kokoyé relates to the limited economic viability of rumba performance in contemporary Cuba (see Bodenheimer 2013). Like many musicians, Mayito is now playing in a son/dance band because it offers better opportunities for financial gain, commercial recording, and international tours than does playing in a rumba group. Robin Moore (1995) describes a similar situation for Havana *rumberos* in the 1920s and 1930s, such as Ignacio Piñeiro, who turned to son performance because of the marginalization of rumba.

63. See Victoria Elí Rodríguez (1989) and Robin Moore (2006) for details about pilón and other rhythms/dance crazes, such as *mozambique*, that emerged after the revolution.

64. Cutumba's earlier albums, *Ritmos Cubafricanos Volume 1* and *Ritmos Cubafricanos Volume 2* (both released in 2005) focused respectively on Afro-Haitian rhythms and songs, and a mix of Bantu-derived songs, Afro-Haitian songs, and rumba songs.

65. As discussed above, the scholarship seems to concur on this point as well.

66. Mayito estimated that the Casa del Caribe event began sometime in the early 1990s.

67. Puyas are traditionally associated with the more combative, male-dominated columbia style.

68. "Al final tú no sabes si eres chino, o si eres cubano, o si eres francés, o si estás en verano o si llovió . . . tú no sabes si estás en otoño. Tú no sabes en qué época del año tú estás, porque tú no respetas ni eso y te vistes de cualquier modo, para estar a la moda."

69. It also reminded me of the tensions between calypso and soca advocates in Trinidad, specifically the critiques of soca issued in songs such as Mighty Chalkdust's hit "Kaiso Sick in de Hospital."

Chapter 4

1. See the introduction for a brief discussion of how I distinguish between space and place.

2. Spain was dealt a huge blow with the successive and rapid independence of all its former American colonies except Puerto Rico and Cuba between 1822 and 1824. However, by this time, the economic value of the Cuban-based sugar trade was greater than that of all of the former colonies' wealth combined, which explains why Spain fought several wars to maintain possession of Cuba in the later nineteenth century and why Cuba's independence took thirty years to achieve.

3. As a result of policies enabling gradual emancipation, the total slave population in Cuba fell by 46 percent between 1862 and 1877, but this decline varied widely from province to province, and it was precisely these two high-producing sugar zones, Matanzas and Santa

Clara, that had the highest rates of persisting slavery until official emancipation in 1886 (Scott 2000, 86).

4. See Delgado 2001 for a detailed discussion of *Iyesá*, a subgroup of the Yoruba whose religious practice and music is related to that of Santería in many ways. See Vinueza 1989 for a detailed discussion of *Arará*, the culture and religious practice associated with the ancient kingdom of Dahomey in modern-day Benin. See Elí Rodríguez 1997 for information on *Bríkamo*, a rarely practiced tradition related to Abakuá, the male secret society derived from the Cross River region of Nigeria. Unlike Abakuá, where only men are allowed to be initiated or participate in ceremonies, women play an important role in Bríkamo ceremonies. I was fortunate to see a Bríkamo ceremony in Matanzas in January 2007, the only locale where it is currently (and rarely) practiced, and noted that women were the most active participants, especially in the dancing. See *Atlas de los instrumentos de la música folclórico-popular de Cuba* (Elí Rodríguez 1997) for information on *Olokún*, a religious practice honoring a mysterious orisha (Yoruba-derived deity) who is associated with the depths of the ocean, and also with the Middle Passage, as so many Africans died aboard slave ships bound for the Americas and were thrown into the ocean.

5. Afro-Cuban religions do not require that practitioners adhere to only one worship practice. As one member of Afrocuba de Matanzas explained, practitioners use the different religions for distinct purposes (Dreke Reyes, pers. comm. 2005). See Vélez 2000 for a biography of a Matanzas ritual drummer initiated into the three principal Afro-Cuban religions: Santería, Palo, and Abakuá.

6. The main distinctions between the three styles are to be found in their respective tempos—yambú is the slowest, guaguancó has a medium tempo, and columbia has the fastest tempo—and in the different dance steps of each style: the first two are couples dances, representing different relationships between the man and the woman, and the third is a solo male dance. There are also certain distinctions in vocal style between the three. I will be speaking mainly about rumba guaguancó, as it is the principal platform for the innovations I analyze in chapter 5. In the nineteenth century, there were several "mimetic" rumbas regularly danced that are collectively categorized under the term *rumba del tiempo de España*, or rumbas from the colonial era. They are no longer performed by contemporary rumba groups, although occasionally they are danced in folkloric representations by groups such as the Conjunto Folklórico Nacional. *Batarumba*, the rumba hybrid that I discuss in chapter 5, might be considered another, newer genre within the rumba complex.

7. One of the Cutumba songs features famed Havana rumba singer Carlos Embale.

8. This song can be found on *The Legendary Los Van Van: 30 Years of Cuba's Greatest Dance Band* (1999).

9. This song can be found on the album *Control* (2008).

10. This is not to suggest that danzón emerged in a vacuum in Matanzas. It is a derivative of the contradanza that displays more Cuban (i.e., Africanized) rhythmic elements, and these innovations were not the creation of only one person. However, "Las Alturas de Simpson"—which translates to "The Heights of Simpson" (Simpson is the name of a Matanzas neighborhood)—is the first piece universally recognized as a danzón.

11. As discussed in the previous chapter, there is a scholarly debate about whether the cinquillo rhythm was introduced to Cuba by Franco-Haitian immigrants fleeing the Haitian Revolution or by Africans brought directly to Cuba as slaves.

12. Miguel Bretos presents yet another nickname for the city, "the Tyre of the Western Seas" (2010, 87), another allusion to an ancient city. He suggests that this epithet predated the Athens nickname.

13. This discursive celebration of Afro-Cuban culture by the state has not always translated into practical support for black expressive or religious practices, nor has it precluded continuing policies of repression and policing of them.

14. I heard this song, which has not been commercially recorded, performed twice in February 2007.

15. As discussed in chapter 1, one of the ways that popular discourse paints Havana as the seat of modernity is by talking about the rest of the country, including large cities, as el campo (the countryside), which implicitly assumes backwardness.

16. Interestingly, Rebecca Scott notes that the free population of color in western Cuba was overwhelmingly urban (65 percent), while it was largely rural (over 50 percent) in the east (2000, 8).

17. This does not mean that Cubans do not recognize that there is a mix of racial identities in each province—whites, blacks, and mulatos—but rather that popular discourse tends to gloss over these specificities and paint different places on the island in more simplified racial terms.

18. I present a more detailed comparison of the different discourses of blackness attached to Matanzas and Oriente, respectively, in chapter 6.

19. Cubans of Spanish ancestry historically constituted a large proportion of the population in Pinar del Río (Helg 1995). However, while the proportion of whites in Pinar hovered around 78–80 percent throughout the twentieth century, it was not the "whitest" region statistically: in 1953, the central province of Las Villas was 82 percent white (Oficina Nacional de Los Censos Demográfico y Electoral 1953), and the 1981 census showed five provinces with a higher proportion of whites than Pinar del Río, including the eastern province of Holguín (Comité Estatal de Estadísticas 1984). Cuba's most recent published census figures (Oficina Nacional de Estadísticas 2013) suggest a continuation of this trend. In terms of the black population, Pinar del Río has the fourth-highest figure of the sixteen provinces; interestingly, it also has one of the lowest percentages of mixed-race people in the country (Oficina Nacional de Estadísticas 2013).

20. This song can be found on Clave y Guaguancó's album La Rumba Que No Termina (2006). The Spanish lyrics are taken from the album's liner notes, and the English translation is my own.

21. It is common to list these three African ethnic groups (in addition to Arará) when discussing the roots of Afro-Cuban culture, as they are thought to have constituted the majority of slaves brought to Cuba.

22. Andalusians made up a large proportion of the Spaniards who traveled to and settled in Cuba throughout the colonial period (Guanche 1996).

23. Although probably not the author's intention, I would note that the notions of "spontaneity" and "institutional" have racialized overtones, where the former corresponds

to essentialist notions about Afro-diasporic expressive practices and the latter implies a "whiter," more formalized version.

24. Writing about the CFN, Robin Moore quotes several Cuban scholars who have been critical of the group's artistic objectives of presenting relatively fixed representations of various traditions that do not allow for the spontaneity or improvisation that have always been a part of these practices (2006, 187–88).

25. Kenneth Schweitzer presents a lengthy musical comparison of batá drumming styles in Havana and Matanzas, but he does not link the different playing styles to discourses of place. Nonetheless, similar to ways that musicians have often described these styles to me, he characterizes the Matanzas example as the most "conservative" of the three he analyzed (2003, 227).

26. All information is drawn from an interview that took place on February 12, 2007, at Minini's home in Matanzas.

27. *Inventar* literally means "to invent." However, it is a polysemic word in the context of post-Soviet Cuba and is used often to refer to making ends meet. In reference to economic problems and the inadequacy of wages in state jobs, it is very common to hear someone say, "Tengo que inventar algo" (I have to find some way of making money), and this often alludes to an engagement with the black market. In the folkloric music scene, *inventar* can be used as a neutral or positive term, meaning "to make something up" or "to create something," or it can have a negative connotation, highlighting a lack of authenticity and/or knowledge about traditional music and dance practices. A common example of the latter is, "Los habaneros siempre están inventando" (People from Havana are always making stuff up).

28. All information is drawn from an interview that took place on March 8, 2007, at Wichichi's home in Matanzas.

29. Bembé is one type of ceremony and instrumental ensemble within the Lucumí pantheon in Cuba that is practiced more in Matanzas and the central Cuban provinces than in Havana.

30. "No porque yo sea matancero, que vivo orgulloso de serlo, y no por ser regionalista, ni tampoco por pecar ni de pretensión ni de superlativo, y mucho menos de autosuficiente, pero él que tenga la oportunidad de escuchar lo que se percute en La Habana y lo que se percute en Matanzas, aunque no sea muy buen entendedor en la materia, puede darse cuenta que lo que se percute o se toca aquí en Matanzas tiene más riqueza, es más, como te voy a explicar, más agradable de escuchar y de ver. . . . Porque en La Habana se percute y se toca muy rápido, corriendo, muy a prisa, y muchas cosas no se alcanzan a entender. Y bailando igual, bailan muy acorde con la intensidad con la que tocan y con la que cantan. Sin embargo, aquí en Matanzas se toca más asentado, se canta más asentado, se baila más asentado, se entiende mejor, y el ritmo es distinto."

31. "Si nos dedicaríamos a cosechar un folklore, una cosa que no es nuestra, nos identificaríamos como habaneros, no como matanceros, perderíamos nuestra identidad como tal."

32. All information is drawn from an interview that took place on March 2, 2007, at Dolores's home in Matanzas. Unfortunately, I did not take a picture of Dolores, as she was no longer performing with Afrocuba when I interviewed her. However, there are many YouTube videos of her performances, and a few images can be found here: http://www.afrocubaweb.com/photopages/doloresgallery.htm, accessed October 2014.

33. The Catholic saint San Lázaro is syncretized with the Yoruba orisha Babalu-Ayé and is one of the most fervently worshipped within both Santería and Cuban Catholicism because of his association with disease and epidemics—and thus his symbolization of suffering—and for his curative powers. See Hagedorn 2002 for a detailed ethnographic account of the significance of San Lázaro to religious practitioners, and the annual pilgrimage to the Sanctuary of San Lázaro in Rincón, a town on the outskirts of Havana.

34. See my dissertation (Bodenheimer 2010) for more information on this shift in Afrocuba's repertoire.

35. All information from Daniel is drawn from our many conversations between September 2006 and May 2007 and two formal interviews conducted on October 6 and October 26, 2006, in various locations in Havana.

36. As was discussed in chapter 1, there is a common perception that there are no more "pure-bred" habaneros (defined by the criteria of having both parents be Havana born) in the capital anymore and that they have all left the country, principally for Miami. Ironically, despite the antagonism toward people from el campo, many habaneros have at least one parent who migrated from another province.

37. All information is drawn from an interview that took place on December 23, 2006, near Gerardo's home in Arroyo Naranjo, one of the outlying municipalities of Havana.

38. All information is drawn from an interview that took place on October 24, 2006, at Amado's home in Havana.

39. *Día de los Reyes*, or Day of Kings, celebrations have been well documented by Fernando Ortiz and other scholars (Ortiz [1921] 1984; Bettelheim 2001). In colonial times, they took place on January 6, Epiphany Day in Catholicism, and formed the basis for what would become Cuba's carnival tradition. It was on this one day a year that slaves and free blacks were allowed to publicly perform their music and dance traditions, and the celebrations generally included competitions between the different African ethnic groups.

40. *Coros de clave* (literally, "clave choirs") were ambulatory groups of singers who paraded in the streets of Havana and Matanzas in the late nineteenth century, particularly during the Christmas holidays. Their repertoire and vocal style are thought to be an important predecessor of rumba guaguancó. For more information, see León 1984. Nancy Grasso González (1989) discusses their history in Matanzas, referring to them as "coros de rumba."

41. All information is drawn from an interview that took place on December 1, 2006, at Geovani's home in Havana.

42. All information is drawn from an interview that took place on April 18, 2007, at Ronald's home in Havana. A photo of Ronald appears in chapter 5.

43. I discuss this new singing style in chapter 5.

44. This type of privilege is most obviously evidenced in the racial politics of musical appropriation in the United States and Europe, where musicians often perform or borrow from non-Western traditions (i.e., not "their own" musics) without any critique directed at them, while non-Western musicians who do the same are accused of "selling out" or betraying their cultural heritage.

45. Hall states, "An articulation is thus the form of a connection that can make a unity of two different elements, under certain conditions. It is a linkage which is not necessary, determined, absolute and essential for all time" (Grossberg [1986] 1996, 141).

46. Nonetheless, as chapter 1 argued, people of mixed-race ancestry were/are actually a much larger percentage of the population in southeastern Oriente than in Havana.

47. Daniel's fieldwork was conducted in the 1980s, and I am not sure if this rule is still in effect at the CFN. However, I can say, based on the many performances of the group that I have attended, that its repertoire generally continues to emphasize "traditional" folkloric representations.

48. Vélez states that there are no records concerning the first set of batá drums in Matanzas (2000, 53).

49. Cárdenas is the second-biggest city in Matanzas Province. Both the city of Matanzas and Cárdenas were important port cities that received shipments of slaves directly from Africa during the nineteenth century. The Abakuá religion has always had a stronghold among stevedores working on the docks in Havana, Matanzas, and Cárdenas.

50. While slaves from Dahomey were not as predominant in Cuba as Bantu and Yoruba slaves, they made up the most important African ethnic group among slaves sent to Haiti. Thus, aside from Arará, there are other Dahomey-derived traditions practiced in eastern Cuba among descendants of Haitians.

51. *Cabildos de nación* were colonial-era mutual aid societies formed by African slaves and their descendants, which were formed principally along ethnic (national) lines.

52. I discuss batarumba's musical elements and history in more detail in chapter 5.

53. Sister of Afrocuba singer Dolores Pérez, Ana is a longtime singer and dancer with Los Muñequitos de Matanzas. Afrocuba has been filled with other members of the Pérez family, including Ana's daughter, another sister, an uncle, an aunt, a nephew, and one of her sons (Sandy Pérez, who moved to the United States in the late 1990s).

54. Historian Miguel Bretos, a native of Matanzas, similarly characterizes his hometown as racially diverse, "a place of meeting" for various nationalities, although he refers to a different historical period than Martínez Furé, the mid-nineteenth century (2010, 100).

55. The song made reference to a popular Cuban comic strip of the 1950s.

56. While remembered primarily for their work with Los Muñequitos, Virulilla and Saldiguera joined Afrocuba de Matanzas for a period of time later in their career. Nancy Grasso González, whose fieldwork was conducted in the 1980s, mentions both of them as members of Afrocuba at that time.

57. Juan García was instrumental in elucidating the details of Los Muñequitos' innovations in rumba style, which, beyond the singing format, also included Esteban "Chachá" Vega's revolutions in *quinto* (improvising drum) playing and the expansion of its role within the ensemble. See also Grasso González's thesis (1989) on professional rumba groups in Matanzas for details regarding Los Muñequitos' innovations.

58. The *claves* are two wooden sticks beat against each other to play the clave rhythm that constitutes the rhythmic timeline for all styles of rumba. The *catá* is a hollowed-out piece of sugarcane against which drumsticks are beat to play a complementary rhythm with

the clave. The *shékere*, which is also used to accompany singing in Santería ceremonies, is a hollowed-out gourd covered in beads. In rumba performance, the shékere usually punctuates beat one of a four-beat measure and doubles in density during the montuno section.

Chapter 5

1. Rumba is an inherently hybrid practice. Thus, when I use the term *hybridizing practices*, I do not mean to suggest that hybridity is something new in the performance of rumba, only that I will be discussing more recent innovations.

2. While my focus here is on recent innovations, and not on the larger rumba scene, in other publications (Bodenheimer 2010; 2013) I provide ample details about the broader socioeconomic dynamics of the contemporary rumba scenes in Havana and Matanzas.

3. Nonetheless, in comparison with the nationalist discourses in the other parts of the Spanish Caribbean—Puerto Rico and the Dominican Republic—Cubanidad is the most racially progressive of the three, and folklorists have been more active in recognizing and celebrating the African roots of and contributions to the nation.

4. Unless otherwise noted, all of the information pertaining to batarumba was gleaned through interviews with six current or former Afrocuba musicians—Francisco Zamora, Pedro Tápanes, Dolores Pérez, Reinaldo Alfonso, Miguel Angel Dreke, and Sandy Pérez—over a period of several years.

5. Minini's assertion that Afrocuba was the first to use batá drums within a secular musical context may not be accurate. First, jazz fusion group Irakere was also mixing batá drums with secular instruments and songs in the 1970s. Second, as early as the 1940s there were radio programs featuring live batá drumming, although these performances simply involved the performance of Santería songs and drumming in a nonreligious context and did not use the drums in a nontraditional manner like the later fusions did.

6. Yvonne Daniel's book on rumba dance (1995) is probably the first published mention of batarumba. Unlike the few other sources, she discusses it in some depth, albeit primarily as an innovation in rumba dance.

7. Unless otherwise indicated by a source credit, all the photos that appear in this chapter were taken by me.

8. See Delgado 2001 for details on the Iyesá religion and percussion tradition. Although the Yoruba/Lucumí are often discussed as an African ethnic group, it would be more accurate to categorize the term "Yoruba" as a "meta-label" (Delgado 2001), since several West African ethnic groups are subsumed under this categorization. One of Hagedorn's interviewees, Carlos Aldama (founder of the Conjunto Folklórico Nacional), asserts that chachalokofún actually emerged from a combination of Iyesá and bembé rhythms, both of which are Matanzas-based traditions (Hagedorn 2001, 125).

9. For examples of Dolores's batarumbas entitled "Caridad" and "Tambor," see Afrocuba's *Raíces Africanas* (1998) and the compilation album *¡La Rumba Está Buena!* (1994). Other Afrocuba vocalists sing batarumba, but Dolores's songs have generally been the most popular because of their dissemination on commercial recordings.

10. Bolero is a balladic genre centered around themes of romantic love.

11. The histories and musical elements of rumba and comparsa are very much intertwined, as exemplified by the fact that the conga drum was first associated with comparsa music and only later made its way into the rumba ensemble in the mid-1940s (Alén Rodríguez 2002).

12. In the wake of these imitations, some veteran members think they should have a patent on the term "batarumba," that is, that no other group should perform pieces with this name (pers. comm. with musicians, 2007).

13. Sandy is son of Ana Pérez (longtime singer/dancer for Los Muñequitos de Matanzas) and nephew of former Afrocuba singer Dolores Pérez.

14. I'm not sure exactly what Sandy meant by "Congo" other than that it is a rhythm related to Bantu music (*Congo* is the Cuban term used to refer to Bantu-derived culture). It is not a rhythm associated with either of the two most recognizable Bantu-derived genres, Palo and makuta (both of which Afrocuba regularly perform). Incidentally, Sandy noted that in Havana this same batá rhythm (Ochosi) is used to play for a different orisha, Ogún.

15. For all three songs, I reproduce the lyrics of the canto section in their entirety, but I do not present the soloist's calls/improvisations in the montuno section, just the main coro. All transcriptions and translations of the lyrics are my own.

16. The meaning of this popular proverb can be interpreted in many ways. Although I have never asked members of Afrocuba what it means to them, my observations concerning the way this proverb is used in rumba song and popular discourse lead me to believe that it asserts that everyone in Cuba has some kind of African ancestry. The fact that Bantu and Calabar slaves were brought to Cuba in larger numbers than other African ethnic groups— particularly in the crucial period of the late eighteenth century through the late nineteenth century (Klein 1978; Bergad et al. 1995)—also seems pertinent to the proverb. Furthermore, Bantu- and Calabar-derived music and dance practices are the primary African influences on rumba.

17. The decision to mix Abakuá and Lucumí rhythms is a fairly controversial choice, as is evident in my discussion in this chapter of the Oyá-Abakuá fusion performed by Clave y Guaguancó.

18. While attempting to find a transcription of the lyrics of this song on the Internet, I came across no search results related to Afrocuba but instead discovered that Cuban exile Gloria Estefan released a song called "Morenita" that reproduces the lyrics and melody of the introduction and first verse of "Caridad." This song can be found on her album *90 Millas* (2007). This is not the first time Estefan has borrowed from traditional Afro-Cuban music: the song "Tradición" from her first Spanish-language album, *Mi Tierra* (1993), begins with a rumba that eventually turns into a comparsa.

19. One of these Iyesá rhythms, heard at 1:00 when the montuno section begins, is also played in Havana; Sandy referred to the other style, heard at 2:13, as the "traditional Matanzas-style Iyesá" (García Pérez, pers. comm. 2014).

20. As noted earlier in the chapter, these latter two traditions enjoy a much closer connection to one another (they are both considered to be meta-Yoruba traditions) than Lucumí and Abakuá do.

21. Two of these genres—rumba and comparsa—were considered popular during the late nineteenth and early twentieth centuries, in the sense that they constituted the main "party music" for poor and working-class Afro-Cubans at the time (rumba for house and spontaneous street parties, and comparsa for carnival celebrations). However, since the 1960s, rumba and to a lesser extent comparsa have undergone a process of folklorization, in that the government and certain folkloric groups have sought to preserve traditional Afro-Cuban percussion practices and have included rumba in this purview (Daniel 1995).

22. Guaguancós tend to draw more from the Yoruba-derived repertoire, while columbias (which are often described as the most Africanized rumba style) draw more from Palo and Abakuá repertoires. Yambús generally include only Spanish lyrics.

23. See chapter 3 for a discussion of Espiritismo and the cajón de muerto ceremony.

24. Cuban music scholars have generally taken a softer stance toward Cruz's ideological leanings, as evidenced by the fact that she was included in Radamés Giro's comprehensive four-volume encyclopedic dictionary of Cuban music (2009).

25. The band was founded in 1924 in Matanzas as La Tuna Liberal (changed in 1932 to La Sonora Matancera), and came to be one of the most popular bands on the island during the "golden era" of Cuban popular music, the 1940s and 1950s. Cruz joined the band in 1950. The band, including Cruz, went to Mexico for a tour in 1960 and never returned to Cuba. In 1961 they moved to the United States, and Cruz stayed on as their principal singer until 1965 (Díaz Ayala 2002). Although the group is still performing in the United States, many feel that its essence died with the 2001 passing of Rogelio Martínez, who had been the director of the group since 1932.

26. According to the invaluable discographic resources collected by Cuban scholar Cristóbal Díaz Ayala (2002), "Mata Siguaraya" was originally released by Seeco as a single in 1950; in fact, it was Cruz's first major hit with Sonora Matancera. "Chango ta' Veni" was also originally recorded as a single by the group in 1958. "Lalle Lalle" was originally released on the LP *La Dinámica Celia Cruz, Acompañada de la Sonora Matancera* (Seeco, 1960); "Óyeme Agayú" first appeared on the LP *Homenaje a Los Santos* (Seeco, 1964); and "Rinkinkalla" was originally released on the LP *Sabor y Ritmo de Pueblos: Celia Cruz con la Sonora Matancera* (Seeco, 1965). Except for the song "Mata Siguaraya," composed by Sonora Matancera pianist Lino Frías, none of these songs were composed by Celia Cruz or Sonora Matancera.

27. Musicians and composers from the city or province of Matanzas have had a vital impact on the emergence and/or evolution of the three most important popular music genres of the late nineteenth through the mid-twentieth centuries. As noted in chapter 4, the first danzón was composed by an Afro-Cuban native of Matanzas, Miguel Faílde. Arsenio Rodríguez, the blind, black tres player/composer who revolutionized son both through the introduction of conga drums to the ensemble and the incorporation of African-derived religious themes and texts, was born in the Matanzas countryside. Finally, there is Damaso Pérez Prado, who became famous and received credit for the invention of mambo in the 1950s. Despite his incredibly significant contribution to mambo's musical style, he is now recognized not as its creator but as its principal disseminator in Mexico and the United States.

28. A performance of this piece can be found on the DVD *Afrocuba de Matanzas: 50 Years On* (Weaver 2007).

29. This is an innovation that can *only* be performed in a folkloric context. To do this in a ritual context would violate religious precepts.

30. Some might argue that the inability to pin down a meaning for guarapachangueo is evidenced in most musical practices in their emergent years, before they become standardized. Standardization may well happen eventually with guarapachangueo, but currently it lacks a stable definition.

31. The standard rumba ensemble includes three congas: the low-range *mayor* (or *tumbador*), the mid-range *tres-dos* (or *segundo*), and the high-pitched, improvising *quinto*.

32. Van Nispen adds that at the time of the cajón's emergence, it was often used in many different Afro-Cuban religious ceremonies to substitute for the particular percussion instruments associated with each practice that were not available and/or prohibited due to the criminalization of practitioners (2003, 29).

33. Cuban musicologist Argeliers León noted that in West and Central African percussion traditions, the low-range drum, rather than the high-pitched drum, usually functions as the lead and improvising drum of the ensemble. This African approach is still evidenced in Afro-Cuban sacred practices such as the batá and Palo musical traditions, where the largest, lowest-pitched drum is the main improviser of the ensemble. León suggested that the transition from the African philosophy of low-register improvisation to the tendency in Afro-Cuban secular music to improvise on the high-pitched drum relates to the influence of Western music, where instruments/voices in higher registers tend to perform with more ornamentation (1984, 141–42).

34. Unless otherwise indicated, all information about Los Chinitos and their creation of guarapachangueo is drawn from an interview with Irián on May 8, 2007, at his home in San Miguel del Padrón.

35. Beginning in the 1990s, religious practice was decriminalized as the revolution declared itself a "secular" rather than an "atheist" state. Since that time there has been a much greater official tolerance for religious practice.

36. Although Daniel drew connections between different Afro-Cuban religions and particular Havana municipalities and neighborhoods, this is not to say that these practices are not widespread in more centralized parts of Havana such as Habana Vieja, Centro Habana, and the Vedado neighborhood. Havana has a high proportion of Santería and Abakuá practitioners in general.

37. *Mambises* is the term for the Cuban rebels who rose up against the Spanish colonial regime in the late-nineteenth-century wars of independence.

38. This is just one of countless examples of the famed Cuban resourcefulness, born of necessity and many people's inability to afford a replacement when a household appliance (or car part) breaks. Common examples include fashioning homemade fans using motors taken from washing machines or other appliances, and using appliance motors to keep 1950s-era American cars running.

39. I am grateful to ethnomusicologist Eliot Bates, who digitized my transcriptions for this chapter.

40. Most of the rumba musicians I know use the term *guarapachangueo*, as does Van Nispen (2003) in his thesis. *Atlas de los instrumentos de la música folclórico-popular de Cuba*

(Elí Rodríguez 1997), a comprehensive encyclopedia of Cuban instruments, uses the variant *guarapachanguero* but mentions the style only once in a passing reference.

41. The cajón maleta can be substituted for the low-range conga drum, and the conical tres-dos cajón can take the place of the mid-range conga drum. I did not ask Irián when the quinto cajón emerged, but it is now common in rumba performance to see a quinto conga drum be replaced with or played in addition to a quinto cajón (which also has a conical shape but is smaller and shorter than the tres-dos cajón; see figure 5.2).

42. It was not clear to me during my interview with Irián whether the first conical cajón was created or developed first by his brother Pedro, who adapted the cajón maleta for their guarapachangueo style, or by Yoruba Andabo percussionist Pancho Quinto. Paul Van Nispen asserts that the tres-dos cajón was introduced by Pancho Quinto in 1970 and that before this time there only existed two cajones—the maleta and the quinto cajón (2003, 41). Whether or not this is the case, guarapachangueo had not yet been created, so Pancho Quinto would not have originally adapted this instrument for use with Los Chinitos' style.

43. Some works (Elí Rodríguez 1997; Wielecki 2001; Schweitzer 2003) do not mention Los Chinitos in their narrative about guarapachangueo, leading the reader to assume that it was Pancho Quinto who invented the style.

44. Kenneth Schweitzer's dissertation focuses on Quinto's role as a teacher of ritual batá drumming rather than his membership in and innovations with Yoruba Andabo. Schweitzer's more recent book (2013) includes more information about Quinto's career as a rumbero and recognizes Los Chinitos' role as the creators of guarapachangueo.

45. See my dissertation (Bodenheimer 2010) for more details on the history of the group.

46. Interestingly, Schweitzer conceives of both batarumba and guarapachangueo as batá-based fusions (not rumba-based fusions like I do), no doubt because his work is more focused on batá drumming. He states, "Unlike the Afrocuba de Matanzas creation, which requires three batá players in addition to the normal complement of rumba drummers, Pancho plays all the drums by himself" (2003, 158). However, as should be evident by now, batá drums are not always used when playing guarapachangueo. Schweitzer's dissertation and book (2003; 2013) reproduce a wonderful and unique image of Quinto with his entire guarapachangueo ensemble (i.e., the cajón, batá drums, and cowbell), a photo that I also used in my dissertation. The original image, however, was not a photo but a screenshot from a video taken by Steve Bloom, and its resolution was simply too low for me to reproduce in this book. The image I use here does not show all the elements in Quinto's guarapachangueo configuration, but it was the best high-resolution photo I could find.

47. Although Quinto died in 2005, he left Yoruba Andabo around 1994–1995 (Del Pino Rodríguez, pers. comm. 2007).

48. Here, the cowbell is clearly visible in front of the percussionist's left foot.

49. For examples of these routines, see "Capricho de Abuela" and "Ña Francisca" on Clave y Guaguancó's album *Déjala en la Puntica* (1996).

50. Many reggaetón scholars view Panamanian rapper El General as the first recognized proponent of the style. However, as it has grown in popularity, reggaetón has become increasingly associated with Puerto Rico, and Puerto Rican reggaetón singers currently enjoy the most popularity and economic success.

51. A few of the best-known Cuban reggaetón artists and groups are Gente de Zona, Eddy K, Cubanito 20.02, and Elvis Manuel.

52. The word "tuba" (like the band instrument) has a double meaning in this song, alluding to the penis. In April 2008, Elvis Manuel, his mother, and fifteen other Cubans left the island on a raft bound for Miami. The US Coast Guard rescued Manuel's mother and thirteen others two weeks later, but Manuel and several others were never found and were eventually presumed dead.

53. The group's identity as preservers of tradition does not always go uncontested. Notably, it was a younger singer who inserted the reggaetón lyrics into this performance, someone who has expressed the desire to inject new styles and trends into Afrocuba's repertoire.

54. I have not examined in depth the issue of generational difference in speaking about the respective views of Havana and Matanzas musicians, a factor that in many cases (not that of Geovani) can be more influential than one's regional/local affiliation.

55. The Trio Matamoros was a popular son group of the 1930s.

56. "Como género vivo también tiene derecho a evolucionar . . . y no deja de ser rumba. Hay quién está abrazado a que, si no se toca como aquel tiempo, no es rumba. Yo no estoy de acuerdo con ese criterio. Porque entonces diríamos que lo que toca Adalberto Álvarez hoy no es son. Nadie se atreve a decirle a Adalberto Álvarez que lo que toca hoy no es son, porque no toca igual que, que el Matamoros. . . . No hay quién se atreva a decirle a Arsenio Rodríguez que lo que él hizo después con el son, que le incluyó piano, que le incluyó tumbadoras, que le incluyó trompetas . . . que lo que él tocaba no era son. . . . Hubo quién lo pensó . . . pero se impuso. Y se impondrá lo nuevo, aunque muchos viejos no lo quieran . . . ¿tú sabes porqué? Porque no tienen las posibilidades de ejecutar de la manera que lo hace un joven. Y como que no tienen las posibilidades de hacerlo, no quisieran que eso sucediera. Pero los jóvenes se imponen, y se impondrán siempre. . . . La rumba no ha muerto por eso, porque evolucionó, evolucionó con la época."

57. The *tonada trinitaria* is a lesser-known Afro-Cuban folkloric genre that emerged in the mid- to late nineteenth century in the central Cuban city of Trinidad, now a major tourist destination. Like rumba, it involves only percussion and song and has been likened to the coros de clave that are thought to be a predecessor of rumba guaguancó (see León 1984); unlike rumba, however, it has remained a regional tradition that is not even widely practiced anymore in Trinidad. For more on the tonada trinitaria, see Frías 2010. Interestingly, one of Afrocuba's most popular yambú songs, "Pa' los mayores," recorded on the group's *Raíces Africanas* (1998), may have its origins in the tonada trinitaria repertoire (Cox 2008).

58. I have never heard of *catumba* as a style of rumba or a distinct Afro-Cuban drumming tradition. I have not been able to find any references to this term in the context of Cuban music.

59. *Lambada* was a Brazilian dance craze of the late 1980s. *Batucada* is a Brazilian drumming tradition and style of samba that includes strong African influence; its sound is similar to Cuban comparsa, and thus the rhythms complement each other well.

60. This song, entitled "De Oyá a Abakuá," also appears on one of Clave y Guaguancó's albums, *Noche de la Rumba* (1999).

61. To contextualize this discussion, I should mention that this percussionist has been initiated into Santería and perhaps other Afro-Cuban sacred religions, as are the director of Clave y Guaguancó and all the musicians I spoke with regarding this fusion.

62. Unfortunately, I wasn't aware of the Abakuá drumming in the Afrocuba song at that time and thus didn't think to question the musician further about it.

63. Perhaps one's opinion is also dependent upon the degree of fusion. For example, in the Afrocuba batarumba song, while Abakuá drumming is mixed with other styles for brief moments during the song and there is never an explicitly stated intention to mix this tradition with batá drumming, the title and lyrics of the Clave y Guaguancó song purposefully link these two practices. Furthermore, the latter song includes singing and chanting in both the Lucumí and Abakuá languages—alternating sections in the montuno feature one or the other.

Chapter 6

1. On the island, this renewed global interest in son has precipitated the proliferation of neotraditional groups—particularly in Old Havana but also in Santiago and other tourist destinations—that cater to tourists' desires to see "real" son played in Cuba.

2. See Perna 2005 for a detailed analysis of the *Buena Vista Social Club* phenomenon, the ways it is usually juxtaposed to timba, and a discussion of tensions between musicians associated with each movement.

3. See my dissertation (Bodenheimer 2010) for more details on each of these events.

4. As I argue elsewhere (Bodenheimer 2013), outside of the discursive realm, rumba is still a heavily racialized practice that is denigrated by upper-class Cubans.

5. The Permanent Army, Cuba's first national military force, was established in 1908 during a second US occupation of the island (the first was right after independence, from 1898 to 1902), and was designed to replace US troops. Troops from western Cuba were often stationed in the east and vice versa following the racially motivated massacre of members of the Partido Independiente de Color.

6. Acosta also critiques the ethnocentrism of Cuban musicology (including his own previous work), which has traditionally linked son to similar Caribbean genres through León's notion of a "zone/area of son," thus privileging the Cuban manifestation of what is more accurately a pan-Caribbean way of combining string and percussion music.

7. Acosta also notes that the danzón complex includes both antecedents (like contradanza) and descendants/derivations (like mambo), so the choice of the term "danzón" to represent this group of musical styles is arbitrary, as it is neither the first nor the last genre to emerge. What he does not mention is that danzón not only emerged at a historically significant time (during the struggle for independence), but also constituted a much more Cubanized (read: Africanized) derivation of the European contredanse tradition. This suggests that genres become prominent not only for their musical originality or innovations but because of how they are linked to national history.

8. Various Cuba scholars have discussed this mislabeling as intentional, and not accidental. For example, Robin Moore (1995) suggests that the principal actors in the rumba

craze—such as white Cuban bandleader Don Azpiazu and Spanish bandleader Xavier Cugat—were quite aware that their representation of "rumba" had nothing to do with the original Afro-Cuban genre. Ned Sublette (2004) suggests that "rumba" was simply a sexier marketing term than "son," a word that could be potentially confusing to the American public because its spelling is identical to the English word "son."

9. For details on the emergence and history of Congolese popular music, see Bob White's *Rumba Rules* (2008) and Gary Stewart's *Rumba on the River* (2000).

10. Explaining the anticipated bass of son, Manuel states that it "is remarkable not only for its silent (or tied) downbeat, but also for the manner in which the final note of the bar anticipates the harmony of the following bar" (1985b, 250).

11. Perna views NG La Banda's sound as the hallmark of timba style, discussing—in addition to the rumba influences—the virtuosity of instrumentalists, particularly the horn section, and the lyrical content of their songs, which often related to the everyday experiences of black Cubans.

12. See my article on rumba and racial politics for more details (Bodenheimer 2013).

13. In *Contrapunteo cubano* ([1940] 1999), Ortiz famously likened tobacco to the rebellious spirit of the indigenous natives and enslaved Africans in Cuba, while sugar represented Spanish oppression, slavery, and capitalism.

14. Furthermore, many of timba's most important innovators, such as José Luís "El Tosco" Cortés and Adalberto Álvarez, were trained in national music conservatories where the core curriculum is heavily oriented toward Western art music idioms.

15. Lisa Knauer (2005) introduced this term, and I also discuss the phenomenon in chapter 2 of my dissertation.

16. As noted in chapter 5, rumba has historically appropriated songs from popular genres such as guaracha, son, and bolero.

17. To be clear, both are hybrid practices, although son clearly displays more European and North American influence, especially in its instrumentation.

18. Although the version of Lapique's essay that I consulted and am citing is taken from a 1998 edition of *Panorama de la música cubana*, this anthology (edited by Radamés Giro) was originally published in 1995.

19. Despite the fact that claves were introduced in the 1920s in Havana and that conga drums were later added in the 1940s, I would argue that the bongó is the percussion instrument most closely associated with son, if only because it is unique to this genre and related styles like changüí. Claves and congas, on the other hand, are also essential instruments in the rumba ensemble.

20. Benjamin Lapidus (2008) and the *Atlas de los instrumentos de la música folclórico-popular de Cuba* (Elí Rodríguez 1997) are only two of the many sources that confirm the bongó's eastern origins. Lapidus notes that an earlier version of the instrument, the *bongó de monte* ("mountain bongó"), is used in traditional changüí (2008, 21–22).

21. The province of Pinar del Río is, in fact, the primary site of Cuba's ecotourism industry, and the discourse of "pristine," natural beauty that is used to draw tourists to places like Viñales and Soroa is clearly entangled with romanticized notions about rural life.

22. Although the Abakuá tradition in particular never spread beyond western Cuba, Carabalís, Africans from the same ethnic group and region, were brought to Oriente during

slavery, establishing societies in the nineteenth century such as the still-extant Carabalí Isuama in Santiago.

23. Among the several differences he discusses in depth, the most obvious is the absence of clave, or any kind of timeline, in changüí.

24. There has been recent debate among Cuban cultural officials and in the national media about how to combat the "reggaetón menace."

25. One of the ways that reggaetón is commonly derided is by comparing it unfavorably with timba, a musically sophisticated and complex practice that requires performers to have formal training.

26. A short article on the drink states, "Usually prepared as a homemade brew, it begins with the fermentation of several plant roots, along with chinaberry, Chinese root, pepper leaves, brown sugar, cinnamon, pine sprouts and water" (Milanes Despaigne 2011). The author also asserts that the drink was originally introduced to Oriente by Franco-Haitian migrants fleeing the Haitian Revolution.

27. Baker's use of the word "immigrants" to refer to eastern Cubans is clearly erroneous, although quite telling: as discussed in chapter 1, they are often discussed by habaneros not as fellow Cuban citizens but as immigrants, invading a completely separate national territory.

28. While it is another example of the tendency of foreign (and national) researchers to focus on the capital's musical scene to the exclusion of other parts of the island, I appreciate Baker's specificity when speaking about "Havana reggaetón" (not "Cuban reggaetón"), and thus his recognition that the capital's musical identity does not stand in for that of the nation as a whole.

29. While the nationalist hybridity discourses acknowledge the different racial components that make up the nation—namely, Spanish and African ancestry—these distinct elements are considered to belong to Cuba's past, and to have now been discarded and replaced by one hybrid populace. This notion is key to Fernando Ortiz's conceptualization of "transculturation."

30. The female orisha Ochún is syncretized with the Virgin of Charity, Cuba's patron saint.

31. There continues to be debate about where the most popular style of rumba, guaguancó, emerged (Havana or Matanzas), but no one contradicts its identity as a western Cuban tradition.

32. Some of the most outspoken Cuban scholars on this issue are Tomás Fernández Robaina, Roberto Zurbano, Esteban Morales Domínguez, and Pedro Pérez Sarduy.

33. Rumba is of course also a hybrid genre, but it is not always recognized as such.

34. This song can be found on the 2010 album *El Son de Altura*.

35. Because the title references son while the sounds clearly reference salsa, the song also constitutes a conflation of these two genres and an implicit assertion that Cuban son is the heart and soul of salsa, a controversial issue within salsa historiography that has created a rift between some Cuba- and Puerto Rico–based scholars.

Conclusion

1. They are also still evident in some academic publications, even when the authors claim a knowledge of critical race theory and assert the fact that "race" is a constructed category.

2. This is not to suggest that there is one Latin American racial formation that can be applied to the whole region, for every country has its specificities, but only to emphasize that there are shared histories of colonization and racial and cultural characteristics that bind it together in many ways, and that distinguish it from the United States.

3. For example, see works by anthropologists Kristina Wirtz (2007) and Grete Viddal (2010, 2012).

4. The similarity of early Congolese rumba to son is evident when listening to "classic" groups from the 1950s like OK Jazz and African Jazz (who released a song called "Independence Cha Cha Cha" in 1960 to celebrate the independence of the Democratic Republic of Congo from Belgium).

References

Books, Articles, Theses, and Internet Sources

Acosta, Leonardo. (1983) 1991. "The Rumba, Guaguancó, and Tio Tom." Translated by Peter Manuel. In *Essays on Cuban Music: North American and Cuban Perspectives*, edited by Peter Manuel, 49–73. Lanham, MD: University Press of America.

———. 2004. *Otra visión de la música popular cubana*. Havana: Editorial Letras Cubanas.

Adalberto Álvarez: El Caballero del Son. At http://www.adalbertoalvarez.cult.cu/main.htm. Accessed January 2008. Site discontinued.

Alén, Olavo. 1986. *La música de las sociedades de tumba francesa en Cuba*. Havana: Casa de las Américas.

Alén Rodríguez, Olavo. 1995. "Rhythm as Duration of Sounds in Tumba Francesa." *Ethnomusicology* 39 (1): 55–71.

———. 1998. "Cuba." In *The Garland Encyclopedia of World Music*. Vol. 2, *South America, Mexico, Central America, and the Caribbean*, edited by Dale Olsen and Daniel Sheehy, 822–39. New York: Garland Publishing.

———. 2002. "A History of the Congas." Afrocubaweb. At http://www.afrocubaweb.com/cid muc.htm#History. Accessed March 2004.

Alonso Yodú, Odette. 1986. "Una polémica innecesaria." In *Criterios al pie de la obra*, 14–19. Havana: Universidad de La Habana.

Álvarez Estévez, Rolando, and Marta Guzmán Pascual. 2008. *Cuba en el Caribe y el Caribe en Cuba*. Havana: La Fundación Fernando Ortiz.

Álvarez Vergara, Rosa Esther. 1989. "Caracterización de las agrupaciones de rumba de ciudad de La Habana." Bachelor's thesis, Instituto Superior del Arte.

Averill, Gage. 1989. "Haitian Dance Bands, 1915–1970: Class, Race, and Authenticity." *Latin American Music Review* 10 (2): 203–35.

———. 1997. *A Day for the Hunter, a Day for the Prey: Popular Music and Power in Haiti*. Chicago: University of Chicago Press.

———. 1999. "Caribbean Musics: Haiti and Trinidad and Tobago." In *Music in Latin American Culture: Regional Traditions*, edited by John Schecter, 126–91. New York: Schirmer Books.

Baker, Geoffrey. 2011. *Buena Vista in the Club: Rap, Reggaetón, and Revolution in Havana*. Durham, NC: Duke University Press.

Barcia Zequeira, María del Carmen. 2004. "El tema negro en la historiografía cubana del siglo XX." *Del Caribe* 44: 102–10.

Bardach, Ann Louise. 2002. *Cuba Confidential: Love and Vengeance in Miami and Havana.* New York: Random House.

Barreiro, José. 1989. "Indians in Cuba." *Cultural Survival Quarterly* 13 (3): 56–60. At http://www.hartford-hwp.com/archives/41/014.html#N2. Accessed August 2011.

Bennett, Andy. 2000. *Popular Music and Youth Culture: Music, Identity, and Place.* New York: St. Martin's Press.

Berenguer Cala, Jorge. 2006. *El Gagá de Barrancas: una comunidad de descendientes haitianos en el oriente de Cuba.* Santiago de Cuba: Ediciones Santiago.

Bergad, Laird W., Fe Iglesias García, and María del Carmen Barcia. 1995. *The Cuban Slave Market, 1790–1880.* Cambridge: Cambridge University Press.

Bernabé, Jean, Patrick Chamoiseau, and Raphaël Confiant. 1990. "In Praise of Creoleness." *Callaloo* 13 (4): 886–909.

Betancur Álvarez, Fabio. 1993. *Sin clave y bongo no hay son: musica afrocubana y confluencias musicales de Colombia y Cuba.* Medellín: Universidad de Antioquia.

Bettelheim, Judith, ed. 2001. *Cuban Festivals: A Century of Afro-Cuban Culture.* Kingston: Markus Wiener Publishers.

Blue, Sarah A. 2007. "The Erosion of Racial Equality in the Context of Cuba's Dual Economy." *Latin American Politics and Society* 49 (3): 35–68.

Bodenheimer, Rebecca. 2009. "'La Habana No Aguanta Más': Regionalism in Contemporary Cuban Society and Popular Music." *Musical Quarterly* 92 (3–4): 201–41.

———. 2010. "Localizing Hybridity: The Politics of Place in Contemporary Cuban Rumba Performance." PhD diss., University of California, Berkeley.

———. 2013. "National Symbol or 'a Black Thing'? Rumba and Racial Politics in Cuba in the Era of Cultural Tourism." *Black Music Research Journal* 33 (2): 177–205.

Bretos, Miguel A. 2010. *Matanzas: The Cuba Nobody Knows.* Gainesville: University Press of Florida.

Brown, Jacqueline Nassy. 2005. *Dropping Anchor, Setting Sail: Geographies of Race in Black Liverpool.* Princeton, NJ: Princeton University Press.

Cabrera, Lydia. 1973. *La laguna sagrada de San Joaquín.* Madrid: Ediciones Madrid.

Carpentier, Alejo. 2001. *Music in Cuba.* Translated by Alan West-Duran. Minneapolis: University of Minnesota Press.

Casey, Matthew. 2001. "Haitians' Labor and Leisure on Cuban Sugar Plantations: The Limits of Company Control." *New West Indian Guide* 85 (1–2): 5–30.

Castro, Fidel. 1976. *Angola, África Girón.* Havana: Editorial de Ciencias Sociales.

Castro Monterrey, Pedro Manuel. 2010. "La situación del negro en Santiago de Cuba durante el primer decenio del siglo XX." *Del Caribe* 54: 29–31.

Centro de Investigación y Desarrollo de la Cultura Cubana Juan Marinello. 1999. *Atlas etnográfico de Cuba.* Havana: Centro de Investigación y Desarrollo de la Cultura Cubana Juan Marinello. CD-ROM.

Chen, Kuan-Hsing. 1996. "The Formation of a Diasporic Intellectual: An Interview with Stuart Hall." In *Stuart Hall: Critical Dialogues in Cultural Studies,* edited by David Morley and Kuan-Hsing Chen, 484–503. London: Routledge.

Chomsky, Aviva. 2000. "'Barbados or Canada?': Race, Immigration, and Nation in Early-Twentieth-Century Cuba." *Hispanic American Historical Review* 80 (3): 415–62.

Clifford, James. 1992. "Traveling Cultures." In *Cultural Studies*, edited by Lawrence Grossberg, Cary Nelson, and Paula Treichler, 96–116. London: Routledge.

Cohen, Sara. 1994. "Identity, Place, and the 'Liverpool Sound.'" In *Ethnicity, Identity, and Music: The Musical Construction of Place*, edited by Martin Stokes, 117–34. Oxford: Berg Publishers.

Comité Estatal de Estadísticas, República de Cuba. 1979. *Atlas demográfico de Cuba*. Havana: Instituto Cubano de Geodesia y Cartografía.

———. 1984. *Censo de la población y viviendas, 1981*. Havana: Oficina Nacional del Censo.

Connell, John, and Chris Gibson. 2003. *Sound Tracks: Popular Music, Identity, and Place*. London: Routledge.

Corbea Calzado, Julio. 1996. "La Virgen de la Caridad del Cobre: construcción simbólica y cultura popular." *Del Caribe* 25: 4–11.

———. 2004. "Historia de una familia haitiano-cubana." *Del Caribe* 44: 62–70.

Cox, Barry. 2008. "Tonadas Trinitarias." Esquina Rumbera. At http://esquinarumbera. blogspot.com/2008/08/tonadas-trinitarias.html. Accessed April 2009.

Crook, Larry. 1992. "The Form and Formation of the Rumba in Cuba." In *Salsiology: Afro-Cuban Music and the Evolution of Salsa in New York City*, edited by Vernon W. Boggs, 31–42. Westport, CT: Greenwood Press.

D-maps.com. "Cuba, República de Cuba: Boundaries, Provinces, Names, Color." At http:// d-maps.com/carte.php?&num_car=38497&lang=en. Accessed November 2013.

Daniel, Yvonne. 1995. *Rumba: Dance and Social Change in Contemporary Cuba*. Bloomington: Indiana University Press.

De la Fuente, Alejandro. 2001. *A Nation for All: Race, Inequality, and Politics in Twentieth-Century Cuba*. Chapel Hill: University of North Carolina Press.

———. 2008. "The New Afro-Cuban Cultural Movement and the Debate on Race in Contemporary Cuba." *Journal of Latin American Studies* 40 (4): 697–720.

Del Real, Patricio, and Joseph Scarpaci. 2011. "Barbacoas: Havana's New Inward Frontier." In *Havana beyond the Ruins: Cultural Mappings after 1989*, edited by Anke Birkenmaier and Esther Whitfield, 53–72. Durham, NC: Duke University Press.

Delgado, Kevin Miguel. 2001. "Iyesá: Afro-Cuban Music and Culture in Contemporary Cuba." PhD diss., University of California, Los Angeles.

Diago Urfé, Virgilio. 1997. "Virulilla, El de Los Munequitos." *Tropicana Internacional* 5: 26–29.

Díaz Ayala, Cristóbal. 2002. *Cuba canta y baila: Encyclopedic Discography of Cuban Music*. Miami: Florida International University. At http://latinpop.fiu.edu/discography.html. Accessed April 2009.

———. 2003. *Música cubana: del areyto al rap cubano*. San Juan: Fundación Musicalia.

Dodson, Jualynne E. 2008. *Sacred Spaces and Religious Traditions in Oriente Cuba*. Albuquerque: University of New Mexico Press.

Domínguez, Jorge I., Omar Everleny Pérez Villanueva, and Lorena Barberia, eds. 2004. *The Cuban Economy at the Start of the Twenty-First Century*. Cambridge: David Rockefeller Center for Latin American Studies, Harvard University Press.

Elí Rodríguez, Victoria. 1989. "Apuntes sobre la creación musical actual en Cuba." *Latin American Music Review* 10 (2): 287–97.

———, ed. 1997. *Atlas de los instrumentos de la música folclórico-popular de Cuba*. Havana: Centro de Investigación y Desarrollo de la Música Cubana.

Esquenazi Pérez, Martha. 2001. *Del areíto y otros sones*. Havana: Editorial Letras Cubanas.

Faro, Rachel, and Rebecca Mauleón. 1999. *The Legendary Los Van Van: 30 Years of Cuba's Greatest Dance Band*. Ashé, liner notes.

Fernandes, Sujatha. 2006. *Cuba Represent! Cuban Arts, State Power, and the Making of New Revolutionary Cultures*. Durham, NC: Duke University Press.

Fernández Retamar, Roberto. (1971) 1989. *Caliban and Other Essays*. Translated by Edward Baker. Minneapolis: University of Minnesota Press.

Fernández Robaina, Tomás. 2005. "The Term *Afro-Cuban*: A Forgotten Contribution." In *Cuban Counterpoints: The Legacy of Fernando Ortiz*, edited by Mauricio Font and Alfonso Quiroz, 171–80. Lanham, MD: Lexington Books.

Ferrer, Ada. 1999. *Insurgent Cuba: Race, Nation, and Revolution, 1868–1898*. Chapel Hill: University of North Carolina Press.

Forman, Murray. 2002. *The 'Hood Comes First: Race, Space, and Place in Rap and Hip-Hop*. Middletown, CT: Wesleyan University Press.

Foucault, Michel. 1977. "Nietzsche, Genealogy, History." In *Language, Counter-memory, Practice: Selected Essays and Interviews*, edited and translated by Donald Bouchard, 139–64. Ithaca, NY: Cornell University Press.

Frías, Johnny. 2010. "History and Evolution of the Tonadas Trinitarias of Trinidad de Cuba." Master's thesis, University of Florida.

Gaínza Moreno, Eglis. 2013. "Cándido Fabré: 'Soy un hombre que anda al ritmo de la vida con mis temas.'" *Cubadebate*, August 13, 2013. At http://www.cubadebate.cu/opinion/2013/08/12/candido-fabre-soy-un-hombre-que-anda-al-ritmo-de-la-vida-con-mis-temas/#.VNmi3LCMmLo. Accessed October 2014.

Gannett, Henry. 1900. "The Results of the Cuban Census." *Journal of the American Geographical Society of New York* 32 (3): 281–86.

Giro, Radamés. (1994) 1998. "Los motivos del son: hitos en su sendero caribeño y universal." In *Panorama de la música popular cubana*, edited by Radamés Giro, 198–209. Havana: Editorial Letras Cubanas.

———. 2009. *Diccionario enciclopédico de la música en Cuba*. Havana: Editorial Letras Cubanas.

Goldberg, David Theo. 2008. *The Threat of Race: Reflections on Racial Neoliberalism*. Oxford: Blackwell.

Gómez Cairo, Jesús. (1980) 1998. "Acerca de la interacción de géneros en la música popular cubana." In *Panorama de la música popular cubana*, edited by Radamés Giro, 111–24. Havana: Editorial Letras Cubanas.

González Bello, Neris, Liliana Casanella Cué, and Grizel Hernández Baguer. 2008. "El reguetón en Cuba: un análisis de sus particularidades." Paper presented at the Fifth International Colloquium of Musicology at La Casa de las Américas, Havana, April 2008.

Gramsci, Antonio. 1971. *Selections from the Prison Notebooks of Antonio Gramsci*. London: Lawrence and Wishart.

Grasso González, Nancy. 1989. "Folklore y profesionalismo en la rumba Matancera." Bachelor's thesis, Instituto Superior del Arte.

Gregory, Steven. 1999. *Black Corona: Race and the Politics of Place in an Urban Community*. Princeton, NJ: Princeton University Press.

Grenet, Emilio. 1939. *Popular Cuban Music: 80 Revised and Corrected Compositions*. Havana: Southern Music Publishing Company.

Grossberg, Lawrence. (1986) 1996. "On Postmodernism and Articulation: An Interview with Stuart Hall." In *Stuart Hall: Critical Dialogues in Cultural Studies*, edited by David Morley and Kuan-Hsing Chen, 131–50. London: Routledge.

Guanche, Jesús. 1996. *Componentes étnicos de la nación cubana*. Havana: Ediciones Unión.

Guanche, Jesús, and Dennis Moreno. 1988. *Caidije*. Santiago de Cuba: Editorial Oriente.

Guilbault, Jocelyne. 1994. "Créolité and the New Cultural Politics of Difference in Popular Music of the French West Indies." *Black Music Research Journal* 14 (2): 161–78.

———. 2007. *Governing Sound: The Cultural Politics of Trinidad's Carnival Musics*. Chicago: University of Chicago Press.

Gupta, Akhil, and James Ferguson. 1992. "Beyond 'Culture': Space, Identity, and the Politics of Difference." *Cultural Anthropology* 7 (1): 6–23.

Guss, David M. 2000. *The Festive State: Race, Ethnicity, and Nationalism as Cultural Performance*. Berkeley: University of California Press.

Hagedorn, Katherine. 2001. *Divine Utterances: The Performance of Afro-Cuban Santería*. Washington, DC: Smithsonian Institution Press.

———. 2002. "Long Day's Journey to Rincón: From Suffering to Resistance in the Procession of San Lázaro/Babalú Ayé." *British Journal of Ethnomusicology* 11 (1): 43–69.

———. 2003. "Drum Talk: Sweet and Tasty Rhythms for the Orichas." *Emergences: Journal for the Study of Media and Composite Cultures* 13 (1–2): 95–104.

Hall, Stuart. (1986) 1996a. "Gramsci's Relevance for the Study of Race and Ethnicity." In *Stuart Hall: Critical Dialogues in Cultural Studies*, edited by David Morley and Kuan-Hsing Chen, 411–40. London: Routledge.

———. (1989) 1996b. "New Ethnicities." In *Stuart Hall: Critical Dialogues in Cultural Studies*, edited by David Morley and Kuan-Hsing Chen, 441–49. London: Routledge.

Helg, Aline. 1995. *Our Rightful Share: The Afro-Cuban Struggle for Equality, 1886–1912*. Chapel Hill: University of North Carolina Press.

Hernandez-Reguant, Ariana. 2009. "Multicubanidad." In *Cuba in the Special Period: Culture and Ideology in the 1990s*, edited by Ariana Hernandez-Reguant, 69–88. New York: Palgrave Macmillan.

Hill, Donald R. 1998. "West African and Haitian Influences on the Ritual and Popular Music of Carriacou, Trinidad, and Cuba." *Black Music Research Journal* 18 (1–2): 183–201.

Hill Collins, Patricia. 2009. *Another Kind of Public Education: Race, Schools, the Media, and Democratic Possibilities*. Boston: Beacon Press.

Hintzen, Percy. 2002. "Race and Creole Ethnicity in the Caribbean." In *Questioning Creole: Creolisation Discourses in Caribbean Culture*, edited by Verene Shepherd and Glen Richards, 92–110. Kingston: Ian Randle Publishers.

Howe, Genevieve. 1998. "Cuba: Regulating Revolution." *Z Magazine* 11 (4): 32–38.

Isfahani-Hammond, Alexandra. 2005. *The Masters and the Slaves: Plantation Relations and Mestizaje in American Imaginaries*. New York: Palgrave Macmillan.

James, Joel, José Millet, and Alexis Alarcón. 2007. *El vodú en Cuba*. Santiago de Cuba: Editorial Oriente.

Klein, Herbert S. 1978. *The Middle Passage: Comparative Studies in the Atlantic Slave Trade.* Princeton, NJ: Princeton University Press.

Knauer, Lisa Maya. 2005. "Translocal and Multicultural Counterpublics: Rumba and La Regla de Ocha in New York and Havana." PhD diss., New York University.

Knight, Alden. 2000. "Tackling Racism in Performing Arts and the Media." In *Afro-Cuban Voices: On Race and Identity in Contemporary Cuba*, edited by Pedro Pérez Sarduy and Jean Stubbs, 108–17. Gainesville: University Press of Florida.

Krims, Adam. 2007. *Music and Urban Geography.* New York: Routledge.

La Rosa Corzo, Gabino. 2003. *Runaway Slave Settlements in Cuba: Resistance and Repression.* Chapel Hill: University of North Carolina Press.

Lago Vieito, Ángel. 1996. "El espiritismo de cordón en el Bayamo colonial." *Del Caribe* 25: 16–18.

———. 2001. "El espiritismo en la región oriental de Cuba en el siglo XIX." *Del Caribe* 35: 72–79.

Lapidus, Benjamin. 2005. "Stirring the *Ajiaco*: *Changüí*, *Son*, and the Haitian Connection." In *Cuban Counterpoints: The Legacy of Fernando Ortiz*, edited by Mauricio Font and Alfonso Quiroz, 237–46. Lanham, MD: Lexington Books.

———. 2008. *Origins of Cuban Music and Dance: Changüí.* Lanham, MD: Scarecrow Press.

Lapique, Zoila. 1998. "Aportes franco-haitianos a la contradanza cubana: mitos y realidades." In *Panorama de la música popular cubana*, edited by Radamés Giro, 137–54. Havana: Editorial Letras Cubanas.

León, Argeliers. 1952. *El patrimonio folklórico musical cubano.* Havana: n.p.

———. (1982) 1991. "Notes toward a Panorama of Popular and Folk Musics." Translated by Peter Manuel. In *Essays on Cuban Music: North American and Cuban Perspectives*, edited by Peter Manuel, 1–23. Lanham: University Press of America.

———. (1982) 1998. "Notas para un panorama de la música popular." In *Panorama de la música popular cubana*, edited by Radamés Giro, 27–42. Havana: Editorial Letras Cubanas.

———. 1984. *Del canto y el tiempo.* Havana: Editorial Letras Cubanas.

López, Pedro. 2007. Interview by Antoine Miniconi, translation by Barry Cox. Manley Lopez. At http://manleycvenglish.blogspot.com/2007/03/pedro-lpez-in-this-interview-con ducted.html. Accessed March 2014.

Madrid, Alejandro L., and Robin D. Moore. 2013. *Danzón: Circum-Caribbean Dialogues in Music and Dance.* New York: Oxford University Press.

Malkki, Liisa. 1997. "National Geographic: The Rooting of Peoples and the Territorialization of National Identity among Scholars and Refugees." In *Culture, Power, Place: Explorations in Critical Anthropology*, edited by Akhil Gupta and James Ferguson, 52–74. Durham, NC: Duke University Press.

Manuel, Peter. 1985a. "Formal Structure in Popular Music as a Reflection of Socio-economic Change." *International Review of the Aesthetics and Sociology of Music* 16 (2): 163–80.

———. 1985b. "The Anticipated Bass in Cuban Popular Music." *Latin American Music Review* 6 (2): 249–61.

———, ed. 1991. *Essays on Cuban Music: North American and Cuban Perspectives.* Lanham, MD: University Press of America.

————. 1994. "Puerto Rican Music and Cultural Identity: Creative Appropriation of Cuban Sources from Danza to Salsa." *Ethnomusicology* 38 (2): 249–80.

————. 2009a. *Creolizing Contradance in the Caribbean*. Philadelphia: Temple University Press.

————. 2009b. "From Contradanza to Son: New Perspectives on the Prehistory of Cuban Popular Music." *Latin American Music Review* 30 (2): 184–212.

Martínez Furé, Rogelio. 1979. *Díalogos imaginarios*. Havana: Editorial Arte y Literatura.

————. 2000. "A National Cultural Identity? Homogenizing Monomania and the Plural Heritage." In *Afro-Cuban Voices: On Race and Identity in Contemporary Cuba*, edited by Pedro Pérez Sarduy and Jean Stubbs, 154–61. Gainesville: University Press of Florida.

————. 2004. *Briznas de la memoria*. Havana: Editorial Letras Cubanas.

Martínez Rodríguez, Raúl, and Pedro de la Hoz González. 1977. "From the Columbia to the Guaguancó." *Direct from Cuba* 168 (May 1): 1–7.

Marx, Anthony W. 1998. *Making Race and Nation: A Comparison of South Africa, the United States, and Brazil*. Cambridge: Cambridge University Press.

Massey, Doreen. 1994. *Space, Place, and Gender*. Minneapolis: University of Minnesota Press.

————. 2005. *For Space*. London: Sage Publications.

Massón Sena, Caridad. 2009. "Los partidos políticos y el problema racial en Cuba." *Caliban* 3. At http://www.revistacaliban.cu/articulo.php?article_id=31&numero=3. Accessed January 2012.

McAlister, Elizabeth A. 2002. *Rara! Vodou, Power, and Performance in Haiti and Its Diaspora*. Berkeley: University of California Press.

McLeod, Marc C. 1998. "Undesirable Aliens: Race, Ethnicity, and Nationalism in the Comparison of Haitian and British West Indian Immigrant Workers in Cuba, 1912–1939." *Journal of Social History* 31 (3): 599–623.

Milanes Despaigne, Jorge. 2011. "A Special Drink Made in Cuba: Pru Oriental." *Havana Times*, September 2, 2011. At http://www.havanatimes.org/?p=50033. Accessed July 2014.

Miller, Ivor L. 2009. *Voice of the Leopard: African Secret Societies and Cuba*. Jackson: University Press of Mississippi.

Millet, José. 1996. *El espiritismo: variantes cubanas*. Santiago de Cuba: Editorial Oriente.

————. 2000. "El foco de la santería santiaguera." *Del Caribe* 32: 110–19.

Millet, José, and Rafael Brea. 1989. *Grupos folklóricos de Santiago de Cuba*. Santiago de Cuba: Editorial Oriente.

Millet, José, Rafael Brea, and Manuel Ruiz Vila. 1997. *Barrio, comparsa y carnaval santiaguero*. Santiago de Cuba: Ediciones Casa del Caribe.

Milstein, Lani. 2013. "Toward an Understanding of Conga Santiaguera: Elements of La Conga de Los Hoyos." *Latin American Music Review* 34 (2): 223–53.

Mitchell, Don. 2000. *Cultural Geography: A Critical Introduction*. Malden, MA: Blackwell.

Moore, Carlos. 1988. *Castro, the Blacks, and Africa*. Los Angeles: Center for Afro-American Studies, University of California, Los Angeles.

————. 2008. *Pichón: Race and Revolution in Castro's Cuba; A Memoir*. Chicago: Lawrence Hill Books.

Moore, Donald S. 2005. *Suffering for Territory: Race, Place, and Power in Zimbabwe*. Durham, NC: Duke University Press.

Moore, Robin. 1995. "The Commercial Rumba: Afrocuban Arts as International Popular Culture." *Latin American Music Review* 16 (2): 165–98.

———. 1997. *Nationalizing Blackness: Afrocubanismo and Artistic Revolution in Havana, 1920–1940*. Pittsburgh: University of Pittsburgh Press.

———. 2006. *Music and Revolution: Cultural Change in Socialist Cuba*. Berkeley: University of California Press.

Oficina Nacional de Estadísticas, República de Cuba. 2006. *Censo de población y viviendas, Cuba 2002*. Havana: Oficina Nacional de Estadísticas.

———. 2013. *Censo de población y viviendas 2012: informe nacional*. Oficina Nacional de Estadísticas. At http://www.one.cu/informenacional2012.htm. Accessed January 2014.

Oficina Nacional de Los Censos Demográfico y Electoral, República de Cuba. 1953. *Censos de Población, Viviendas, y Electoral*. Havana: Oficina Nacional de Los Censos Demográfico y Electoral.

Omi, Michael, and Howard Winant. 1986. *Racial Formation in the United States: From the 1960s to the 1980s*. New York: Routledge.

Orovio, Helio. 1981. *Diccionario de la música cubana: biográfico y técnico*. Havana: Editorial Letras Cubanas.

Ortiz, Fernando. (1921) 1984. "Los cabildos afrocubanos." In *Ensayos etnográficos*, edited by Miguel Barnet and Angel Fernández. Havana: Editorial de Ciencias Sociales.

———. (1940) 1999. *Contrapunteo cubano del tabaco y el azúcar*. Madrid: Editorial Música Mundana Maqueda.

———. (1950) 1998. *La africanía de la música folklórica de Cuba*. Madrid: Editorial Música Mundana Maqueda.

———. 1965. *La africanía de la música folklórica de Cuba*. Havana: Editora Universitaria.

Pasmanick, Philip. 1997. "Décima and Rumba: Iberian Formalism in the Heart of Afro-Cuban Song." *Latin American Music Review* 18 (2): 252–77.

Pedro, Alberto. 1967. "La semana santa haitiano-cubana." *Etnología y folklore* 4: 49–78.

Pérez, Lisandro. 1984. "The Political Contexts of Cuban Population Censuses, 1899–1981." *Latin American Research Review* 19 (2): 143–61.

Pérez, Louis A. 2006. *Cuba between Reform and Revolution*. New York: Oxford University Press.

Pérez Sarduy, Pedro, and Jean Stubbs, eds. 1993. *AfroCuba: An Anthology of Cuban Writing on Race, Politics and Culture*. Melbourne: Ocean Press.

———, eds. 2000. *Afro-Cuban Voices: On Race and Identity in Contemporary Cuba*. Gainesville: University Press of Florida.

Perna, Vincenzo. 2005. *Timba: The Sound of the Cuban Crisis*. Burlington, VT: Ashgate Publishing.

Pratt, Mary Louise. 1992. *Imperial Eyes: Studies in Travel Writing and Transculturation*. London: Routledge.

Puri, Shalini. 2004. *The Caribbean Postcolonial: Social Equality, Post-Nationalism, and Cultural Hybridity*. New York: Palgrave Macmillan.

Queeley, Andrea. 2010. "*Somos Negros Finos*: Anglophone Caribbean Cultural Citizenship in Revolutionary Cuba." In *Global Circuits of Blackness: Interrogating the African Diaspora*, edited by Jean Muteba Rahier, Percy C. Hintzen, and Felipe Smith, 201–22. Champaign: University of Illinois Press.

Robbins, James. 1990. "The Cuban 'Son' as Form, Genre, and Symbol." *Latin American Music Review* 11 (2): 182–200.

Rodríguez Ruiz, Pablo, and Claudio Estévez Mezquía. 2006. "Familia, uniones matrimoniales y sexualidad en la pobreza y la marginalidad: el 'llega y pon,' un estudio de caso." *Catauro* 8 (14): 5–31.

Ruiz, Raúl R. 2001. *Matanzas: surgimiento y esplendor de la plantación esclavista, 1793–1867.* Matanzas: Ediciones Matanzas.

———. 2003. *Retrato de ciudad.* Havana: Ediciones Unión.

Sánchez Lussón, José. 1996. "Los cordoneros de orilé: presencia histórica y alcance cultural en Manzanillo." *Del Caribe* 25: 20–22.

Sawyer, Mark Q. 2006. *Racial Politics in Post-Revolutionary Cuba.* New York: Cambridge University Press.

Schweitzer, Kenneth. 2003. "Afro-Cuban Batá Drum Aesthetics: Developing Individual and Group Technique, Sound, and Identity." DMA diss., University of Maryland.

———. 2013. *The Artistry of Afro-Cuban Batá Drumming: Aesthetics, Transmission, Bonding, and Creativity.* Jackson: University Press of Mississippi.

Scott, Rebecca J. 2000. *Slave Emancipation in Cuba: The Transition to Free Labor, 1860–1899.* Pittsburgh: University of Pittsburgh Press.

Sheriff, Robin E. 2001. *Dreaming Equality: Color, Race, and Racism in Urban Brazil.* New Brunswick, NJ: Rutgers University Press.

Smith Mesa, Jorge. 2005. "'Mi linda habanera': nuevo disco de Adalberto Álvarez." *Periódico Cubarte,* September 26, 2005. At http://www.cubarte.cult.cu/periodico/noticias/133940/133940.html. Accessed October 2014.

Stewart, Gary. 2000. *Rumba on the River: A History of the Popular Music of the Two Congos.* London: Verso.

Stokes, Martin. 1994. "Introduction: Ethnicity, Identity, and Music." In *Ethnicity, Identity, and Music: The Musical Construction of Place,* edited by Martin Stokes, 1–28. Oxford: Berg Publishers.

Sublette, Ned. 2004. *Cuba and Its Music: From the First Drums to the Mambo.* Chicago: Chicago Press Review.

Sweeney, Philip. 2001. *The Rough Guide to Cuban Music.* London: Rough Guides.

Taylor, Timothy. 2007. *Beyond Exoticism: Western Music and the World.* Durham, NC: Duke University Press.

Trincado Fontán, María Nelsa. 2007. "La obsesión de Joel fue la historia de Cuba." *Del Caribe* 48–49: 93–100.

Turino, Thomas. 2000. *Nationalists, Cosmopolitans, and Popular Music in Zimbabwe.* Chicago: University of Chicago Press.

Urfé, Odilio. (1977) 1984. "Music and Dance in Cuba." In *Africa in Latin America: Essays on History, Culture, and Socialization,* edited by Manuel Moreno Fraginals and translated by Leonor Blum, 170–88. New York: Holmes and Meier.

Van Nispen, Paul. 2003. "El *cajón*: la persistencia de un instrumento de percusión en La Habana." Bachelor's thesis, University of Leiden.

Vélez, María Teresa. 2000. *Drumming for the Gods: The Life and Times of Felipe García Villamil, Santero, Palero, and Abakuá*. Philadelphia: Temple University Press.

Venegas Delgado, Hernán. 2001. *La región en Cuba: un ensayo de interpretación historiográfica*. Santiago de Cuba: Editorial Oriente.

Viddal, Grete. 2010. "Haitian Migration and Danced Identity in Eastern Cuba." In *Making Caribbean Dance: Continuity and Creativity in Island Cultures*, edited by Susanna Sloat, 83–93. Gainesville: University Press of Florida.

———. 2012. "Vodú Chic: Haitian Religion and the Folkloric Imaginary in Socialist Cuba." *New West Indian Guide* 86 (3–4): 205–35.

Vinueza, María Elena. 1986. "Matanzas, Tradición y Memoria." *Clave* 1 (March): 43–47.

———. 1989. *Presencia arará en la música folclórica de Matanzas*. Havana: Casa de las Américas.

Wade, Peter. 1993. *Blackness and Race Mixture: The Dynamics of Racial Identity in Colombia*. Baltimore: Johns Hopkins University Press.

———. 2000. *Music, Race and Nation: Música Tropical in Colombia*. Chicago: University of Chicago Press.

———. 2005. "Rethinking 'Mestizaje': Ideology and Lived Experience." *Journal of Latin American Studies* 37 (2): 239–57.

Warden, Nolan. 2006. "Cajón Pa' Los Muertos: Transculturation and Emergent Tradition in Afro-Cuban Ritual Drumming and Song." Master's thesis, Tufts University.

Watts, Michael. 2003. "Alternative Modern: Development as Cultural Geography." In *Handbook of Cultural Geography*, edited by Kay Anderson, Mona Domosh, Steve Pile, and Nigel Thrift, 433–53. London: Sage Publications.

Waxer, Lise. 1994. "Of Mambo Kings and Songs of Love: Dance Music in Havana and New York from the 1930s to the 1950s." *Latin American Music Review* 15 (2): 139–76.

White, Bob W. 2008. *Rumba Rules: The Politics of Dance Music in Mobutu's Zaire*. Durham, NC: Duke University Press.

Whiteley, Sheila, Andy Bennett, and Stan Hawkins. 2004. *Music, Space and Place: Popular Music and Cultural Identity*. Burlington, VT: Ashgate Publishing.

Wielecki, Mikolaj. 2001. "El fenómeno de la persistencia de la rumba en ciudad de La Habana." Bachelor's thesis, University of Warsaw.

Wirtz, Kristina. 2007. *Ritual, Discourse, and Community in Cuban Santería: Speaking a Sacred World*. Gainesville: University Press of Florida.

Zurbano, Roberto. 2009. "El Rap Cubano: Can't Stop, Won't Stop the Movement!" Translated by Kate Levitt. In *Cuba in the Special Period: Culture and Ideology in the 1990s*, edited by Ariana Hernandez-Reguant, 143–58. New York: Palgrave Macmillan.

Sound and Video Recordings

Adalberto Álvarez y Su Son. 2005. *Mi Linda Habanera*. Bis Music, compact disc.

———. 2010. *El Son de Altura*. Bis Music, compact disc.

———. 2013. *Respeto pa' los Mayores*. Bis Music, compact disc.

Afrocuba de Matanzas. 1998. *Raíces Africanas*. Shanachie, compact disc.

Ballet Folklórico Cutumba. 2005a. *Ritmos Cubafricanos, Volume 1*. Academy of Cuban Folklore and Dance, compact disc.

———. 2005b. *Ritmos Cubafricanos, Volume 2*. Academy of Cuban Folklore and Dance, compact disc.

———. 2007. *Orishas: Música para Danzar*. Academy of Cuban Folklore and Dance, compact disc.

Ban Rarrá. 2002. *Con Sabor al Guaso*. Salsa Blanca, compact disc.

Clave y Guaguancó. 1996. *Déjala en la Puntica*. Egrem, compact disc.

———. 1999. *Noche de la Rumba*. Tumi, compact disc.

———. 2006. *La Rumba Que No Termina*. Cuba Chévere, compact disc.

Cruz, Celia. 1993. *Azucar! Caliente*. Seeco, compact disc.

———. 1994. *Homenaje a Los Santos*. Polydor, compact disc.

Cruz, Celia, and Johnny Pacheco. 1974. *Celia & Johnny*. Vaya, compact disc.

Cruz, Celia, and Willie Colón. 1977. *Cruz & Colón: Only They Could Have Made This Album*. Vaya, compact disc.

Estefan, Gloria. 1993. *Mi Tierra*. Sony, compact disc.

———. 2007. *90 Millas*. Sony/BMG, compact disc.

Los Muñequitos de Matanzas. 1994. *Congo Yambumba*. Qbadisc, compact disc.

Los Van Van. 1999. *The Legendary Los Van Van: 30 Years of Cuba's Greatest Dance Band*. Ashé, compact disc.

Manolito y Su Trabuco. 2008. *Control*. Egrem, compact disc.

NG La Banda. 1992. *En la Calle*. Qbadisc, compact disc.

Ricardo Leyva y Sur Caribe. 2005. *Credenciales*. Egrem, compact disc.

Ritmo y Canto. 2004. *Ritmo y Canto*. Everloving, compact disc.

Various artists. 1993. *Cuban Gold: Que se Sepa, ¡Yo Soy de La Habana!* Qbadisc, compact disc.

———. 1994. *¡La Rumba Está Buena!* Corasón, compact disc.

Weaver, Christian, producer. 2007. *Afrocuba de Matanzas: 50 Years On*. La Timbala Films, DVD.

Yoruba Andabo. 1993. *El Callejón de los Rumberos*. Ayva, compact disc.

Interviews and Personal Communication

Alfonso García, Reinaldo. Interview with author, Matanzas, Cuba, March 8, 2007.

Anonymous. Conversation with author, Camagüey, Cuba, May 9, 2008.

Averill, Gage. Email exchange with author, February 2009.

Brinner, Benjamin. Conversation with author, Berkeley, California, March 2009.

Corbea Calzado, Julio. Conversation with author, Santiago de Cuba, June 13, 2011.

De Arma Sarria, Gerardo. Interview with author, Havana, December 23, 2006.

Dedeu Hernández, Amado. Interview with author, Havana, October 24, 2006.

Del Pino Rodríguez, Geovani. Interviews with author, Havana, December 1, 2006, and January 12, 2007.

Dreke Reyes, Miguel Angel. Conversations with author, Matanzas, Cuba, July 28, 2005, and October 17, 2006.

García Fernández, Juan. Interview with author, Matanzas, Cuba, March 2, 2007.

García Pérez, Ramón "Sandy." Interview with author, Oakland, California, July 6, 2014.

Giro, Radamés. Conversation with author, Havana, June 24, 2011.

González Coba, Ronald. Interview with author, Havana, April 18, 2007.

López Rodríguez, Irián. Interview with author, Havana, May 8, 2007.

Manuel, Peter. Conversation with author, June 2014.

Márquez Domínguez, Ramón. Interview with author, Santiago de Cuba, June 17, 2011.

Moncada Merencio, Lázaro. Various conversations with author, Havana and Oakland, California, September 2006–January 2010.

Pablo (pseudonym). Interview with author, Santiago de Cuba, June 14, 2011.

Pérez Herrera, Dolores. Interviews with author, Matanzas, Cuba, March 2, 2007, and August 9, 2013.

Portuondo Zúñiga, Olga. Conversation with author, Santiago de Cuba, June 15, 2011.

Rodríguez Morales, Daniel. Interviews with author, Havana, October 6, 2006, and October 26, 2006. Multiple conversations with author, September 2006–May 2007.

Rojas Ramírez, Isaias. Interview with author, Havana, June 26, 2011.

Seguí Correoso, Mario. Interview with author, Santiago de Cuba, June 14, 2011. Conversation with author, Santiago de Cuba, July 2005.

Tápanes, Pedro. Interview with author, Matanzas, Cuba, February 2, 2007.

Zamora Chirino, Francisco. Interview with author, Matanzas, Cuba, February 12, 2007. Conversation with author, Matanzas, Cuba, February 21, 2007.

Index